The Rise of Tamil Separatism in Sri Lanka

Among the examples of civil wars, armed secessionist movements and minority uprisings in the world today, many involve conflict between a minority group's aim for political self-determination and the nation state's resistance to any diminution of sovereignty. With the expansion of the international regime of human rights, minority groups have reconceptualised their struggle with the understanding that a minority that is linguistically, religiously or ethnically distinctive is entitled to self-determination if its aspirations cannot be met.

This book explores the relationship between minority rights, self-determination and secession within international law, by contextualising these issues in a detailed case study of the rise of Tamil separatism in Sri Lanka. Welhengama and Pillay show how Tamil communalism hardened into secession and assess whether the Sri Lankan government has met its obligations with respect to the right to self-determination short of secession. Focusing on the legal and human rights arguments for secession by the Tamil community of the north and east of Sri Lanka, the book demonstrates how the language of international law and international human rights played a major role in the development of the arguments for secession. Through a close examination of the case of the Tamil's secessionist movement the book presents valuable insights into why modern nation states find themselves threatened by separatist claims and bids for independence based on ethnicity.

Gnanapala Welhengama is now retired but was previously Principal of Toxteth Community College in Liverpool. He was a lawyer and judge in Sri Lanka and was a magistrate in England and Wales.

Nirmala Pillay is Senior Lecturer in law at Liverpool John Moores University, UK.

Routledge Research in International Law

Available:

International Law and the Third World
Reshaping Justice
Richard Falk, Balakrishnan Rajagopal and Jacqueline Stevens (eds.)

International Legal Theory
Essays and Engagements, 1966–2006
Nicholas Onuf

The Problem of Enforcement in International Law
Countermeasures, the Non-Injured State and the Idea of International Community
Elena Katselli Proukaki

International Economic Actors and Human Rights
Adam McBeth

The Law of Consular Access
A Documentary Guide
John Quigley, William J. Aceves and Adele Shank

State Accountability under International Law
Holding States Accountable for a Breach of Jus Cogens Norms
Lisa Yarwood

International Organisations and the Idea of Autonomy
Institutional Independence in the International Legal Order
Richard Collins and Nigel D. White (eds.)

Self-Determination in the Post-9/11 Era
Elizabeth Chadwick

Participants in the International Legal System
Multiple Perspectives on Non-State Actors in International Law
Jean d'Aspremont

Sovereignty and Jurisdiction in the Airspace and Outer Space
Legal Criteria for Spatial Delimitation
Gbenga Oduntan

International Law in a Multipolar World
Matthew Happold (ed.)

The Law on the Use of Force
A Feminist Analysis
Gina Heathcote

The ICJ and the Development of International Law
The Lasting Impact of the Corfu Channel Case
Karine Bannelier, Théodore Christakis and Sarah Heathcote (eds.)

UNHCR and International Refugee Law
From Treaties to Innovation
Corinne Lewis

Asian Approaches to International Law and the Legacy of Colonialism
The Law of the Sea, Territorial Disputes and International Dispute Settlement
Jin-Hyun Paik, Seok-Woo Lee, Kevin Y L Tan (eds)

The Right to Self-determination Under International Law
"Selfistans," Secession, and the Rule of the Great Powers
Milena Sterio

Reforming the UN Security Council Membership
The Illusion of Representativeness
Sabine Hassler

Threats of Force
International Law and Strategy
Francis Grimal

The Changing Role of Nationality in International Law
Alessandra Annoni and Serena Forlati

Criminal Responsibility for the Crime of Aggression
Patrycja Grzebyk

Regional Maintenance of Peace and Security under International Law
The Distorted Mirror
Dace Winther

International Law-Making
Essays in Honour of Jan Klabbers
Rain Liivoja and Jarna Petman

Resolving Claims to Self-Determination
Is There a Role of the International Court of Justice and Other Legal Tribuals?
Andrew Coleman

The Rise of Tamil Separatism in Sri Lanka
From Communalism to Secession
Gnanapala Welhengama and Nirmala Pillay

Forthcoming titles in this series include:

International Law, Regulation and Resistance
Critical Spaces
Zoe Pearson

The Cuban Embargo under International Law
El Bloqueo
Nigel D. White

The Changing Nature of Customary International Law
Methods of Interpreting the Concept of Custom in International Criminal Tribunals
Noora Arajärvi

Technology and the Law on the Use of Force
New Security Challenges in the Twenty First Century
Jackson Maogoto

Criminal Diversity in International Law
The Effectiveness of the UNESCO Convention on the Protection and Promotion of the Diversity of Cultural Expressions
Lilian Hanania

The United Nations and Collective Security
Gary Wilson

The Rise of Tamil Separatism in Sri Lanka

From Communalism to Secession

Gnanapala Welhengama and Nirmala Pillay

Routledge
Taylor & Francis Group
LONDON AND NEW YORK

First published 2014
by Routledge
2 Park Square, Milton Park, Abingdon, Oxon OX14 4RN

and by Routledge
711 Third Avenue, New York, NY 10017

Routledge is an imprint of the Taylor & Francis Group, an informa business

British Library Cataloguing in Publication Data
A catalogue record for this book is available from the British Library

Library of Congress Cataloging in Publication Data
Welhengama, Gnanapala.
The rise of Tamil separatism in Sri Lanka : from communalism to secession / Gnanapala Welhengama, Nirmala Pillay.
pages cm.—(Routledge research in international law)
Includes bibliographical references and index.
ISBN 978-0-415-85486-3 (hardback)—ISBN 978-0-203-79718-1 (ebk)
1. Self-determination, National—Sri Lanka. 2. Tamil (Indic people)—Legal status, laws, etc.—Sri Lanka. 3. India, South—Politics and government. 4. Secession—Sri Lanka. I. Pillay, N. (Nirmala) II. Title.
KZ1269.W43 2014
341.6'8—dc23

2013027801

ISBN: 978-0-415-85486-3 (hbk)
ISBN: 978-0-203-79718-1 (ebk)

Typeset in Baskerville by
Keystroke, Station Road, Codsall, Wolverhampton

Contents

Abbreviations

A/C.3/SR	Summary Reports of the 3rd Committee of the General Assembly of the United Nations
AC	appeal cases (of Privy Council)
ACTC	All-Ceylon Tamil Congress
CHJ	Ceylon Historical Journal
CJHSS	Ceylon Journal of Historical and Social Studies
EPRLF	Ealam People's Revolutionary Liberation Front
FP	Federal Party
GNLF	Gorkha National Liberation Front
ICLQ	International and Comparative Law Quarterly
JAS	Journal of Asian Studies
JHU	Jatika Hela Urumaya
JVP	Janatha Vimukthi Peramuna
LC	Legislative Council of Ceylon
LSSP	Lanka Samasamaja Party
LTTE	Liberation Tigers of Tamil Ealam
MEP	Mahajana Eksath Peramuna
PA	Peoples' Alliance
PC	Privy Council
SC	Soulbury Commission
SLFP	Sri Lanka Freedom Party
TELO	Tamil Ealam Liberation Organisation
TNT	Tamil New Tigers
TUF	Tamil United Front
TULF	Tamil United Liberation Front
UCHC	University of Ceylon History of Ceylon
UCR	University of Ceylon Review
UNP	United National Party
WLR	Weekly Law Reports

1 Introduction

Sir Ivor Jennings was the first Vice-Chancellor of the University of Ceylon and the chief architect of the Soulbury Constitution (1947–1972). Commenting on the *nationalism* prevalent in his time in Ceylon (since 1972, Sri Lanka) he stated in 1950:

> What historical students in Ceylon ought now to do is to remove recent history from its emotional context. Neither the view that 'British imperialism' was always nefarious and iniquitous nor the opposite view that British policy was invariably enlightened and beneficial will stand the test of history. British rule had many advantages and many disadvantages. How the historian reads the balance will depend in some degree upon his own prejudices, for all history involves a selection of materials, and subjective influences cannot be entirely avoided either in the selection or in the emphasis. In writing about the seventeenth century conflicts in England, as I have been doing lately, I find that I have to guard against the bias due to my Nonconformist background . . . It is all the more necessary to take precautions against interpreting in such a manner as to feed one's own emotions.[1]

Considering the severity of ethnic prejudices that currently obtain in every community and in the political discourse in the island we are aware that our task cannot be an easy one in the presentation of facts without arousing anger in one or other ethnic camp. Those who dare to tread a path strewn with lies and misinterpretation of historical facts must indeed shed their own prejudices before even trying to enter the debate on the ethnic conflict in Sri Lanka.

Misunderstanding of how political 'communalism' evolved from a non-violent bipartisan approach into a more destructive violent force often leads to superficial and erroneous conclusions.[2] Moreover, it has become difficult for any independent

1 Sir Ivor Jennings, 'Nationalism and Political Development in Ceylon The Background of Self-Government', *Ceylon Historical Journal*, 3, 1953–54, p.63.

2 C. Palley, *Constitutional Law and Minorities, Report no. 36*, Minority Rights Group: London, 1978, p.10.

observer to assess the situation due to the strength of feeling and prevalence of distorted facts and figures.[3]

What factors have induced us to write this book?

What motivated me, G. Welhengama, to tackle a book on the ethnic conflict in Sri Lanka? The apparent reason, perhaps, was Professor Dominic McGoldrick's insistence that I should write a separate chapter in my PhD thesis on Sri Lanka's ethno-tribal conflict. My thesis concerned ethnic conflicts in general and how demands by ethno-tribal groups for greater political power in the form of *autonomy* and *secession* contributed to the escalation of ethnic violence in multi-ethnic polities in the contemporary nation state system. However, I resisted his request for fear that I might not be able to rise above my own prejudices and present an objective analysis as an impartial observer. I am also myself indirectly a party to the present conflict, for the simple reason that I had lived for 40 years in Sri Lanka until I was forced, in 1990, to flee my country owing to political reasons. When I was writing Chapter 11 of my PhD thesis, I finally made up my mind and entitled it: 'A Case Study: Ethnic Conflict in Sri Lanka'.

Writing a book on Sri Lanka while in exile was no easy task since most primary and secondary data on Sri Lanka are not available in the UK. Most significantly, some primary data and resource materials relating to the period 1900 to 1946 are still available in Sri Lanka alone. In particular, parliamentary Hansards are still difficult to obtain even through the inter-library loan scheme. Nonetheless, we managed to secure most materials, both primary and secondary, which helped us complete the project.

Surprisingly, there exists hardly any serious and impartial discussion about what part Tamil politicians played in the escalation of violence that prevailed in Sri Lanka. Of course these events have taken place over a century in which both major communities, Sinhalese and Tamils, have been interlocked in each other's downfall. Political leaders from both sides made fateful decisions before and after independence, perhaps, without realising the dire consequence for future generations, which set the scene for the rise of one of the most dangerous secessionist movement in the world and a prolonged civil war.

Why do we focus only on Tamil 'communalism'?

Our analysis of Sri Lanka's ethnic conflict is not meant to form the basis of yet another historical textbook. This work attempts to show that of the ethnic struggle in Sri Lanka mirrored changing global attitudes to minorities in

3 See, for example, S. Ponnambalam, *Sri Lanka: The National Question and the Tamil Liberation Struggle*, Tamil Information Centre with Zed Books: London, 1983. S.J. Tambiah, *Sri Lanka: Ethnic Fratricide and the Dismantling of Democracy*, University of Chicago Press: Chicago and London, 1986.

nation states in the developing regime of international law on minority rights and on the changing attitude of nation states to devolution and grants of autonomy.

Our primary objective is to examine the self-understanding of Tamils as a separate nation and their determination to 'share power' in the constitutional settlements in Sri Lanka before and after independence. The book examines how separatist ideology progressed, first of all, from 'communalism' then to *federalism* and finally to a *secessionist* armed struggle. Most of the literature about the Sinhalese involvement in this adventure recorded both by indigenous scholars and by western observers, published especially after 1966, present only one side of this tragic saga. Even though many of these writers are scholars of international repute their failure to present an impartial analysis of what has happened on the island is due mainly to the fact that almost all of them, in one way or another, have been deeply affected by the conflicts. The frustration and anger felt by distinguished Tamil scholars such as Professor A.J. Wilson, Professor Arasaratnam and Professor S.J. Tambiah is sometimes visible in their writings. The sheer quantity of competing narratives in Sri Lanka has made it[4] difficult to tell the difference between history and propaganda. The creation of nations is also the creation of an historical narrative that seamlessly links together territory with language and ethnicity. Likewise, liberation struggles also try to recapture the past so that historical facts, embellished by myths and legends create for the fledgling nation a clear identity, on the basis of which political and legal claims for territory can be founded. For example, Sachi Ponnambalam's *National Question and the Tamil Liberation Struggle*[5] published in the aftermath of the riots of July 1983 is a partisan account of someone who has been part of the Tamil struggle for some time.

Professor Tambiah, an eminent Tamil scholar and an internationally reputed anthropologist left the country due to the ethnic riots that took place in the late 1950s, to take up the Chair of the Department of Anthropology at the University of Harvard. Some of his post-1970 articles and monographs on the crisis in Sri Lanka are aimed at the Sinhalese, in general, and Sinhalese Buddhists, in particular. His later works are replete with exaggerations[6] such as the clear parallel he drew between the Holocaust in Nazi Germany and massacres in Tamil-inhabited areas of Sri Lanka. The late Professor A.J. Wilson, the chief ideologist in Tamil federal politics until the LTTE began to dominate politics in the north and east has also succumbed to this trend from the early 1980s. He strenuously supported demands for federal status for the north and east in his writings from the late 1960s onward. Sinhalese domination in post-independence Sri Lanka has frustrated him and most of his contemporaries. In his *Break-up of*

4 The dependence in this work of the self-same writers testifies to the fact that they were still capable of being remarkable observers of the developing situation and their perspicacious and insightful comments, worthy of note.

5 Ponnambalam, *Sri Lanka: The National Question*, 1983.

6 See, for example, Tambiah, *Sri Lanka: Ethnic Fratricide and Betrayal of Sri Lanka*, 1986

Sri Lanka,[7] he reports on events that he was personally acquainted with between the years 1947 to 1987 such as his association with the upper echelons of the traditional Tamil leadership and his close acquaintanceship with J.R. Jayawardene, former President of Sri Lanka. In this book, he discusses broken promises, the betrayal of Tamils by Sinhalese politicians, the colonisation of traditional homeland by Sinhalese peasants, and so forth. Most of his post-1970 work reflects his deep feelings about the Tamil cause and appear one-sided and lacking the scholarly approach he had quite remarkably demonstrated in his earlier works. This is equally true of Arasaratnam, Sabaratnam and many other contemporary writers, almost all of them self-exiled Tamil scholars. These scholars are of the view that Sinhalese chauvinism alone generated the ethnic crisis. The main thesis seems to be that Tamil 'communalism' emerged as a result of the defensive politics adopted by the Sinhalese. The role Sinhalese politicians and Sinhalese nationalists played in escalating and exacerbating ethnic tensions is well documented both in the works of Sinhalese and Tamil scholars (including the ones mentioned), and in the official records and personal journals of the main political actors. But the issue is not so simple.

Sri Lankan Tamils feared becoming an ethnic minority in post-independence Sri Lanka. Like other ethnic minorities in nation states elsewhere in the world they had difficulty fitting into a democratic unitary state in which, on account of their numerical inferiority, they became a minority in perpetuity subject to the political will of the Sinhalese majority. What is missing, in published accounts of the Sri Lankan crisis, is a clear narrative about the way the Tamils as an ethnic minority resisted since the beginning of the twentieth century to address their loss of status and minority position in an emerging nation state.

Amidst the vast amount of excellent work produced by western scholars who have attempted to write about the tragic tale of post-independence Sri Lanka, such as W. Howard Wriggins,[8] Robert Kearney[9] Paul Sieghart[10] and Virginia Leary,[11] there are also several who have failed to grasp the complexity of the political situation on the island. Their problem has been an over-reliance on western news reports and hurriedly executed 'fact-finding missions'. Edgar O'Ballance's *Cyanide War, Tamil Insurrection of Sri Lanka 1973–88*,[12] is an example. Other problems have

7 See A.J. Wilson, *The Break-up of Sri Lanka: The Sinhalese Tamil Conflict*, C. Hurst & Co.: London, 1988. See also his other post-1970s' work, *Politics in Sri Lanka, 1947–1979*, Macmillan: London, 1979.

8 W.H. Wriggins, *Ceylon: Dilemmas of a New Nation*, Princeton University Press: Princeton, NJ, 1960.

9 R.N. Kearney, *Communalism and Language in the Politics of Ceylon*, Duke University Press: Durham, NC, 1967.

10 See his *Sri Lanka, A Mounting Tragedy of Errors*, Report of a Mission to Sri Lanka in January 1984 on behalf of the International Commission of Jurists and its British Section, Justice, Dorchester, 1984.

11 Ethnic Conflict and Violence in Sri Lanka: report of a mission to Sri Lanka in July–August 1981 on Behalf of the International Commission of Jurists, International Commission of Jurists, 1983.

12 E. O'Ballance, *Cyanide War: Tamil Insurrection in Sri Lanka*, RUSI and Brassey's Defence Publishers: London, 1989.

been a lack of context or accuracy in the reporting. For example, UN Special Rapporteur Professor Palley's allegation that Tamil students were not allowed to study medicine in the medical faculties in Sri Lanka. There were certainly policies aimed at restricting the admission of Tamil students at Sri Lankan universities, which generated a major political problem, but it was well known that there has been a medical faculty attached to the University of Jaffna for nearly two decades, of which almost all the entrants are Tamil students. In other medical faculties at the University of Colombo, the University of Peradeniya, the University of Kelaniya and the University of Matara (Galle campus) Tamil students have been studying without experiencing any trouble. Although there is a medical faculty in the University of Jaffna, some Tamil medical students preferred to go to Peradeniya and other faculties even though they are located in the areas predominantly inhabited by the Sinhalese.

It is very rare that an author can escape what Jennings has described as subjective influences. Emotions and prejudices will creep imperceptibly into one's thinking and play a huge role as one starts recording what he or she has learnt and heard. I left my country for political reasons in 1990 with my family. However, this had nothing to do with the Sinhalese – Tamil conflict. We have both presented the facts and came to our own conclusions based on our first-hand experiences of the countries in which we were born and through relying on both primary and secondary sources of eminent scholars. Fortunately, Bandaranaike's *Handbook*, Michael Roberts' documents, works by Sir Ivor Jennings, Dr I.D.S. Weerawardana, Dr G.C. Mendis, B.H. Farmer and Jane Russell provided invaluable materials not otherwise available.

From a different perspective?: Gnanapala Welhengama

I was born in the southern part of Sri Lanka. I had my university education during the early 1970s in the capital of the island, Colombo, although I never really enjoyed its cosmopolitan surroundings and all the hustle and bustle typically associated with an Asian metropolis. Neither was I able to savour the essence of city life. So, after one year in the wilderness among strangers, both the Sinhalese and the Tamils, I left Colombo and returned to my village to take up a teaching position at a very junior level. It was another ten years before I returned to Colombo, this time to qualify as a lawyer, after being disappointed with the degree of political interference in the teaching profession by politicians. On this occasion I spent exactly a decade in Colombo even after qualifying as an attorney-at-law of the Supreme Court of Sri Lanka. My time at the Sri Lanka Law College proved to be a very useful one, during which I had the opportunity for the first time to interact with the main minority groups, the Ceylon Tamils and Muslims.

Although I never experienced any difficulties mixing with my Tamil colleagues, at times language barriers became an obstacle for us both, Tamil and Sinhalese students alike. Yet, in our social intercourse, we somehow managed to cooperate with each other in very friendly and congenial surroundings. We were invited to Tamil student union meetings and they, in turn, had always willingly accepted our invitations. After completion of my legal studies I worked at a chamber, in which Tamil lawyers also practised, as junior counsel.

Above all, I have a strong blood relationship with the Tamil community, although it came about in a rather unexpected way. One pleasant evening I was informed that one of my brothers had married a Tamil lady, which did not accord well with my parents. Now they have been happily married for 30 years. Neither my family members nor I had found any difficulty in coming to terms with it, because the Tamils, just like my forefathers from whom the Sinhala race originated, came ultimately from the Indian subcontinent. They established settlements in this beautiful country, known very appropriately, as the pearl of the Indian ocean for centuries, even though early migrants of Tamil origin had journeyed much later than the Sinhalese. A great chunk of Tamil conurbation outside the northern and eastern provinces is located in the Western Province, which is principally inhabited by the Sinhalese. It became customary that whenever there was an attack against Tamils, by extremists of both camps or when faced with the wrath of the LTTE, Tamil civilians sought refuge in and around Colombo.

Dr Nirmala Pillay

I was born in Durban, South Africa, at the height of apartheid. In that country, the ethnic problem was the reverse of Sri Lanka. The minority ethnic Afrikaaners and English, numbering only about four million people were firmly in political control of a government that ruled a country of some 35 million Africans, 800, 000 Indians and two million people who were classified as 'coloured'. It was ostensibly a democratic government since it was elected into power by the white minority. In 1992 Nelson Mandela, leader of the African National Congress (ANC), the banned African liberation movement, was released from jail after 27 years and the country embarked on the process of writing a new constitution in terms of which the 1994 election would be held. Although it was clear that the constitution would apply to a unitary state, there were threats of secession from both the Inkatha Freedom Party, the party dominating Natal and representing ten million Zulus, and the conservative Afrikaaners. Neither threat materialised. Behind the scenes negotiations by Prime Minister F.W. De Klerk with the King of the Zulus, isolated Chief Gatsha Buthelezi and neutralised the threat. As it turned out the ANC garnered most of the Zulu vote. The plans of the separatist Afrikaaners never really garnered enough support to make good their threat either.

The South Africans avoided a disaster in spite of years of abject deprivation, poverty and oppression because the President was a reconciling figure who set himself the task to promote harmony between the races. The drafters of the constitution entrenched a bill of rights and took wise decisions, albeit not practical ones, regarding language policy. South Africa has 11 official languages. As election officer in the 1994 South African general election, I was able to revel in the peaceful air of celebration of that election and of a great conflict, averted.

Emergence of Velupillai Prbhakaran and Junious Richard Jayawardene (JR)

A new kind of politics emerged from the late 1970s onward, with devastating consequences for the generation to come. This originally started in the Jaffna Peninsula with the killing of the former Mayor of Jaffna and a parliamentarian, Alfred Duraiappah, on 27 July 1975 by a hitherto, unknown Tamil insurgent group, *Tamil New Tigers* (TNT) headed by a 20-year-old 'boy', Velupillai Prabhakaran.[13] Duraiappah was killed on his way back from a Hindu temple. Such terrorist activities directed against elected representatives in the province was previously unheard of. Writing about the incident and the LTTE's evolution since then, T. Sabaratnam commented, 'The first murder of the ethnic conflict had been committed. It shocked the Tamils. It shocked the Sinhalese. The armed revolt began' with a number of Tamil militant groups emerging out of the shadow of the Tamil United Front led by Samuel James Velupillai Chelvanayakam. However, it was Prabhakaran who emerged as the dominant rebel leader in the north and east and who later became, as it were, a killing machine in South East Asia. His group went on a killing spree from 1975, destroying his political opponents whatever their religion or ethnic backgrounds. He was responsible for the murders of Appapillai Amirthalingam (the leader of TULF), Rãjiv Gãndhi (Prime Minister of India) and Ransinghe Premadasa (President of Sri Lanka). Subsequently, the entire leadership of TULF was annihilated and all political parties, both democratic and armed groups, fighting for *Tamil Eelam* were banned. Prabhakaran was afterwards implicated in murders, robberies, organised crime and terrorism. He was sought by INTERPOL and the Sri Lankan and Indian courts. A death warrant was issued by Chennai High Court for his part in the assassination of Rãjiv Gãndhi and he was convicted by the Colombo High Court for his participation in the bombing of the Central Bank of Sri Lanka and sentenced to a 200-year prison sentence.

In the south another revolution took place towards the end of the 1970s with the gradual ascendancy of the then opposition party, the UNP, led by J.R. Jayawardene (JR). The country was in a difficult situation, the economy faring badly and unemployment rising. Generally, people were not satisfied with the coalition government (UF), led by Sirimao Bandaranaike, that included the country's most dominant Marxist parties, the Communist Party (CP, Moscow wing) and the Lanka Samasamaja Party (LSSP). The government extended its mandate by two years by amending the former Soulbury Constitution. JR, having noted the mood of the people, deployed a number of eye-catching promises during the general

13 He is also referred to as Pirapaharan or Priabaharan.

election held in 1977 and managed to capture power through democratic means, quite literally, by popular will. In the 1977 general election his political party polled 50.9 per cent of the total vote. He became President of Sri Lanka in 1978 by an amendment made to the 1977 Constitution. Equipped with these enormous powers he once famously told party members that he could change anything, apart from a man into a woman and vice versa. Not surprisingly, politics became a blood sport played and executed by ruthless men whose sole aim was to control power by whatever means they could muster. Owing to both Prabhakaran and JR's violent and undemocratic politics during the 1980s, the political atmosphere lurched from crisis to crisis, both in the south-west and the north-east. Both resorted to violence to establish themselves above accepted democratic institutions and destroyed the finer fabric of civic society that was deeply ingrained in both the Jaffna Peninsula and the southern part of the country for many centuries. JR's draconian and undemocratic policies created a terrible 'Frankenstein's monster'[14] in the shape of Prabhakaran replacing the traditional 'half-hearted, tea-cup Tamil leadership' and inaugurating a new era engulfed with blood, tears and misery.

The July 1983 riots in the island gave unexpected impetus to Tamil insurgent groups. This was the turning point in the Tamils' armed struggle against the Sinhalese and the Sri Lankan government. The July riots allowed Tamil insurgents to recruit foot soldiers to their cause. By this time the Liberation Tigers of Tamil Ealam (in 1976 the TNT was renamed as LTTE) had become the most dominant, insurgent group. V. Prabhakaran's 'liberation fighters' identified themselves as *Tigers*. So an unending war between government forces *Tigers* against *Lions* began.

1989 – a turning point in both my life and country

One fine morning in 1989 I went to the Magistrates' Court in Embilipitiya to engage in my daily legal work. I was informed by the Chief Clerk of the Court that Mr Mahinda Rajapakse was waiting at the Hambantota Katchcheriya (administration centre) and wanted to talk to me. I contacted Rajapakse on the phone and found that he wanted me to contest the general election for the Hambantota parliamentary seat from the Sri Lanka Freedom Party list, of which he was the leader. I did not accede to his request, saying that it was not possible to do so considering the situation that existed in the south then. The JVP, a Marxist insurgent group, similar to that of the LTTE in the north and east was in full command in the south. Its edicts were usually to be obeyed. Candidates who would contest the general election would be killed. Rajapakse was considered the number one traitor by the JVP and was on its hit list. I had been previously warned by one of my lawyer friends, Wickramasinghe, that I should not contest the 1989

14 Prabhakaran was very appropriately identified with this term by A.J. Wilson in a Canadian Tamil online journal.

election from SLFP or UNP lists; and if I failed to heed his advice, I would be killed by the JVP.

My pleading with Rajapakse did not work, as he wanted me to become one of the SLFP candidates for the Hambantota District. I finally agreed. Not surprisingly, we, the SLFP, lost the general election to our main rival, the UNP, led by R. Premadasa. (Rajapakse went on to become the President of Sri Lanka 17 years later, in 2006.)

The 1989 general election was won by the then ruling party led by R. Premadasa by fraudulent means and by resorting to violence. Those who had stood in the election as candidates from opposition parties were intimidated, some were forced to leave the country and a few of them were actually killed. A few months later, paramilitary forces broke into my house on the instructions of the high-ranking military commander for Embilipilitya military zone, Col. Liyanage, with a clear mandate from top government politicians seeking my family and me. As it transpired, they instead found Wickramasinghe and another youth, my nephew, in my house on that fateful night – where they were hacked to death. I was fortunate enough to escape with my life, although subsequently I was forced to leave my country. I learnt later that the former Defence Minister, Ranjan Wijerathne, was in the Embilipitiya army camp on the previous night talking to Col. Liyanage about how to destroy those who stood against atrocities committed by government forces. (Ironically, he was assassinated by the Tigers a few years later.) Thus, 1989 became an *annus horribilis* in my life.

By then, the southern part of the island was virtually engulfed in violence. The combatants this time round were Sinhalese versus Sinhalese. A large section of unemployed Sinhalese young people rose up against the oligarchic and dictatorial UNP regime led first by JR and then subsequently by Premadasa. By the end of the 1990s, more than 60,000 Sinhalese youths had been brutally massacred. The JVP rebellion was destroyed with extraordinary brutality. Yet, the government was unable to constrain Tamils insurgent groups who were by this time fighting for an Ealam, a separate State within a State with full sovereignty.

In January 1999 it was reported that ethno-tribal conflicts in Sri Lanka had already cost 62,000 lives or more[15] and that 126,281 people had become internally displaced refugees since 1983, while many thousands more had sought asylum in India and some also in the west.[16] According to some unofficial figures it is estimated that there were, by 2002, at least 850,000 Tamils living in western Europe.[17] This number has increased ever since. It gained notoriety as 'South Asia's longest secessionist war'.[18] Regrettably, it was through a brutal war that the armed conflict was finally brought to an end in 2009.

15 Namini Wijedasa, 'Sri Lanka Government Draft Constitution', in http://dailynews.yahoo.com/h/ap/ 20000803/w1/sri_lanka_civil_war_3.html, 4 August 2000.

16 *Daily News*, 28 January 1999.

17 *Himal Magazine*, June 2000.

18 *Himal Magazine*, June 2000.

In our analysis concerning the conflict in Sri Lanka, attempts had been strenuously made to avoid the pitfalls mentioned earlier. We have tried, at all times in this monograph, to present an impartial view of how events reached such a pass that violence engulfed the country. We focus on the evolution of the Tamils' political position. Important to this narrative are also the people (leaders) involved – their education, caste and temperament.

2 Conceptual setting

Separatism, secession and irredentism rights

State building in the modern world

The concept of the 'post-modern tribal state' was first popularized by Thomas M. Franck but was later seized on by Rosalyn Higgins and Antonio Cassese. An unprecedented scale of 'tribal revivalism' in contemporary nation states was feared by many to represent a form of struggle to establish ethnically defined new 'tribal states'.[1] However, some scholars have questioned the suitability of such a term, notably Patrick Thornberry[2] and the UN Special Rapporteur, Asbjórn Eide.[3] Thornberry noted that when 'tribal' in the descriptive sense is used, it might carry some negative connotations. He preferred the use of the expression 'ethnic fundamentalism' to 'tribalism'. Special Rapporteur Asbjórn Eide also uses 'ethnic fundamentalism' to identify this new ethno-tribal phenomenon and the resulting trend towards *secession*. One might argue that 'ethnic fundamentalism' also has negative connotations since 'fundamentalism' suggests a type of fringe group extremism currently prevalent in many parts of the globe. However, since the 1990s, with the end of the Cold War and the break-up of many eastern European states, attitudes to the demands of minority groups in various parts of the world, for some form of self-government, changed. The economic and cultural aspirations of ethnic minorities became a legitimate political issue both domestically and internationally:

Empire-building and its subsequent dissolution, particularly in Asia, Africa and Eastern Europe has been largely instrumental in the de-stabilization of

1 See T.M. Franck, 'Postmodern Tribalism and the Right to Secession', in C. Brölmann et al. (eds.), *Peoples and Minorities in International Law*, Martinus Nijhoff: Dordrecht, 1993, pp.3–28. See also R. Higgins, 'Postmodern Tribalism and the Right to Secession, Comments', in Brölmann, *Peoples and Minorities 1993*, pp.29–36. A. Cassese, *Self-Determination of Peoples*, Cambridge University Press: Cambridge, 1995, p.338.

2 See P. Thornberry, 'The Democratic or Internal Aspect of Self-Determination with Some Remarks on Federalism', in C. Tomuschat (ed) *Modern Law of Self-Determination*, Martinus Nijhoff: Dordrecht, 1993, p.105.

3 See *Possible Ways and Means of Facilitating the Peaceful and Constructive Solution of Problems Involving Minorities*, 2nd Progress Report, UN Doc. E/CN.4/Sub.2/ 1992/37, prs.16–22. Same author in 'In Search of Constructive Alternatives to Secession', in Tomuschat (ed.), *Modern Law of Self-Determination*, 1993, pp.139–176.

heterogeneous, ethnically diverse nation-States across the globe.[4] Many ethnic groups argue that the post-Westphalian State system created in the post-war period, especially in the former Empires, virtually ruined their socio-political structure. So, struggles for new nation-States have been on the increase for many decades.[5]

The 1990s: A decade of secessionist movements worldwide

> We want a country, we will wait a bit, but not for long.

One state representative memorably noted that most secessionist movements pursue 'the path of the gun' and are eventually 'locked in a life-or-death struggle'[6] against the contemporary nation state system to achieve their ultimate goal, namely, the creation of new ethnic states. Some of these secessionist movements, observed the Armenian delegate to the UN, 'have escalated into long-standing conflicts or civil wars'.[7] The campaign of the Serbs to create the Republika Srpska, seceding from the Republic of Bosnia Herzegovina resulted in one of the bloodiest wars, in fact, the 'first general war since 1945',[8] that was witnessed in recent history. Ethnic Albanians living in the Kosovo province fought a virulent war against the Serbian forces for independence 'to preserve their language, educational system and traditional culture'.[9] These secessionist movements justified their struggles with arguments based on religious, linguistic and cultural identities.[10]

From Angola to Somalia . . .

On the African continent, ethnic conflicts erupted in Angola, Somalia, Burundi, Rwanda, and Liberia.[11] A former Namibian Foreign Minister's anguished assessment was that 'Africa is bleeding . . . the African people are burning in misery and mayhem.'[12] Human tragedy and the massacres of innocent people 'have gone

4 See, for example, Hendrik Spruyt, 'The Origins, Development and possible Decline of the Modern State.', *Annual Review of Political Science*, 5, June, 2002, pp.127–149.

5 See, generally, Dr G. Welhengama, *Minorities' Claims: From Autonomy to Secession, International Law and State Practice*, Ashgate: Aldershot, 2000; see, further, R. Müllerson, 'Minorities in Eastern Europe and the Former USSR: Problems, Tendencies and Protection', *MLR*, 56, 1993, p.799.

6 A/C.3/49/SR.8/, 25 Oct. 1992, pr.12, p.5.

7 A/C.3/48/SR. 21, 26 Nov. 1993, pr.11, p.4.

8 B. Denitch, *Ethnic Nationalism: The Tragic Death of Yugoslavia*, University of Minnesota Press: Minneapolis/London, 1994. For more details, D.P. Moynihan, *Pandemonium: Ethnicity in International Politics*, Oxford UP: Oxford, 1994, p.72.

9 A/C.3/47/SR.8, 19 Oct. 1992, pr. 48, p. 13 (Albania). See also Russia's Foreign Minister, Sergey Lavrov's statement on Kosovo's secession, in International Herald Tribune, 15 Feb. 2008. See also Accordance with International law of the Unilateral Declaration of Independence in respect of Kosovo. ICJ Summary. Advisory Opinion 2010/2 para 83.

10 See, generally, H. Kohn, 2nd ed. *Nationalism, Its Meaning and History*, Van Nostrand: Princeton, NJ, 1965.

11 A/51/PV.20, 3 Oct. 1996, p.9 (Senegal).

12 A/51/PV. 14, 30 Sept. 1996, p.6.

beyond the bounds of all reason'.[13] It is common knowledge that in the Democratic Republic of Congo, Rwanda, Uganda, Burundi, Algeria, Ethiopia, Somalia, Papua New Guinea and Sudan many thousands of non-combatants have cruelly suffered as a result of secessionist violence. In Somalia, the government was overthrown in 1991 and 'freelance gunmen', operating on a tribal basis brought Somalia to total anarchy. It appeared that Somalia was going to break up into several, separate states along the lines of tribal and clan allegiances. Secessionists in the northern part of Somalia succeeded in claiming independence for a semi-desert territory on the coast of the gulf of Aden called 'Somaliland' and although this area has developed fairly stable institutions of government, its independent status was never actually recognised either by Somalia or the rest of the world. Now that a new federal parliament has replaced the transitional government in Somalia whose term ran out in August 2011, leaders of Somaliland agreed in June 2012 to talks with the Somali government over the status of Somaliland.

Secessionist wars in Sudan's southern and eastern regions entered a different phase under an umbrella organization called 'the National Democratic Alliance' – consisting mainly of non-Muslim groups in the southern[14] and eastern parts of the country. Even the neighbouring countries, Ethiopia, Eritrea and Uganda, are alleged to have been involved in assisting the southern Sudanese.[15] After years of conflict, the most recent being the war that lasted from 1983 to 2005, which caused the deaths of two million people, the peace settlement between north and south agreed to settle the matter of secession through a referendum. On 1 July 2011, following the referendum in which 99.57 per cent of voters chose secession, south Sudan became an independent state. However, armed disputes with north Sudan over some border regions and the Helig oil fields continue. South Sudan itself is also mired in a war with seven armed groups of rebels in nine of its ten states. These wars have displaced thousands of people.

Clearly, with new claimants emerging year after year newly independent states are not safe from the threat of secession. This proliferation of states along tribal and religious lines sometimes took on an outlandish aspect, for example, when the new South African Republic was established in 1994 with the first fully democratic election. The South African white settler communities, the Afrikaners, declared their determination to fight for a 'white homeland or peoples' state' (*volkstaat*), effectively wishing to break away from the newly formed Republic of South Africa.[16] Support for a *volkstaat,* was led by the 'Freedom Front'. Professor Hendrik Robbertz, the Chairman of the *Volkstaat* Council, believed that 'self-determination for Afrikaners will determine whether South Africa will survive as a stable

13 Reference to Somali situation by Mr. Al-Eryany, the Yemen Deputy Prime Minister's address to the UN, DHA News, *UN Department of Humanitarian Affairs*, Special Edition, Jan/Feb 1994, p.12.

14 B. Whitaker, 'The Southern Sudan and Eritrea' in B. Whitaker (ed.) *The Fourth World: Victims of Group Oppression*, Sidgwick & Jackson: London, 1972, pp.80–94. In November 2012 the UK government discontinued aid to Rwanda on account if its continuous involvement in civil unrest in neighboring Congo.

15 *Financial Times*, 9 Feb. 1997.

16 R.W. Johnson, 'Afrikaners' Rights of Hopes in Bluff and Bluster', *The Times*, 27 Dec. 1993.

community of secure peoples'. The main reason for a white homeland was the Afrikaaners' rejection of 'a pot where you throw everything in and then you will have a new nation'.[17] The movement gained ground initially but has since lost momentum completely.

From eastern Europe to central Europe

In Europe, particularly in eastern and central Europe, secessionist movements gained ground after the break-up of the former USSR.[18] New nation states emerging out of the ruins of the former USSR are also grappling with secessionist claims by ethnic groups in their midst. The Chechen separatists' armed struggle against the Russian Federation is a classic case in point. When Boris Yeltsin, the former President, offered the separatists greater autonomous powers, including the right to have plenary powers to establish relations with the international community and other economic and cultural organisations; the right to govern in terms of their constitutional structure; the right to determine their flag and national anthem, Chechen and Tartastan ethnic rebels rejected his offer, arguing they were not satisfied with anything less than complete and undiminished statehood.[19] The Chechen secessionist movement still functions in the form of sporadic terrorism despite the death of its one-time charismatic leader, Basayev.[20] The Ossetians and the Abkhazians, who represent respectively 3 and 1.9 per cent of the population of the Republic of Georgia, have declared Ossetia and Abkhazia respectively as independent states. The Abkhazians have attempted several times to break away from Georgia. In 1990 the Abkhaz Supreme Soviet declared Abkhazia a sovereign Republic.[21] In the hope that the Abkhazians would remain in the Georgian Republic, they were offered 'disproportionate representation' by the Georgian government in the legislative council of Abkhazia. This constitutional arrangement has been rejected by the Abkhazian separatist politicians making it abundantly clear that it does not fully reflect their ambitions. Secessionist Crimean Tartars in the Crimean peninsula of Ukraine are not satisfied with mere administrative and territorial autonomy for Crimea.[22] The Armenian minorities' campaign for an independent State in the Nagorny Karabakh region in Azerbaijan resulted

17 S. Kiley, 'Afrikaners Win Backing for Separate Homeland', *The Times*, 7 Aug. 1998.

18 See, generally, Peter Radan, *The Breakup of Yugoslavia and International Law*, Routledge: London, 2002; S.J. Kaufman, *Modern Hatreds: The Symbolic Power of Ethnic War*, Cornell University Press: Cornell, NJ, 2001; S.M. Birgeson, *After the Breakup of a Multi-Ethnic Empire. Russia, Successor States, and Eurasian Security*, Praeger Publishers: Westport, CT, 2002.

19 *Washington Post*, 1 April 1992, cited in D. P. Moynihan, *Pandaemonium* ,1993 p.71.

20 Council of Foreign Relations, www.cfr.org/publication/11095.

21 See *The United Nations and the Situations on Georgia*, UN Department of Information: New York, DPI/1693, April 1995, p.1.

22 A/C.3/51/SR.28, 19, Sept. 1997, pr.14, p.5 (Ukraine). See details, J. Packer, 'Autonomy Within the OSCE: The Case of Crimea', in M. Suksi (eds.), *Autonomy: Applications and Implications*, Kluwer Law International: The Hague, 1998, pp.312–314.

in a large-scale war between Azerbaijan and Armenia. The Turkish Cypriot secessionists were not even satisfied with the 'bicommunal and bi-zonal federation' proposed by the Greek government based on the seemingly equitable principle that the future political structure of Cyprus should be composed of two politically equal entities.[23]

Similarly, despite already having an autonomous province, Euskadi Ta Askatasuna (ETA) secessionists in the Basque country fought for a separate state for many decades. Tunku Vardarajan, columnist for the *Guardian* once concluded from ETA's political philosophy that they desire nothing short of total sovereignty: 'How can we accept political consensus within the Spanish State if we do not accept that State in the first place.'[24] However, on the eve of the elections in the Spanish regions of Catalonia, which in November 2012 voted for independence, ETA offered to enter talks with the Spanish government to bring an end to their operations. Spain rejected this offer insisting that it would not negotiate with terrorist organisations and demanded the 'unconditional dissolution' of ETA. Interestingly while the momentum seems to have abated from the Basque separatist movement, the movement for Catalonian independence has grown. The Catalonians have a different culture and language from the rest of Spain.[25]

UK and Canada

Separatist tendencies are prevalent even in the most advanced of democratic countries, such as in the UK and Canada. In Great Britain, although the Scots already enjoy extensive devolved powers through the Scotland Act of 1998,[26] the Scots have made their desire for complete independence known. Devolution appears to have increased the desire for independence rather that diminished it. In October 2012 the Prime Minister of England, David Cameron, with his Scottish counterpart, the leader of the Scottish Nationalist Party (SNP), Alex Salmond, resolved to put the question of Scottish independence to a referendum. In 2014 Scots over the age of 15 will vote on whether they remain in the United Kingdom.[27]

23 A/51/PV. 10, 26 Sept. 1996, p.3. See further A/C.3/47/SR.9, 27 Oct. 1992, pr.89, p.19.

24 *The Guardian*, 23 July 1996.

25 Jon Henley, 'Catalonia Tales: "Independence began as something small in my heart"', 23 November 2012, Guardian.co.uk.

26 An Introduction to Devolution in the UK. *Research Paper* 03/84, 17 November 2003. House of Commons Library. http://www.parliament.uk/documents/commons/h6/reserach/rp2003/rp03-084.pdf.

27 There are a number of recent studies such as Gudrun Ostby, 'Polarisation , Horizontal Inequalities and Violent Civil Conflict', *Journal of Peace Research* March, 4pp.5(2), 2008, 143–162; or Joan Esteban, Laura Magoral, Debraj Ray, 'Ethnicity and Conflict: Theory and Facts', *Science*, 18 May 2012, 336, 858–865; and Christa Diewiks, Lars-Erik Ciderman and Kristian Skrede Gleditsch, 'Inequality and Conflict in Federations', *Journal of Peace Research*, 49(2), 2012, pp.289–304, that have sought to find underlying causes for the ethnic violence such as poverty or weak institutions and in many instances these studies do shed light on a large number of conflicts, however, as the Scottish and Catalonian cases show ethnic or cultural affiliations may be irreducible to underlying causes.

The attempts by Republicans in Northern Ireland to achieve a United Ireland are well documented. While a gentler assertion of national pride is also active in Wales in the form of the 'Welsh language groups', the Welsh are not as robust as the Scots in their demand for independence.[28]

In Canada, Francophile Quebecois have been trying to secede from Canada for some considerable time, even though the Quebec province enjoys greater autonomous power within a federal structure in perhaps the most decentralised constitutional structure in the world.[29] Nevertheless, the majority of Quebecois are in favour of secession; further constitutional arrangements may well not suffice to quell secessionists' desires for an independent Quebec. 'We want a country, we will wait a bit, but not for long', said Jacques Parizeau.[30] In the Americas, Puerto Rican and Alaskan secessionist movements are also campaigning for independent statehood.[31]

Indian subcontinent

Predictably, the Indian subcontinent is beset by a great number of ethnic separatist movements.[32] Given the diverse nature of the various ethnic and tribal populations, especially in northern and eastern parts of the subcontinent, it is not at all surprising that these demographic diversities inevitably make the region unstable and politically volatile. Secessionist armed struggles by ethnic groups in Sri Lanka, India, Bangladesh, Pakistan and Myanmar (previously known as Burma) have a long history. Most ethnic groups in the region share the view that they have been deprived of their right to have their own nation states, first by the British Raj, and then subsequently by the newly created nation states. These diverse resentments have resulted in widespread violence engulfing several states in the region.

Not surprisingly, secessionist armed struggles have resulted in border clashes among states causing a deterioration of inter-state relations. For example, India has had many such clashes with Pakistan since its independence in 1947. India has supported separatist movements in Pakistan and Pakistan has, in turn, supported secessionist movements operating in India, each with the view to destabilise the

28 In 2003, 21 per cent of those who were questioned told that they would prefer independence. See *Public Attitudes, Devolution and National Identity, Devolution and Constitution Change*, ESRC Research Project, 5 September 2004.

29 A. E. Buchanan, *Secession: The Morality of Political Divorce, From Fort Sumter to Lithuania and Quebec*, Westview Press: Boulder, CO/San Francisco, 1991, p.128. See, further, J. Porter, 'Ethnic Pluralism in Canadian Perspective', in. N. Glazer and D.P. Moynihan (eds.), *Ethnicity, Theory and Experience*, Harvard University Press: Cambridge, MA, 1976, pp.267–304.

30 http://www.usatoday.com/news/index/inque, 16 March 1999.

31 Moyniham *Pandemonium*, 1994, p.76.

32 This includes India, Pakistan, Bangladesh, Bhutan, Maldives, Nepal and Sri Lanka. See Ashutosh Varshney 'Ethnic Conflict and Civil Society: India and Beyond', *World Politics*, 53(3), 2001.

enemy.[33] It has been widely reported that many separatist movements in the northern and eastern regions of India[34] have been supported financially, ideologically and militarily by the Republic of China as well as by Pakistan. In 2012 the redrawing of the Chinese border in passports issued by the Chinese authorities to include disputed territory between India and China continues this low-intensity quarrel.

Violation of Sri Lanka's air space by the Indian Air Force (code named, 'Operation Poomalai' or 'Eagle Mission 4') in 1987 on the instruction of the former Indian Premier, Rãjiv Gãndhi, in support of Tamils in the Jaffna Peninsula almost brought Sri Lanka and India to the brink of war. When, in pursuance of the Indo-Lanka Peace Accord 1987,[35] the Sri Lankan government made an offer of autonomy to the merged north-eastern provinces of the island, the Tamil separatist group LTTE rejected it outright, making it clear that such a move would not fulfill the Tamil nation's aspiration to have their own nation state, Tamil Eelam. The struggle for a homeland was prosecuted violently by the Tamils for more than 22 years until the Rajapakse government crushed the LTTE militarily in 2009.

The Chitagongs in the Chitagong Hill Tracks were at first prepared to accept greater autonomous status within Bangladesh. In 1997 a peace accord was signed but owing to the 'spiral of government repression and armed resistance', Chitagong secessionist groups are now fighting for an independent Chitagong. Secessionists in Kashmir and Jammu,[36] the Nagas and the Mizos in the Republic of India have also been fighting for independent statehoods, respectively, for Nagaland and Mizoram. The Nagas commenced their campaign for independence before India had even attained her independence. Naga national leaders, on the eve of the declaration of Indian independence by the British Raj made a declaration of independence of their own. Both the British and post-independent Nehruvian governments refused to grant independent status to Nagaland. A short-lived, independent, sovereign 'Federal Government of Nagaland' has never been militarily, or politically, able to defend its proclaimed statehood. Nonetheless, with the encouragement of Pakistan and sometimes with the suspected clandestine military assistance from the Republic of China, the Nationalist Socialist Council of Nagaland has resorted to violence to create a Christian Socialist state within greater Nagaland. Analysing this unusually protracted military struggle, Mahmud Ali writes: 'Nagas have fought Indian forces for more than three decades and, despite immense odds, continue to do so.'[37] The Manipur secessionist struggle led by the

33 A/C.3/50/SR.50, 12 Jan. 1996, pr.43, p.8 (Indians' allegation against Pakistan).

34 There has been ongoing analysis of the crisis in the northeast of India. See Krishna C. Vadlamannathi, 'Why Indian Men Rebel? Explaining Armed Rebellion in the North Eastern States of India. 1970-2007', *Journal of Peace Research*, 48(5), 2011.

35 See the full text of the Accord, *ILM*, 26, 1175 [1987], pp.1175–1183. See also S. Thamilchelvan, Head of Political Division of the LTTE, *Tamil Net*, 25 June 2007.

36 A/C.3/47/SR.9, 27 Oct. 1992, pr.52, p.12 (Pakistan).

37 S.M. Ali, *The Fearful State: Power, People and Internal Wars in South Asia*, Zed Books: London and New Jersey, 1993, p.37. See also E. Aspinall and E. Berger, 'The Breakup of Indonesia Nationalism after

Meitei tribal group is yet another candidate seeking independence. Having recognised the legitimacy of some of the claims made by the Meitei secessionists the Indian government established the Manipur Hill Council and granted it greater autonomous powers within the Indian federal structure. Yet, both the People's Liberation Army (PLA) and the People's Revolutionary Government of KunglaPak (PREPAK), the main separatist groups of Meitei, are not satisfied with limited autonomous status. The secessionists' claimed that, 'we are beasts of burden under Mayang colonial rule; let us throw out Mayang rule and build a new society. We want independence, we want liberalism.'[38] Extremely concerned with the Marxist–Leninist leaning of both factions, the PLA and PREPAK, the Indian government has not been willing to reach a compromise with them.

In Darjeeling, in West Bengal, the Gurkhas's struggle for an independent state commenced as early as 1907. They first tried, peacefully, to secure a separate constituency to voice their grievances within the National Assembly. Later, the campaign turned to the liberation of Gurkhaland. The militant group's struggle has 'transformed Darjeeling from being a peaceful tourist haven into a potential tinder-box'.[39] Pranta Prashad and the Gurkha National Liberation Front (GNLF) were prominent among secessionist groups in the 1980s. Even though the central government of India was able to persuade some moderate leaders of the GNLF to accept autonomous status for 600,000 Gurkhas by establishing the 'Darjeeling Gurkha Hill Council' in 1988, the military wing of the GNLF and other small secessionist groups were not satisfied with such a constitutional arrangement. So the hit-and-run guerrilla campaign against state authorities has continued, although success seems unlikely, at least in the near future.[40] Baluchis and Pathans in Pakistan have also been unsuccessfully fighting for their own nation states for many decades now.

South East Asia

Myanmar, Thailand, Indonesia and the Philippines have also not been free of aggressive secessionist struggles. Myanmar's unitary structure has been threatened mainly by the Karens since Myanmar gained its independence from the British Empire in 1948. There were more than 16 secessionist groups operating against Myanmar. Separatist ethnic secessionist groups increased their military campaigns against Myanmar after the military coup in 1962. Constitutional changes also triggered secessionists' struggles since Myanmar was declared a unitary

Decolonization and the Limits of the Nation State in Post-Cold War South East Asia', *Third World Quarterly*, 2001, 22(6), pp.1003–1024.

38 Ali, *The Fearful State*, 1993, p.47.

39 Ali, *The Fearful State*, 1993, pp.53–54.

40 Ali, *The Fearful State*, 1993, pp.53–56. A recent confirmation of the Gurkha position not to give up the fight is recorded in Anuradha Sharma, 'A Conversation With Gorkha leader Bimal Gurung', *New York Times*, 27 March 2012. http://topics.nytimes.com/topics/reference/timestopics/subjects/g/gurkhas/index.html.

state by the 1974 Constitution.[41] After decades of isolation, the country held its first elections in 2011 and since then relations with the US have thawed with the President of the US making an historic visit to Myanmar in November 2012. The EU has also eased sanctions against Myanmar. Yet tellingly the war between the Burmese Army and the Kachin Independence Army (KIA) has intensified rather than eased. The June report of Human Rights Watch put the figures of displaced civilians in Kachin at 75,000 and claim that about 10,000 Kachin refugees are in temporary refugee camps along the Chinese border. Suu Kyi in her Nobel Prize speech also sounded a note of caution about 'blind faith' in Burma's future direction.

Although only a few secessionist groups have been successful in forming new states there remains no sign of any decrease in these secessionist struggles. While some have admittedly lost their momentum others have, by contrast, become increasingly active. Ultimately, success or failure depends on the extent to which these groups are prepared to continue with their struggles and on the determination of nation states to continue to resist their claims.

Triggers and incentives

There are a multitude of different reasons for the escalation of armed struggles by ethnic groups against contemporary nation states. However, there has to be an explanation for the sudden increase of secessionist movements in more than a third of all states in the 1990s. In some places the reasons are clear. The mishandling of crucial issues affecting sections of the population caused disaffection. In the former USSR, ruthless policies adopted by former dictators created temporary peace but the liberation struggles that erupted in that part of the world exposed the hidden allegiances of different ethnic groups, which manifested in a series of splinter wars.[42] When a segment of a population has been subjected to discriminatory treatment and kept within an artificially created nation state structure,[43] such as the former Socialist Republic of Yugoslavia and the Republic of Iraq, it is predictable, sooner rather than later, that a popular uprising may spring up.[44]

There is a pattern to be discerned in ethnic groups' claims for greater political power. These claims usually start with a demand for the political recognition of

41 R. Milne, 'South East Asia', in R.A. Jackson and A. James (eds.), *State in a Changing World: Contemporary Analysis*, Clarendon Press: Oxford, 1993, p.183.

42 See C. Schreuer, 'The Waning of the Sovereign State: Towards a New Paradigm For International Law', *EJIL*, 4(4), 1993, p.448.

43 See W. Soyinka, *The Open Sore of a Continent*, Oxford University Press: Oxford, 1996.

44 C.S. Leff, 'Democratization and Disintegration in Multinational States: The Breakup of the Communist Federations', *World Politics*, 51(2), 1999, p.206. See also R. P. Cinolla, R. Engleman and P. Anastasioin, 'The Security Demographic: Population and Civil Conflict After the Cold War', Pdf Url: ADA 422694, 2003. DTIC online; Ronald Axtmann, 'The State of the State: The Model of the Modern State and its Contemporary Transformation', *International Political Science Review*, 25(3), 2004, pp.259–279.

minority aspirations usually through some form of *autonomy*; this may proceed to *separatism* in terms of a federal or confederal structure, while a final progression would be *secession* or *irredentism*. When a compromise can be achieved through mutual understanding between an ethno-nationalist group (or groups) and the state, autonomy may develop within a unitary, federal or confederal structure creating a union of states. But when claims for autonomy fail, the resentments of ethnic groups may develop into *separatism*, that is rebellion against the sovereign state, which, if successful, might result in a new state. Contrariwise, autonomy might be used by ethno-tribal groups as a stepping stone towards creating ethno-tribal states. Even assuming that an ethno-tribal group achieved autonomy with shared sovereignty within a federal or confederal structure, tendencies towards an independence might still operate. Indeed, autonomous power might help ethnic groups strengthen their power base.

Already in 1944 Cobban noted that nationalism had developed from the era of state building to state breaking. He observed how 'dormant nationalities' were coming to the surface thus posing a threat to the nation state structure.[45] His prescient comments anticipated the upheavals in contemporary global polities beset by secessionist violence. Nationalism created states but the same nationalism is now leading to the 'the break-up or serious weakening of states'.[46]

Some contemporary research reveals that in the last quarter of the twentieth century there were active movements fighting either for secession or for greater autonomy in more than 60 nation states, which is almost one-third of the international community.[47] This phenomenon has now reached the point where even the smallest ethno-tribal groups, previously unheard of, are fighting for new nation states. Buchheit refers to an amazing case in which a declaration of secession was served on the Australian government by as few as 29 individuals living in the Hutt River Province Principality situated 595 km north of Perth in Western Australia.[48] This new 'nation state' (about 75 km in size) was founded on 29 April 1970 by Leonard George Casley. He and his associates later claimed independence from Australia. The Principality claims worldwide citizenry of 13,000. Unsurprisingly, Australia's response was that the new nation state was not more than a farmland controlled by a maverick businessman and his henchmen.[49]

45 A. Cobban, *National Self-Determination*, Oxford University Press: London, 1944, Preface, p.xi.

46 I. Bremmer and A. Bailes, 'Sub-Regionalism in the Newly Independent States', 74 (I) *International Affairs* 1998, p.131.

47 M.H. Halperin, D.J. Scheffer and P.L. Small, *Self-Determination in the New World Order*, Carnegie Endowment for International Peace: Washington DC, 'Forward', 1992, p.xi. See, generally, L.C. Buchheit, *Secession: The Legitimacy of Self-Determination*, Yale University Press: New Haven/London, 1978.

48 Buchheit, *Secession*,1978, p.ix. Now this is called the Hutt River Principality, which was founded on 21 April 1970 by Leonard George Casley.

49 See details, http://en.wkipedia.org/wiki/Hutt_River_Province.

Moral justification

It is argued that secession, or the right to establish a separate nation or region, can be justified on moral grounds. The philosophy behind this argument is that individuals or groups have the inherent right to decide whether to stay or leave and subsequently set up their own states. Arguments based on morality are also based on liberal principles. Secessionists claim that the right to secession flows from natural rights, the same rights that underpin the American Declaration of Independence and the French Declaration of the Rights of Man and of the Citizen. The right to determine one's own political system, if secession does not harm the other communities or groups or individuals, states have a moral obligation not to be obstructionist. According to liberal political philosophy, secessionists should be allowed to achieve their aspirations to the maximum without interference by states. For this reason, therefore, both groups and individuals have an inherent right to decide or select the kind of society, community or the state which they would like to live in. The right to participate in the political process is one of the essential rights to which any individual is entitled. The state cannot simply violate these basic rights – it is morally bound to safeguard rights conducive to the enhancement of individual wellbeing. Individuals acquire rights not as citizens of the state, but by virtue of being human beings. Therefore, an individual's decision matters in determining whether he or she should join a society or a polity or a breakaway any time he or she chooses to do so. On these grounds, secession is a morally justifiable right.[50]

Human factor

The ideologies of secessionist campaigners have proved attractive to a wide range of people. Honour and pride, mixed with aggression and militancy, play a significant role in the psychology of such movements. Yet no single factor can be attributed to the secessionists' motives. Dov Ronen argues convincingly that ethnic groups often try to exploit 'primordial' loyalties to fight against the dominance of other groups. Group identity is based on 'a sense of collective destiny on the basis of a collective past and a common biological descent'.[51] Preserving this identity is seen as a constant struggle, the purpose of which is to control their own lives by themselves without any interference from 'outsiders'. Ethnic identity thus gradually

50 See details, Buchanan, *Secession: The Morality of Political Divorce*, 1991, chapter 2; V. van Dyke, 'The Individual, The State, and Ethnic Communities in Political Theory', in W. Kymlicka (ed.), *The Rights of Minority Cultures*, Oxford: Oxford University Press, 1995, pp.44–45; D. Murswiek, 'The Issues of a Right of a Secession-Reconsidered', in Tomuchat (ed), *Modern Law of Self-Determination*, Dordrecht, 1993, pp.21–40.

51 S. Lawson, 'Self-Determination as Ethnocracy: Perspectives from the South Pacific', in M. Sellers (ed.), *The New World Order, Sovereignty, Human Rights and the Self-Determination of Peoples*, Berg: Oxford/Washington, DC, 1996, p.156.

becomes a rallying point for confrontations with other similar groups.[52] As Stephanie Lawson rightly argues, 'the single-minded assertion of ethnic differences can overwhelm all other aspects of identity, resulting in the total domination of social and cultural life.'[53] This may, according to Ronen, gradually increase pressure toward secession and the establishment of an independent ethno-tribal state[54] or, as pointed out by Franck more bluntly, constitute new 'uni-national and uni-cultural – that is, post-modern tribal-states'.[55] Existing state structures are perceived as being insufficient to cater for ethno-tribal demands or else seen as an obstacle to development as a separate nation. Such an environment puts pressure on both ethno-tribal groups and states, and in extreme cases escalates into secessionist violence.[56] This has become a concern for many states at present because secessionist movements do not hesitate to challenge the legitimacy of the existing structure of multi-ethnic polities. This is an age when nation states find themselves continually harassed by ethnic groups threatening to alter territorial boundaries.[57]

Separatism, irredentism and secession

'Separatism', 'secessionism' and 'irredentism' generally have negative connotations. It is claimed that it was General de Gaulle who popularised these terms during the Algerian war.[58] Various definitions are offered by political commentators and social scientists to identify the phenomenon of *secession*, and to analyse how secession is different from kindred concepts such as *separatism* and *irredentism*. It is common to find these terms used interchangeably. 'Separatism', while inherently embedded in ethno-national politics,[59] nevertheless indicates two different ideologies.[60] One is that of the demands of an ethnic group for a new nation state. Secessionist Tamil guerrillas in Sri Lanka, and the Basque (ETA) in Spain fell into this category. The second option allows separatists to pursue their claims for a lesser alternative, that is, for autonomous status of the region. Kurdish separatists in Iraq and the Catalans

52 D. Ronen, *The Quest for Self-Determination*, Yale University Press: New Haven/London, 1974, pp.42–43. See, further, H.R. Isaacs, 'Basic Group Identity: The Idols of the Tribe', in N. Glazer and D. P Moynihan (eds.), *Ethnicity, Theory and Experience*, 1976, p.30.

53 S. Lawson 'Self-Determination as Ethnocracy: Perspectives from the South Pacific' in M. Sellers (ed.), *The New World Order*, 1996, p.156.

54 Ronen, *The Quest for Self-Determination*, 1974, 54, p.xii.

55 Franck, in Brolman et al., *People and Minorities*, 1993, p.21.

56 Ronen, *The Quest for Self-Determination*, 1974, 54, p.xii and p.49.

57 F.L. Shiels, 'Introduction', in F.L. Shiels (ed.), *Ethnic Separatism and World Politics*, University Press of America: Lanham, MD, 1984, p.1.

58 Details J. Tubiana, 'The Linguistic Approach to Self-Determination', in I.M. Lewis (ed.), *Nationalism and Self-Determination in the Horn of Africa*, Ithaca Press: London, 1983, p.23.

59 Sigler argues that minority rights, 'for the sake of clarity and logic', should not be identified with 'separatism'. See J.A. Sigler, *Minority Rights: A Comparative Analysis*, Greenwood Press: London, 1983, 31, p.191.

60 See, Z.T. Irwin, 'Yugoslavia and Ethnonationalists', in F.L. Shiels (ed.), *Ethnic Separatism and World Politics*, 1984, p.105.

in Spain, the moderate Sikh nationalist movements in Punjab and some Tamil political parties such as TULF in Sri Lanka fell into the second category. When the second option is exercised, separatism does not necessarily lead to the establishment of a new nation state. However, the nature of the claims made is dependent on the level of mutual understanding achieved between the separatists and the state concerned.

Secession

The word *secession* is derived from the Latin word *secessio* – which means literally 'going away or apart from'. *Secession* is the most dangerous phenomenon threatening the modern nation state structure. It is as Albert Taylor Bledsoe pointed out, one and a half centuries ago, 'pregnant with such unutterable calamities'.[61] According to Cobban secession is 'generally a work of destruction and breaking down of established connexions'.[62] Heraclides offers the following more detailed definition of secession:

> [S]ecession is a special kind of territorial separatism involving States. It is an abrupt unilateral move to independence . . . In secession there is a formal act of declaration of independence on the part of the region in question. Secession thus defined can be called secession *stricto sensu* or secession *simpliciter*.[63]

Secession can result in civil unrest and, at worst, chaos. 'It can shatter old alliances, stimulate the forging of new ones, tip the balance of power, create refugee populations and disrupt international communities.'[64] As Thornberry points out, secessionist movements may lead to 'genocidal policies of so-called ethnic cleansing'.[65] Eide views secession as 'one of the most serious contemporary threats both to a peaceful evolution of the international order and to the advancement of human rights'. Therefore, he suggested that secessionist movements based on ethno-tribalism should be constrained and counteracted.[66] Müllerson presents a more forceful argument when he warns that endless 'tribalization' may increase if secessionism is recognised or encouraged.[67] He also points out that the potential

61 A.T. Bledsoe, *Is Jeff Davis a Traitor?*, Innis and Comp: New York, 1866, p.1, cited in A. Buchanan, *Secession: The Morality of Political Divorce* ,1991, Preface, p.viii.

62 Cobban, *National Self-Determination*, 1995. p.75.

63 A. Heraclides, *The Self-Determination of Minorities in International Politics*, Franck Class & Co. Ltd: London, 1991, p.1.

64 Buchanan, *Secession: The Morality of Political Divorce*, 1991, p.2.

65 Thornberry, 'The Democratic or Internal Aspect of Self-Determination with Some Remarks on Federalism', in Tomuschat (ed.), *Modern Law of Self-Determination*, 1993, p.104.

66 A. Eide, 'In Search of Constructive Alternatives to Secession', Tomuschat (ed.), *Modern Law of Self-Determination*, pp.140 and 144.

67 R. Müllerson, *International Law, Rights and Politics: Developments in Eastern Europe and the CIS*, LSE and Routledge: London, 1994, p. 71.

threat of secessionism to the harmony and balance of the wider international society is too much to warrant its acceptance in international law or political science. The emergence of a multiplicity of micro-states, based on ethno-national ideology, may not help the stability of the international order.[68] Furthermore, Müllerson blames the leadership of the secessionist movements for being selfish and power-crazy ready to exploit any opportunity to satisfy their ambitions at the expense of non-combatant, peace-loving civilians.[69] Above all, argues Cassese, secession dangerously undermines the contemporary nation state world structure, heralding catastrophic consequences for global peace.[70]

Secession is conspicuous for its unpredictability both within the movement and in its impact on the State. Ethno-tribal centered secessionism results in deep divisions and tensions amongst different ethno-tribal groups. Such an environment generates mistrust, fear and insecurity, which do not produce ideal conditions for the development of liberal democracies; neither do they encourage respect for human rights. Aggressiveness, hatred, and intolerance towards other ethnic groups should also not be underestimated. Consequently, other smaller groups are forced either to find protection from the largest ethnic group in the nation or to seek to found their own separate state.[71] For example, Muslims living in the north-east provinces of Sri Lanka had never sought an ethnically based separate territory before the commencement of the Tamil secessionist campaign in the north and east. But not only did they seek protection against Tamil secessionists such as the LTTE but they also demanded a separate province of their own in the eastern region of the island, which is they call *Nasaristan*.

Secessionism is a changing and fluctuating phenomenon generally associated with extremism and destruction. Secessionist movements operate in both forward and reverse directions. They 'slide back and forth between autonomy and independence'.[72] A good example of the latter is the secessionist movement in the province of Madras before Madras was elevated to union state status. The secessionist Dravidian movements in Tamil Nadu reversed their course preferring instead greater political power within a federal structure. A similar route was taken by the northern Nigerian secessionists, mostly the Hausa-Fulani people, who abandoned their secessionist goal in 1966, despite many prominent leaders having felt that secession was the only way that guaranteed 'honour and dignity'.[73] Some separatist groups may move from autonomy to secession as in the case of the

68 Müllerson, *International Law, Rights and Politics*, 1994, p.90.

69 Müllerson, *International Law, Rights and Politics*, 1994, p.90.

70 Cassese, *Self-determination of Peoples*, 1995, p.339.

71 Müllerson, *International Law, Rights and Politics*, 1994, pp.84–85.

72 D.S. Treisman, 'Russia's Ethnic Revival, The Separatist Activism of Regional Leaders in a Post Communist Order', 49 (2) *World Politics* 1997, p.224. See further A. Kohli, 'Can Democracies Accommodate Ethnic Nationalism? Rise and Decline of Self-Determination Movements in India', *JAS*, 56(2), 1997, p.326.

73 D.L Horowitz, *Ethnic Groups in Conflict*, University of California Press: Berkeley, 1985 pp.241 and 243.

Mizo secessionists (Mizo National Front in Mizoram in north-east India) and the Moro National Liberation Front in the Philippines.[74] South Sudan secessionists changed their positions from autonomy to secession and vice versa many times. Secessionist movement does not, by any means, necessarily end in achieving independence. There is no rule that prevents secessionists from coming to a compromise solution, such as greater autonomy – in fact something falling short of independence. Autonomous status in terms of territory might be such a compromise – as happened in Tamil Nadu (Republic of India), the Basque country and in Catalonia (Spain).

The paradoxical nature of this phenomenon is such that secessionist tendencies in suppressed groups may sometimes never develop into full secession. The Lozi homeland in Zambia is an example provided by Horowitz. Even though the imperial or constitutional powers of their monarch were restricted and many other legislative measures were enacted to curtail administrative powers within the region, the Lozis preferred to remain within a unitary Zambia.[75] Secession is rarely mentioned even when political relations deteriorate. Another notable example is the Catalans' stance towards secession. Both the Basques and the Catalans had been subjected to oppression for many decades by Spain equally, yet the Basques reacted far more vigorously than the Catalans to their situation and only recently abandoned their violent struggle while the Catalans have recently become more convinced of the need for greater independence from Spain.[76]

The target population, or the ethnic group, in a secessionist campaign is of great significance. First, secessionists have to keep their region intact and their ardent supporters together. At least the tacit support of the target group is expected. Most importantly, the assistance of the international community is needed. Both these objectives have to be targeted simultaneously. However, it is only the most advanced secessionist groups, those operating over a long period such as the PKK (the Kurdish Workers' Party)[77] the LTTE and the ETA, who manage to reach international organizations through which the justification of their respectively secessionist and irredentist claims can be effectively defended.

As Heraclides notes, violence and propaganda are part and parcel of secessionist armory.[78] Beatings as well as pleadings are used to maintain group control and to achieve group loyalty. All of these tactics were very much on display in the cases of the Tamil Tigers in Sri Lanka, ETA in Spain, and the former IRA movement

74 Horowitz, *Ethnic Groups in Conflict*, 1985, p.230.

75 Horowitz, *Ethnic Groups in Conflict*, 1985, pp.241–243.

76 Horowitz, *Ethnic Groups in Conflict*, 1985, pp.231 and 252. Robert P. Clark describes the Basque separatists as the most violent, intransigent, always assertive and, above all, the 'most difficult to reconcile'. See details, R.P. Clark, 'Spain and the Basques', in Shiels (ed.), *Ethnic Separatism and World Politics*, 1984, p.71.

77 See D. McDowall, 'The Kurdish Question: A Historical Review', in P.G. Kreyenbroek and S. Sperl (eds.), *The Kurds, A Contemporary Overview*, Routledge: London/New York, 1992, p.20.

78 Heraclides, *The Self- Determination of Minorities*, 1991, pp.42–43.

in Northern Ireland. Propaganda is not difficult at the initial stage of the conflict when there is real difficulty in obtaining accurate information. The lack of fact-checking accuracy may be due to the reluctance of both the states and secessionist groups to allow the international media unhindered access to the theatres of ethno-nationalist conflicts.

Coercion and violence, is treated by secessionists as being a kind of 'propaganda by deed'.[79] Human sufferings and the sacrifice of a perceived 'enemy group' appear justifiable prices to pay in the struggle for a worthy cause. The blowing-up of buildings, especially those belonging to the state, the theft of property, the random killings of members of the perceived enemy group, kidnapping and the infliction of fear and uncertainty are some of the more prominent tactics used by secessionists with a view to bringing their cause to the attention of the international community. If the state in question is not prepared to give up a part of its territory in recognition of a secessionist claim, violence is the ultimate choice adopted by many contemporary secessionist groups in the belief that, ultimately, the state will be forced to accept secession.[80] Violence, in the name of group interests, is justified on the assumption that a people have the right to choose their political destiny.[81] Fighting, is not only 'intrinsically important', but also instrumentally valuable' for protection against the enemy group, for the survival of the group,[82] and in pursuit of their life as a free people.[83]

The campaign of the secessionists is for the independence of a region of the nation state in which they live, and, if this campaign is successful the boundaries of the state concerned is redrawn. Generally, secessionists neither claim the whole territory of the state nor are they pleased only with the changes to the political and constitutional structure of the state in question. Most importantly, as Buchanan correctly points out, the state's authority to govern a province or a region that is predominantly inhabited by the group represented by leaders backing secession is severely challenged.[84] The state in question is identified and described as an occupying force in a given territory. Secession based on territorial claims presents more complexities and difficulties than any other form of domestic unrest. Although they are often referred to as liberation armies, as in the case of the LTTE in Sri Lanka, secessionist groups are different from national liberation movements. In the latter case, the purpose is to take over the whole territory and state structure by either peaceful or violent means from the control of an illegitimate government.

79 Buchheit, *Secession: The Legitimacy of Self-Determination*, 1978, p.19.

80 Buchheit, *Secession: The Legitimacy of Self-Determination*, 1978, p.19. For example, ETA secessionist groups in the Basque country in Spain are so far, from 1968 to date, alleged to have killed 763. See details, D. White, 'Basque Politicians Under the Gun', *Financial Times*, 27 Jan. 1998.

81 P. Gilbert, *Terrorism, Security and Nationality: An Introductory Study in Applied Political Philosophy*, Routledge: London/New York, 1994, see particularly chapter 6. See, further, A. Margalit and J. Raz, 'National Self-Determination', in W. Kymlicka (ed.), *The Rights of Minority Cultures*, 1989, p.89.

82 Margalit and Raz, 'National Self-Determination', p. 89. The whole article appeared in *Journal of Philosophy*, 87(9), Oxford University Press: Oxford, 1990, pp.439–461.

83 Ronen, *The Quest for Self-Determination*, 1974, p.47.

84 See Buchanan, *Secession: The Morality of Political Divorce*, 1991, pp.10–11.

Secession may occur within a province or provinces in the state itself. Demands can be made on a group or regional basis. Therefore, secession is considered by some as 'a special species of ethnic conflicts'.[85] The movement operates on a regional basis and may comprise many ethno-tribal and religious groups for example, the Eritrean secessionist movement (Arab Beja, Arab Afar, Black African and Christians), Biafran secessionist movements (Ibo,[86] Ibibio, Efik, Ijaw and many other small tribes) and secessionists in southern Sudan[87] (mainly Christian religious groups with the assistance of other ethnic groups).[88] However, the most important element of a secessionist claim, as pointed out by Brilmayer, is the claim for a demarcated territory which would become the basis, if secession succeeded, for the future state.[89]

Secessionists advocate the dismemberment of a state, and 'intend to abandon their current State, and in so doing, to take with them the land on which they live'.[90] Secession often emerges and is organised from below[91] unlike a formal *coup d'état* with which politicians and officials at a higher level are often associated. Sometimes, elite members of secessionist groups provide the necessary leadership, in particular, on the ideological front and especially in the international sphere to win new friends, sympathisers and activists. If the struggle succeeds, the region in question may achieve independent statehood, normally through a unilateral declaration on the part of the secessionists. Independent statehood also occurs with the tacit agreement of the international community. Bangladesh is the prime and most quoted example. More rarely, it may also happen with the consent of the majority community or the state in question. Slovakia seceded with the consent of the Czechs. Eritrea broke away from the Ethiopian state with the blessing of both the UN and the OAS. East Timor[92] gained independence with the blessing of the whole international community.

85 Horowitz, *Ethnic Groups in Conflict*, 1985, p.231.

86 During the Biafran war, the Biafran secession was and is identified as ethnic secession launched by the Ibos. See C.S. Phillips, 'Nigeria and Biafra', in Shiels (eds.), *Ethnic Separatism and World Politics*, 1984, pp.176–177. However, Col. Ojuku who led the separatist campaign rejecting such assertions emphasised that Biafran struggle was between the 'North and South' and between 'Nigeria and the former eastern region'.

87 They are mainly Negroid. Most tribal groups remain pagan. Southerners are divided into three main linguistic groups, i.e. Niloties, Nilo-Hamities, and the Sudanic. Each linguistic group is composed of various sub-tribal groups. For example, the Sudanic includes the Azande, Kreish, Bongo, Moru and Madi tribes. See Whitaker, 'The Southern Sudan and Eritrea', in Whitaker (ed.), *The Fourth World*, 1972, pp. 77–79.

88 See Ronen, *The Quest for Self-Determination*, 1974, p.45.

89 L. Brilmayer, 'Secession and Self-Determination: A Territorial Interpretation', *YJIL*, 16, 1991, pp.187–188.

90 Brilmayer, 'Secession and Self-Determination', 1991, p.187.

91 Horowitz, *Ethnic Groups in Conflict*, 1985, p.273. A classic example is that of the LTTE. Their leadership comes from the lower castes of the Tamils.

92 The new government changed its former name after it has gained independence. It is now identified as the Democratic Republic of Timor-Leste (previously known as East Timor).

Secession and irredentism

Irredentism and *secession* are different. The term 'irredentism' seems to have originated from an Italian word, *irredenta*, whose meaning is equivalent to the 'redemption' of the territory originally conquered by a foreign country.[93] But, in modern political parlance, it stands for territorial claims by a state to another state's region or province. The majority community fears that ethnic minorities may try to amalgamate with like groups beyond the border. This was true of Poland and the allegation has been made that Kosovo might eventually seek more than an understanding with Albania.

Irredentism may also involve alliances of ethnic groups across borders involving kindred ethnic groups in two or more states whose principal aim is to merge with another state. This merger is justified on historical grounds or results from primordial tribal loyalties. Somalia's claims to the Ogaden region in Ethiopia and the Djibouti region in the north-east province of Kenya; Morocco's claims, first to all of Mauritania and later to the Western Sahara, Argentina's claims to Malvinas (Falklands), Spanish claims to Gibraltar, the Irish Republic's claim to Northern Ireland are all good cases in point. Irredentist movements want a merger of the part of a territory they claim with the territory of another state occupied by members of the same group. In the 1950s and 1960s some Tamil separatist movements in Sri Lanka and Chennai (formerly known as Madras) had advocated the merger of the Dravidian nations across the Palk Strait uniting south Indian Tamils and Ceylon Tamils in the North-east Province of Sri Lanka to create a *Dravidastan/Dravidam*. Similar movements are evident in other contemporary multi-ethnic polities.[94] It has been argued that Albanians living in Macedonia and Serbia tried to gain political power within these respective states to create a 'Greater Albania'.[95] Attempts were also made by the Serbs in Macedonia and Bosnia and Herzegovina with a view to establishing a 'Greater Serbia' for Serb nationalities in central and eastern Europe. The consequences of building a greater Serbia were coldly and clinically stated by Vladimir Srebov of the Serbian Democratic Party: 'The plan was for a division of Bosnia into two spheres of influence, leading to a Greater Serbia and a Greater Croatia. The Muslims were to be subjected to a final solution – more than half were to be killed, a smaller segment converted to Orthodoxy while a smaller segment still, those with riches, could buy their lives and leave. The goal was to cleanse Bosnia-Herzegovina completely of Muslim people.'[96] The Transylvanians' desire to merge with Hungary by breaking away from Romania and the Azerbaijanis in Georgia are other well-known instances. Owing to its international dimension, irredentism presents a bigger problem than

93 See details, J. Mayall, *Nationalism and International Society*, Cambridge University Press: Cambridge, 1990.

94 See details, Horowitz, *Ethnic Groups in Conflict*, 1985, p.281.

95 Irwin, 'Yugoslavia and Ethnonationalists', in Shiels (ed.), *Ethnic Separatism and World Politics*, 1984, pp.105–131.

96 See details, E. Vulliamy, 'Bosnia: The Crime of Appeasement', *International Affairs*, 74(1), 1998, p.77.

secession. However, irredentist movements are not in as much abundance in comparison with secessionist movements the world over.

Post-Cold War secession

Secessionist movements achieved significant momentum, after the end of the Cold War and with the collapse of the former USSR and its satellite states in eastern Europe.[97] Since 1990 more than 30 new nation states have emerged and have subsequently been granted membership of the UN. This number is growing. The former Soviet Union dissolved unexpectedly and rapidly, and 15 new nation states emerged. Eastern Europe followed the same path and some ethnic groups have been successful in achieving new nation states.[98] For example, on 22 May 1992 the United Nations General Assembly admitted three new members – Slovenia, Bosnia and Herzegovina, and Croatia. On 17 September 1991 some constituent parts of the former USSR, Estonia, Latvia and Lithuania were admitted to the UN as new members. Azerbaijan, Armenia, Kazakastan, Kyrgystan, Moldova, Tajikistan, Turkistan and Uzbekistan were admitted by the UN on 2 March 1992. Georgia was admitted on 31 July 1992. Belarus (earlier, Byelorussia) and Ukraine had been original UN members and therefore no issues arose as to their membership being recognised by the UN. By 2009 Kosovo was recognized by the US, most of the EU countries and other countries around the world but has yet to be granted a seat at the UN. Elsewhere, notably Eritrea, broke away from Ethiopia with the 'connivance' of the international community in 1993[99] to the delight and satisfaction of ethnic groups in other parts of the world. Some other secessionist struggles succeeded without the usual violence; for example, ethnic Slovaks in the former Czechoslovakia were successful in achieving their Slovak nation state without embarking on a destructive war against the Czechs.[100] But Croatia achieved its independence by seceding,[101] in the context of dissolution, from the former Yugoslav Republic only after a long drawn-out war that claimed the lives of many thousands of men and women. This has become the new paradigm in the international world order. Nakhichevan, Nagorny- Karabakh, Tartastan, Chechnya, Kosovo, Bougainville[102] and Jaffna, previously unheard of names in international

97 K.S. Shehadi, *Ethnic Self-Determination and the Break-up of States*, Adelphi Papers 283, Brassey's (UK): London, 1993, p.6. See further D.E.M. Mihas, 'Romania Between Balkan Nationalism and Democratic Transition', 17 (3) *Politics*, 1997, pp.175–181. See also C. Leff, 'Democratisation and Disintegration', 1999 pp.205–235.

98 See Y.Z. Blum, 'UN Membership of the New Yugoslavia: Continuity or Break?', *AJIL*, 86(4), 1992, pp.830–832.

99 Halperin et al., *Self-determination in the New World Order*, 1992, p.14. See also Shehadi, *Ethnic Self-determination*, 1993, p.8.

100 See E. Stein, 'International Law in Internal Law: Toward Internationalization of Central-Eastern European Constitutions', *AJIL*, 88, 1994, pp.427–450.

101 See the Opinion of Badinter Arbitration Committee on this. This was set up by the Council of Ministers of the European Economic Community in 1991.

102 S. Lawson, 'Ethno-Nationalist Dimensions of Internal Conflict: The Case of Bougainwille

politics emerged out of obscurity as new candidates for 'post-modern tribal states'. As Müllerson notes, secessionist campaigners believe that, 'this is the correct moment to achieve their goals. Now or never.'[103] For many ethnic groups, 'separatism seemed the only vehicle for self-expression.'[104] This new danger, as noted by the former UN Secretary-General Boutros Ghali, creates more unstable and fragmented micro-tribal states. He cautioned, 'rather than 100 or 200 countries, you may have at the end of the century 400 countries, and we will not be able to achieve any kind of economic development, not to mention endless disputes on boundaries.'[105] According to the former US Secretary of State, Warren Christopher, if we fail to respond quickly, 'we'll have 5,000 countries rather than the hundred plus we now have.'[106] Although this may not happen in the near future, secessionist developments have shattered the conventional belief that the UN system would eventually be able to bring peace in the post-war era by respecting and guaranteeing individuals' rights on a universal basis.

No doubt, the establishment of new nation states in Europe and elsewhere encourage ethnic groups to continue their struggles believing that they are entitled to secede from existing states by invoking the doctrine of the right to self-determination. Yet the difficulties – economic, social and political and, most importantly, the fact that the proliferation of ethnic divisions does not stop with the newly created borders that they have to overcome – are enormous and not fully realised.

Secessionism', in K.P. Clements (ed.), *Peace and Security in the Asia-Pacific Region: Post-Cold War Problems and Prospects*, United Nations University Press and Dummove Press: Tokyo, 1993, pp.58–77.

103 Müllerson, *International Law, Rights and Politics*, 1994.

104 Sigler, *Minority Rights*, 1983. p.189.

105 *The Times*, 21 September 1992, cited in Shehadi, *Ethnic Self-determination*, 1993, p.8.

106 Cited in Shehadi, *Ethnic Self-determination*, 1993, p.3.

3 Nation building and minority rights

Secession: a failure to secure adequate protection for minority rights

Since the turn of the twentieth century the international regime of minority rights developed in fits and starts. However, political instability and widespread ethnically based violence in eastern Europe in the 1990s forced a re-examination of assumptions about nations, and minority rights. This re-evaluation occurred in the Sri Lankan situation as well, especially in the late 1990s and in 2000 when concerted efforts were made to provide a constitutional solution to the minority problem there. Unfortunately, these efforts fizzled out. Today the rights of minorities are fairly clearly defined and protected in a series of standard setting UN-sponsored documents. The disruptive potential of disaffected minorities exposed the fact that liberal rights, while they affirm equality and individual freedoms, are ill-fitted to the protection of such rights as language rights, that individuals enjoy by virtue of belonging to a community.

Minority rights attach to those individuals whose status as a member of a community is usually determined by descent. Individual human rights offers little help to preserve the unique culture and language that individuals can only enjoy in community. Even though a minority community may form a significant group in the nation state, they are politically non-dominant and in a vulnerable position if exposed to state-sponsored discrimination. The protection of minority rights would be fundamental to avoid an escalation of conflict such that neither secession nor the crushing of the minority community by the state, like the defeat suffered by the Sri Lankan Tamils in 2009, becomes the only solution.

The protection of minority rights is not straightforward. Minority rights demands that the majority in a nation state do more than merely refrain from interfering with the rights of minorities but respect the desire of the minority to preserve their language, religion, customs and traditions with state support.

The nation and heterogeneity

Not all secessionist movements are motivated by human rights abuses or language differences, such as the recent bid by one of the Scottish parties for independence, however most conflicts are brought on by ethnic clashes involving the domination of one group over another. There are many reasons why separatist movements arise but the common factors are discrimination and mortal threat, both of which have the effect of promoting solidarity and safety in the group and, most importantly, consolidating a group identity such that the ethnic community sees itself as a nation deprived of political expression. Either internal or external self-determination is demanded. Internal self-determination refers to the range of devolved powers to regions – usually implying shared sovereignty between the centre and the regions but external self-determination is about external boundaries and international status.[1]

Ethnic minorities became a serious political problem in the modern nation state.[2] The Roman Empire encompassed peoples of a variety of autonomous ethnicities over a vast territory. Roman citizens were subject to Roman law while Roman subjects were governed according to their own laws. This policy of allowing subjects to 'apply their own laws to themselves' continued into the Ottoman Empire and into the twentieth century.[3] The Ottomans encouraged each ethnic group through the establishment of institutions such as schools, hospitals and places of worship, to continue their customs and cultures. In western Europe, almost as soon as the Roman Empire collapsed, new political arrangements formed loosely around a monarchical system. After the Thirty Years' War ending with the Treaty of Westphalia (1648), the nation state system consolidated itself over time.

The French Revolution inaugurated the modern nation state by changing dramatically the relationship between the citizen and ruler. The republic was a decisive break with monarchy and introduced a political arrangement where rulers became accountable to the 'the people'. The 'sovereignty of the people' was a new political idea, yet the term 'the people' has always remained vague and undefined even though it determines who is included in the nation and who is not. In fact, the definition of 'people' has continued to be a problem in phrases such as the 'self-determination of peoples' found in international rights instruments and has proved to be a major stumbling block in determining the meaning and scope of these rights.[4] The heterogeneous, communal life of human beings was shaped and

1 M. Saul, 'The Normative Status of Self-Determination in International Law: A Formula for Uncertainty in the Scope and Content of the Right', *Human Rights Law Review*, 11(4), 2011, p.609.

2 Sigler, *Minority Rights, A Comparative Analysis*, 1983, p.71.

3 Sigler, *Minority Rights, A Comparative Analysis* 1983, p.71. See also E. Kedourie, *Nationalism*, London, 1960, p.117.

4 Aureliu Cristescu, *The Right to Self-Determination*, UN Doc. E/CN 4/Sub. 2/404/ Rev. 1 (1981) where the question of what are peoples is inconclusive. See also Shehadi, *Ethnic Self-Determination and the Break-up of States*, 1993.

constrained by the new Republic. The state came to be seen as 'the political form that a nation, that is, a culturally distinctive people, takes in the political order'.[5] Smaller ethnic groups became, in this new political state, 'national minorities'.[6] Currently 82 per cent of all independent states are comprised of two or more ethnic groups.[7] R.W. Stirling sums up the new nation state thus: 'The Nationalisms of the United States and of England, France, Germany, Russia and Spain were nationalisms of the majority population. The ethnic minorities lost their traditional status as an accepted part of an otherwise politically undifferentiated mass and became appendages to the new ruling majorities. Without exception, the ethnic majorities attempted to impose their cultural values on the ethnic minorities within the new national jurisdictions.'[8]

Ethnically diverse peoples who had coexisted with each other over the centuries, not always peacefully, found themselves in intense competition with one another.[9] It was a new experience to discover that because of numerical inferiority they had to give way to the will of the majority in ways that threatened their culture and way of life. In many instances, the creation of minorities was artificial depending where the borders were drawn. In order to make the heterogeneity of human life conform to the theoretical construction of a nation state, it was necessary to either assimilate or expropriate minority ethnic identities. Hence, the process of nation building has usually entailed bloodshed, the subjugation of minority populations and the expulsion of peoples in order for the nation to consolidate itself around a shared identity.

Even though the concept of the nation state has endured and the modern world order remains a conglomeration of discrete states, the idea of the nation state as a culturally homogenous state was challenged from the beginning of state formation. It was never universally accepted that minority peoples should have to surrender their culture to belong to the nation. A form of romantic nationalism developed as a reaction to the nation state. It recognized the uniqueness of each culture and encouraged the notion that if the political expression of the nation is the state then every culture should be represented as a nation state.[10] This idea gained ground over the years with an increasing number of groups expecting and demanding some sort of autonomy.

5 James Muldoon, 'The Development of Group Rights', in Sigler (ed.), *Minority Rights a Comparative Analysis*, 1983, p.62.

6 Raymond L. Hall (ed.), *Ethnic Autonomy – Comparative Dynamics. The Americas, Europe and the Developing World*, Pergamon Press: Oxford, 1979, p.xix.

7 M.D. Toft, 'Self-Determination, Secession, and Civil war, Terrorism and Political Violence', 24(4), 2012, p.585.

8 Richard W. Sterling, 'Ethnic Separatism in the International System', in Hall (ed.), *Ethnic Autonomy – Comparative Dynamics*, 1979, p.416.

9 Hall, *Ethnic Autonomy – Comparative Dynamics*, 1979, p.xix.

10 See J. L. Talmon, *Romanticism and Revolt: Europe 1815–1848*, New York: Harold Brace and World, 1967; S. May, *Language and Minority Rights: Ethnicity Nationalism and the Politics of Language*, Longman: Harlow, 2001.

Post-war wariness of minority rights

When the 1919 Paris Peace Conference[11] redrew the borders of several states, an elaborate system of treaties was put in place guaranteeing that the state would respect racial, ethnic, religious and linguistic minorities.[12] This was underwritten by the League of Nations System of Minority Guarantees, which covered both the new state boundaries and mandated territories.[13] However, the system was a dismal failure since it could not prevent the outbreak of World War II. Moreover, Woodrow Wilson, who had championed the cause of self-determination, failed to persuade other nations to include general protections of national, religious and racial minorities into the Charter. Most of the colonies of the imperial powers were simply not covered by the provisions. 'Africa, Asia, most of the Near East, Latin America, the Pacific regions, and North America were not included.'[14]

Human rights and ethnic conflict after World War II

Human rights after World War II succeeded in securing the protection of mainly the civil and political rights of people. The idea that government is a trust whose rationale is to secure the individual rights of people dates to John Locke and Thomes Hobbes. The principle of equality was central to Locke's idea that rights inhere in individuals. However, the rights and freedoms Locke imagined were mainly negative in nature; power would remain in its proper sphere and not encroach on the freedoms of the individual. Individual rights were considered a sufficient check to the domination of the majority in a democracy.

After World War II the desire to entrench individual rights replaced the idea that minorities deserved special protection. The fear after World War II was that if minorities enjoyed protection as minorities this would encourage disruption along ethnic lines, a view shared even by newly independent states as well. So long as non-discrimination provisions are made explicit and entrenched in law this would adequately cover discrimination against individuals including any discrimination a person might suffer on account of being a member of an ethnic minority. What was obvious from the discussions surrounding the proposed UN Charter was that minority protection was completely discredited (there is no mention of minorities in the Charter or in the Universal Declaration of Human Rights (UDHR)). During the discussions on the UDHR, the Soviet delegate's proposal that states guarantee to national minorities the use of their own language and foster minorities' cultures

11 Jennifer Jackson Preece, *Minority Rights*, Polity Press: Cambridge, 2005, p.13.

12 Linguistic minorities had free use of their language in religion, trade, press, and even qualified for limited educational funding in some cases.

13 Countries that signed up to minority rights obligations in their jurisdiction were the Åaland Islands, Albania, Austria, Bulgaria, Czechoslovakia, Greece, Estonia, the Free City of Danzig, Hungary, Iraq, Latvia, Lithuania, Memel, Poland Romania, Serb-Croat-Slovene State and Turkey.

14 Sigler, *Minority Rights: A Comparative Analysis*, 1983, p.75.

through schools, libraries, and museums, was defeated. The general feeling was best expressed by the chairman Eleanor Roosevelt that the rights of minorities did not belong in the current document and that 'so far as the American continents were concerned, the minorities problem did not exist.'[15] Countries continued to conclude bilateral treaties on minority rights guarantees and protections for linguistic minorities in Europe[16] but the paradox was that while the idea of the state as the political expression of a nation remained, there was a marked decline in interest in its corollary, minority rights.[17] The mood after World War II was that if the civil and political rights of individuals are protected the protection of minority rights would be superfluous. But, as Vernon van Dyke correctly points out: 'Individualism, combined with the usual stress on personal merit, is destructive of cultures other than the majority or dominant culture.'[18] Even when minority groups were protected through bilateral and multilateral treaties, these were political arrangements between states and not equivalent to rights.

The Marxist tradition did not fare any better with respect to minority rights. Intermediate loyalties such as to family, community or church had to be overcome[19] since they were obstacles to the international project of making people citizens of the world. Underlying both Liberalist and Marxist theories are modern notions of development and progress where the great nations were seen as the 'carriers of historical development'.[20] The only way for small ethnic groups to modernize was to become part of the progressive nation. This proved to be inimical to minorities since the issue was not only about discrimination but about the cultural and political advantages that the majority community automatically enjoyed that were denied to the rest. Equality and non-discrimination provisions are not sufficient to protect groups from discrimination at the hands of a majority population, for example, with respect to language; much less create an environment for minority languages to thrive.

Discrimination against minorities happens because of attempts made by the state to either assimilate or oppress minorities, for to allow them to thrive would threaten the stability of the state, yet minorities have proved resistant to either solution and have become instead a source of real instability. Conflict with the majority partner has usually had the effect of consolidating the minority group, removing internal differences and making them more effective opponents. Ethnic minorities behaved in the same way as the majority population of the state by consolidating themselves

15 UN Doc. E/CN 4S.R.,73, p.5 cited in Sigler, *Minority Rights: A Comparative Analysis*, 1983, p.67.

16 Jackson Preece, *Minority Rights*, p.115. See also J. Jackson Preece, 'Human Rights and Cultural Pluralism', in G. Lyons and J. Mayall (eds.), *International Human Rights in the 21st century: Protecting the Rights of Groups*, Oxford: Rowman & Littlefield, 2003; J. Jackson Preece, *National Minorities*, 1998.

17 Sigler, *Minority Rights: A Comparative Analysis*, 1983, p.21.

18 Vernon van Dyke, 'The Individual, the State, and Ethnic Communities in Political Theory', in Kymlicka (ed.), *The Rights of Minority Cultures*, 2004, p.10.

19 Minority cultures and languages should be suppressed with 'iron ruthlessness'. Kymlicka (ed.) *The Rights of Minority Cultures*, 2004, p.9.

20 Kymlicka (ed.) *The Rights of Minority Cultures*, 2004, p.5.

into a nation and insisting on recognition as a separate and distinct people. Richard Stirling claims that 'mass nationalism among majorities spawned mass nationalism among minorities. Traditionally inert and politically faceless during the long ascendancy of the elite state, ethnic majorities and minorities subsequently divided into distinct political blocs.'[21] Often this included a claim to territory and in extreme instances minorities demanded, on the basis that they were a distinct people, the right to secede and become an independent nation. The failure of assimilation and exclusion policies to deal with the issue of minorities and the failure to guarantee stability, given the amount of ethnic violence in the world, has required a rethink of some presuppositions with respect to minority populations. The notion of rights inhering in groups as a consequence of certain inalienable characteristics of the group *qua* group is a late modern development.

Language and the nation state

The reason that ethnic identity became the most significant, disruptive phenomenon of the modern world is because the main thrust of nationalism, especially in the nineteenth century, was national unity. Previously divided groups had to be forged into one nation,[22] and the means of doing so invariably meant a direct attack on the ways in which ethnic identities are constituted. The matter of what the official language of the state should be and the differential impact of the official language policy on the different linguistic groups in a country is central to several ethnically based conflicts in the world.

From the time of the French Revolution, language became a matter for government policy. The European idea that the minority will conform to the will of the majority was developed in eighteenth-century political thought and found political expression in the French Revolution. The feudal system was going to be replaced by 'uniformity and order'.[23] Since the Revolution had altered the nature and reach of government, it became necessary for the citizenry to understand the language of the law. A 'common public, language' became the *sine qua non* of democratic government and of liberal thought.[24] A common language was also a necessary requirement of public discourse. According to Jackson Preece, 'it was through a common language that the newly authoritative will of the people could be expressed and communicated.'[25] Therefore, it became the responsibility of government to establish and fund schools to teach the French language and the meaning of citizenship. Minority languages were tolerated in the private domain, but in order

21 Richard W. Stirling, 'Ethnic Separatism in the International System', in Hall (ed.) *Comparative Dynamics*, 1979, p.418.

22 Edward Sagarin and James Moneymaker, 'Language and Nationalist, Separatist and Secessionist Movements', in Hall (ed.) *Ethnic Autonomy*, 1979, p.19.

23 Muldoon, 'The Development of Group Rights', in Sigler, *Minority Rights: A Comparative Analysis*, 1983, p.36.

24 Jackson Preece, *Minority Rights*, 2005, p.108.

25 Jackson Preece, *Minority Rights*, 2005, p.107.

to ensure the full political participation of everybody and the functionality of public institutions 'linguistic minorities ought properly to be assimilated into the official, public language.'[26]

The Republican notion that a commonly spoken language by the electorate was important merely because it served a political and civic purpose was slowly replaced by the idea that language was the way in which individuals and communities mediated the world and each community apprehended that world in a unique way. Since the eighteenth century, the conviction grew in Europe that a nation state is a natural phenomenon – an expression of an organic community. Several nineteenth century German philosophers such as Herder and Fichte greatly influenced the discourse on nationhood. Herder believed that the nation, being a people defined according to their unique national character had a clear 'ethnic connotation', and should not expand 'beyond its natural limits and thereby cause the indiscriminate mingling of various nations and human types'.[27] Clearly, 'the nation' is actively involved in the consolidation of ethnicity as well since issues such as immigration and the granting of citizenship are matters for state policy. For this reason, some authors have pointed out that the state 'ethnifies' the nation. Nationalism is often propagated by the state by 'propagating a myth of common origin', language and other customs.[28] According to Troft, 'Whereas an ethnic group is a latent ethnic nation, a nation is a politically active ethnic group, which tends to demand greater cultural autonomy or self-determination. National self-determination, therefore, is the notion that ethnic groups have the right to determine their own fate.'[29]

Language, which embodies the history, memory and a unique way of understanding the world, defined an organic community.[30] Max Boehm argued that that role of language was the most important factor in modern nationalism and claimed that 'a people not only transmits the store of all its memories through the vocabulary of its language, but in syntax, word, sound and rhythm finds the most faithful expression of its temperament and general emotional life.'[31] A successful nation was a proper alignment of language, community and territory.

Nations were people who occupied a defined territory and who spoke the same language. It meant that borders of states should follow language groupings. The concept of the nation implied popular sovereignty, and a common language, culture and history. Not surprisingly some scholars have come to the conclusion

26 Jackson Preece, *Minority Rights*, 1988, p.109.
27 M. Shahabuddin, 'Ethnicity in the International Law of Minority Protection', 2012, p.895.
28 P.G. Roeder, *Where Nation-States Come From: Institutional Change in the Age of Nationalism*, Princeton University Press: Princeton, 2007, p.31.
29 M.D. Toft, 'Self-determination, Secession and Civil War, Terrorism and Political Violence', 24(4), 2012, p.584.
30 'The State should be the political expression of a culturally homogeneous society', James B. Muldoon 'The Development of Group Rights', in Sigler, *Minority Rights: A Comparative Analysis*, 1983, p.31.
31 Max Boehm cited in Sagarin and Moneymaker, 'Language and Nationalist, Separatist and Secessionist Movements', in Hall (ed.) *Ethnic Autonomy*, 1979, p.19.

that 'the nineteenth century quest for statehood became as much a philological as a political endeavour.'[32] Sujit Choudhry argues that this quest was not confined to the Europe, in fact 'it would be no exaggeration to claim that in South Asia language has been the single most important force driving the reconfiguration of political space in the modern era.'[33] In fact, it persisted into the twentieth century. In Asia and the Middle East, there was the attempt to impose Persian on the Arabistans in Iran, dzonghka on the Nepalese in Bhutan, Burmese on the Mons in Burma and Urdu on the Sindhi in Pakistan.[34] In the 1980s there was a concerted attempt by the Bulgarians to ensure the 'Bulgarisation' of the Turkish minority.[35] In 1990 the Slovak Official Language Law was seen as a means of restricting the use of minority languages.

The Committee on New States at the Paris Peace Conference in 1919[36] was heavily influenced by the idea that the boundaries of nation states should be demarcated along linguistic lines, but, it was impossible to incorporate similar language groups into one territory. This is why linguistic minorities are still found in pockets in all the new states of Europe. Describing the nation as a people sharing of language, community, and territory together leaves little room politically for minorities of different ethnicities speaking other languages. Since the state is an irreducible political entity, minority groups simply had to become part of the nation and had to be assimilated. This was the standard view in the nineteenth century as is exemplified by the Durham Report commissioned by the British government after a rebellion against colonial rule in Canada. Durham states his conviction that the national character of the province should be the majority, which is British and that the British government should incrementally but firmly establish an English population, English language and English legislature in the province. This policy of nation building was pursued even in post-communist states.[37]

Minorities are assimilated through a variety of different processes such as the removal of 'traditional forms' of regional self-government or by forced integration through resettlement policies where 'immigration' is encouraged into areas traditionally settled by the minority, but the restriction of the minority language [38] is often the 'flashpoint' in the relationship of minorities with the nation state. While other distinctive characteristics of people, such as their religion can be relegated to

32 See Jackson Preece, *Minority Rights*, 2005, p.111.

33 S. Choudhry, 'Managing Linguistic Nationalism through Constitutional Design: Lessons from South Asia', *Int. J. Constitutional Law*, 2009, 7(4), 577.

34 Will Kymlicka, 'Models of Multicultural Citizenship' in S. Tan (ed.) *Challenging Citizenship. Group Membership and Cultural Identity in a Global Age,* Ashgate: Farnham, 2005, p.119.

35 Jackson Preece, *Minority Rights*, 2005, p.127.

36 See L. Riga and J. Kennedy, 'Tolerant Majorities, Loyal Minorities and Ethnic Reversals: Constructing Minority Rights at Versailles 1919', *Nations and Nationalism*, 15(3), 2009, 461–492.

37 R. Coupland, *The Durham Report*, Oxford University Press: Oxford, 1945, cited in Jackson Preece, *Minority Rights*, 2005.

38 Kymlicka, 'Models of Multicultural Citizenship', in Tan, *Challenging Citizenship*, 2005, p.120.

the private domain, language cannot be so confined. The language that a state chooses will advantage native speakers of the language since all public and most private intercourse will be conducted in that language. It will dominate the public media, the justice system, trade and education.[39] Depending on which language is favoured as the language of the administration and law it will have an effect on people's prospects for employment, access to justice and political participation.

Language and colonial policy

While language policy was the means of assimilating the minority into the nation state and the guiding principle of nation building in Europe, an entirely different language policy was pursued by the colonial powers in the colonies.[40] There was no intention on the part of the colonial authorities to extend political participation to the masses so there was no need to promote a language policy that would have created a nation on the European model. What was needed in the colonies was a language necessary for the proper functioning of the colonial administrative bureaucracy. Usually this meant that the language of the imperial power became the language of administration – English in British colonies and French in French colonies and so on. The administration of the colonies was carried out by colonial administrators and a local elite proficient in the colonial language and educated in the same way as the colonial elite. Imperial rule was not possible without the cooperation of the locals and this necessitated a 'commensurately "civilised" bureaucracy'.[41] That this was a deliberate policy to create a dependent 'native coterie educated according to "civilised" European principles', and with whom the imperial rulers could do business is apparent from Thomas Babington Macaulay's 1835 Minute on Education for India, 'imperialism demanded the creation of a class of persons, Indian in Blood and colour but English in taste, in opinion, in morals and in intellect.'[42]

This policy was extremely successful. An indigenous colonial elite emerged, which was partially assimilated into the imperial culture and which 'identified themselves with this culture both in their social behaviour and in their appreciation of its values'.[43] They became culturally alienated from the masses. The local elite which was 'was indispensable to the system of colonial exploitation, stands midway

39 Jackson Preece, *Minority Rights*, 2005, p.127.

40 Language had but a small role to play in nation building in the colonial context. The right of peoples to self-determination in the colonial context were people 'under alien rule, and the colonial boundary constituted the land upon which they would exercise their right'. D. Demisse, 'Self-Determination Including Secession vs The Territorial Integrity of Nation States: A Prima Facie Case for Secession', *Suffolk Transnational Law Review*, 20, 1997, p.165.

41 Kymlicka, 'Models of Multicultural Citizenship', in Tan, *Challenging Citizenship*, 2005, p.119.

42 Cited in Jackson Preece, *Minority Rights*, 2005, p.114.

43 Amilcar Cabral, 'Identity and Dignity', in Linda Martin Alcoff and Eduardo Mendieta (eds.), *Identities Race, Class Gender and Nationality*, Blackwell Publishers: Oxford, 1983, p.57.

between the masses of the working class in town and country and the small number of local representatives of the foreign ruling class'.[44]

Since only the elite spoke the language of the colonial rulers the linguistic diversity of the rest of the society was left untouched. Indeed in Sri Lanka, attempts were made for natives to have representation on the Legislative Council on the basis of language community groups as well. At the top of what was a largely heterogeneous society of many spoken languages, but where people were, in the main, illiterate, was an elite group, who were educated to be 'English', and who did not disappoint. They learnt all the colonial ideas and practices necessary to run an efficient bureaucracy. Their training and education placed them at the heart of the western liberal tradition which meant that they assimilated the same ideas about nation building and democracy as that which prevailed in Europe. In many cases the western experiment at nation building was transferred to the colonies after the colonies achieved independence. '(T)he discourse of popular sovereignty and representative government to which the indigenous colonial elites were exposed through their assimilation into the imperial language proved just as powerful and persuasive in Africa and Asia as it had already proved within Europe itself.'[45] This is why democracy as majoritarian rule is often part of the problem.

Majoritarian nationalism has, through most of its history, a poor record concerning the human rights of minorities.[46] Shapiro offers a succinct, practical and political definition of democracy as the say the all people have in the decisions that affect them and that opposition to the current policies are equally legitimate and institutionalised as the loyal opposition. This definition implies majority rule.[47] However, as Shapiro also points out such a definition of democracy does not fit with group identities and aspirations. Post-colonial states inherited an acute problem as far as ethnic minorities are concerned. Borders were not determined as they were in Europe. In post-colonial Africa, for example, where the colonial boundaries remained largely intact, the ethnic composition of the state was fixed by 'imperial fiat'. Considerations such as tribal, ethnic or religious bonds among the populace were ignored and regional 'geographic or economic coherence were wholly subordinated to the building of imperial political units'.[48] After independence, these countries incorporated within its borders several language groups creating problems in perpetuity. Some countries in Asia, such as India, tried to solve the problem by creating federal units, again along linguistic lines thus

44 Cabral, 'Identity and Dignity' in Alcoff and Mendieta (eds.), *Identities, Race*, 1983, p.57.

45 Jackson Preece, *Minority Rights*, 2005, p.115.

46 Sterling, 'Ethnic Separatism in the International System', in Hall (ed), *Ethnic Autonomy*, 1979, p.423.

47 Ian Shapiro, 'Group Aspirations and Democratic Politics', in Harold Hongju Koh and Ronald C. Slye (eds.), *Deliberative Democracy and Human Rights*, Yale University Press: New Haven, NJ, 1999, pp.257ff.

48 Sterling, 'Ethnic Separatism in the International System', in Hall (ed.), *Ethnic Autonomy*, 1979, p.423.

minimising the problem but not eradicating it.[49] However, even though India has achieved a remarkable stability, in spite of there still being several hot spots, other Asian societies have not followed this federal example, taking the view that any form of devolution would be a serious threat to the state. Among the reasons Kymlicka offers for the reluctance of Asian states to move away from a unitary state to accommodating sub-state nationalities, is the belief that the ethnic distinctiveness of minorities is the result of underdevelopment and will become diluted and eventually disappear if there is modernisation and development.[50] Notions of underdevelopment echo the idea of 'primordial loyalties', the expectation being that such loyalties will loosen and disappear when people become part of the nation.

It is now accepted that in a democracy, where the majority population has power in perpetuity, 'sub-state national identities'[51] persist and are increasingly insistent on having their aspirations met by the state. The fact that there is a problem at all with minorities is precisely because the policy of assimilation has been a failure. In fact, most of what the German philosophers claimed about culture, language and community is no less true for ethnic minorities than for ethnic majorities. The form that language and culture give to the personal self[52] is not easily altered. The differences between groups reflect 'distinct outlooks on life, codes of values, and unique customs and traditions that are threatened implicitly or explicitly, by pressures stemming from the majority'.[53] The idea that the nation is a natural phenomenon that flows out of an organic community means that minority cultures that are also 'organic communities' are resistant to assimilation and endure. A major solution to the problem has been to explore the overlapping ideas of devolution of power, minority rights and multiculturalism. More recently, the discourse of multiculturalism has challenged the view that a single language is necessary for the development of national solidarity. The idea that it is necessary to have an official language for administrative affairs is not the same as insisting that only one official language should be protected and promoted in the society.

Kymlicka points out that at the turn of the century in Europe, only Switzerland and Canada had allowed sub-state national groups' self-governing autonomous status and official language status.[54] Today the 1998 Swiss Constitution recognises four official languages German, French, Italian and Romansch. Except for

49 The Indian government originally re-organised states along linguistic lines in 1956. Since then the issue had to be revisited in 1960, 1962, 1966 and 1972. Moreover, India seems to have responded to the different needs of different communities attempting customised solutions to the Kashmiri issue and the issue of tribal territories. Kymlicka, 'Models of Multicultural Citizenship', in Tan, *Challenging Citizenship*, 2005, p.120.

50 Kymlicka, 'Models of Multicultural Citizenship', in Tan, *Challenging Citizenship*, 2005, p.124.

51 Kymlicka, 'Models of Multicultural Citizenship', in Tan, *Challenging Citizenship*, 2005, p.111.

52 For an erudite discussions of community and self, see Charles Taylor, *Sources of the Self: The Making of Modern Identity*, Cambridge University Press: Cambridge, 1992.

53 Muldoon, 'The Development of Group Rights', in Sigler, *Minority Rights*, 1983, p.32.

54 Kymlicka, 'Models of Multicultural Citizenship', in Tan, *Challenging Citizenship*, 2005, p.111.

Romansch, the other languages are spoken by countries that neighbour Switzerland.[55] Other communities that now enjoy autonomous status include the Swedish-speaking Aland Islands in Finland, German-speaking South Tyrol in Italy, Catalonia and the Basque country in Spain, Flanders, Scotland and Wales.[56]

The perennial fear of nation states that devolution will stimulate rather than head off claims for partition is not entirely without foundation. There is historical evidence that that might happen. It was English policy to assimilate French Quebec in culture but in spite of the resistance to the policy no separatist movement developed. Separatism began when the central government devolved powers to the region. The same seems to have happened in Scotland where devolution of powers has created a taste for independence. The main fear of creating autonomous regions is that autonomy is the first step to secession. Indeed, secessionist parties do thrive in autonomous regions, however, they are not involved in a protracted civil war but express their wishes through the party political system or through referenda. According to Kymlicka, had Canada, Belgium and Spain not federalised 'they may not exist as countries today.'[57] In 2014 a referendum will be held to gauge whether Scottish sentiment leans toward complete independence or towards remaining within the United Kingdom. So far no referendum on secession has given a clear light to secession in the west.

It seems that in Europe states have had to accept that sub-state nationalities will always desire the same political independence as the majority ethnic group but they will use the democratic institutions to test the opinion of their own community and to cut deals with the majority ethnic community; the alternative is for the nation state to become involved in a conflict that threatens its very existence. Either way it is no longer feasible to believe that communities will die away as distinct entities as a result of policies pursued by the state. The existence of permanent minorities as a fact of political life has been accepted, the question now is how to adequately ensure their protection. For this reason over the past few decades group rights have made its way into international documents and domestic constitutions.[58]

Change of terminology – from ethno-tribal to ethnic

The focus on ethnicity is a recent phenomenon and dates to the middle of the twentieth century.

In the context of nation building, the recalcitrance of inassimilable minorities was usually explained with respect to their primordial loyalties. Ethno-tribal loyalties result from blood ties, and other racial and cultural phenomena that create fixed identities, which, in turn, become a source of conflict with the loyalties of

55 Sagarin and Moneymaker, 'Language and Nationalist, Separatist and Secessionist Movements', in Hall (ed.), *Ethnic Autonomy*, 1979, p.31.

56 Kymlicka, 'Models of Multicultural Citizenship' in Tan, *Challenging Citizenship*, 2005, p.111.

57 Kymlicka, 'Models of Multicultural Citizenship' in Tan, *Challenging Citizenship*, 2005, p.116.

58 Sigler, *Minority Rights: A Contemporary Analysis*, 1983, p.29.

other tribes. However, this view has been challenged especially in the works of Benedict Anderson and Donald Horowitz.[59] Anderson, in his *Imagined Communities*,[60] rejected the idea that cultural identity is an essential quality. Communities fashion themselves in response to the environment and the manipulation of history and other cultural symbols are the means by which this is accomplished. Identities are socially constructed by 'ethnic entrepreneurs' skilled in encouraging group identity for overtly political reasons. This idea is not very different from post-modernists who claim that ethnicity is a flexible category that changes with time.

In spite of a stream of scholarly works mainstream thinking on minorities and nations did not change until the 1990s. After the collapse of the Berlin Wall in 1989–90, violent, ethnically based conflicts emerged. Under the old regime, ethnic differences were suppressed, but the transition to democracy unleashed old rival-ries as national minorities competed for predominance and the right to define the nation. These destabilizing ethnic conflicts rendered old understandings and definitions of minority loyalties inadequate. Hence, the 'protection of minorities in ethnic terms once again gained attention as a viable pragmatic response to ethnic tension'.[61] The collapse of the Soviet Union and Yugoslavia also forced Europe to take self-determination claims seriously, especially since many such claims had 'deep roots and broad support within the society'.[62] The Conference on Security and Cooperation in Europe (CSCE) issued the 1990 Copenhagen declaration that endorsed 'territorial autonomy as best practice'.[63] It appeared at that time that autonomy was emerging as a right, however, this notion disappeared in declarations by European Organizations such as the Hague, Oslo and Lund Recommendations between 1996 and 1999.[64] In the face of robust opposition to notions of autonomy or secession, European organisations opted to entrench individual rights and to protect the cultures of sub-national minorities.

In recent literature, there has been a concerted effort to disassociate the ideas of nation from those of the organic community. There is a growing recognition that minority peoples and communities are permanent constituents of most nation states. It might also be a permanent feature of the modern state that there will be a tension between the need to create a national consciousness, such as what does it mean to be English, American and so on and the need to recognise the existence of permanent minorities and to take steps to ensure that individuals belonging to such minorities do not suffer unequal treatment in perpetuity. Lord Scarman took

59 See Horowitz, *Ethnic Groups in Conflict*, University of California Press, Berkeley, 1985.

60 B. Anderson, *Imagined Communities: Reflections on the Origin and Spread of Nationalism*, Verso Books: London, 1991.

61 Shahabuddin, 'Ethnicity in the International Law of Minority Protection' *Leiden Journal of International Law*, 2012, p.899.

62 Halperin and Scheffer with Small, *Self-Determination in the New World Order*, 1992, p.77.

63 W. Kymlicka, 'The Internationalisation of Minority Rights', *International Journal of Constitutional Law*, 6(1), 2008, p.19.

64 Kymlicka, 'The Internationalisation of Minority Rights', 2008, p.12.

the view that plural societies are a positive phenomenon. The aim should not be to create 'homogenous societies but to manage them fairly'.[65] There is a growing consensus that it might be possible for people to engage in political life and to enjoy the benefits of citizenship, without necessarily being part of the ethnic majority. In other words, nation building should not require cultural homogeneity. Ethnic minorities only really constitute a threat to the stability of the nation when they become resistant to policies that require sacrifices of them not required of the majority ethnic group. In the modern world, the competing realities of the nation state and the inassimilable minority group have had to come to terms and the increasing recognition of minority rights may offer a way of coping with the tension.

International protection of minority rights

Today the protection of language rights is part of the international protection of minority rights. The early instruments that include special provisions for the protection of minorities are the 1955 Framework Convention for the Protection of National Minorities, the 1966 International Convention on the Elimination of All Forms of Racial Discrimination, and Article 27 of the 1966 International Covenant on Civil and Political Rights, the last two being the standard on minority rights.

Since 1989 several international instruments included special provisions for the protection of minority rights.[66] The 1992 United Nations Declaration on the Rights of Persons Belonging to National or Ethnic, Religious and Linguistic Minorities accommodates 'the post-Cold War consciousness about the ethnic dimension of minority protection'.[67] This declaration requires the state to take positive action with respect to the protection of minority rights. In addition to the provisions for minority language rights it includes the measures states should take to fund the teaching of minority languages.

There are also regional instruments such as the 1992 European Charter for Regional or Minority Languages and the 1993 Copenhagen Criteria which requires that states wishing to accede to the EU must respect and protect minorities within their borders.[68] Some instruments have even tried to tackle the problem of the role of minorities in national life. The 1992 UN Declaration declares that minorities have a right to participate in national and regional decisions. The Lund Recommendations on the Effective Participation of National Minorities in Public Life, sponsored by the CSCE, also offers a few recommendations, such as quotas or the reservation of special seats, to make it possible for minorities to participate

65 Rt Hon. Lord Scarman, 'Minority Rights in a Plural Society', in Whitaker (ed.), *Minorities: A Question of Human Rights*, 1984.

66 See also J. Fawcett, *The International Protection of Minorities*, Minority Rights Group Report: London, No. 41.

67 Shahabuddin, 'Ethnicity in the International Law of Minority Protection', 2012, 899.

68 Jackson Preece, *Minority Rights*, 2005, p.9.

in public life. The idea is to avoid undemocratic outcomes from democratic processes.[69] Other instruments concentrate on provisions that would allow a fair degree of internal self-determination.[70] By such means an attempt is made to retain stability in the international order.

Since 1995 the UN has had an especially dedicated body, the Working Group on Minorities that addressed issues relating to minorities.[71] It has shown its commitment to the issue of minority rights when in 2005 the High Commissioner for Human Rights appointed the first 'Independent Expert on Minority Issues' and in 2007 the Human Rights Council created the Forum on Minority Issues with a mandate 'to provide a platform for promoting dialogue and cooperation' on minority issues.[72]

Sri Lankan Tamils in the context of minority rights and secession

Tamils were not 'communalists' who became separatists as a defensive reaction to Sinhalese government policies. The Tamils saw themselves as a separate nation who were a minority on an island with a majority Sinhalese community. In 1947 Sri Lanka gained independence and was the first colonial country to obtain universal franchise. The Tamils desired political participation in the unitary state as equal partners and insisted on a level of participation that seemed incommensurate with the size of their population. Liberal politicians in Sri Lanka, most of whom had studied abroad, and were well indoctrinated with liberal European ideas by design of the colonial authorities, could not take ethnically based politics seriously. Also, universal franchise based on territorially demarcated constituencies was already an entrenched model for elections in Britain and arguments against it would have seemed idiosyncratic and selfish. The early Sinhalese leaders were not narrowly ethnic in their outlook and neither were the Sinhalese or Tamil electorate inclined, at that time, to vote along 'communal', lines. Hence, Tamil fears that they were vulnerable as a community were dismissed by the Sinhalese and by some Tamils as 'communal politics', and their ethnic loyalties as 'primordial'. Such attitudes had to be shed by the Tamils for them to become true citizens of the state.

In 1998, in Sri Lanka, the Social Scientists Association published *Unitarianism, Devolution and Majoritarian Elitism*, which reflected the revised thinking on sub-nationalities that the ethnic wars in Europe had triggered. They recommended

69 See D.L. Horowitz, 'The Challenge of Ethnic Societies: Democracy in Divided Societies', *Journal of Democracy*, 4(4), 1993, 20ff.

70 Sec. IV (35) of the Copenhagen Document (1990) allows for autonomy in administrative matters. The UN Declaration on the Rights of Indigenous Peoples uses the words 'right to self-determination' in the pursuit of their economic, social and cultural development.

71 C. Chapman and K. Ramsay, 'Two Campaigns to Strengthen United Nations Mechanisms on Minority Rights', *International Journal on Minority and Group Rights*, 18, 2011, p.185.

72 Chapman and Ramsay, 'Two Campaigns', 2011, p.196.

a federal solution as the only way to deal with the ethnic problem in Sri Lanka since the unitary state would necessarily reflect the culture of the majority ethnic group. By now the Sinhalese government were already examining the options of devolution of power and shared sovereignty. The 1995/1997 constitutional package was a progressive solution to the problem but the entrenched ethnic nationalism of Sinhalese Buddhists who are intolerant of any solution that involves the loss of sovereignty and the demand for full partition by the LTTE, scuppered any progress. The failure to resolve the issue peacefully culminated in the 2009 war involving allegations of atrocious human rights abuses of the civilian population.

Separatist movements and the LTTE[73]

Ethnicity is not necessarily the most politically divisive feature of group identity since people enjoy many identities simultaneously.[74] Gender, class or educational status may also be a source of intense political conflict. This is the reason that post-modernists claim that politicized identities are the constructs of circumstances. This might be true but while ethnic communities might become politicized ethnicity is not a creation of politics. It has endured through different political arrangements and history has proved its stubborn reality. Shapiro points out another problem with the post-modern view: even if one concedes that 'politicised identities are historically contingent', how does such an identity become 'demobilised' once it has been created?

Most separatist movements are based on perceived insoluble differences between ethnicities. The literature on ethnic minorities makes a distinction between objective and subjective differences between ethnic groups. Objective differences are differences of wealth, power, religion, and language but this may have little to do with the subjective conviction that people 'share something in common with the enemy',[75] which encourages a movement 'against the enemy to develop'. When a group is willing to take up arms to fight for their own nation there are two arguments that motivate them. One is the argument of cultural preservation and the other the argument of self-defence.[76] The mobilisation of the masses is an

73 The Tamil Liberation Organisation was a resistance cell that came together in 1969. Its members were from the *Karaiyar* caste. It became the Tamil Eelam Liberation Organization (TELO) and then was renamed the Liberation Tigers of Tamil Eelam (LTTE) M. Roberts, 'Caste in Modern Sri Lankan Politics', *The Sri Lanka Guardian*, 12 March 2013.

74 '[A]ll individual identities are at least in part (and whether the individual in question likes it or not) necessarily functions of the communities to which the individuals in question may properly be held to belong and of the roles which they may be thought to occupy in virtue of their community membership(s).' Alan Montfiore, 'Liberlism, Identity, Minority Rights', in Tan (ed.), *Challenging Citizenship*, 2005.

75 McCord and McCord, 'Ethnic Autonomy: A Socio- Historical Synthesis', in Hall (ed.) *Ethnic Autonomy*, 1979, p.427.

76 Buchanan, 'The Morality of Secession', in Kymlicka (ed.), *The Rights of Minority Cultures*, 2004, p.362.

essential element in the quest for secession. It usually involves conflict that heightens the sense of boundary between in-group and out-group.[77]

The way the international order has approached the protection of minority rights over the past few decades was largely influenced by the fluctuations of state dissolution and state building mainly in eastern Europe. However, the role of violence in the break-up of the former eastern bloc sounded a cautionary note. Analyses of the strategies of separatists exposed the extent to which violence plays a role in forcing the separatist option by eliminating political differences internal to groups so that a single, political solution is proposed by the group as a whole.

In modern societies, what is obvious from the terrorist threat and secessionist militancy is that charismatic leaders are able to mobilise the society and ensure that the community speaks with one voice. Reflecting on his Irish experience, Conor Cruise O'Brien, warns that one ought not to 'hypostatise monolithic minorities'. Given the extent of the differences among members of a community and the variety of political opinion represented there would be a number of solutions favoured to address their predicament. When the secessionist element comes to dominate the aspirations of the group, this is because the political pressures external and internal to the community have played a role in producing a dominant political aspiration. According to O'Brien, the minority community looks at its militants with such mixed emotions as 'admiration, sympathy, apprehension, anxiety, guilt, fear and hatred'.[78] This is the main reason why states are urged to arrive at compromise solutions before opinions harden and coercion consolidates group opinion.

In addition to defining the enemy, the community must also identify things it can fight for and around which its identity consolidates. The creation of important symbols and the embellishment of history with myths and legends is an important part of this exercise, but it may also involve violence against moderate and dissenting voices within the community itself. McCord and McCord touch on a very important feature of the development of separatist movements: 'Thus, the success or failure of a separatist movement to develop and grow depends upon whether the leaders can invent and communicate a series of acceptable symbols, ideologies and myths, as well as strategies to counter their defined enemy. This subjective variable, contingent, in part, upon the style, cleverness, or even charisma of the leaders appears as a dominant factor in deciding the fate of separatist movements.'[79]

77 Mike Featherstone, 'Localism, Globalism and Cultural Identity', in Alcoff and Mendieta (eds.), *Identities: Race, Class, Gender and Nationality*, 2003, p.347.

78 Conor Cruise O'Brien, 'What Rights Should Minorities Have?', in Whitaker (ed.) *Minorities: A Question of Human Rights*, 1984, p.17.

79 McCord and McCord, 'Ethnic Autonomy', in Hall (ed.) *Ethnic Autonomy – Comparative Dynamics*, 1979, p.427.

According to Horowitz,[80] minority groups become secessionist or irredentist because their more modest demands are not met. Keiichi Kubo,[81] in his examination of session and ethnic conflict proposes that 'when ethnic groups seek secession, this can be regarded as the radicalization of an ethnic minority *in terms of political goals*. Equally important is the radicalization of an ethnic minority in terms of *the means to achieve their goals*.'[82]

The radicalisation of the Tamil community was as much the result of external pressures as it was irresolvable internal difficulties that Tamil leaders had for too long stubbornly failed to address. Among Sri Lankan Tamils, intra-ethnic divisions were those of caste. The LTTE is a separatist movement that rose up against exclusion by the upper echelons of the Tamil hierarchy in the Jaffna Peninsula and seized the leadership of the Tamil movement by force. Hence, the moderate/radical competition within the Tamil community was resolved in favour of lower caste radicals alienated not only on account of ethnicity but also of caste. They demanded a complete partition of the island. Radicalization is the shift of 'balance of power that takes place within the ethnic group' and migrates outside the political and parliamentary process.

Separatist movements tend generally to be non-democratic in essence since the most important task is to eliminate internal disagreements by eliminating the opposition to become the sole representative of the voice of the people. It is not surprising, therefore, that the first targets of the LTTE were duly elected local and national Tamil MPs. Having consolidated their position the war between the Tamil separatists and the Sinhalese was waged for over 20 years with attempts at peace made in 1985, 1987, 1989, 1990, 1995, 2002 and 2006. They all failed. However, the defeat of the LTTE in 2009 does not mean that the ethnic problem has been resolved or the quest for independence quelled.

80 D.L Horowitz, 'Irredentas and Secessions: Neglected Connections', in Naomi Chazan (ed.), *Irredentism and International Politics*, Lynne Rienner: Boulder, CO, 1991, p.13.

81 Keiichi Kubo, *Secession and Ethnic Conflict*, Ashgate Research Companion to Secession, p.214.

82 Kubo, *Secession and Ethnic Conflict*, p.214.

4 The island

The people and colonial policy

The people

Sri Lanka[1] is a small, yet splendid and beautiful island located in the Indian Ocean, just below India where it hangs like a jewel. The country is 270 miles (435 km) long and 140 miles (225 km) wide and has an area of 25,332 square miles. It is separated from India by the 33-mile (53km) wide Palk Strait.[2] It has a 2,500-year-old known history.

The island[3] has been inhabited, *inter alia*, by the Sinhalese[4] (low-country and up-country) and the Ceylon Tamils, who respectively represent 70 per cent and 11 per cent of the population. In addition, the Indian Tamils, the Moors (Ceylon and coastal) – Muslims who are the descendants of seafaring Arab merchants and migrants from South India – Malays (the descendants of Malay regiments), burghers (the descendants of Dutch and Portuguese settlers), and a few small groups such as Colombo Chetties, the Parawas, the Parsees, Eurasians, and the Mukkuvars have been living in the country for many centuries. It has been pointed out by commentators that the designation of these groups as 'smaller racial groups' was a deliberate policy of the British colonial administration in keeping with the racial stratification current in Victorian scholarship.[5]

1 The word *Ilam* or *Ilankai* is used in Tamil and the original English term, *Ceylon* is derived from *Sihaldwipa*, the meaning of which is 'island of the Sinhalese'. See Encyclopedia Britannica, 'Ceylon', 1978, p.217.

2 See, Encyclopedia Britannica, 'Ceylon', 1978, p.217.

3 See, generally, history of Sri Lanka, C.W. Nicholas and S. Paranavitana, *A Concise History of Ceylon*, Colombo, 1961; K.M. de Silva, *A History of Sri Lanka*, C. Hurst & Company: London, 1981; K.M. de Silva, *Sri Lanka: A Survey*, London, 1976; S. Arasaratnam, *Ceylon*, Englewood Cliffs, NJ: Prentice-Hall, 1964; H.W. Codrington, *A Short History of Ceylon*, London, 1947; E.F.C. Ludowyk, *The Story of Ceylon*, London, 1962; S.A. Pakeman, *Ceylon*, London, 1964; U. Padnis, *Sri Lanka*, New Delhi, 1973; G.C. Mendis, *Early History of Ceylon*, Calcutta, 1932; J.E. Tenant, *Ceylon, An Account of the Island: Physical, Historical and Topographical*, London, 1859.

4 S. Paranavitana, 'Sinhalayo', Lake House Investment: Colombo, 1967; idem, 'The Aryan Settlements: the Sinhalese', Chapter VI, Vol. 1, part 1, University of Ceylon History of Ceylon: Colombo, 1959; J.M. Seneviratne, *The Story of the Sinhalese*, Colombo, 1930; C.A. Wijesinha, *The Sinhalese Aryans*, Colombo, 1932.

5 E. Nissan and R. L. Stirrat, 'The Generation of Communal Identities', in J. Spencer (ed.) *Sri Lanka, History and the Roots of Conflict*, Routledge: London, 1990, p.30.

Politicised historical narratives

Regarding the long and vexed debate about who arrived first, Dr Namasivayam, a reputed Tamil scholar, suggested that it might have been the Sinhalese who inhabited the island first. The claim is that the 'Sinhalese are people of Aryan stock who originally came from India about the sixth century BC.'[6] The Mahavamsa records that the first appearance of the Sinhalese in the island appears to date from the fifth century BC.[7] The first Sinhalese settlement in the island around Puttalam was attributed to Prince Vijaya, the founding father, and 700 of his friends, as remembered in the myths and legends of the Sinhalese. Whatever the truth of this story, it is now readily accepted by both Indian[8] and Sri Lankan historians[9] that there was large-scale migration of people of Indo-Aryan extraction to Sri Lanka from the fifth century. The settlements of the descendants of Prince Vijaya and his followers in the island were referred to in the old chronicles such as *Dïpavamsa* (c. fourth to fifth century AD) and the *Samanthapasadika* (c. fifth century AD).[10] Referring to the Indo-Aryan settlements in the island, K.M. de Silva, an authority on the history of Sri Lanka, states that the descendants of Vijaya and his friends had gradually been able to establish settlements inland; first south, then east, and then throughout the island. The island came to be known as 'lankădïpa' and the descendants of the Vijayan dynasty were called 'Sîhala' or 'Simhala' (the people of the lion). They are now called Sinhalese. R.A.L.H. Gunawardana comments:

> The term Sinhala (Păli Sîhala, Skt. Simhala) occurs for the first time in Sri Lankan sources in the Dîpavamsa which has been assigned to the fourth–fifth centuries A.D. In this chronicle the term occurs only once, and in this cryptic verse it is stated that the island was known as Sihala 'on account of the lion' (lankădipo ayam ăhu sihena sihaăa iti). The term Sâihaladipa or the 'Sinhala island' occurs in the Samanthapăsădikă the commentary on the Vinaya section of the Pali Canon, written by Buddhagosa in the fifth century A.D. The text states that the earlier commentaries used by Buddhagosa had been written in the language of Sihaladipa. Fa-Hian, who visited the island in the fifth century, refers to it by the name 'the country of the lions'. The term Heladivi, the equivalent of the Păli Sîhaladipa, occurs in one of the graffiti at Sîgiri which have been assigned by Paranavitana to a period extending from the eighth to

6 See Namasivayam, *The Legislature of Ceylon*, 1951. See also Jennings, 'Nationalism and Political Development in Ceylon, the Background of Self-government', 1953, pp.63–64.

7 W. Giger (ed.) *Mahăvamsa*, Colombo, 1950.

8 See a frequently cited essay on this: A.L. Basham, 'Prince Vijaya and the Aryanisation of Ceylon', 1(3), *Ceylon Historical Journal*, 1952, pp.172–191.

9 S. Paranavitana, 'Aryan Settlements: the Sinhalese', Chapter V, Vol. 1(I) University of Ceylon; History of Ceylon; R.A.L.H. Gunawardana, 'The People of the Lion: the Sinhala Identity and Ideology in History and Historiography', *Sri Lanka Journal of Humanities*, 1(2), 1979, pp.1–36; G.C. Mendis, 'The Vijaya Legend', in N.A. Jayawickrama (ed), *Pranavitana Felicitation Volume*, 1965, pp. 263–292.

10 See Gunawardana, 'The People of the Lion', 1979, pp. 2–3.

> the tenth century A.D. By the eighth century the name was being used to denote a group of people, as is evident from an inscription found at a ruined monastic site in the Raubaka Platau in Central Java, which refers to the Simhala.[11]

The *Tamils* are a 'Dravidian' people who migrated to Sri Lanka from various parts of south India. The exact period in which they began to migrate to the island is not known. Nonetheless, most historians speculate that significant movements of Dravidians from South India took place after the eleventh century AD, even though a thin stream of migration to the Jaffna Peninsula may have occurred much earlier. Wave after wave of migrating peoples from south India, particularly of the *Pandyas*, the *Pallavas* and the *Colas* changed the monolithic, homogeneous nature of the population of the island. The main objective of these intermittent invasions appeared to be a sort of treasure hunting. Permanent settlements did not seem to be the intention of the migrants. Nonetheless, many remained in the northern region, particularly around the Jaffna Peninsula. An authority on this issue, K. Indrapala (a Tamil historian) claims that there was no permanent Tamil settlement in the island even by the tenth century AD. By around the thirteenth and fourteenth centuries the Jaffna Peninsula had become the centre of the Ceylon Tamils; and by the time that the Portuguese invaded the coastal areas of the island there was a well-established autonomous Tamil governing structure in the Jaffna Peninsula.[12] According to S. Namasivayam:

> Tamils in Ceylon are of Dravidian stock and, like the Sinhalese, came over from India, though at a much later date. They are descended from the Tamil invaders who accompanied South Indian Kings and Chieftains in their periodic invasions of Ceylon. As a result of these invasions Tamil rule was established in the northern and eastern parts of the country.[13]

It should be remembered that the exact nature of the Tamils' settlements in the island prior to the eleventh century is difficult to gauge since any inscriptions or early chronicles on the Tamil settlements have not yet been found. Rajanayagam offers interesting details about the Jaffna Tamils' historical past. In her view, it was a Dutch governor, Klaas Isaacsz, who in the seventeenth century cajoled a native Jaffna Tamil called Mayilvakana Pulavar to write the history. *The Yalppana Vaipava Malai*[14] (the Garland of Jaffna Events) was the result of this enterprise based on oral

11 Gunawardana, 'The People of the Lion', 1979, pp.2–3.

12 The most authoritative work on this is Professor K. Indrapala's (Tamil historian) work, 'Dravidian Settlements in Ceylon and the Beginnings of the History of Jaffna', unpublished PhD Thesis, University of London.

13 See Navasivayam, *The Legislature of Ceylon*, 1951. See also Jennings, 'Nationalism and Political Development in Ceylon, the Background of Self-government', 1953, p.63–64.

14 Mayilvakana Pulavar (ed.), *Yalppana Vaipava Malai*, Colombo, 1953. The English translation of this work was provided in 1879, by C. Brito, *The History of the Kingdom of Jaffna*, 1879 reprinted in 1999, Asian Educational Service: New Delhi.

traditions and palm leaf manuscripts of uncertain dates. Rajanayagam observes that:

> This jumble of myth and tradition, ending with the conquest of Jaffna by the Portuguese and the death of the last king, Cankili, became the standard work of Tamil history in the nineteenth century. While in the Sinhala chronicles the Tamils were the enemy, conversely in these Tamil chronicles, the Sinhala were the adversaries who had to be overcome in order to enable the civilized Tamils to settle, who had to be prevented from polluting Tamil holy places, and had therefore to be driven out, and who instigated rebellions and usurpation against the lawful rulers. The contradiction in this account is that it says that the Tamils got their country as a fief from the 'king of Kandy' in the first place. As this is certainly historically impossible, one has to assume that the author meant by the 'king of Kandy' the only Sinhala king he knew.

A large corpus of literature, produced by Tamil scholars, followed this effort but most of them remained principally based on Mayilvakana Pulavar's original work.[15] In the 1970s the literature on the history of the Ceylon Tamils and the Jaffna Peninsula were written mainly by Tamil politicians. This has made it difficult to separate the political rhetoric from scholarly claims. For example, Satchi Ponnambalam, a Tamil politician, asserts that it was the Tamils who first arrived and colonised the island. The Sinhalese were descendants from Tamils who were later converted to Buddhism.[16]

K.M. de Silva, in his major work *A History of Sri Lanka*,[17] admits the difficulty in establishing a 'compilation of a reasonable and accurate chronological list of the rulers of this northern kingdom'. Even though the post-Portuguese era history of the 'Jaffna kingdom' can be surveyed accurately, nevertheless the pre-sixteenth-century history of the Jaffna Peninsula/the history of the Ceylon Tamils was entirely open to speculation. Even in certain details about this phase, 'there are problems with regard to regnal dates'. He concludes, 'Who ruled this kingdom and the regnal years of those identified as rulers are matters of scholarly controversy.'[18] The debate between P.A.T. Gunasinghe[19] and S. Pathmanathan,[20] both lecturers

15 See Indrapala, 'Dravidian Settlements in Ceylon and the Beginnings of the History of Jaffna', 1965; K. Velluppillai, *Yalppana Vaipava Kaumuti*, Vasavilan: Jaffna, 1918. See also S. Pathmanathan, *The Kingdom of Jaffna*, Arul M. Rajendran: Colombo, 1978 and a rejoinder to it by P.A.T. Gunasinghe, 'Review Article of S. Pathmanathan's Kingdom of Jaffna', *Sri Lanka Journal of the Humanities*, 4, 1978, pp.99–112.

16 See, for example, Ponnambalam, *Sri Lanka: the National Question and the Tamil Liberation Struggle*, 1983, p.19.

17 de Silva's *A History of Sri Lanka*, 1981, is a *magnum opus* in the literature of Sri Lanka's past. It is considered by many as being the best work after the famous English scholar, Sir James Emerson Tennent's, *Ceylon, An Account of the Island: Physical, Historical and Topographical*, Longman: London, 1859–60.

18 de Silva, *A History of Sri Lanka*, p.570.

19 See Gunasinghe, 'Review Article of S. Pathmanathan's Kingdom of Jaffna', pp.99–112.

20 See Pathmanathan's reponse to Gunasinghe, S. Pathmanathan, 'The Kingdom of Jaffna –

in history at the University of Ceylon, Peradeniya campus, demonstrates how difficult it can be to find the exact period in which permanent Tamil settlement occurred in the island. Gunasinghe, however, rejects the assertion that most works on the 'well-established Jaffna kingdom' were no more than propaganda by some Tamil scholars.

Both Sinhalese and Tamil historians agree that earlier settlers of the island were the Sinhalese with the Tamils arriving later and that their presence in the island was originally limited to areas of the Jaffna Peninsula and the Eastern Province.[21] The existence of a long dynasty of a Tamil kingdom in the north and the east is difficult to establish but is useful politically for Tamil activists and politicians. The history is not of interest only for scholarly reasons but in order to establish a lineage and an historical homeland.

Colonisation generally and British colonialism specifically

With the colonisation of Sri Lanka (previously called Ceylon) by the Europeans since the early sixteenth century[22] the demographic structure of the island underwent enormous changes. When the island was absorbed into the British Empire in 1815[23] the situation changed irretrievably. Under the British colonial government, the establishment of a centralised bureaucracy required the movement of peoples and many Tamils moved to the capital Colombo to take up civil servant positions and established themselves there.

There was hardly any communal conflict among the major ethnic groups in the island for a further 100 years. This changed during the first two decades of the twentieth century within the emergence of 'communal' rivalries in Sri Lanka. One of the main causes of this was the policies adopted by an insensitive colonial government during the years 1833 to 1920 to perpetuate British power on the island. According to a report of a government agent, the colony was run 'as though it were a public school, and its administration a game conducted like

Propaganda or History?', *Sri Lanka Journal of the Humanities*, 5, 1979, pp.105–125. Pathmanathan, *The Kingdom of Jaffna*, 1978.

21 See Navasivayam, Indrapala and Rajanayagam.

22 See, on the Portuguese period, T.B.H. Abeysinghe, *Portuguese Rule in Ceylon 1594–1612*, Lakehouse Investments: Colombo, 1966; C.R. de Silva, *The Portuguese in Ceylon 1617–1638*, H.W. Cave: Colombo, 1972; see, on the Dutch period, A. Arasaratnam, *Dutch Power in Ceylon*, S. Publisher: Amsterdam, 1958; K.W. Gunawardene, *The Foundation of Dutch Power in Ceylon*, Djambatan: Amsterdam, 1958. See, on the British period, G.C. Mendis, *Ceylon Under the British*, 2rd edn., Apothecaries: Colombo, 1952; L.A. Mills, *Ceylon Under British Rule, 1795–1932*, Oxford University Press: Oxford, 1933; Colvin R. de. Silva, *Ceylon Under the British Occupation, 1795–1832*, 2 volumes, Apothecaries: Colombo, 1941–1942; Sir Ivor Jennings, *The Dominion of Ceylon*, Cambridge University Press: London, 1952; I.D.S. Weerawardana, *Government and Politics in Ceylon, 1931–1946*, Economic and Research Association: Colombo, 1951.

23 See P.E. Pieris, *Tri Sinhala: the Last Phase, 1795–1815*, 2nd edn., Apothecaries: Colombo, 1939; P.E. Pieris *The Sinhalese and the Patriots, 1815–1818*, Apothecaries: Colombo, 1950; K.M. de Silva, *A History of Sri Lanka*, C. Hurst & Co.: London, 1981, pp.220–225.

cricket with its own arcane rules'.[24] There cannot be any doubt that successive governors favoured the divide *et impera* to prevent the emergence of a nationalist movement similar to that of the Indian nationalist movements. Administrative policies were formed in terms of the racial differences on the island that were advantageous to British rule.

As soon as the whole island was brought under one centralised system with Executive and Legislative Councils[25] and with the governor leading the administrative hierarchy, as proposed by the Colebrooke Commission in 1832, representation to these institutions were based on communal and/or racial differences.[26] The result was that a few Ceylonese from the wealthiest families were selected: one from each community (a higher caste Tamil, a low-country Sinhalese and a burgher) appointed by the governor to the Legislative Council (LC) to assist the government in an unofficial capacity. The 'communal' representation in the island thus began 'with unfortunate results to Ceylon politics'.[27]

In 1889 further communal differences were recognised with the appointment of two more (unofficial) representatives to the LC, one from the Kandyan Sinhalese community and one from the Moors. By the first decade of the twentieth century communal representation in the island's political structure was a well-entrenched policy of the colonial administration. The first decade also saw the fine tuning of representation to accommodate the western educated new elite of the low-country Sinhalese, Kandyan Sinhalese and the Ceylon Tamils, as well, as is evidenced by a despatch sent to the Secretary of State for the Colonies by Governor MacCallum (1907–13).[28] His successors Sir Robert Chalmers (1913–1916), Sir John Anderson (1916–1918), and Sir William H. Manning (1918–1925) pursued this policy robustly. New constitutional reforms introduced in 1912, 1921 and 1923 for the island retained communal representation in the face of a great deal of opposition from the main communities of the island. Colonial officials defended the policy of communal representation to the LC, which consolidated a perception that the population of the island was deeply divided along communal and religious lines and that it was essential to recognise these differences and to give a voice to each community in government affairs. Inevitably group consciousness was fostered and communal rivalry perpetuated. According to E. Nissan and R.L. Stirrat, the 'British rule substantialized heterogeneity, formalizing cultural differences and

24 Cited in C.T. Blackton, 'Empire at Bay: British Attitudes and the Growth of Nationalism in the Early Twentieth Century', in M. Roberts (ed.), *Collective Identities, Nationalisms and Protest in Sri Lanka*', Marga Institute: Colombo, 1979, p.365.

25 The LC was created by an Order in Council by the Crown in 1833. See Jennings, 'Nationalism and Political Development in Ceylon 1953–1954', p.73. The Legislative Council was composed of 15 members, of which nine were official members and six were selected by the governor on communal basis.

26 See S.D. Bailey, *Ceylon*, Hutchinson: Stratford Place, 1952, pp.92–97. See further, L.A. Mills, *Ceylon Under British Rule 1795–1932*, Oxford University Press: London, 1933, pp.65–67; S.A. Pakeman, *Ceylon*, Earnest Benn Ltd: London, 1964, see particularly Chapter 5, pp.59–68.

27 Navasivayam, *The Legislatures of Ceylon, 1928–1948*, 1950, pp.9–10.

28 The Papers on Constitutional History of Ceylon 1908–24, p.8.

making it the basis for political representation'.[29] Naturally constituted communities had become formalised political constituencies even though such ethnically based elections to the Legislative Council was rejected by many politicians of the day as 'barbaric' and 'racist'.[30] The consequence was communal competition and rivalries with the elite of both the Sinhalese and the Tamil communities competing for a share of the spoils of government service, the learned professions and business enterprises.

The policies adopted and perpetuated, especially by the two governors who ruled the island during the first two decades and a half of the twentieth century, left a lasting legacy of ethnically entrenched politics in the island. Of these governors, the roles played by Sir H.E. McCallum and Sir William H. Manning, both staunch opponents of any substantial conferment of power to the native elite deepened the divide among the principal communities in the island, that is, the Sinhalese and Tamils. They appointed colonial civil servants from among the Tamil and Sinhalese elites and trusted them with the running of the administration of the colony. At the same time, the English-educated Sinhalese and Tamil elite, particularly those with political aspirations, were perceived as 'an unrepresentative group . . . alienated by their education from the culture and communal obligations of the common people'.[31]

The colonial policy of political representation based on communal affiliation certainly laid the basis for ethnically based political conflicts at the dawn of the twentieth century but it did not create fierce communal loyalties since, in the main, the different communities lived according to different religious beliefs and customs. The proximate cause of the communal tension and hatred that gradually developed between the Tamils and Sinhalese was the politicisation of ethnicity in the early twentieth century.

Ethnic relations on the island before the twentieth century

Many Europeans of the nineteenth century reported that there had once been a remarkable unity among the various communities in the island. One Englishman, William Digby, observed in the 1870s: 'The diverse races in the island, instead of seeking to acquire dominance over the other, are being drawn together to think and act as one people.'[32] The local newspaper, *The Ceylon Standard*, reported on June 8, 1899, 'among the different races to be found in Ceylon, the existing relations

29 Nissan and Stirrat, 'The Generation of Communal Identities', in Spencer (ed.) *Sri Lanka: History and Roots of Conflict*, 1990 p.29.

30 See E.W. Perera's submission to the Donoughmore Commission on November 22–23, 1927.

31 C.T. Blackton, 'The Empire at Bay,' in Roberts (ed.), *Collective Identities, Nationalisms and Protest in Sri Lanka*, 1979, p.363.

32 See W. Digby, in *Calcutta Review*, 1870, cited in D.B. Jayatilaka's Presidential Address to the Congress, 21–22 Dec. 1923, S.W.R.D. Bandranaike, *The Handbook of the Ceylon National Congress, 1919–1928*, H.W. Cave & Co: Colombo, 1928, p.583.

are perhaps the more cordial than . . . in any other British dependency in the East.'[33] Cultural or historical diversities, as John D. Rogers says, which existed among different racial and community groups in the island, had hardly given rise to communal frictions. 'Sinhala-Tamil clashes', argues Rogers, 'were very rare'.[34] In particular, there is no evidence to suggest that the propagandist activities of the Sinhala Buddhists, since the latter half of the nineteenth century, had much to do with exacerbating communal conflict on the island in pre-independence Ceylon.[35] Indeed, as correctly observed by E. Nissan and R.L. Stirrat: 'None of the clashes of the colonial era . . . involved violence between Buddhists and Hindus, the violence was of a different nature to that found today.'[36] Remarkably, leaders were particularly sensitive on issues relating to race and religion.[37] Relations between the Sinhalese and Tamils were extremely friendly since it was not considered sophisticated to appear to be communally minded. John D. Rogers in his remarkable essay on historical background to communalism points out:

> The existence of a strong sense of historical continuity, coupled with the assumption that the Sinhalese people had a great past, did not, however, mean that other aspects of what is now referred to as the ideology of Sinhala-Buddhist cultural nationalism, including the explicit racialism found in some of Dharmapala's writing, were widely adhered to at this time. Images of ethnic conflict in the past had little direct influence on ethnic relations among ordinary people around the turn of the century. Neither the Ceylon Tamils nor the Indian Tamils were identified with the invaders from southern India who had fought Sinhala kings. Although there were a good many small riots along ethnic, religious, and caste lines, Sinhala-Tamil clashes were very rare.[38]

One of the pioneering historians of pre-independence Ceylon, G.C. Mendis offers a class based argument for the rise of communalism in the first four decades in the twentieth century. His thesis is that the emergence of divisive communalism in the island was due purely to economic reasons, which was essentially a recent phenomenon. During the first few decades of the twentieth century, which

33 Cited in de Silva, *A History of Sri Lanka*, 1981, p.369.

34 J.D. Rogers, 'Historical Images in the British Period', in Spencer (ed.), *Sri Lanka, History and the Roots of Conflict*, 1990, pp.101–102.

35 See also Elizabeth J. Harris, *Theravada Buddhism and the British Encounter, Religious, Missionaries and Colonial Experience in Nineteenth Century Sri Lanka*, Routledge: Abingdon, 2001.

36 See Nissan and Stirrat, 'The Generaration of Communal Identities', in Spencer (ed.), *Sri Lanka, History and the Roots of Conflict*, 1990, p.31.

37 P. Tremayne, 'Sri Lanka: The Problem of the Tamils', in RUSI and Brassey's Defence Yearbook, (ed.) The Royal United Services Institute for Defence Studies: London, 1987, p.217.

38 J.D. Rogers, 'Historical Images in the British Past', in J. Spencer (ed.), *Sri Lanka, History and the Roots of Conflict*, 1990, p.101.

witnessed the birth of communalism in its ugliest aspects, it was only the elite of both the Sinhalese and Tamils who competed with each other to strengthen and advance themselves socially and politically. Ordinary people, as observed by Governor Manning in one his despatches to the Secretary of State for the Colonies, had been no more than 'spectators watching an interesting game'.[39]

Most were involved in trying to eke out a meagre existence in their day-to-day lives. Mendis argues that communalism 'came into existence as a result of the rise of the middle class, and the conflicts are mainly due to a struggle within this new class for the spoils won from the British through constitutional reforms'.[40] Furthermore, he states 'That communalism of the type we see today is a recent development is supported by many. European writers such as de Queyroz (Portuguese), Robert Knox and James Cardiner (Englishmen)', have left us with pictures of Ceylon with its various divisions of society, but none of their writings indicates that there were communal conflicts commensurate with recent developments.[41] While there is truth to some of what Mendis claims, most of the Tamils in politics were upper caste people, not the recently arrived middle class. However, Mendis also, without being explicit, dates the rise of communalism to the period when the Sri Lankans were beginning to consider post-colonial politics. What would government in an independent Ceylon be like? S.J. Tambiah agrees that 'Communalism and communalist conflict in the island is of relatively recent manufacture – a truly twentieth century phenomenon'.[42] It has been systematically and intentionally encouraged by those who engaged in 'elite politics' in the early twentieth century.

Dagmar Hellmann-Rajanayagam, an internationally reputed Tamil researcher at the German Historical Institute in London, also confirms the conclusions arrived at by Roger, Mendis and Tambiah. Quoting an Administrative Report of 1883, which records 'very little animosity in Ceylon between the Sinhala and Tamils', she concludes: 'As police reports from the time show, both Tamil and Sinhala were generally concerned with themselves and consequently preferred to assault people of their own "race".'[43] Referring to the current perception of the Sinhalese among the Tamils she says:

> What, then, is the Tamil perception of the Sinhala? It is obvious that today they are perceived firstly as cruel, bent on killing or at least driving out the Tamils, and as having been so for centuries; and secondly, as encroaching on

39 C.O. 1882, Confidential Print, Eastern, No. 138, p. 48, cited in Blackton, 'Empire at Bay', in M. Roberts (ed.), *Problems of Collective Identities*, 1979, p.367.

40 G.C. Mendis, 'The Causes of Communal Conflict in Ceylon', *University of Ceylon Review*, vii(i),1943, pp.41–42.

41 Mendis, 'The Causes of Communal Conflict in Ceylon', 1943, p.42.

42 Tambiah, *Sri Lanka: Ethnic Fratricide and the Dismantling of Democracy*, 1986, p.7.

43 D. Hellmann-Rajanayagam, 'The Politics of Tamil Past', in Spencer (ed.), *Sri Lanka, History and Roots of Conflict*, 1990, pp.109–110.

> Tamil land thus threatening the concept of the 'traditional homeland'. But this perception seems to be a fairly recent one.[44]

Ethnic rivalry between the Tamils and Sinhalese did not surface on the political or national landscape of the island during the early decades of the twentieth century at a level of hostility existing at present. If there had been any conflict it was against western cultural values and the influence of Christianity on indigenous values. Not surprisingly, there was no significant involvement by the political elite in this matter. Only ordinary people, both Hindu Tamils and the Sinhala Buddhists, were involved in fighting the alleged supremacy of the western values and mores that they believed was devoid of spiritual values.

Rise and influence of the political elite

From about the middle of the nineteenth century onwards there emerged a politically elite class of both the Sinhalese and Tamils. This was due mainly to the introduction of English education and the opportunities provided for those who could access this education and the commercial activities of the colonial government. A new class of people emerged who amassed wealth, prestige and social status through governmental professions or through newly opened up business opportunities. Both the Tamils and the Sinhalese benefitted enormously.

The emergence of a professional elite among the high-caste Ceylon Tamils (almost all of them belonged to the *Vellala* caste) in the Jaffna Peninsula occurred much earlier than their Sinhalese counterparts since their exposure to western influence dated from the time of the Portuguese arrival in the sixteenth century. The involvement of American missionaries in higher education in the Jaffa Peninsula from about the middle of the nineteenth century was also a major factor in the advancement and greater achievements of Tamils in government employment and other learned professions such as the legal and medical fields in comparison with the Sinhalese, both low-country and Kandyan. It should not escape attention that until 1869 education was run by the missionaries without the direct involvement of government aid. It is no exaggeration to say that the non-intervention of government policy had, quite ironically, contributed to the advantage of the Tamils whereas a lack of English education had severely reduced opportunities for the Sinhalese.

Thus, exposure to English education placed the Ceylon Tamils in a more competitive and more advantageous position than the Sinhalese. The elite of the Ceylon Tamils who could afford to go to British universities embraced that opportunity while other, less privileged Tamils, went to Calcutta and Madras for a university education. Thus, many were able to enter the professions reserved for the educated.

44 Hellmann-Rajanayagam, 'The Politics of the Tamil Past', in Spencer (ed.), *Sri Lanka, History and Roots of Conflict*, 1990, p.108.

This was especially the case for those coming from the Jaffna province, which had been the centre of Tamil habitation since the fourteenth century AD and had concentrated on government employment and other learned professions, such as law, medicine and engineering. The geography of Jaffna played a major role in this. The rugged terrain of the north, in particular, in the Jaffna Peninsula had not been beneficial for the inhabitants of the region, because the land was, in terms of productivity, no inducement to those who aspired to climb to the top of the socio-political structure. There was no environment conducive to an emergence of business enterprise in those areas inhabited principally by the Ceylon Tamils.

The Sinhalese elite emerged from among the low-country low-caste Sinhalese families such as Karãva (especially from Moratuwa),[45] Durãva, Salãgama as well as from the highest caste Goyigama. However, it was the first of these groups who became the most powerful clan in the island until, perhaps, 1930. Unlike their counterparts, the Jaffna Tamils, they benefited from new business enterprises, such as the plantation and mining industries, as well as transport, toddy and arrack businesses. Most importantly, nearly all of these industries were located in the southern and western provinces.[46] The emerging elites were not satisfied merely with wealth, which they amassed without much ado, but they also realised that in order to maintain their advantageous position in society they needed to have political influence as well.

While some of the new Sinhalese elite entered the colonial civil service, a significant proportion took up medicine, law and engineering.[47] Some individuals, notably, Dr Marcus Fernando, a very prominent Sinhalese, having practised as a physician for a while, entered the plantation industry, which had then become the most lucrative business among the emerging elite in the island. At the beginning of the twentieth century the educated elite preferred business and trade to politics.

The emergence of a new English educated elite of Jaffna Tamils in the Sinhalese-dominated areas contributed to the creation of conflict between the Sinhalese and Tamils. Both these groups were able to dominate not only government employment but also economically more important areas such as export and import, banking, textile, food, transport, brokerage and small and large-scale businesses. This gradually resulted, since the second decade of the twentieth century, in ethnically based competition for government jobs and political influence.[48]

Enthusiasm for politics also arose out of the belief that with educational and professional qualifications and wealth it was not difficult to compete with colonial officials to gain a foothold in the colonial administration. Some of the elite had

45 See M. Roberts, 'The Rise of the Karava', Ceylon Studies Seminar, 1968–1969.

46 See also J. Ferguson, *Ceylon in 1883*, Colombo, 1883, p.64, cited in de Silva, *A History of Sri Lanka*, 1981, p.334.

47 The Ceylon Medical College was opened in 1870, and the Ceylon Law College was opened in 1874.

48 L. Sabaratnam, 'The Boundaries of the State and the State of Ethnic Boundaries: Sinhala Tamil Relations in Sri Lankan History', *Ethnic and Racial Studies*, 10, 1987, p.302.

already, by the dawn of the twentieth century, served their political apprenticeship by acting as unofficial members of the Legislative Council, *the* corridor of power, where the top colonial officials gathered to decide everything, from cleaning the metropolis to the security of the island. By the same token, some of the elite from both the Sinhalese and Tamils communities[49] were exposed to Westminster politics in England where they were educated. Universities such as Cambridge, Oxford or the University of London nurtured the future presidents and prime ministers of Ceylon, whose sole ambition was to become *imperator esse in regno suo* in their own post-colonial mini-empire.

It is, therefore, hardly surprising that some of them, for example, the Ponnambalam brothers (Ceylon Tamil elite), James Pieris and Marcus Fernando (both of the low-country Sinhalese elite) showed an interest in politics already since the beginning of the twentieth century. At the turn of the century, with a change of government in Britain and the Liberal Party's ascension to power, the political ambitions of the emerging elite increased.

When conflict first emerged it developed, not between the Europeans and the natives, or between the Tamils and Sinhalese but between the low-caste Sinhalese and highest caste Sinhalese *Goyigamas*. Later, this extended to the Sinhalese and Tamil elite. Other groups in the island, notably the burghers, Moors and Indian Tamils were mere spectators in the 'internal affairs' of the elite groups, that is, 'the two majority communities' in the island.

Cross-boundary movements – from the north to the west and south

The introduction of a centralised civil service in the island brought English-educated Ceylon Tamils from the Jaffna Peninsula, since the middle of the nineteenth century to areas that were predominantly Sinhalese. Until this time there had not been any significant cross-boundary movements between the Sinhalese and the Tamils regions, apart from some occasional trading between them. Most importantly, this cross-boundary movement occurred from the north to the south and west thus creating Tamil pockets in predominantly Sinhalese areas.

By the turn of the twentieth century rivalries between the Sinhalese and Tamil elites began to emerge. Most of the elite showed little interest in the welfare of their fellow countrymen. By way of example, when the unofficial member of the Legislative Council, John Ferguson (European), tried to launch an organisation to agitate for the constitutional reforms for the island his attempts were thwarted owing to the lack of cooperation and opposition he faced from the new elite Sinhalese. He complained: 'The Sinhalese are our great difficulty. S.C. Obeysekere

49 de Silva, *A History of Sri Lanka*, 1981, Chapter 24, pp.327–338; M. Roberts, 'A New Marriage, an Old Dichotomy: the 'Middle Class' in British Ceylon', in *F.T. Ratnam Felicitation Volume*, Jaffna, 1980, pp.32–63.

objects to elections and James Pieris has not replied at all . . . They would not entrust power to their countrymen.' Most surprisingly, when he moved a motion in the LC in 1904 demanding an additional seat for the low-country Sinhalese, it lapsed due to want of a seconder. Even though no one knows exactly what motivated Pieris not to cooperate with Ferguson, it was suggested in some quarters that he was, by this time, seriously thinking about a judicial post. Any involvement in constitutional reforms would have been detrimental to his ambitions. By contrast S.C. Obeysekere, the unofficial member in the LC, whose responsibility it was to look after the interests of the Sinhalese, kept opposing proposals aimed at enhancing the representation of the low-country Sinhalese.[50]

The behaviour of the Sinhalese and Tamil 'self-made men,' as K.M. de Silva noted, was often, perhaps quite rightly, scoffed at by the colonial officials for their conservative outlook in social and political matters. Governor Sir Henry MacCallum wrote in 1910:

> Even for many who have not found it possible to visit Europe, education of a purely European type has become more easily accessible and has been sought with eagerness. This had led, in my opinion, not to the working of any marked transformation in the bulk of the population, but to the creation of a class of natives which formerly was almost a negligible quantity.
>
> [It] is precisely the acquisition of European ideas and the adoption of European in preference to Ceylonese civilization that differentiates this class of Ceylonese from their countrymen [and separates them] by a wide gulf from the majority of the native inhabitants of the Colony. Their ideas, their aspirations, their interests are distinctly their own, are all moulded upon European models, and are no longer those of the majority of their countrymen.[51]

Alas! It was between the *Goyigamas* and the *Karavas* that the conflict was most prevalent

At the beginning of the century it was the low-caste *Karava* who dominated the economic and trading fields. It helped them climb to the upper echelons of the society to challenge the alleged supremacy of the highest caste *Goyigamas*. From the high-caste Sinhalese elite's point of view, the most burning issue was how to dominate and maintain their hold on politics over the low-caste Sinhalese groups. The caste rivalry between the low-caste and high-caste Sinhalese families was, either deliberately or inadvertently, supported by the colonial administration whose policies kept the majority community divided against each other thus preventing any threat rising against the colonial administration. This was achieved by making appointments to the LC only from the high-caste *Goyigama* Sinhalese, even though

50 See detail, de Silva, *A History of Sri Lanka*, 1981, p.365.

51 Cited in de Silva, *A History of Sri Lanka*, 1981, p.327.

from the third quarter of the nineteenth century, the elite of the *Karava* had unsuccessfully tried to persuade the governor to appoint one of them to the LC as unofficial member/s. Most remarkably, colonial administrators kept the *Karavas* at bay while promoting the *Goyigamas*. When Sir James Pieris, the most prominent star of the low-caste Karava and a highly respected civil servant, stood for the LC he was overlooked both in 1900 and in 1905 in favour of arch-conservative S.C. Obeysekara, the star of the *Goyigama* caste.

The approach adopted by the governor in respect of the Sinhalese was in stark contrast to the stance he took with the Tamil community. Nevertheless, it was only the elite of the highest caste *Vellalas* who were selected as the unofficial members to the LC, during the third quarter of the nineteenth century, and changed when a low-caste Tamil, Mr W.G. Rockwood was selected after the expiration of the term of office of Mr Ponnambalam Ramanathan.

During the period 1905 to 1919 there seemed to have been a kind of mutual understanding between the elite of the Sinhalese *Goyigamas* and Tamil *Vellalas* against their 'common enemy', the rising elite of the Sinhalese, the low-caste *Karava*. The 1906 and 1911 elections to the educated Ceylonese seat provide some evidence to conclude that there was a *pactum* between these two elite groups to keep political power between them. In both these elections, the high-caste Tamil elite candidate Sir Ponnambalam Ramanathan was widely supported by the *Goyigama* elite. This resulted in a campaign by the *Goyigama* elite against the Sinhalese candidate Sir Marcus Fernando (*Karava* elite) of Moratuwa, in favour of Ramanathan. Clearly, some members of the Tamil and the Sinhalese high castes were able to cooperate and keep political and economic power to themselves.

However, the alliance between the high-caste Tamil and Sinhalese elites proved to be short-lived, as communal loyalties overtook other concerns. The decisive breakthrough came from the Jaffna Tamils (also called the Ceylon Tamils) who from about the second decade of the twentieth century, began to organise under the banner of the 'Jaffna Association' to preserve the status quo of the Tamils in government employment and other learned professions. This no doubt instilled fear into the hearts of both the low- and up-country Sinhalese elite.

The most urgent task for the Sinhalese elite was how to keep the Tamil elite from dominating prestigious positions in the employment sector and in mostly white-collar jobs which, since European conquest of the island was 'monopolised' by the Ceylon Tamil elite. Animosity between the principal rivals thus gradually increased when more opportunities became available between 1912 and 1931.

5 The evolution of 'communalism'

Patriots

During the second half of the nineteenth century there emerged a small caucus of Sinhalese, Ceylon Tamils, burghers (the descendants of Dutch extraction) and other small minority groups who attempted to create a 'Ceylonese' national identity, encompassing all the ethnic and racial groups. A semi-political campaign to achieve constitutional reforms for the island was enthusiastically initiated resulting in the formation of the 'Ceylon League'.[1] The pioneering reformists had realised that the existing practice of electing representatives on the basis of communal and racial differences to the Legislative Council (LC) would have a baneful influence on harmony among the inhabitants of the island. The appointment of the unofficial members to the pre-1912 LC was underpinned by communal differences, as is shown in Table 5.1.[2]

Predictably, every governor between 1900 and 1921 maintained the composition of the LC on a communal basis. When the constitutionalist reformists proposed that the elections of the representatives to the LC be appointed on a non-communal basis, it was vehemently opposed by Governor Sir H.E. McCallum. Having noticed that some elements of the Tamil leadership in the Jaffna Association were interested

Table 5.1 Composition of unofficial members in the Legislative Council, 1909

Ethnic group	*Total number*	*Allocated seats*
Europeans	6,500	3
Burghers	24,780	1
Moors	250,000	1
Tamils	1,127,000	1
Sinhalese (both Kandyan and low-country Sinhalese)	2,551,000	2

1 See E.W. Perera, 'Ceylon Under British Rule', 1796–1906, in *The 20th Century Impressions of Ceylon*, an extract published in *The Handbook*.

2 *Handbook*, p.24

in maintaining communal representation, he suggested, in his despatch of 26 May 1909 to the Secretary of State for the Colonies, Earl of Crew KG, that the existing system of communal representation should be maintained. His justification for communal representation was that 'The races inhabiting this island are numerous and divisive.'[3] Therefore, 'he was strongly of the opinion that, in the best interests of the country, and especially those of the bulk of the native inhabitants, appointments to seats upon the Legislative Council should continue to be made, as at present, by means of nomination, and not by recourse being had to popular franchise.'[4] The Governor's approach was considered prudent by the Secretary of State for the Colonies. In his correspondence with the Governor on 24 December 1909 he wrote: 'I consider, therefore, that the members who are to represent these communities must continue to be nominated until Ceylon is ripe for a wide extension of the franchise on democratic lines.'[5]

The result was that the composition of the membership of the LC was disproportionate. For instance, while the smallest community in the island, that is the European settlers, had three seats, only two members from the largest community, the Sinhalese (both low-country and the Kandyans), were nominated to the LC.

Against communal representation

Communal representation to the LC was not universally accepted. Such representation was perceived by many as dividing people along racial lines and was a mechanism designed to prolong the colonial administration. The *Karăva* caste among the Sinhalese (a relatively low caste in the cast hierarchy in Ceylon) led the campaign for the abolition of communal representation. Sir James Peiris, one of the leading constitutionalists of the *Karăva*,[6] in his memorial of 12 December 1908, to the Under-Secretary of State said that the existing system of representation in the LC was underpinned by inequality and was an injustice which was 'utterly indefensible'.[7] What is needed, argued Peiris, 'is a system of local representation which enable the inhabitants of the different districts to place their wants before the council through their representatives'. He urged that the people should be given the right to choose their own representatives – and that the Governor's prerogative right in the selection of individuals on purely communal grounds should be

3 McCallum's dispatches to the Secretary of State for the Colonies Earl of Crew, KG, on 26 May 1909. *Handbook*, p.61.

4 *Handbook*, p.59.

5 See the Colonial Secretary's dispatches to Governor McCallum, 24 Dec. 1909, *Handbook*, and p.66.

6 He was educated in Cambridge gaining a double first. During his time at university he became its President. When he returned to the island he entered the Colonial Civil Service. Later he served as a member of the Legislative Council and was elected President of the Ceylon National Congress.

7 *Handbook*, p.9.

abolished.[8] In another memo (of 19 April 1909) from A. Alwis, A. St. Jayawardene and F.J. de Mel, writing on behalf of the Ceylon National Association to the Colonial Secretary, the Secretary of State for the Colonies was urged 'to direct that such measures be taken so as to place the Legislative Council of Ceylon on an elective basis'.[9] The strongest opposition to the continuation of communal representation came from the Chillaw Association. In its memo of 5 May 1909 to the LC, C.H. Senevirathna and J.A.E. Corea, on behalf of the Chillaw Association pleaded with the Colonial Secretary:

> Your memorialists humbly conceive that it is essential, in order to correct such legislative blunder as the above, and to prevent similar errors in the future, that the existing form of Government should be re-formed on constitutional lines, and respectfully submit that:
>
> (i) racial representation and the appointment of non-official members of Council on the Governor's nomination should be discontinued;
> (ii) the non-official members should be elected by the people to represent each revenue district and each chief town of a province. Provision may be made for more than one member to represent important centres, such as the city of Colombo, Kandy.[10]

The Chillaw Association was not totally indifferent to the concerns of the Tamils. It was suggested that a limited number of Tamils be elected 'by means of an electoral association, approved by the Government, such as the Planters' Association, Chambers of Commerce etc'.[11] A memorial by H.J.C. Pereira of 18 March 1909 with 760 signatures and also H.L. de Mel's memo on behalf of the Low Country Products Association both urged the Secretary of State for the Colonies to replace communal representation with a more radical territorial, electoral system.[12]

Even though the Ceylon Tamils' loyalty to the *throne* and to the colonial administration was strong, the leadership of the Ceylon Tamils in the Jaffna Association was also unhappy with the way communal representation was maintained since it seemed to exist mainly for the advantage of the colonial administration. It was alleged that the racial representation to the LC was 'likely to perpetuate class feelings, and was not calculated to introduce the best talents into the Council'.[13] On 10 April 1909, A. Sabapathy, M.A. Arulanandan and J.M. Hensman, the leading stars of the Jaffna Association, made their view known to the Secretary of

8 *Handbook*, p.9.
9 *Handbook*, p.37.
10 *Handbook*, pp.39–46.
11 *Handbook*, p.46.
12 *Handbook*, pp.22–27.
13 A memorial to the Colonial Secretary sent by A. Sabapathy, M.A. Arulanandan and J.M. Hensman on behalf of the Jaffna Association on 10 April 1909, *Handbook*, pp.27–32.

State for the Colonies that the continuation of communal representation could have pernicious effects for the island. However, they did not object to having some elements of communal representation on a temporary basis. It was suggested that, 'two or three seats might be reserved for nomination by the Governor for the representation of minorities'. It is interesting to note that the term 'minorities' was used to identify small community groups such as the burghers and the Moors but not the Tamils who comprised 11 per cent of the population. The Ceylon Tamil leadership never saw themselves as a minority and thought that together with the Sinhalese they would comprise the *majority* on the island.[14]

In the post-1912 constitutional reform movement, the campaign against communal representation steadily, if slowly continued. N. Salvadurai, a Jaffna Tamil politician, addressing the Congress of the Literacy Association in 1914 reminded the audience that all nationals of Ceylon should work as 'one solid whole', or as 'one united people' to create a Ceylonese identity. Such a unitary approach would, in his view, enable them to win more rights in the affairs of the colonial administration.[15] Powerful Sinhalese, liberal voices supported unity between the majority and the minorities in the struggle for more reforms for the island. Aramand de Zouza, a prominent member of the Sinhalese community, urged everyone interested in reforms to 'dissipate cliquism' so as to create trust between the communities with a view to becoming 'a single united unit and one community' so that they could fight for reforms.[16] In the view of another Sinhalese leader, E.W. Perera, 'the Sinhalese, Tamils, burghers and Mohammedans are all one race in their love for this island. In this respect they form one community.'[17]

The Ponnambalam factor

P. Ramanathan's election in 1912, as the first representative for the educated Ceylonese seat in the LC, played a major role in assuaging any fears that might have been entertained by the Ceylon Tamils that elections would be conducted on a strictly communal basis. He was a well-known Tamil respected among all community groups in the island. To the surprise of many Tamils, it was the Sinhalese elite who guaranteed Ramanathan's victory in the election campaign. His rival, Dr Marcus Fernando, a highly respected Sinhalese medical practitioner and businessman, was unable to win the support of the Sinhalese even though he made much of the ethnic difference between himself and his rival. A significant factor in Ramanathan's election success was the role he played in the 1915 Sinhalese–Muslim riots in bringing justice to Sinhalese leaders who had been

14 Sabapathy's letter, in *Handbook*, p.32.

15 Roberts, 'Problems of Collective Identity in a Multi-ethnic Society: Sectional Nationalism vs Ceylonese Nationalism 1900–1940', in Roberts (ed.), *Collective Identities, Nationalism and Protests in Sri Lanka*, 1979, p.345.

16 Roberts, 'Problems of Collective Identity in a Multi-ethnic Society', 1979, p.345.

17 Roberts, 'Problems of Collective Identity in a Multi-ethnic Society', 1979, p.345.

imprisoned and persecuted. The reluctance of the *Karãva* caste to spearhead the reform campaign as they had done before the 1912 constitutional reforms campaign also militated against any chance of securing Fernando's victory, in spite of Fernando being of that caste. The *Karãva* held back their support from the reform campaign because they felt that the main beneficiaries would be a rival Sinhalese caste, the *Goyigama*.

The 1915 riots had considerably weakened the Sinhalese elite's reform campaign because many of them were jailed for their suspected collusion with the rioters. The best part of the next three to four years was spent by both the Sinhalese and Ceylon Tamil elite travelling between Whitehall in London and Colombo to get a special commission to inquire into the brutal methods employed by the colonial officials against only the Sinhalese Buddhists. Colonial officers had committed atrocities against the Sinhalese Buddhist leaders and peasantry in the suppression of the riots.

The sudden withdrawal of the *Karãva* elite from the agitation for constitutional reform movement also came as a surprise to many observers, given their indefatigable campaign in securing constitutional reforms between the years 1908 to 1910. It has been suggested that their reluctance to provide leadership to the reform campaign may also have been a reaction to the sudden rise of *Goyigama*, regarded as the Sinhalese aristocracy, with the covert support of the Governor. This was perceived as a real threat to the further advancement of the *Karãva* elite in both trade and in white-collar jobs in the colonial administration on account of the traditional rivalry between these castes. Also, by this time, there had emerged a number of prominent *Goyigama* leaders such as the Senanayake brothers (D.S. and F.R.) and D.B. Jayatilaka. Considering the rivalry between the *Karãva* and *Goyigama* castes, the reluctance of the former to play a subservient role to the latter was not at all surprising. As a consequence, between 1910 and 1916 there was hardly any agitation for constitutional reforms from the Sinhalese. Significantly, there was little rivalry between the Sinhalese and the Tamils during these years as well.

Indian influence

Around 1916 a few prominent Sinhalese and Tamil people such as Sir James Peiris, E.J. Samarawickrame and Sir Ponnambalam Arunachalam, Ramanathan's brother, resurrected the campaign for constitutional reforms. No doubt, developments in the neighbouring country, India, might have influenced the Sri Lankan elite forcing them to reconsider their strategies for winning self-rule. (Chapter 7 explores Arunachalam's leadership in greater detail.) Arunachalam's plea to all who were concerned about constitutional reforms to come forward in the struggle for the self-rule for the island was so powerful that he was able to bring the leading players of the respective communities, Sinhalese, Tamils, Moors and burghers into a united front. Leadership for this front was provided by the Ceylon Reform League and the Ceylon National Association, with Arunachalam providing moral support and political leadership. 'The Legislative Council of Ceylon shall be enlarged and re-constituted', it was argued, 'so as to contain a substantial majority of members elected upon the basis of territorial electorate with a broad franchise, with due safeguards for the minorities'.[18]

Sir Ponnambalam Arunachalam was a widely respected Tamil politician in pre-1921 Ceylon. His reputation as a national leader and, most importantly of all, his liberal outlook, had been instrumental in influencing, both Jaffna Tamils and cosmopolitan Tamil elites to work together with the Sinhalese constitutional reformists. Arunachalam's insistence that in future constitutional reforms representation to the LC should be based purely on a territorial basis became a rallying cry that most found attractive. His generosity was also demonstrated when he suggested that members from 'small minorities of our population', be elected on a communal basis. This won the backing of Sinhalese reformists much to the delight of Arunachalam. By 'smaller minorities',[19] Arunachalam meant the burghers, the Moors, the Malays and the Europeans but not the Ceylon Tamils whom he grouped with the Sinhalese as one of the island's majorities. He urged:

> We ought to have at once a large increase in the number of elected members of the Legislative Council. While the general principle should be local representation, there must be adequate safeguards for minorities. The Burghers, for example, the Europeans and Mohammedans should have a special electorate . . . So do we in Ceylon desire that Government shall be a Ceylonese Government, that our rulers shall identify themselves entirely with Ceylonese interests and, in the, striking words of the, Mihavama, 'be one with the people'.[20]

In his presidential address to the Conference on Constitutional Reforms convened by the Ceylon National Association and the Ceylon Reform League on 15 December 1917, Arunachalam reiterated the need for the elimination of communal representation from the LC. 'We all feel', said Arunachalam, 'that racial representation is pernicious and has operated to widen cleavages in the community and to obstruct that unity and harmony which we should all do our best to promote'. [21]

The formation of the Ceylon National Congress (Congress) in 1919 was the culmination of the tireless attempt of Sir Ponnambalam Arunachalam and a few of the Sinhalese elite to create a body with more autonomy to fight for self-government 'by constitutional methods for a reform of the existing system of government and administration'.[22] This should, however, not be regarded as full

18 This was resolution No. 4 of the First Conference's resolutions, *Handbook*, p.128.

19 See his address to the Annual General Meeting of the Ceylon National Association on 4 February 1917, *Handbook*, p.80.

20 Arunachalam's address on 4 February 1917, *Handbook*, p.86.

21 Presidential address by Arunachalam to the Conference on Constitutional Reforms, *Handbook*, p.111.

22 Article 1 of the Constitution of the Ceylon National Congress, Appendix H, cited in Kearney, *Communalism and Language in the Politics of Ceylon*, 1967, p.27. See, further , B.H. Farmer, *Ceylon:*

independence, *purna swaraj*, as was demanded by the then radical political group, the Young Lanka League. The formation of Congress was considered the first big attempt after the 1870s at uniting the Tamils, the Sinhalese, the Moors and other minority groups around a common national front.[23] Most importantly, it was meant to be used as 'a vehicle of expression of truly Ceylonese aspirations since its founding in 1919'.[24]

The twin pillars of Congress

Thus the twin pillars of Congress, as K.M. de Silva points out, were to build communal harmony and to win self-rule for the island.[25] Congressmen seriously began to urge unity among the various communities. D.B. Jayatilaka (later, Sir D.B. Jayatilaka, a Sinhalese Buddhist scholar, who became the President of Congress, 1923 to 1924, and the leader of the State Council, 1931 to 1942), emphasised that it was necessary that the Sinhalese and Ceylon Tamils fight shoulder to shoulder, as one people.[26] He urged his fellow Congressmen:

> We are bound to win on one condition – we are bound to win if we sink our petty differences, if we give up our personal considerations, if we prepare to renounce our personal ambitions, if we prepare to do our best for the common good. The battle has been simplified enormously for us. The whole fight rests with the low-country Sinhalese and the Ceylon Tamils. We have taken up the challenge on the main point as regards constituencies. The Sinhalese and Tamils can fight shoulder to shoulder. The past few years have shown us that the Sinhalese and the Tamils are one people.[27]

Thus, the struggle for constitutional reforms during the early years of Congress was structured on a bipartisan approach with a liberal outlook.[28] But this unity was not to last. Not long after the formation of Congress, cracks began to emerge among the Sinhalese and Tamil reformists. There were three main factors that created communal rivalry: the insistence that communal representation be maintained to

A Divided Nation, London Institute of Race Relations, p.55; and G.C. Mendis, *Ceylon Under the British*, 2nd rev. ed., Apothecaries Co. Ltd: Colombo, 1948, pp.124–125.

23 S. Arasarathnam, 'Nationalism, Communalism and National Unity in Ceylon', in P. Mason (ed.), *India and Ceylon: Unity in Diversity, A Symposium*, Oxford University Press: London/New York/Bombay, 1967, p.262.

24 V. Samaraweera, 'Land, Labour, Capital and Sectional Interests in the National Politics of Sri Lanka', *Modern Asian Studies*, 15(1), 1981, p.140.

25 K.M. de Silva, 'The Ceylon National Congress in Disarray, 1920–1921: Sir Ponnambalam Arunchalam Leaves the Congress', *CJHSS*, 2(2), 1972, p.115.

26 D.B. Jayatilaka's address to Congress, *Handbook*, p.237.

27 Jayatilaka's address to Congress, *Handbook*, p 237.

28 Namasivayam, *The Legislators of Ceylon, 1928–1948*, 1950, p.18.

the LC; the demand for an extra seat for Colombo Tamils within the western region and the colonial administration's policy of divide and rule.

Communal representation

Even though unity between the Tamils and Sinhalese prevailed during the first two decades of the twentieth century a difference of opinion began to surface concerning representation to the LC. During the pre-1916 period differences between the communities were kept at a manageable level since both the Sinhalese and Tamil leadership rose above communal prejudices to attract loyalty to the wider cause, namely, the struggle for the self-rule.

It should be noted that most of the Tamil and Sinhalese reformist leaders had their political base in and around Colombo. Most of them were exposed to western liberal traditions but their thinking was also shaped by their own cultural values. There were other political leaders such as the Tamil politicians who were born and raised in the provincial cities of the Jaffna Peninsula and whose political outlook was quite different to those of the constitutionalist reformists. It was these provincial leaders who eventually determined the future direction of the island.

The Ceylon Tamils in the Jaffna Association faced a dilemma. On the one hand, they did not want to be identified with communalism. On the other, they could not come to terms with the notion of territorial representation that would bolster the numerical strength of Sinhalese representation in the LC, thus reducing the parity that had hitherto existed between the Ceylon Tamils and the Sinhalese. In a memorial (of 6 April 1910) to the Earl of Crew, the Secretary of State for the Colonies, the Jaffna Association stated that even though they were 'disappointed and grieved' to find that the communal representation was to continue they would not ask 'Your Lordship to revoke that decision'.[29] It is easy to understand this dilemma. Communal representation is not the best way to secure minority interests. It secures the minority by actually entrenching the differences between the communities and induced various communities in the island 'to consider themselves as separate entities rather than as citizens of Ceylon'.[30] Other prominent commentators, B.H. Farmer[31] and Sir Ivor Jennings,[32] reached similar conclusions.

The reformists, or as they were popularly known, territorialists were not able to influence the colonial administration and communal representation continued in the constitutional reform introduced to the LC, in 1912. In addition to 11 official members, another ten unofficial members were appointed to the LC. Of the ten,

29 C.O. 54/733, Despatch no. 179, Memorial of the Jaffna Association to Crew, 6 April 1910, cited in R.A. Ariyaratne, *Communal Conflict in Ceylon and the Advance towards Self-government 1907–32*, PhD Thesis, Cambridge, 1973, p.60.

30 Mendis, *Ceylon Under the British*, 1948, p.122.

31 See B.H. Farmer, *Ceylon: A Divided Nation*, 1963, p.54.

32 Jennings, 'Nationalism and Political Development in Ceylon', 1953, p.73. W.H. Wriggins, *Ceylon: Dilemmas of a New Nation*, 1960, p.82.

four members were elected from communal constituencies (one rural European, one urban European, one burgher, one educated Ceylonese). The remaining six were nominated by the governor who took into account communal affiliations (one Kandyan Sinhalese, one low-country Sinhalese, two Ceylon Tamils, one Moor).[33] Sir P. Ramanathan was elected to the educated Ceylonese seat with the support of a large majority of Sinhalese voters so the ratio of Tamil representation to Sinhalese representation in the LC was 60 to 40 per cent.

There were some progressive elements in the 1912 constitutional reform. For the first time in the history of the LC, educated Ceylonese were given the opportunity to select their representative through an election even though it was confined to a privileged few. The 'educated Ceylonese seat', as it was known, however, allowed for one member only to represent the non-European native population. The election of Ramanathan, a Tamil, to represent the whole of the native population mainly through the strength of the Sinhalese vote is evidence that in spite of years of communally based representation, the people of Ceylon did not vote along ethnic lines. Political judgement still remained independent of ethnic considerations.

1912–1917: the system of communal representation continued

For the next five years (1912–1917) there was no discernible tension between the Sinhalese and Ceylon Tamil communities. However, this situation changed when the Jaffna Tamils' feared that their representation in the LC might diminish if communal representation were abolished in future constitutional reforms.

When the Ceylon Reform League for constitutional reforms was formed at the initiative of Arunachalam and a few low-country Sinhalese elitists, only two Tamils, C. Gunasekeram and E.V. Ratnam, actually attended the meeting. For most of the early discussion, the Jaffna Association 'kept aloof from the League'.[34] For example, when the Conference on Constitutional Reform was launched (comprising members of both the Ceylon National Association and Ceylon Reform League), of the 144 delegates who attended representing various provincial organisations, there were only 17 Tamils – a majority of whom represented non-communal 'open societies' outside the Northern and Eastern Provinces. Only two representatives, W. Duraiswamy and G.C. Tambiah, were sent by the Jaffna Association at the insistence of Arunachalam. 'Such meagre support', observed Ariyaratne, 'looked all the more glaring when provincial organisations like the Chillaw Association and Galle Association had sent more than ten delegates each'.[35] Arunachalam failed to secure the support and loyalty of the Jaffna Association to the extent he would have liked. From 1917 to 1920 the Jaffna Association

33 Jennings, 'Nationalism and Political development in Ceylon', 1953, p.73.

34 Ariyaratne, *Communal Conflict in Ceylon, 1907–32*, 1973, p.63.

35 Ariyaratne, *Communal Conflict in Ceylon, 1907–32*, 1973, p.64.

opposed territorial representation favoured by the reformists. It was determined to oppose any further increase of territorial representation because any such arrangement would have resulted in the domination of the Sinhalese *vis-à-vis* other community groups. In 1918, opposing both the Ceylon National Association and the Ceylon Reform League, the Jaffna Association passed a resolution proposing that the existing formulae for Sinhalese and Tamil representation in the LC be maintained in any future constitutional reforms. On 2 January 1918 the following was recorded:

> That . . . the scheme of constitutional reform contained in the joint memorial of the Ceylon National Association and the Ceylon Reform League adopted at the Conference held in Colombo on the 15th December 1917, is not acceptable to the Tamil community, and that a memorial be forwarded to the Right Honourable the Secretary of State for the Colonies, praying, among other administrative reforms, for the reform of the Executive and Legislative Council of the Island on an extended elective basis, whilst maintaining as far as possible, the existing proportion of Sinhala and Tamil representation in the Legislative Council.[36]

It was proposed that one Councillor be elected by the unofficial members and another member be nominated by the Governor from 'a different race to that of the elected member'.[37] Ariyaratne argues that '(t)he underlying idea, it is clear, was to assure themselves of the presence of a Tamil unofficial in the Executive Council thereby maintaining equal representation should the unofficial elector be a Sinhalese.'[38] Had their demand been accepted, communal representation would have been further strengthened. Future constitutional reforms, in particular the campaign for self-rule, would have been difficult to achieve.

It was proposed by the Jaffna Association that if the Secretary of State for the Colonies were going to introduce reforms to the LC, the membership of the Council should consist of 16, of which 11 would comprise elected members and five nominated by the governor. Of these two categories, it was urged that Ceylon Tamils' representation should be no fewer than six. A suggestion by the Ceylon National Association and First Conference Scheme for an increase of the representatives, at least, to 30 in the LC, was also opposed. It was argued that any such increase would reduce their numbers as compared with the Sinhalese.[39] This

36 C.O. 54/810, memorial of the Jaffna Association to the Colonial Secretary for the Colonies. See, further, K.M. de Silva, 'The Formation and Character of the Ceylon National Congress 1917–1919', 1967, p.92.

37 C.O, 54/810, Memorial of the Jaffna Association.

38 Ariyaratne, *Communal Conflict*, 1973, p.65.

39 According to the Ceylon National Association the total numbers of the members of the Legislative Council should be increased to 31. Except for the Europeans (two), the burghers (one) and the Moors (one) other representatives should be elected on territorially based electorates. The First Conference Scheme also suggested that the membership of the Legislative Council should increase

had, according to Ariyaratne, a devastating effect on the credibility of constitutional reformists' alleged claim that *they* were the true representatives of the population of the island.

The influence exercised by the stalwarts of the Jaffna Association such as A. Kanagasabhai and A. Sabapathy over the Ceylon Tamils was immense. Addressing P. Arunachalam, they wrote that under any constitutional reforms to the island 'the present ratio of Tamil to Sinhalese members should be maintained.'[40] The presidents of the Ceylon Reform League and the Ceylon National Association pleaded with the Jaffna Association not to press for 'a system of racial representation' for fear that such a move might have a baneful effect on the communal harmony in the island.[41]

Governor Manning seemed to agree with this argument. Writing to Secretary of State for the Colonies, the Duke of Devonshire, Manning suggested that the existing system of communal representation be continued given the diverse nature of the communal groupings of the island. The Duke replied to Manning thus:

> I am in accord with the opinion expressed by you that, in view of existing conditions and of the grouping of population in the Colony, representation must for an indefinite period of time be in fact communal, whatever the argument of constituencies may be . . . It appears to me to be clearly established that in Ceylon the organization of society is communal, and that if this fact is not clearly expressed, one of the essential considerations on which my decision must be based might be obscured.[42]

Ramanathan appeared willing to provide the leadership for both the retention of communal representation to the LC (1921 election) and an extra electorate for the Tamils in the predominantly Sinhalese-inhabited Western Province.[43] Both of these were strongly resisted by Sinhalese Congressmen such as Sir James Peiris, Sir Baron Jayatilaka, E.J. Samarawickrame, H.J.C. Pereira, and Francis de Zoysa, who argued that the retention and extension of the principle of communal representation would give rise to ethno-tribal conflicts and would not help the struggle

up to 33. It was suggested that a communal representation should be allowed in the case of the Europeans (two), the burghers (one), and the Moors (one). See Ariyaratne, *Communal Conflict*, 1973, p.67.

40 de Silva, 'The Formation and Character', 1967, p.91.

41 See a letter sent to Jaffna Sabhai through Sir Ponnambalam Arunachalam by Ceylon Reform League and Ceylon National Congress, cited in de Silva, 'The Formation and Character', 1967, Appendix B, p.102.

42 Dispatch to Manning on 11 Jan. 1923, ibid. p.120.

43 Kearney *Communalism and Language in the Politics of Ceylon*, 1967, p.28. See, A.J. Wilson, 'The Tamil Federal Party in Ceylon Politics', *Journal of Commonwealth Political Studies*, 4(2), 1966, p.117. See also *Handbook*, pp.522–527. See also R.N. Kearney, 'Political Mobilization in Contemporary Sri Lanka', in R.N. Kearney (ed.), *Political Mobilization in South Asia*, Syracuse University Press: Syracuse, NY, 1973, p.44.

for self-government.[44] Such a move would also obstruct any attempt at fostering a Ceylonese identity.

The demands for constitutional reforms were, therefore, not straightforward. Minority and communal interests got in the way. When the reformists' demands for the grant of greater political power to Ceylon was considered favourably, which was in keeping with the spirit of the constitutional reforms introduced in 1917 by the Montagu-Chelmsford reforms for India, the communalists discouraged this move. An Assistant Under-Secretary, G.E.A. Grindle, made the following observation about the demand for reform: 'We shall have to take the Ceylon Reform League demand seriously . . . We cannot put off the request as inopportune.' Nonetheless, this attitude began to change when the Jaffna Association started to put pressure on the colonial government in Whitehall to maintain the status quo. Divisions between the reformists and the Jaffna Association were so great that the Parliamentary Under-Secretary of State, W.A.S. Hewins, felt compelled to make a statement in the House of Commons that 'until the time is more opportune' further constitutional reforms would not be introduced.[45] Moreover, 'a question of this difficulty and complexity could only be discussed usefully after careful investigation by a Commission.'[46]

An extra electorate for Ceylon Tamils

From the second decade of the twentieth century, Tamil politics centred on securing an extra electorate for the Ceylon Tamils in the Western Province. The Tamils were aggrieved by the suggestion of the governor for an additional representative for the low-country Sinhalese to the LC. The Jaffna Tamils were also shocked to hear that an 'educated Ceylonese seat' was going to be created within the Sinhalese-dominated Western Province. It would appear that the Jaffna Association sent a memorial to the Secretary of State for the Colonies expressing their anxiety and anger that the educated Ceylonese seat would 'fall to the lot of the Sinhalese'.[47]

The Ceylon Tamil elite argued that without a special Tamil seat in the Western Province they could not work any more with the Sinhalese constitutionalist reformists. This eventually came to threaten the unity between the Sinhalese and Tamil leadership. The founding father of Congress, Sir Ponnambalam Arunachalam, was a victim of this struggle. He came under enormous pressure from the Ceylon Tamils to reconsider whether he should continue to work with the Sinhalese constitutional reformists. This resulted in the resignation of

44 The dispatches to Amery in August 1920 by the leaders of Sinhalese Congressmen, see details, *Handbook*, p.312.

45 Hansard, the House of Commons, 1918, vol. 108, cited in Ariyaratna, *Communal Conflict in Ceylon*, 1973, p.66.

46 C.O 54/810, Cowell's minute, 20 April 1918, on the memorial sent by the Jaffna Association.

47 C.O. 54/733, the Memorial of the Tamil inhabitants of Ceylon to Crew, 27 April 1910, cited in Ariyaratne, *Communal Conflict in Ceylon*, 1973, p.60.

Arunachalam from Congress. At an emergency meeting held in Arunachalam's Colombo house it was decided by 11 leading Ceylon Tamils that Arunachalam should send a memorial to the Secretary of State for the Colonies, the Duke of Devonshire, explaining the reason for his resignation. It was noted in the memorial that 'unfortunately, owing to personal differences between Sir P. Arunachalam and the Hon. James Peiris in regard to the representation of the city of Colombo, Sir P. Arunachalam withdrew from Congress.'[48]

Role of Governor Manning

The campaign for an extra electorate within the Western Province found a strong supporter in Governor Manning. In his dispatches to the Colonial Office he recommended the introduction of a 'communally elected Tamil seat for Colombo Town'.[49] It later emerged that Manning had quietly collaborated with the aforementioned Tamil organisations to prepare his draft constitutional reforms.[50] This is clear from Manning's own remarks reported by the *Times of Ceylon* when he thanked Sir Ponnambalam Ramanathan for the assistance rendered in drafting the reform proposals. The seats given to them, he said, were their birthright and they were justified in fighting for them.[51] Commending the role played by Manning, a leader of the Jaffna Association and a member of the Ceylon Tamil Mahajana Sabahi (CTMS), Sir K. Kanagasabai observed:

> [I]t was His Excellency Sir William Manning who had actually fought their cause for them after having shown and advised them what they should do. And it was His Excellency who obtained for the Tamils the *preferential treatment and concessions* as outlined in the Draft Scheme of Reforms. Such being the case it was their bounden duty to show their gratitude to Sir William Manning and accord him a fitting welcome.[52]

The *Times of Ceylo*n reported Manning 's words to the Tamils when he secured the seat as follows: '[I]t would please them to hear that all his recommendations, including the seat in the Western Province, had been sanctioned and that the Secretary of State had further thanked the Tamils for simplifying his task.'[53]

Nearly all the community groups protested a special electorate for the Ceylon Tamils. Most notably, Mr G.A. Wille, the leader in the burgher community, stressed that the concessions granted to 'backward communities', such as the Mohammedans, the Kandyans and the Indians, should not be exploited as an

48 The memorial sent to the Secretary of State for the Colonies on 23 May 1923, *Handbook*, p.524.

49 *Handbook*, p.540.

50 See the memorial submitted to the Secretary of State, W. Churchill by the Congress on 31 Aug. 1922, *Handbook*, p.439.

51 *The Times of Ceylon*, 13 June 1923.

52 Emphasis added. *Ceylon Daily News*, 12 June 1923.

53 *The Times of Ceylon*, 13 June 1923.

excuse for demanding a special Tamil seat in the Western Province. He stressed that the 'Tamil community had no right to place themselves in the position of a backward community in their demand for a seat in Colombo. So long as they were sure that the Tamils would be strongly represented in Council they could not sacrifice the basic foundation on which the Congress was based.'[54] Another burgher representative, Mr. Drieberg, supported this stance. More remarkably, S. Pasupathy, a Tamil, representing the Kurunagala Association, opposed any form of communal representation. He pointed out in rather flowery language, but his meaning is quite clear that:

> Communalism in any form, in any sphere would benefit neither the granter nor the grantee, but would be a permanent source of frictions and conflict. Communalism and national advancement was a contradiction of forms. It might even be described as political brigandage. Therefore anyone who would surrender to that gilded glamour would be opposing the goddess of democracy. That would lead them down the incline of political moribundity. That was the travesty of history.[55]

Pasupathy believed that communalism continued a divide-and-rule policy. Moreover it would destroy the 'amity of the races' on the island which was a 'far greater treasure' than the reforms that entrenched communal camps. 'The idea of race should be immolated at the altar of the motherland.'[56]

During the debate at the LC over the proposal for a special seat for the Tamils in the Western Province, the Tamil representative of Eastern Province, Mr. Tambimuttu, also vigorously opposed it. Desertion of the Ceylon Tamil leadership, including Sir P. Arunachalam, from Congress to take up the cause of the Tamil community was criticised as desperate action over communal politics.[57] However, according to Ponnambalam, it was his 'Sinhalese brethren' who should be blamed for the spilt of Congress. Referring to the new direction of Congress he alleged that Congress 'had destroyed the feelings of mutual confidence and co-operation between the various communities'.[58]

Ceylon Tamil Mahajana Sabhai

In 1921 the majority of the Ceylon Tamil leaders, most of whom were of the Jaffna Association, left Congress.[59] They subsequently formed the *Ceylon Tamil Mahajana*

54 *Handbook*, p.412.
55 *Handbook*, p.513.
56 *Handbook*, p.513.
57 Kearney (ed.), *Political Mobilization in South Asia*, 1973, p.44.
58 M. Vythilingam, *Ramanathan of Ceylon: The Life of Sir Ponnambalam Ramanathan*, vol. II, Chunnakam, 1977, p.538.
59 Kearney (ed.), *Political Mobilization in South Asia*, 1973, p.44. See also Jennings, *Nationalism and Political Development in Ceylon*, 1953, p.75.

Sabhai (CTMS, Tamils' Peoples' Union) on 15 August 1921. Some Colombo Tamil elites also joined them. The Union was composed only of Ceylon Tamils and was principally controlled by the highest caste *Vellãlas* of Jaffna Tamils. Its effect was to demarcate clearly the boundaries between the Tamils and Sinhalese. In 1923 another Jaffna Tamil organization, the *Ceylon Tamil League*, was formed by Ponnambalam Arunachalam to further the cause of the Ceylon Tamils. The Ceylon Tamils now had three major political organisations advocating for them. Tamil politicians, fearing political marginalisation chose to represent their community through their own organisations, thereby distancing themselves from mainstream politics. For 20 years, between 1920 to 1940, the partisan interests of the various communities dominated the political landscape militating against the fostering of national unity or a Ceylonese identity in the island.[60]

Post-Congress communal politics – fight for the restoration of pre-1921 communal representation

The reforms introduced into the LC, in 1921 meant that representatives were elected mainly on a territorial basis. The existing balance of power between the Sinhalese and Tamils was dramatically changed giving a decided advantage to the Sinhalese. For example, only three Tamil representatives were elected to the LC as against 13 Sinhalese. Dissatisfied with this 'legislative discrimination' as it was later dubbed by many Tamil politicians, notably G.G. Ponnambalam, Tamil politicians campaigned for a restoration of the old communal representation.[61] It was always in the minds of Tamil leaders that they needed to secure enough power to influence political policy and constitutional amendments so that their interests both in politics and in employment opportunities in the colonial administration would not be seriously diminished. Tamil leadership confronted this new danger by turning to subtler strategies, as Kearney notes, 'to curb the potential powers of the Sinhalese majority'.[62]

Colonial factor: His Excellency Governor Sir William H. Manning's role – 'adding fuel to smouldering coals?'

Sir William Manning (1918–1925) is regarded by some as one of the most reactionary governors to rule the island. His military background, perhaps, might have shaped his political thinking against the Ceylonese who was eager for independence from Britain. Before his appointment to the position of governorship of the island he served in the military in Somaliland and the North-west Frontier, and later became an ardent supporter of the continuation of the British Empire.

60 Tremayne, 'Sri Lanka: The Problem of the Tamils', London, 1987, p.217.
61 de Silva, '*The Ceylon National Congress in Disarray*', 1972, p.106.
62 Kearney, *Political Mobilization in South Asia*, 1973, p.32.

He did not approve of the constitutional reforms agitated for by Congress, neither did he believe that the colonial government should delegate its powers to competent natives. Congress, in his view, was no more than a political instrument manipulated by a group of western educated, low-country Sinhalese and a few of the Ceylon Tamil elite. He was of the view that the island could be governed with the assistance of government Agents and *durbas*[63] – such a system would not create any problem for the British Empire.[64] He also had a low opinion of the Sinhalese and Tamil leadership in Congress. His perception of the reformist elitists was negative. For example, he branded E.W. Perera, one of the leading figures in Congress, who later become its president and an elective member of both the Legislative and State Councils, as a 'shifty' and 'dishonest' low-country Sinhalese. According to Blackton, Manning 'generally cut Ceylonese politicians down to size in his despatches to the Colonial Office',[65] often generalising about them:

> The patronizing reservations Governor West Ridgeway had expressed were sharpened and defined in the unflattering terms of Governor Manning's analysis. The Ceylonese were unreliable, nervous when faced with contentious or unpopular decisions, hypersensitive, mutually mistrustful and liable to be self-serving in positions of authority. What the unofficials said in the Legislative Council was considered to be '90% rubbish'.[66]

Manning tried to block any implementation of substantial constitutional reforms and his management divided Congress by exploiting the caste, religious and communal differences that existed among its leadership.[67] In this he succeeded in creating permanent divisions among the various communities in the island, most notably among the Sinhalese and Tamils. Manning was determined to stop low-country Sinhalese gaining political power in the LC and therefore, looked at the demands of the Tamils with sympathy. He was apprehensive of the scenario in which Sinhalese dominance over the Tamils would continue *ad infinitum*. Manning warned, 'no single community can impose its will upon the other communities.'[68] In this endeavour, he had been able to win the support of the Duke of Devonshire, the Secretary of the State for the Colonies. In response to Governor Manning's reservations the Duke of Devonshire recommended that:

63 They were appointed from the natives and functioned in an inferior role to that of the government agents and British civil servants. More correctly, they were the strongest link between the native population and the colonial government.

64 See Manning dispatches to Fiddes, 31 Dec. 1918, C.O 54/814; Manning to Milner, C.O 54/819, 17 May 1919, cited in de Silva, 'The Ceylon National Congress in Disarray', 1972, 31, p.98.

65 CO 1882, Confidential Print, Eastern, No. 138, p.48, cited in C.T. Blackton, 'The Empire at Bay', in Roberts (ed.), *Collective Identities*, 1979, p.367.

66 Blackton, 'The Empire at Bay', in Roberts (ed.), *Collective Identities*, 1979, p.367.

67 Blackton, 'The Empire at Bay', in Roberts (ed.), *Collective Identities*, 1979, p.99.

68 See Wilson, *The Break-up of Sri Lanka*, 1988, p.7.

> If, on the other hand, these Unofficial Members had been elected by purely territorial constituencies, the Sinhalese community would almost certainly have been in a majority (disproportionate even to their numerical superiority in some respects) over all other sections of the Legislative Council including the Government. It would therefore appear to be clear that adherence, pure and simple, to the territorial basis of representation would be strongly opposed by all communities except the Sinhalese, and I am satisfied that the former are sincerely persuaded that their vital interests require serious limitation of the territorial basis of representation.[69]

Both Manning's and the Duke of Devonshire's responses are interesting. They appear to appreciate the problem of creating a majority in perpetuity without the necessary checks and balances in place. But ultimately, there was no doubt in the minds of the colonial administration that for a considerable period of time, whatever system of election was going to be applied the majority of the representatives would be chosen based on their communal background.[70] It was Manning who, to the dismay of the territorialists, exercising his influence over the colonial machine at Whitehall in London, determined the shape of the constitutional reforms. Thus the new reforms for LC in 1920 maintained the policy of racial representation.[71] He was also instrumental in abolishing the 'educated Ceylonese' seat thus effectively reversing the progressive element introduced by the 1912 constitutional reforms.[72]

Dissatisfied with the new constitutional reforms of 1921, Congress began to campaign more vigorously for more territorial representation. As a matter of urgency, a motion was debated in the LC in 1921 to abolish communally based seats in the Western Province. It was defeated by the votes of Tamil members and the official members (the latter being European members). Manning also appointed one member of each community to act in the committees of the LC.[73]

Balanced representation

Manning's scheme for the reform of the LC was based on 'balanced representation'. This became the main argument used later by the Ceylon Tamil politicians whenever the issue of constitutional reforms was raised by Congress. His scheme was supported by the CTMS in its memoranda Nos. 3 and 15, the Ceylon Tamil

69 *Handbook*, p.441.

70 Cited in Wilson's *Break-up of Sri Lanka*, 1988, p.7.

71 See ss 5(2), 5(3) and 5(4) of the Ceylon (Legislative Council) Order in Council 1920.

72 See the Ordinance enacted by the Governor with the advice and consent of the LC, no. 13, 1910, s.3.

73 *Handbook*, p.439.

League, memo. No. 4 and the Tamils of Ceylon memo. No.14.[74] According to Manning's plan the seats in the LC would be allocated as shown in Table 5.2.[75]

The reforms introduced by the Ceylon (Legislative Council) Order in Council 1923, continued a tradition of racial representation. Of 23 elected members from the territorial constituencies, 11 were to be elected from specially created communal constituencies.[76] The new reforms were seen by some political commentators as a further continuation of 'invidious distinctions between communities'.[77]

Manning's continuation of 'the existing racial and other differences' was seen as a deliberate attempt to 'arrest the growth of the sense of common citizenship' by giving new life to the existing racial representation in the LC. The policy of Manning was 'originated and fostered' by his predecessors.[78] The Ceylon Reform Deputation complained:

> In fact, the Governor's recommendations and the reasons with which he supports them offer plain encouragement to each community to go on fighting for its own advantage. Furthermore, they invite the minorities to regard the possible predominance in the Legislative Council of representatives belonging to the majority population, namely the Sinhalese, as a latent source of danger against which they must combine for their own safety.[79]

Table 5.2 Manning's plan for Legislative Council seat allocation

Community	*Population number*	*Seats*
Europeans	8,300	3
Burghers	29,100	2
Moors	265,000	3
Indian Moors	33,100	2
Indian Tamils	606,700	2
Ceylon Tamils	514,300	8
Sinhalese	3,016,400	14

74 In fact, the Ceylon Tamil League and Tamils of Ceylon were the brainchild of the Ramanathan and Arunachalam Ponnambalam brothers and were created to further the cause of the Tamil community and for communal representation. The same members of the CTMS and the JA served in both these organizations, the origin of which has been questioned. See *Handbook*, p.544.

75 *Handbook*, p.537.

76 See Namasivayam, *The Legislature of Ceylon*, 1951, p.19.

77 Farmer, *Ceylon: A Divided Nation*, 1963, p.55.

78 See the memorial submitted to the Principal Secretary of State W. Churchill by the Congress on 20 Sept. 1922, in *Handbook*, p.439.

79 The First Memorandum sent to the Duke of Devonshire KG, Principal Secretary, London, by the Ceylon Reform Deputation (created as a special body by Congress to advance the reform scheme of Congress) in May 1923, *Handbook*, p.535.

Governor Manning and the 'Minorities Conference'

Manning noticed 'with deep interest and satisfaction' the emerging gulf between the leadership of the Sinhalese and the Ceylon Tamils. He reported to the Colonial Office that the leaders were: '[V]iolently squabbling among themselves as to the representation of the Western Province electorates . . . one of the most patent facts which has been brought out is that there is very considerable division between the Tamils and Sinhalese.'[80]

With the tacit encouragement of Manning, a 'Minorities Conference' was initiated, which was an attempt to bring every minority group under one umbrella group under the leadership of the Ceylon Tamils.[81] Unofficial Tamil members of the LC together with some Tamil leaders of both the Jaffna Association and the CTMS were involved in this project. They sent a joint memorial supporting the reform scheme of Manning, popularly known as the 'Minorities Scheme',[82] to W. Churchill, the Principal Secretary of State for the Colonies, pleading that the pre-1921 communal representation in the LC be maintained in any future constitutional reform.[83] It was later revealed that the memorial was sent on the advice of Manning. One of the leaders of this new campaign, P. Ramanathan, who was by now *the* leader of the Tamils insisted that 'no two communities should be in a majority in the Council'.[84] Later, in a letter to Manning, Arunachalam, contrary to the patriotic stance taken in pre-1920s' reformist campaign, maintained that his position had always been that there should be adequate safeguards for minorities, particularly a system based on 'communal representation which guarantees equal proportion of members'.[85] Manning's contribution to the fact that Tamils would not suffer from being outnumbered was praised by Sir Ponnambalam Ramanathan as a 'well-thought-out proposal' which would secure the balance of power.[86] However, Manning's collaboration with Tamil groups was regarded with suspicion by the Singhalese and condemned as immoral and unjustifiable. It was alleged by Congress leadership that:

> An attempt to establish a 'balance of power' based upon no principle, but devised for the avowed purpose of preventing the possible predominance of

80 C.O 54/849, Manning's dispatch to J.R.Cowell, 14 Feb. 1921, cited in de Silva, 'The Formation and Character', 1972, p.106. See also Blackton, 'The Empire at Bay', in M. Robert (ed.), *Collective Identities*, 1979, pp.363–385.

81 Tremayne, *Sri Lanka: The Problem of the Tamils*, 1987, p.217.

82 It was submitted pretending that the 'Minorities Scheme' was approved and adopted by the European, the burgher, the Tamil, the Moors and the Indian Tamils in the LC. *Handbook*, p.447.

83 See details in the *Handbook*, p.439.

84 *Handbook*, p.445.

85 Arunachalam's letter to Governor Manning, 13 June 1923, cited de Silva, 'The Ceylon National Congress in Disarray, 1920–1921', *CJHSS*, 2(2), 1972, p.115.

86 P. Ramanathan, 'The Memorandum of Sir Ponnamablam Ramanathan on the Recommendations of the Donoughmore Commissioners appointed by the Right Honourable the Secretary of State for the Colonies to Report upon the Reform of the Existing Constitution of the Government of Ceylon 1924–1930', London, 1930.

> Sinhalese territorial representatives in the Legislative Council, which contingency for some unexplained reason is regarded as a dreadful evil to be averted even at the cost of justice and fair play.[87]

Opposition to the minorities' scheme came from all sections of the island. Divisions, especially among the Jaffna and Colombo Tamils, emerged about the way in which the whole affair was manipulated by the former. The Ceylon Tamils in the Western Province and other regional provinces in the north and east protested when they heard that their organisations' names were added to the petition sent to the Colonial Secretary. A prominent Tamil politician, Dr E.V. Rutnam, the President of the Colombo Tamil Association (which represented all sections of the Tamil community), immediately sent a dispatch to the Colonial Secretary condemning this scheme saying that the so-called memorialists had no authority to submit such a divisive scheme without having the consent of all sections of the Tamil population in the island.[88]

Another alleged signatory to the 'Minorities' Scheme', W.D. Duraiswamy, who was later knighted and became the Speaker of the State Council, distanced himself from any alleged collaboration with the memorialists, saying that he had no part whatsoever in the Minorities Scheme. He remarked, 'My telegram to Sir Ramanathan shows that I was opposed to the very essentials of that absurd scheme . . . No sane Tamil un-obsessed by personal magnificence could have been guilty of such a woeful exhibition of political absurdity.'[89] Moreover, no sooner did the Minorities Scheme become known to the Ceylon Muslim Association that that Association disassociated itself from any involvement with it stating that it had not authorised any of its members to collaborate with the Minority Scheme.[90]

Manning's exacerbation of the communal cleavages between the Sinhala and Tamils was described by Roberts as the case of 'adding fuel to already smouldering coals'.[91]

Manning's role in dividing the Sinhalese against one another

Manning also succeeded in creating mistrust and divisions among the low-country Sinhalese and the Kandyan Sinhalese (also called up-country Sinhalese). He regarded the up-country Sinhalese as high caste and decent and who would suffer at the hands of manipulative low-country Sinhalese if they failed to secure

87 Cited in Wilson, *Break-up of Sri Lanka*, 1988, p.8.

88 Wilson, *Break-up of Sri Lanka*, 1988, p.446.

89 Wilson, *Break-up of Sri Lanka*,1988, pp.445–446.

90 Wilson, *Break-up of Sri Lanka*, 1988, pp.446–447.

91 See Roberts, 'Problems of Collective Identity in a Multi-ethnic Society', in Roberts, (ed.), *Collective Identities: Nationalism and Protest in Sri Lanka*, 1979, p.353.

representation to the LC as a separate community. He agreed with the Kandyans that they, like the Moors and Tamils, were a minority.

In a dispatch to the Secretary of State for the Colonies, Milner, he claimed: 'Unless the high caste men will sink their prejudices and come forward for election, there would be a Council composed, on the elected side, largely of men of the lower castes who would not carry with them the respect of the general community.'[92] In his second reform proposal presented in May 1919, he stressed that the demands of the Kandyans were justified. At least six seats for the Kandyans, claimed Manning, should be created and there should be further constitutional safeguards for the low-country, high-caste Sinhalese as against the 'irresponsible and inexperienced politicians' of the low-country Sinhalese.[93]

Again, with the tacit encouragement of Governor Manning, a rival organisation, the Kandyan National Assembly, was established in 1923 by the Kandyan Sinhalese to fight for Kandyan representation. Manning urged the Kandyans, at a dinner party given in his honour that they should fight for their cause against the encroachments of low-country Sinhalese. They were assured by Manning that 'In any question in connection with the reforms which are in the air at the present moment, their wants and their aspirations will not be forgotten.'[94] A columnist of the *Ceylon Daily News* commented that 'the counter-reformers . . . flit like shadows with memorials hidden in secret sleeves.'[95] The essence of the demands of the Kandyans was that there should be electorates exclusively for the Kandyan Sinhalese.

Manning urged the Kandyan Sinhalese to unite with other minority groups to send a delegation to the Secretary of State for the Colonies to claim their historic rights – they dutifully did what they were requested. A delegation of the Kandyan Sinhalese informed the Secretary for the Colonies that the Congress had no authority to represent them because they were a separate community.[96] It is remarkable that the Kandyan National Assembly claimed that since they were a separate 'ethnic/racial group' distinct from the low-country Sinhalese, their province should be granted a separate provincial status in line with a federal structure.[97]

If they could not get their constitutional rights, they argued, further constitutional reforms were not necessary – such constitutional reforms being branded as an 'expensive and needless luxury'.[98] The Kandyan National Assembly pleaded with

92 C.O. 54/818, Manning to Milner, 7 February 1991.

93 C.O. 54/819, Manning to Milner, 18 May 1919, cited in Ariyaratne *Communal Conflict*, 1973, p.79.

94 *The Ceylon Daily News*, 25 January 1919, cited in Ariyaratne *Communal Conflict*, 1973, p.75.

95 *The Ceylon Daily News*, 24 January 1919, cited in Ariyaratne *Communal Conflict*, 1973, p.75.

96 *Handbook*, p.646. See, further, L.A. Wickramaratne, 'Kandyan and Nationalism in Sri Lanka: Some Reflections', *CJHSS*, 5, 1975, pp.49–67.

97 de Silva, *A History of Sri Lanka*, p.395. See also Wickramaratne, 'Kandyan and Nationalism',1975, pp.49–67.

98 See Attygalle's letter to the Ceylon Observer, 30 December 1918, cited in Ariyaratne, *Communal Conflict*, 1973, p.72.

the British colonial officials to protect them from the dominance of the low-country Sinhalese.

The demands of the Kandyan aristocracy that the areas coming under Kandyan law be recognized as a separate Kandyan province became a serious threat to the constitutional reformists in the Congress. As pointed out by Attygalle, a prominent Kandyan, under any reforms under the existing system the Kandyans would have 'not the ghost of a chance of being elected'.[99] During the debate at the Legislative Council, another leading star of the Kandyan aristocracy, Meedeniya Dissava, stressed that 'in any scheme of reforms that may be put forward for the Kandyan provinces, Kandyans must be represented by themselves'.[100]

The traditional conservative leadership of the Kandyan aristocracy Panabokke, J.H. Meedeniye Dissava, J.N.O. Attygalle, A.F. Molamure, Dr T.B. Kobbakaduva, P.B. Ratnayake, J.A. Halangoda, G.E. Madawala and T.B.L. Moonamalle were moving in a direction opposite to the non-communalist approach taken by the low-country Sinhalese in Congress. Therefore, it was not difficult for Manning, and his successors, Sir Hugh Clifford (1925–27) and Sir Herbert J. Stanley (1927–31) to treat the Kandyan National Assembly as a countervailing force against the constitutionalist reformists of Congress. Thus, it was not only Manning and the Jaffna Tamils, but parts of the Sinhalese community as well who demanded representation on a communal basis. The Tamils based their demand on culture and language and the Kandyans on caste.

Congress' attempt to bring back Arunachalam

Arunachalam's resignation from Congress came as a great shock to the reformist camp in Congress. Attempts to bring him back back into the fold of Congress did not succeed. Reminding him of his lofty speeches D.B. Jayatilaka, a leading Congressman, appealed to Arunachalam in his presidential address to the Congress on 21–22 December 1923 'to be true to what he then said'. He begged him to join 'in our work for the political emancipation of our country'.[101] These attempts did not succeed. Arunachalam had by now joined his brother, Ramanathan. In a letter to Governor Manning, Arunachalam explained that his position had always been that there should be adequate safeguards for minorities, particularly a system based on 'communal representation which guarantees an equal proportion of members'.[102] Indeed, there is evidence that some Tamil leaders did not want to break away from the British Empire so soon fearing that in an independent Ceylon their position and prestige would be weakened.[103]

99 *The Ceylon Observer*, 30 December 1918, cited in Ariyaratne, *Communal Conflict*, 1973, p.73.

100 The Debate of the Legislative Council, 11 December 1918, cited in Ariyaratne, *Communal Conflict*, 1973, p.89.

101 *Handbook*, p.576.

102 Arunachalam's letter to Governer Manning, 13 June 1923, cited in de Silva, 'The Ceylon National Congress in Disarray, 1920–1921', 1972, p115.

103 de Silva, 'The Formation and Character', 1967, p.78.

6 The Ponnambalam brothers

Arunachalam: from national unity to Tamil communal politics

Sir Ponnambalam Arunachalam and his brother, Sir Ponnambalam Ramanathan, were part of the *crème de la crème* of the Ceylon Tamil elite of national politics and the learned professions in the island from the last quarter of the nineteenth century and perhaps to the end of the second decade of the twentieth century. Both men were distinguished scholars (the former a Cambridge graduate), who served in the Ceylon Civil Service, at that time the pinnacle of public life. Aurnalchalam was liberal in his political outlook and devoted the later parts of his remarkable career to the betterment of all sections of Ceylonese society without regard to any racial or religious considerations until he resigned from Congress, suddenly.

The Ponnambalam brothers had been in the forefront of national politics from the last quarter of the nineteenth century and had become examples of patriotic figures *nulli secundus*. In fact, they were also considered by Sinhala Buddhist leaders as the natural leaders of Ceylon. Of these two eminent scholars and Tamil politicians, it was Ponnambalam Arunachalam who was *primus inter pares* in pre-1920s' Sri Lankan national politics.

Sinhalese constitutionalist elites

When Ponnambalam Arunachalam first began to address issues of national significance the Sinhalese leadership (except the Buddhist organisations)[1] and Tamil leadership was remarkably uninvolved in national politics or constitutional reforms. The Ceylon National Association, in the years before 1918, was 'nearly moribund'. Anything associated with radical movements for constitutional reforms was not welcome.[2] Its indolent and indifferent attitudes to national issues had, in fact, been

1 Nationalist groups were those who were mainly concerned with cultural and religious matters. Some nationalist figures such as Anagarika Dharmapala wanted *swaraj* for the island. But they were in the minority. Most were happy with their nationalist campaign against missionary works, western culture and its attendant vices.

2 K.M. de Silva, *A History of Sri Lanka*, 1981, p.379.

an obstacle to those who strove for radical changes to the constitutional structure of the island. It is worth noting that its president in 1918 was a person of the calibre of Sir James Peiris. Other regionally based organisations such as the Dutch Burgher Union, the Low Country Products Association of Ceylon, the Congress of Literary Association, the Jaffna Association and the Chillaw Association confined themselves to local issues. Even though they were keen to raise issues concerning political and constitutional matters, they were unable to stand up against the Ceylon National Association. Not even A.E. Gunasinha's Young Lanka League, which was the first political organisation to emerge in the island with a militant outlook and radical programme against the colonial government, could mobilise a mass movement unaided by the elites. In fact, without the support of the Ceylon National Association it was futile even to think of agitating for political reforms since the Ceylon National Association acted as intermediary between the people of the island and the colonial administration and they were averse to anything radical;[3] neither did the Ceylon National Association have a wide membership or programme of change that would have turned it into a national movement in the true sense. Most of its meetings were limited only to certain wealthy, elite families in the vicinity of Colombo and its meetings confined to reading reports and passing nugatory resolutions that did nothing to serve a wider campaign for achieving constitutional reforms.

In fact, some prominent pro-constitutional reformists such as Sir D.B. Jayatilaka, H.J.C. Pereira and Sir James Peiris were deeply worried about the possible infiltration of the CNA by elements of 'seditious Indian politics' into the island's orderly social and political life. Jayatilaka's attempt to convince Whitehall officials in London of his loyalty to the Empire, in the aftermath of the communal riots in 1915, was an example of their relaxed attitudes. Reiterating his and his countrymen's loyalty to the British Empire he defended the temperance movement[4] as not 'disloyal or seditious in any sense of the word'.[5] W.A. de Silva's appeal to the governor after his release from prison for his alleged role in the communal riots in 1915 was an example of how far the pro-constitutional reformists were prepared to go to assure the British colonial administration that they would, under no circumstances, resort to seditious activities against the British Empire. When Arunachalam proposed a non-cooperation movement against the colonial administration in 1920, Sir James Peris thought that such a movement was 'contrary to the traditions of the people of this country', and 'unhesitatingly condemned' it.[6] Other constitutional reformers such as E.J. Samarawickreme, E.W. Jayawardana and men of a younger generation such as D.B. Jayatilaka, F.R. Senanayaka and D.S. Senanayaka were of the same mind with respect to more radical constitutional

3 See de Silva, *A History of Sri Lanka*, 1981, pp.379–380.

4 It was an anti-alcohol movement seen by the British as anti-colonial since they rented out the taverns.

5 de Silva, 'The Formation and Character',1967, p.74.

6 *Handbook*, p.230.

reforms. As K.M. de Silva observed even the harassment meted out to this elite group of the Sinhalese by the British would not be enough for them to recognise the importance of a strong, committed campaign against imperialism.[7] All the strategies envisaged by the Sinhalese constitutional reformers were moderate and unprovocative.[8] Any suggestion of a boycott of the Legislative Council or the colonial administration was out of the question. The constitutional reforming elites were determined to play the game according to rules set by the governor and the Whitehall officials in London.[9] Quite rightly, the 'timidity' and 'child-like faith' of these leaders in colonial officials were mocked by Arunachalam.

It was in any case difficult to create any meaningful unity among the Sinhalese since caste rivalries hindered the emergence of a unified voice. The revival of Buddhism in the eighteenth and nineteenth centuries exacerbated the tensions between the castes. The high-caste *Goyigama* from whose ranks the Buddhist monks were drawn were challenged by the *Karãva, Salãgama* and *Durãva* castes – professionals and entrepreneurs but of the 'low caste' – who began to ordain their own people.[10] By the early part of the twentieth century the 'low-caste' *Karãva, Salãgama* and *Durãva* castes had ascended into the upper reaches of the Ceylonese society. Also, within the highest caste, *Goyigama,* were divisions between the up-country *Goyigama* (Kandyan aristocracy) and low-country *Goyigama.* There is evidence that there was a deep-seated hatred between the up-country and low-country *Goiygama* families. The former collaborated with the colonial administration with the notable exception of the anti-colonial position they took in the great rebellions of 1818 and 1848. However, the elites of both these groups appeared to be content with the colonial administration for the chance to participate in the public life of Sri Lanka. Of these *Goyigama* families, the Obeysekeras and Bandaranaikes enjoyed the special trust of the colonial administration. As a gesture of goodwill some of these families replaced their traditionally inherited family names with that of the governor.[11] The Obeysekera family, for example, had enjoyed particular privileges, since the beginning of the twentieth century. S.C. Obeysekere, in particular, was elected as a member to the Legislative Council simply because he was a trustworthy gentleman in the eyes of the colonial administrators. He, in turn, perhaps out of gratitude, ceded to almost every legislative or executive measure taken by the governor, even though peasants and rural communities were adversely affected.

The new leaders emerging from the lower castes were also not keen to be seen as *agents provocateurs,* neither did they want to associate with the then emerging Sinhalese nationalists. The Buddhist revivalist campaign, for example, was kept

7 de Silva, 'The Formation and Character', 1967, p.79.
8 de Silva, 'The Ceylon National Congress in a Disarray', 1972, p.102.
9 de Silva, 'The Ceylon National Congress in Disarray', 1972, p.105.
10 Nissan and Stirrat, 'The Generation of Communal identities', in Spencer (ed.), *Sri Lanka History and Roots of Conflict,* 1990, p.31.
11 See, for example, the former Prime Minister, S.W.R.D. Bandaranaike. The initials stand for Solomon West Ridgeway Dias.

at arms' length for fear that any hint of their connivance with popular activities might hinder social progress. Any reforms to the existing Legislative Council (LC) should be at the initiative of the British administration in London, not the other way round. This conservative, illiberal outlook of both the Sinhalese and Tamil leadership and the level of compliance with the colonial status quo moved even some governors, British civil servants and the national newspapers of Ceylon to be critical. The *Ceylon Morning Leader*, a most conservative newspaper, felt obliged to criticise the social elites for their reluctance to take part in an active campaign for constitutional reform.[12] The people especially mentioned were Sir James Peiris, H.J.C. Pereira, E.W. Perera and Sir Marcus Fernando. This may have had the effect of encouraging their subsequent involvement in the constitutional reform campaign.[13] In the 1920s Kandyan noblemen such as J.A. Halangoda, T.B.L. Moonemalle, G.E. Madawala, A.F. Molamure, Dr T.B. Kobbakaduwa and P.B. Ratnayake also showed no enthusiasm for constitutional reforms. Indeed, they looked on the low-country Sinhalese with disdain and complained that the latter were trying to undermine their position on the island. They eschewed joining any other ethnic or racial group to agitate for political change. They were enamoured of British justice and mesmerised by western institutions and values. As a consequence, they collaborated with Governor Manning in the 1920s, to further their own interests and stood against the low-country Sinhalese in Congress.

It was mainly due to Arunachalam's unremitting efforts that there emerged, in the second decade of the twentieth century, a serious campaign aimed at achieving greater constitutional reforms for the Legislative Council. He was able to muster enough support from the elites of both the Sinhalese and Jaffna Tamils to form a united front for more constitutional reform.

Arunachalam had entered politics as a nominated official member of the Legislative Council in 1906. Subsequently, he was appointed member of the Executive Council in 1912. His idea of politics was different to that of other regional and national organisations and he began to organise a political movement that would agitate effectively for constitutional reform for the island. Inspired by the Indian National Congress led by M.K. Gandhi, his mind was set on self-rule. His efforts were helped by the role he played when faced with the brutal suppression of the anti-Muslim 1915 communal riots by the colonial administration. Ruthless and harsh treatment was meted out to Sinhala Buddhist leaders [14] and many leaders

12 *The Morning Leader*, 13 June 1908, was one of the most influential English newspapers at the time. Cited in K.M. de Silva, 'The Reform and National Movements in the Early Twentieth Century', *UCHC*, 3, 1973, p.379.

13 See, further, de Silva, 'The Reform and National Movements in the Early Twentieth Century', *UCHC*, 3, 1973, pp.381–395.

14 See, for the causes of the riots, M. Roberts Hobgoblins, 'Low-Country Sinhalese Plotters, or Local Elite Chauvanists? Directions and Patterns in the 1915 Communal Riots', p.86, available at http://thakshana.nst.ac.ik/pdf/JSS1, accessed 20.1 2012. Also, Command Paper 8167, Correspondence relating to Disturbances in Ceylon, London,1916, Chalmers to Secretary of State (No. 15) 11 July,1915, p.35ff.; de Silva, 'The Formation and Character',1967, p.73.

were imprisoned.[15] Heavy fines were imposed on those suspected of any involvement in communal riots through the enactment of new legislations, such as the *Riots Damages Ordinance of 18 October 1915.*[16] Arunachalam's brother, Ramanathan, came to the rescue of the beleaguered Sinhalese leaders[17] while Sinhalese representatives in the Legislative Council, notably S.C. Obeysekere, remained supportive of the governor. It seemed that Obeysekere was happy to see his rival Sinhalese elites behind bars.[18] Very few people, one notable example being, E.W. Perera, a Sinahlese Christian, campaigned passionately for justice for the Sinhala Buddhist leaders who had been subjected to torture and inhuman treatment at the hands of colonial forces. Unfortunately, in the aftermath of the riots the 'constitutionalist camp', remained determined not to let the 'nationalist camp' disrupt the benign political culture which had served their interests so well.[19] Against this background, Ramanathan's long and tireless campaign to secure justice for the prosecuted and imprisoned Sinhalese leaders revealed an indifference to Tamil /Sinhala prejudices. His condemnation of the excesses of the British forces during the debate at the Legislative Council and his opposition to the *Act of Indemnity*, which was enacted to exonerate the military forces' involvement in suppressing the rioters, was also politically fearless and generous towards the Sinhalese.[20]

Ethnic prejudice did not dominate the different communities at this time. The Tamil leadership recognised and reacted to the injustice done to their fellow countrymen and condemned it. The focus of their attention was the abuse of power by the colonial government, not each other. The Sinhalese 'constitutionalists' gradually joined the campaign for incremental constitutional reform from which they could no longer stand aloof. Indeed, there were personal advantages to be gained from any reforms to the structure of the Legislative Council, in particular for those English educated elite groups. In the years between 1910 and 1920 new elites realised that the Legislative Council could be exploited to improve their economic and professional lives. Membership of the Legislative Council was official recognition at the highest level that enabled the educated and wealthy elite to stand as the de facto 'representatives' of the native population. There is no doubt that national interests alone did not propel the educated elites into national politics.

Arunachalam embraces radical politics

Arunachalam realised that it was essential for a vigorous, politically effective organisation to unite together all the other regional and national organisations that

15 Among them, Senanayake brothers (F.R., D.S. and D.C.), D.B. Jayatilaka, W.A. de Silva, C. Batuwantudawe, A.E. Gunasinhe, C.A. Hewavitarane and Edmond Hewavitarane were prominent figures of the day. All of them became later trusted figures of the colonial administration.

16 An ordinance to make provision for the payment of compensation in the case of damages caused by riots. Sri Lanka Online Legal Library. Blackhall Publishing, 2010.

17 P.T.M. Fernando, 'The Post-Riots Campaign for Justice', *JAS*, xxix(2),1970, pp.255–266.

18 See details de Silva, *A History of Sri Lanka*, 1981, pp.381–384.

19 de Silva, 'The Formation and Character',1967, p.74.

20 Ramanathan later published *Riots and Martial Law in Ceylon* (St Martin's Press: London, 1915).

were operating as separate interest groups. This was not easy to achieve especially persuading his Sinhalese brethren of the necessity of a new national organisation. Predictably, there was strong opposition from many quarters. *The Morning Leader*, a local paper controlled by Sir Marcus Fernando, questioned why another organisation was necessary since the Ceylon National Association could raise issues with the colonial administration whenever it was necessary and that organisation was committed to working for the wellbeing of the native population. The constitutionalists were clearly concerned about the possibility that if a new national organisation were to form it could become the political platform for Sinhalese Buddhist nationalists.[21] Due to his determination and his status as a national leader among the constitutionalists, Arunachalam successfully launched a new political organisation in 1917, the Ceylon Reform League, with himself as its first president. In December a public meeting was held to 'consider the nature of reforms that should be demanded'.[22]

His speech of 2 April 1917 at the annual general meeting of the Ceylon National Association entitled *Our Political Needs*, in which he urged his fellow countrymen to form a more radical and effective national political organisation than the Ceylon National Association, is regarded as a *locus classicus*. The speech was a clearly articulated argument for embracing a Ceylonese identity. Arunachalam was not the first person to make this argument. Sinhalese Buddhist leaders and the temperance movement in Sri Lanka had already attempted this before him. Addressing the theme of Ceylonese identity he said: 'So do we in Ceylon desire that Government shall be a Ceylonese Government, that out rulers shall identify themselves entirely with Ceylonese interests, and, in the striking words of the Mahavamsa, "be one with the people".' To achieve success the leading national figures of all nationalities should be 'prepared to work strenuously and systematically. It is not enough to hold spasmodic meetings, make long speeches and go to sleep. Let us have a minimum of talk and a maximum of action, action well-weighed and persisted in.'[23] Also, in this famous speech he emphasised the need of mass movements throughout the island with a network of branches to keep the people aware of the political situation. He was clearly urging his Sinhalese and Tamil brothers to mount a more vigorous struggle against British colonial rule similar to that of the Indian independence movement. He was determined to launch an effective 'political association' to achieve home rule for the island, 'otherwise . . . we shall be at the mercy of the Dominion.'[24] This was hardly palatable to the Sinhalese elite whose ambition was to become more British and to subordinate their 'Ceylonese' identity. Opposed to Arunachalam were men such

21 The *Ceylon Morning Leader*, 6 May 1916, cited in de Silva, 'The Formation and Character', 1967, p.77.

22 Mendis, *Ceylon Under the British*, 1952, p.187.

23 *Handbook*, p.97.

24 October 1916 entry in his diary, St Nihal Singh, unpublished biography of Sir P. Arunachalam, cited in de Silva, 'The Formation and Character', 1967, p.80.

as H.L. de Mel, who maintained that due to deep divisions among different racial, religious and castes groups, it was not advisable to make any changes to the existing political and constitutional structure. Unfortunately, Mel quietly kept the governor informed of what was happening within the reformist camps – he was later knighted. Ironically, Mel was one of those who benefited when the constitutional reforms that were eventually introduced to the Legislative Council. Apart from a few individuals such as Arunachalam and Ratman, the Ceylon/Jaffna Tamils' participation in the reformist group was very weak.

Arunachalam was faced with enormous problems inside and outside the Ceylon Reform League whenever he tried to introduce his radical ideas into the new movement. Still, he had to work cautiously so as not to alienate Sinhalese 'constitutionalists', most of whom were remarkably backward in their attitudes to the colonial administration. The prevailing wisdom was that if anything was to be achieved it should properly be done by pleading with the colonial administration. Of course, many were quite happy about their 'fortune and blessings', which they were able to achieve owing to 'excellent services' rendered by the British Empire.[25] The myopic, political inertia within the Sinhalese constitutionalist elites forced Arunachalam to brand them 'our Tories' who needed to be educated and enlightened regarding social and political issues.[26]

Even the national newspapers questioned the wisdom of forming more new organisations. Why could they not work with the Ceylon National Association? Were these people who were crying out for new organisations really mad? Was it not the case that these people simply wanted to improve their prestige? Arunachalam and those of his allies, who were instrumental in the formation of the Ceylon Reform League, were singled out for criticism. They were mocked and ridiculed, and branded as lunatics who did not have any 'useful occupation'. to engage in. Their efforts were seen as the purely self-indulgent acts of an immature bunch of individuals who could not do anything 'without forming a society, and electing a President'. The *Ceylon Saturday Review* commented, 'same public spirited gentlemen are generally met in most of the other consequential societies, the president of one society happens to be only the secretary of another or an ordinary member in a third. But this cannot be helped. We live in an age of republics and every man should have his chance of high office.'[27]

Arunachalam's vision in the formation of the Ceylon Reform League was to lay a foundation for a more vigorous national political organisation with a view to achieving home rule for the island. A more popular movement, in his view, was necessary to attract a wider audience if they were to succeed. He and his Sinhalese constitutionalist brethren were forced to wait for another two years. In the interim various other insignificant issues had to be addressed. One such issue was whether

25 See, for example, secret memorandum sent by H.L. de Mel to Governor Anderson. Cited in de Silva, 'The Formation and Character', 1967, p.82.

26 *The Times of Ceylon*, 28 April 1919, cited in de Silva, *Congress in Disarray*, p.116.

27 *Ceylon Saturday Review*, 30 June 1917, cited in de Silva, 'The Formation and Character', 1967, p.83.

they should name the next organisation a 'conference' or 'congress.' Any reference to 'national congress' terrified some prominent personalities of the existing organisations because of its connotations of sedition and disloyalty.[28] Many were of the view that 'conference' was gentler than 'congress'. Above all, they had to make sure that the colonial administration and the sympathisers in London would not doubt their loyalty to the Empire. Thus, during the years 1917 to 1919 it was suggested by many that the new organisation should be named 'constitutional reform conference.' In fact, these seemingly retrogressive ideas served only to hamper Arunachalam and younger advocates for reforms, such as, A.E. Gunasinha.

Some leaders of the Ceylon National Association, such as James Peiris and the leading figure of the Ceylon Reform League, E.J. Samarawickreme, agreed with Arunachalam that there should be a truly national organisation to agitate for greater constitutional reforms. In December 1919 the Low Country Sinhalese, Tamils, and representatives of other communities formed the Ceylon National Congress.[29] K.M. de Silva concludes: 'Indeed in the years 1917 to 1921 the leadership in the agitation for constitutional reform was in Arunachalam's hands, as was the movement for the formation of a Ceylon National Congress. During this period his prestige was at its height; his leadership was ungrudgingly acknowledged by the most prominent Sinhalese of the day, and was not seriously challenged till 1921.'[30]

Arunachalam becomes first president of Congress

When the Ceylon National Congress was formed in 1919, Arunachalam was inaugurated as its first President. It was hoped that Congress would become the embodiment of racial harmony and spearhead the constitutional struggle for the island. No one was better placed than Arunachalam to lead a national movement when the country needed a united organisation.

He gave all his energies to the new organisation; organising meetings, collecting money for publishing materials and travelling around the island to promote national unity with a view to achieving self-rule. He even succeeded in bringing the Jaffna Association into the fold of Congress. Circumstances forced him to act as a mediator between the Jaffna Tamils and the Sinhalese to reconcile these two groups, which had become poles apart in their political outlook and attitudes to constitutional reforms. When other were taking a cautious approach to agitation it was Arunachalam who insisted that it was essential to follow in the footsteps of the Indian national liberation movement, the Indian National Congress. His radicalism, even though ridiculed by some influential Congressmen such as Sir James Peiris, Sir Marcus Fernando and H.J.C. Perera, attracted some of the

28 See *The Speeches and Writings of Sir Ponnambalam Arunachalam*, vol. 1, 1943, pp.162–163.
29 Mendis, *Ceylon Under the British*, 1952, p.187.
30 de Silva, *A History of Sri Lanka*, 1981, pp.386–387.

younger generation. The preferred policy of the Sinhalese in the Ceylon National Congress was to achieve constitutional reforms through memoranda, petitions, deputations and agitations within the law without hurting the feelings of the governor and the British officials at Whitehall. For instance, Sir James Peiris was quite happy with holding an annual conference to draw the attention of the colonial officials to the need for greater political reforms for the island. To adopt the tactics of mass agitation or rouse public opinion similar to what the Indian National Congress was doing was beyond their wildest imagination. Most members of the CNA were still dreaming about becoming the most trusted member of the British Empire. If only they could keep tighter control over constitutional agitation without politicising the masses, they would have no problem with the colonial administration. After all, some of them were also, in one way or another, part of this administration which they did not want to see unsettled.

This curiously submissive outlook of the elite constitutionalists was demonstrated by S.W.R.D. Bandaranaike and R.S.S. Gunawardane, joint secretaries and rising stars of Congress when they asserted that: 'Ceylon is one of the few British possessions in which the demand for political reform has never passed from constitutional agitation to hostile demonstration. Our appeal has always been to reason and justice.'[31] Thus any mass movement against colonialism was rejected (see art. 1 of the CNC Constitution) Even though Arunachalam, on a few occasions, spoke of working towards the 'realization of responsible government in Ceylon as an integral part of the British Empire',[32] he had proved to be much more radical in his political outlook in comparison with other leading congressmen of the day or his friends in the Jaffna Association. On a number of occasions, he openly advocated *swaraj*, by which he meant full independence.[33] His colleagues' attitudes, contrariwise, was captured in H.J.C. Pereira's presidential address to the Ceylon National Congress on 28 October 1922, when he expressed the gratitude that they felt was owed to the British Empire: 'Let us first of all set our own house in order; let us show ourselves entitled to claim from the British Empire that Home Rule which has been granted to Canada, Australia and the Cape colony. The only way we can do it – to my mind – is to become true Britishers in the broad sense of that word (loud cries of 'No No' from members of the Young Lanka League) Britishers first (cries of 'No No') – Ceylonese afterwards (cries of 'No').'[34] H.L. de Mel (later Sir Henri de Mel) was full of admiration of the British Empire. He said that his ultimate goal in public life was to 'serve the state which . . . has served us excellently and brought nothing but fortune and blessings and to await the future glory of the Empire and the destiny which imperial policy will lay down for us must be our chief purpose and desire.' Those who were demanding constitutional reform were: '(M)en with no useful occupation and with certain idiosyncrasies of their own,

31 *Handbook*, p.814.

32 Arunachalam's address to the Ceylon National Congress in 1919, see *Handbook*, p.555.

33 See his article in *The Times of Ceylon*, 14 December 1921.

34 *Handbook*, p.392.

without practical knowledge of the country are most ready to cry for far-reaching reforms and certain others are ready to say ditto.'[35] This attitude was not very different to that of the Jaffna Association. On 10 April 1909 a memorandum was submitted to the Colonial Secretary at Whitehall in which their loyalty to the British Empire was expressed. 'Ceylon has always been loyal to the throne and person of the sovereign, and has always been proud of being a British Crown Colony.'[36] Agitation for self-rule was scoffed at as no more than 'a foolish experiment doomed to disaster'.[37] The elites of the Sinhalese and Jaffna Tamils vied with each other to demonstrate their loyalty to his majesty's Empire.

The Jaffna Association's reluctance to cooperate with the Ceylon Reform League and the Ceylon National Association to form a new non-communal national organisation was a barrier even Arunachalam found difficult to overcome. Leading Tamil figures of the Jaffna Association such as A. Sabapathy and Sir Ambalawanar Kanagasabhai obstructed any unity between the two. 'The Tamils of Ceylon have hitherto, in spite of their inferiority in numbers, maintained a position of equality with their Sinhalese brethren, whether in official or unofficial life.'[38] The expectation that the Tamils will still have a major role in the country's politics made them reluctant to unite for political reform. Against this political and historical background the role played by Arunachalam was immense, but short-lived. First he had to work with his Sinhalese counterparts, most of whom were backward-looking conservatives in their approach to political reforms, second he had to overcome the intransigence of the Jaffna Association over any cooperation with the Sinhalese. It was common knowledge that the latter would work only with the Sinhalese elite groups on a *quid pro quo* basis. Arunachalam's attempt to reconcile these opposite points of views did not work because neither group showed any enthusiasm to accommodate the other's concerns. The promises made by Sir James Peiris and E.J. Samarawickrame to Arunachalam on behalf of the Ceylon National Association and the Ceylon Reform League, that they would support the demand of the Jaffna Association for a special seat for the Tamils, were not honoured owing to strong opposition from other members of the Ceylon National Congress. Therefore, it was natural for Arunachalam to feel betrayed by his Sinhalese brethren. Second, his hope for a mobilisation of a radical mass movement against colonial rule met with strong opposition from the constitutionalist groups – quite surprisingly, most of them were younger generation Sinhalese. In fact, when the Constitution of the Ceylon National Congress was drafted it was made very clear that constitutional reforms should be achieved through the 'existing system of government and administration'.[39] It must also be said that there was a group

35 Mel's memorandum was sent by Governor Anderson to W. Long on 2 August 1917, printed in C.O. 54/854. This was quoted in de Silva, 'The Formation and Character', 1967, p.82.

36 See the memorandum sent by the President of the Jaffna Association, *Handbook*, pp.29–30.

37 *The Times of Ceylon*, 24 November 1917.

38 The memorial sent by the Jaffna Association to W.H. Long on 2 January 1918.

39 See art. 1 of the CNC.

of politically ambitious Sinhalese who were simply not content to being led by a Tamil. In fact, the Ponnambalam brothers were branded by F.R. Senanayake as egocentric and self-indulgent, whose only desire was to lead the Ceylonese nation. Also, by this time, F.R. Senanayake had formed another rival Sinhalese organisation entitled 'Lanka Mahajana Sabha' with himself as the President. In its organisational patterns and its appeal to grassroots activists it was far ahead of the Ceylon National Congress.

Arunachalam's turn

It is not surprising, therefore, that Arunachalam resigned from Congress within two years of its formation. First, he had experienced how difficult it was to launch any radical campaign beyond self-imposed limits by the leading Congressmen. Second, and perhaps more importantly, it was the 'betrayal of his Sinhalese brethren' that broke his heart. The promises made to Arunachalam by James Pieris and Samarawickreme in December 1918 as Presidents of the Ceylon Reform League and the Ceylon National Association respectively, that they would support the demand of the Jaffna Association for a special seat for the Tamils were not honoured. In fact, when the issue was raised within the executive committee meetings of Congress both denied that they had committed themselves to this demand at all. Arunachalam quite justifiably felt that he had been manipulated by the Sinhalese constitutionalist elites for their own personal gain. Arunachalam had played a difficult political game attempting to form a national movement against imperial rule while at the same time trying to secure the future of the Tamils. Ultimately, he failed.

He departed from Congress when he realised that if election to the Legislative Council were to be based on territorial representation it would reduce Tamil representation. This would inevitably weaken the position of the Ceylon Tamils in future politics. Having failed to win Sinhalese support for his demands for a special seat in the Western Province, as promised by Peiris and Samarawickreme, he suddenly departed from Congress in 1921. Before his departure, however, Arunachalam delivered a biting attack on the leadership of Congress:

> We hear a great deal nowadays about the Ceylon National Congress as a power in the island, which it no doubt is. People are almost falling over each other's heels to join it and to bless it. But there was a time not so long ago, when things were different. The very name gave a shock, even to gentlemen some of whom are now Congress leaders. They objected to the word 'Congress' as savouring of Indian disloyalty and sedition and would have nothing to do with the word. Then, 'National,' was an absurd and ludicrous epithet. Some of our reformers had to walk warily. The first meeting of delegates from various parts of the Island in December 1917, was, in deference to these feelings, called a Conference on Constitutional Reforms. By December 1918, the prejudice against 'National' had dissipated; the term might pass, but

> Congress no, not for the world. So that meeting had to be called the Ceylon National Conference. After the lapse of another year it was possible to call the meeting of December 1919, the Ceylon National Congress.; and now it is the rage.
>
> . . . I dread to think of the consequences if some of us who were advocates of full self-government had proposed the name Home Rule or Swaraj League. It would have scattered to the four winds many of the big men in our camp. But the time is not far off when all of us will be working for Swaraj as vigorously as we are doing for the moderate programme of the Congress. Has not his majesty the King used the word and blessed it in his message of last month to the Indian people? The word can no longer be banned by the most timid among us.[40]

Arunachalam had been put in a difficult position by the leading Congressmen among the Sinhalese. It was Arunachalam's assurances that had led the Jaffna Association to temporarily discard their differences and work with Congress. When Congress rejected the demand for a Tamil seat in the Western Province, the Jaffna Tamils saw it as a serious threat to their status in any future constitutional reforms.

By this time, an internal transformation of Jaffna Tamil politics was already underway. The role of the Jaffna Association seemed to have reached its end. It was felt by the leadership of the Jaffna Tamils that a new organisation focusing more vigorously on Tamil interests was necessary. This resulted in the formation of the Tamil Mahajana Sabhai under the leadership of Sir Ambalawanar Kanagasabhai. All the other members were simply transferees from the Jaffna Association. The new organisation was, in effect, a rival ethnically based organisation to the Lanka Mahajana Sabha of F.R. Senanayake.

It was to the delight of the Jaffna Mahajana Sabhai that Arunachalam left Congress. Kanagasahai wasted no time in approaching him and Arunachalam soon found himself collaborating with his brother Ramanathan and other Jaffna Tamils. Just before his withdrawal from the Ceylon National Congress there was a meeting at Arunachalam's Colombo residence attended by 11 leading members of the Tamil Mahajana Sabhai.[41] This gathering agreed to send a memorial to the Duke of Devonshire indicating that the Sinhalese leadership of Congress was determined to obstruct the progress of Tamils in Sri Lanka: 'Unfortunately, owing to personal differences between Sir P. Arunachalam and the Hon. Mr James Peiris in regard to the representation of the city of Colombo, Sir P. Arunachalam

40 *Speeches and Writings of Sir Ponnambalam Arunachalam*, Colombo, 1925, pp.162–163, cited in de Silva, 'Congress in Disarray',1972, p.107.

41 By this time it is apparent there was a transformation of Jaffna Tamil politics. The dominant role played by the Jaffna Association seemed to have reached the final destination. Jaffna Tamils rally round a new organisation called the Tamil Mahajana Sabhai, which was formed under the leadership of Sir A. Kanagasabhai. This was, in effect, aimed at becoming a rival communal organisation to the Lanka Mahajana Sabha of F.R. Senanayake.

withdrew from the Congress.'[42] Arunachalm's departure was a great loss to both Congress and to the home rule campaign for the island. H.L. de Mel, CBE, and D.B. Jayatilaka of Congress made passionate pleas to Arunachalam to reconsider his withdrawal. At the fifth session of Congress held in December 1923 Mel pleaded with Arunahalam to return.[43] Some prominent Tamil politicians also urged those who had broken away from Congress to reconsider their decisions. The feeling that Sinhalese dominance inside and outside Congress would weaken the status of Tamils was challenged in a speech by J.N. Vethavanan whose words were reported thus: 'He felt that they were wrong. He did not think that the time would ever come when the Sinhalese people would be so powerful as to swallow the Tamils. Numerically they might be but he felt that the Tamil cause and the Sinhalese cause was one. He felt that they would fall or rise together.'[44]

Analysing the reasons for Arunachalam's departure from Congress, K.M. de Silva claimed that by the end of 1921 Arunachalam had become the 'co-belligerent' of his brother Ramanathan. A 'Gladstonian Liberal' throughout his public career, he now associated himself with narrow and sectional politics. A man of 'radical outlook and a strong social conscience, he . . . had been reluctant to associate himself too closely in political activity with his brother, and yet the pressures of elite conflict drove him in the twilight of his distinguished public career into the camp of "communal" politics – though he was never comfortable in its ranks.'[45] Perhaps it would be a fairer commentary on Arunachalam's his career to say that his assumptions about the political position of the Tamils were rather rudely corrected. He realised that the Tamils would be relegated to minority status and he took up the cause of the Tamils sacrificing his larger and grander political vision.

All attempts at changing Arunachalam's mind had failed. He subsequently set up the Ceylon Tamil League in 1923 but this never became a serious political movement. Nonetheless, Arunachalam's move from national politics to local Tamil politics was complete with this.[46] In a speech to the Ceylon Tamil League in 1922, he urged his fellow countrymen to rally round his organisation and to the Tamil cause:

> We should keep alive and propagate those ideals throughout Ceylon and promote the union and solidarity of what we have been proud to call *Tamil Eelam*. We desire to preserve our individuality as a people, to make ourselves worthy of our inheritance. We are not enamoured of the cosmopolitanism which would make of us 'neither fish, flesh, fowl not red-herring'. That does not mean that we are to be selfish and work only for the Tamil

42 *Handbook*, p.524.
43 *Handbook*, p.576.
44 *Handbook*, p.409.
45 de Silva, *A History of Sri Lanka*, 1981, p.391.
46 See de Silva, *A History of Sri Lanka*,1981, pp.393–394.

> community. We have done more for the welfare of all-Ceylon than for the Tamils . . . We do object, however, strongly to being under-dogs. We mean to make ourselves strong to defend ourselves and strong also to work for the common good.[47]

In this declaration, Arunachalam also tried to convince the Ceylon Tamils and especially those of the Jaffna Peninsula that even though he lived in Colombo and had worked with Congress, his commitment to the Tamil community was genuine. This was his defence against those who had dismissed the Colombo Tamils as 'an isolated community in the south-west of the island, which has little in common with the people of the main Tamil territory in the North'.[48] In fact, in the eyes of the Jaffna Tamils, the Tamil living in Colombo were 'willing to barter away his Tamil birth-right for a mess of Sinhalese pottage'.[49] The word *Eelam,* in Arunachalm's speech immediately laid him open to the charge that he desired some form of Tamil independence. A.J. Wilson claimed that the premise of Arunachalam's Ceylon Tamil League was to achieve a *Tamil Eelam*, the mythical Tamil kingdom that was claimed to be prevalent in the northern and eastern parts of the island. Hellmann-Rajanayagam[50] points out that the word was not in common usage before Arunachalam coined the term, *Tamil Eelam,*[51] which was later to become such a politically explosive expression of the Tamil secessionist groups. Wilson speculates that even though it was not possible to discern what this means *ex ante,* he nevertheless concludes that it was a 'separate sovereign Tamil State which Arunachalam intended by it'.[52] It is interesting to note that even as early as 1918 Arunachalam was mooting an idea that Ceylon should be federated with India in order to liberate the island from the British overlords. In his interview with *The Daily News* on 29 July 1918, he suggested that unless the island was federated with India, nothing could be achieved as far as the political reforms were concerned. Not surprisingly, this view was subjected to vigorous criticism by the press[53] and Sinhalese constitutionalists. Arunachalam hurriedly backtracked but

47 M. Vythilingam, *The Life of Sir Ponnambalam Ramanathan*, Ramanathan Commemorative Society: Colombo, 1971, pp.540–541.

48 *The Times* (London), cited in J. Russell, *Communal Politics under the Donnoughmore Constitution, 1931-1947*, Thisara Prakasakayo: Colombo 1982, p.80.

49 *The Hindu Organ*, 14 March 1938, cited in A.J. Wilson, *Break-up of Sri Lanka*, 1988, p.62.

50 Hellmann-Rajanayagam, 'The Politics of the Tamil Past', in Spencer (ed.). *Sri Lanka: History and the Root of Conflict*, 1990, p.114.

51 Hellman-Rajanayagam writes: 'In the 1920s and 1930s, the term Tamil Eelam comes into vogue increasingly, indicating the areas inhabited by Tamils and considered as belonging to them. It seems that P. Arunachalam, Register General of Ceylon and later a founder-member of the Ceylon National Congress, coined the term "Tamil Eelam" in 1923, but I have no doubt that the term was widely used in the late 1930s, and it is in this meaning of "belonging to the Tamils" that the term is currently used in Tamil nationalism.' See her 'The Politics of the Tamil Past', in Spencer, *Sri Lanka: History and Root of Conflict*, 1990, p.114.

52 Wilson, *Break-up of Sri Lanka*, 1989, p.8.

53 See, for example, *The Times of Ceylon*, 2 August 1918.

he did suggest to *The Times of Ceylon* on 3 August 1918 that it would be better if people on both side of the argument could consider the pros and cons of a federation with their neighbour, India, in the campaign for home rule for the island. Arunachalam seemed to be seeking common cause with the Indian Congress struggle for *swaraj*. But in the eyes of the Sinhalese this would mean a situation where the Tamils of Sri Lanka and the Tamils of south India together would automatically become the numerical majority. The island was perceived by many Tamils as an appendage of south India with which the Tamils share an ancient culture.[54] Some Tamil politicians and scholars insist even today that the island does not have an independent origin. Any suggestion that the island was once a separate geopolitical entity is dismissed as a 'racial myth' concocted by Sinhalese chauvinists.[55]

Even though his organisation never became the mainstream Tamil organisation, Arunachalam's efforts to temper the dominance of the Sinhalese was unabated. His next political battle was against the conferment of universal suffrage, which he feared would perpetuate Sinhalese dominance over Tamils in the Legislative Council.

Ponnambalam Ramanathan

Ramanathan first served in the Legislative Council as a nominated member, selected by the governor. When the constitutional reforms of 1912 created an 'educated Ceylonese seat', he was the first Ceylonese elected to represent the native population of the island as a whole.

He was a devoted Hindu Tamil and a revered scholar who was keen to protect and propagate Tamil culture and religion. In the early years of his political career he worked tirelessly for the national cause. Although he was first appointed to represent Tamils as an unofficial member to the Legislative Council, he was not parochial in his social and political outlook. In fact, like his brother, he was quickly recognised as a national leader with the interests of all the communities at heart. He was duly rewarded by the Sinhalese when he became their elected member for the educated Ceylonese seat. 'In Council he would appear garbed in the attire of an Indian prince, wearing a gold embroidered turban and long silk coat, and his handsome presence and colourful clothes gave a touch of distinction to the proceedings of the House.'[56]

Even though, in the twilight days of his political career, he sought the support of British officials to protect the Tamils from the yoke of 'Sinhalese imperialism', he had never been an enthusiast of British culture neither did he regard western values highly. His attitude to the west is best summed up in his remark that

54 See Wilson, *Break-up of Sri Lanka*, 1989, p.25. See also Russell, *Communal Politics*, 1982, p.6.

55 See Wilson, *Break-up of Sri Lanka*, 1989, p.18; Tambiah, *Sri Lanka Ethnic Fratricide*, 1986; Ponnambalam, *Sri Lanka: The National Question*, 1983.

56 Namasivayam, *The Legislature of Ceylon*, 1950, p.28.

'Westerners have been revolutionised several times and have not abolished themselves out of existence.'[57] He was determined to protect the indigenous culture and its values from western influence. He exhorted the Sinhalese to do likewise. Why could the Sinhalese not promote their own language, culture and traditional values? Addressing a gathering early in the nineteenth century, at Ananda College, the premier Sinhala Buddhist education centre in the capital, he poured scorn on those who attempted to become a 'true westerner':

> A Sinhalese man is not a tailor-made figure, who puts on a frock-coat, broad collar, a top hat and patent leather boots. He is not a person born only to spread out his shoulders thus dressed, carry an umbrella in a particular way, have a cigar in his mouth, and say 'haw' every now and then (laughter). That is not a Sinhalese man. That is something other than Sinhalese. The man who can speak Sinhalese like the two reverend monks whom we all have had the pleasure of hearing a few minutes ago without any admixture of foreign language, who can roll out sentence after sentence in pure Sinhalese, charged with sober sense, inspiring and grand to hear, is a Sinhalese man indeed . . . It is your duty to cultivate the study of the Sinhalese language to the best of your power, and to speak it, ignoring the English language on all occasions and at all places where English has no business. If you do so, then I say you will be doing your duty to your nation.[58]

He warned the gathering that unless the Sinhalese reconstructed themselves as a nation, in accordance with their great traditions and moral values, they would 'soon dwindle down to nothing. The nation will be ruined, and we must await with trembling knees the early destruction of the Sinhalese language'. He reminded them that there were enough precedents proving that those nations that did not protect their cultural heritage and value systems disappeared altogether. 'Have not the Anglo-Saxons passed away? Have not the Normans passed away? Has not many a great nation passed away? Where are the Phoenicians? Where are the Assyrians, the Grecians and Romans? Where are they? All have been swept off the face of the earth . . . (B)ecause they were only too ready to open their doors to the inflow of foreign ideals, and practices, not in harmony with their civilizations.'[59]

Ramanathan's integrity and independence as a politician, first as a nominated unofficial member and subsequently as the elected, educated representative in the LC were remarkable. He had no desire to be a loyal servant of the British Empire[60] neither did he approve of policies that might affect traditional moral values, culture and social structure. In 1926 when the idea of the establishment of a university in the island was first mooted, he warned the pioneers that in the event that such an

57 Cited in Blackton, 'The Empire at Bay', in Roberts (ed.), *Collective Identities*, 1979, p.379.

58 M. Vythilingam, *The Life of Sir Ponnambalam Ramanathan*, vol. 1, 1971 pp.482–483.

59 Vythilingam, *The Life of Sir Ponnambalam Ramanathan*, vol. 1, 1971, pp.482–483.

60 Sir Charles Jeffries, *Ceylon: The Path to Independence*, Pall Mall Press: London, 1962, p.67.

academic institution was to be set up, Asian values and morals should form the backbone of the curriculum. If the new university were to allow western values to dominate its curriculum it would bring 'trouble, trouble, trouble'.[61] Whenever it was necessary, as the representative of the Tamil community, to protest against the policies adopted by the governor and his administration Ramanathan was the only one who stood up against them in the State Council. When 'toddy taverns' began to appear in every town and village in both Sinhalese and Tamil areas, with the encouragement of the colonial administration, Ramanathan burnt with anger, and questioned the Colonial Secretary, Sir Hugh Clifford, in the LC:

> If my honourable friend says that he himself does not know what the localities are where the taverns are to be established, I say, sire, that it is a confession that is appalling in character. He, the mouthpiece of the government – he, the person who is charged with this Exercise reform, and who is under a promise to the people of Ceylon to do what is just and proper confess publicly, without seeing the enormity of that confession, that he does not know what the localities are where the taverns are going to be established.[62]

His anti-British rhetoric did not go down well with the colonial administration. On one occasion in 1887, when Ramanathan took on the cause of the Ceylonese in the LC, he was mocked by the governor for putting himself forward as the sole representative of the nation. Why could Ramanathan not concentrate only on his community's wellbeing, the Tamils? Why did he want to defend other community's interests and so forth?:

> Now we all know that my honourable friend represents only the Tamil community, and we won't admit he has any right to represent any other section, and indeed I am quite aware that he has no desire to pose as an idol receiving the adoration of thousands of poor Sinhalese and Tamils, as their friend and saviour from a corrupt and despotic government. We all know that he is not the general representative of the whole community, but nevertheless that impression is sometimes conveyed.[63]

This predictably provoked a sharp riposte from Ramanathan: 'I have no desire to change my nationality. I pride myself on being (a) Tamil. I hope a Sinhalese gentleman will always pride himself on being (a) Sinhalese.'[64] He asked the governor if anything was wrong with that.[65]

During the pre-1920 years of his political career Ramanathan saw himself as a national politician. Whenever the Sinhalese were subjected to unfair treatment at

61 Vythilingam, *The Life of Sir Ponnambalam Ramanathan*, 1971, pp.482–483.
62 Legislative Council debate, 1912–1913, session, pp.213.
63 Hansard, 1887 cited in Russell, *Communal Politics*, 1982, p.335.
64 Hansard, 1887 cited in Russell, *Communal Politics*, 1982, p.339.
65 Hansard, cited in Russel, *Communal Politics*, 1982, p.339.

the hands of the colonial administration, it was Ramanathan who defended them on the floor as well as outside it. For example, in the aftermath of the 1915 riots, his fierce attack against the then Inspector General Dowbiggin for his cruel tactics against the Sinhalese is worthy of note. He argued in the LC in support of an impeachment brought against Dowbiggin that, as a politician, his priority should have been to serve *the nation* without bias towards any particular community. He insisted that the cruelty committed against the Sinhalese during the 1915 riots should be remedied forthwith, and he also demanded that the chief 'culprit', Dowbiggin, should be punished for having issued illegal orders to shoot innocent Sinhalese peasants. 'How can we live in Ceylon with a man as heartless and narrow-minded as Mr. Dowbiggin, who is given . . . to carry out his cruel, tyrannical orders and exposes every man here to the direst troubles.'[66]

During the last quarter of the nineteenth century, there was no one among the Sinhalese leadership who could match the charisma, independence and maturity of Ramanathan. Sinhalese leaders such as James D'Alwis and S.C. Obeysekare were reluctant to question the policies adopted by the colonial administration, let alone political reforms for the island, but Ramanathan was prepared to take on these matters in public debate. So much so, that the prominent Sinhalese journal of the day *Sarasavi Sandarasa* published an article in 1899 paying glowing tribute to the service rendered by this eminent national leader to the cause of the Sinhalese. In its view, Ramanathan:

> Not only looks after the welfare of his own constituencies, but also all matters connected with various interests on the island . . . It might well be said, judging from the active part he has taken, and the amount of time and labour he has devoted to questions in Council affecting the Sinhalese alone, that he was their representative . . . The Buddhists owe Mr. Ramanathan a deep debt of gratitude. His interest in the question of the Wesak holiday and the Buddhist Temporalities Bill . . . and a host of other services towards Buddhism have endeared him immensely to the Buddhists of Ceylon. [67]

Ramanathan's transformation from a national leader to a 'hardened communalist'

The Sinhalese leadership of the day actively supported Ramanathan's candidature twice in his bid to become the sole representative for the educated Ceylonese constituency as against a Sinhalese 'man of excellent reputation',[68] Sir Marcus Fernando. In fact it was the Sinhalese elite who persuaded Ramanathan to stand again for the educated seat when he was considering his retirement. As he later

66 M. Vythilingam, *The Life of Sir Ponnambalam Ramanathan*, vol. 2, Ramanathan Commemorative Society: Chunnakam, 1977, pp.327–328.

67 *Sarasavi Sandaresa*, 28 May 1889.

68 Wilson, *Break-up of Sri Lanka*, 1989, p.56.

recorded in his memoir that while he was in a sanctuary in India, he had come under enormous pressure from the Sinhalese and more interestingly from the Sinhala Buddhist organisations to stand again. The first person to approach him was the Kandyan Sinhalese Proctor, J.R. Molligodde.[69] Other prominent Sinhalese leaders, namely Donald Obeyskere, H.A. Jayawardene, A.D. Seneviratne, C. Batuwantudawe, Francis de Soyza, De Alwis and Ramanathan's opponent, Fernando, were unable to muster enough support from the Sinhalese elite. Even though Fernando was the proprietor of a powerful local paper, *The Morning Leader*, which supported his candidacy for nearly a year and a half, nothing positive materialised from it. Fernando was unable to even find Sinhalese leaders willing to sign his nomination papers. Ramanathan won the election because the Sinhalese and other minority groups had appreciated his capacity to serve the Ceylonese nation without partiality.[70]

In 1917 when the election was held for the educated Ceylonese seat, Ramanathan was again asked by the Sinhalese to represent them. This time another member of the Sinhalese elite, a barrister, St Justus Sextus Jayawardene, found to his cost how hard it was to challenge Ramanathan. Jayawardene lost, since the Sinhalese voted for Ramanathan. Even Jayewardene's three older brothers, E.W. Jayawardene, St V. Jayawardene and Hector Jayewardene, joined other Sinhalese notables, A. de Sneviratna, Francis de Soyza, D.G. Obeysekara, W.A. de Soysa, B.F. de Silva, James Peris, C. Dias, D.C. Senanayaka, R.L. Pereira, D.C. Pedris, in opting to support Ramanathan.[71] In this predominantly Sinhalese constituency, Ramanathan's victory was secured by 1,704 votes to 48. Ramanathan had demonstrated his capacity to act on behalf of the native population without bias and the people of Ceylon returned the favour by choosing the most worthy candidate without consideration to creed or language. Ethnic consciousness had

69 It says: My Dear Mr. Ramanathan, We are all desirous of having you for the educated Ceylonese seat. A large number of the educated Ceylonese here are ready to support you. I hope you will have no objection to our putting forward your name. With kind regards, Yours J.R. Molligodde Cited in Vythilingam, *The Life of Sir Ponnambalam Ramanathan*, 1971, p.562.

70 After his well-deserved victory, glowing tributes came from every corner of the island. Most notably, the Colombo based Sinhalese and Tamil elite expressed their joy as follows: Honourable Sir, On behalf of your friends and well-wishers, we beg to offer you our warmest congratulations on your election as the first Ceylonese Member in the Reformed Legislative Council. Your exceptional abilities, your high intellectual attainments and your unswerving and unselfish devotion to your country's course left no doubt in the minds of the large and educated masses of the Ceylonese, that you were the fittest person to be elected to the Ceylonese Seat in the newly-constituted Legislative Council. The overwhelming majority by which you have been returned bears eloquent testimony to their high appreciation of your extraordinary talents and sterling qualities. We have every confidence that you will apply yourself as assiduously to the amelioration of the country as you have hitherto done and that your tenure of office will be signalized by the realization of the hopes and aspirations of the different communities of the island. Trusting that you will be long spared in your career of usefulness to the pubic of Ceylon, and that all happiness and prosperity may ever attend on you. We beg to remain, Sir, sgd. By the leaders of the all communities, Colombo, 15 January 1912. Vythilingam, *Ramanathan of Ceylon*, 1977, p.562.

71 Vythilingam, *Ramanathan of Ceylon*, 1977, p.360.

not infiltrated the Sinhalese elite or the heart of national politics even though, by this time round, the Jaffna Association was enthusiastically calling for the retention of communally elected members to the LC.

Ramanathan's election victory also seemed to be a victory for those interested in creating national unity in their struggle against the British Empire. To his credit, Ramanathan took on a leading role in the LC in his capacity as the unofficial member. He was in his 70s but continued, more or less, as the national leader of the island. However, this was not to last much longer. To his great dismay, he was challenged by a younger generation of the politically ambitious Sinhalese elite, eventually forcing him to sever his relationship with Sinhalese constitutionalists and revert 'to the role of defender of the Ceylon Tamil interests'.[72] The sudden appearance of a galaxy of political stars among the Sinhalese and Tamils undermined Ramanathan's place both within the LC and outside it. Of these, F.R. Senanayaka, looked to being the potential future leader of the island. Unfortunately, he died early, while in his mid-40s and the mantle of leadership fell to his younger brother, D.S. Senanayaka, who became the first Prime Minister of an independent Ceylon.

Both Ramanathan and Arunachalam had legitimacy as representatives of their community. They had insisted, especially between 1920 and 1924, on an especially reserved seat in the Western Province for Ceylon Tamils. This became a bone of contention, to which the leadership of Congress could find no satisfactory solution acceptable to both Tamils and Sinhalese. The objections against such a reservation were not levelled against the Ponnambalam brothers, but their insistence was seen as a barrier against a united nationalist front in the campaign for achieving a responsible government for the island. In this political climate, it was not surprising that unity among the elites could not last.

Ramanathan thought that considering the service he had rendered to the cause of the Sinhala Buddhists, in particular, after the 1915 Sinhalese Buddhist–Muslim riots, his demands should have been met with a more generous response from the Sinhalese leadership. Instead, he was identified with Tamil sectional interests. He was, in fact, the main link between the Colombo and the Jaffna Tamil 'communalists'. Unfortunately Ramanathan's achievements as a member of the Legislative Council for over half a century came to be overshadowed by the attitudes he clung to and views he expressed in his later years. The culture and ethos of the Ceylon Tamils he represented were the traditions practised by high-caste Hindu *Vellalas*. He found real difficulty acknowledging that low-caste Tamils had legitimate grievances that should also be addressed.

Social reforms, urged by oppressed groups in the Jaffna Peninsula such as the Depressed Tamils Service League[73] and the Jaffna Youth Congress were resisted by him but more in the manner of an 'Old Testament Prophet than a politician'.[74]

72 Wilson, *Break-up of Sri Lanka*, 1989, p.57.

73 This way led by N. Selvadurai with the help of the Jaffna Youth Congress. Dr Paul and J. Hensman were also instrumental in the formation of this organisation. See Russell, *Communal Politics*, 1982, p.19.

74 Russell, *Communal Politics*, 1982, p.19.

Of these, equal seating in Jaffna schools, universal education irrespective of caste differences, the right of temple entry for the *Harijans*, were according to Ramanathan, evil attempts by the lower end of society to destroy the whole social fabric of society. He led a deputation to the governor in 1930, regarding commensuality among castes at Copay Training College. Jane Russell suggests that Ramanathan in his later years 'had become rigidly orthodox in his religious and social views to the point of being a "dyed in the wool" reactionary'.[75] Ramanathan lived by and endorsed the social hierarchy of Tamil society. In his later years he had to confront the fact that low-caste Tamils were objecting strenuously to their status and treatment. He reacted to this and did not appreciate that his representation of Tamil interests was, in fact, the interests of a narrow band of the upper end of the Tamil social hierarchy.

When Congress, in the 1920s, began its agitation in earnest for constitutional reforms, it was Ramanathan who objected, arguing that there was no need for new constitutional reforms since the Mannning Constitution was working well, to the satisfaction of all. Criticising E.W. Perera, a Sinhalese Congressman and a member of the LC, for his agitation for self-rule Ramanathan said, 'I am perfectly certain the country is not ready for this as yet. It has now got all it needs for some years to come. My countrymen ought to be satisfied with what has been given to them, in regard to the Legislative council.'[76] He was also not sanguine about a Westminster-style parliament observing that its three pillars, namely, a territorially based electoral system, universal franchise and majority rule, would not fit in with the demographic and political configuration of the island. His *volte face* on issues that he had previously held dear appeared remarkable especially when he suggested that 'the democracy proper to Ceylon is the government of Ceylon by officials selected by the King and by representatives selected by six different communities who justly desire to protect efficiently their respective interests.'[77] The basis for his anxiety was that if changes were made to the Manning Constitution, such as a territorially based electoral system, minorities would be 'enslaved' by the majority Sinhalese community. He rejected the idea that the majority have an automatic advantage: 'My honourable friend the member for the "B" division of the Western Province keeps harping on that as the vast majority of the people of Ceylon are Sinhalese, they must have an overwhelming voice in the government of the country. Is such glorification of the Sinhalese community, to the utter detriment and degradation of the other five communities, humane or just?'[78]

Ramanathan, together with the Ceylon Tamil Mahajana Sabhai and other minority groups, was the architect of the infamous *Minorities' Scheme*, which was offered as a counter to the reform proposal of 1923. The scheme was presented to the Secretary of State for the Colonies through Governor Manning by a hitherto

75 Russell, *Communal Politics*, 1982, p.16.
76 Cited in Vythilingam, *Ramanathan of Ceylon*, 1977, p.576.
77 Vythilingam, *Ramanathan of Ceylon*, 1977, p.578.
78 Vythilingam, *Ramanathan of Ceylon*, 1977, p.579.

unheard of organisation called the 'Minorities Conference'. It tried to give the impression that, apart from the Sinhalese, all the other 'five minority groups', that is, the Tamils, Moors, burghers, Europeans and the Indian Tamils, had subscribed to the scheme. It stated: 'We hereby agree to the scheme of Representation which, we understand, has been adopted by the members of the Legislative Council, who represent the European Burgher, Tamil, Mohammedan and Indian community.'[79] The principal plank of the scheme was to guarantee an equal representation of the Tamils compared with the Sinhalese in a future legislative assembly. This should be done by adhering to a communal representation. It was pleaded in the memorandum that 'no two communities should be in a majority in a Council.'[80]

Ramanathan experienced the worst crisis in his political career when he engineered the minorities' scheme. It immediately came under attack from almost all the community groups. Some Tamil representatives of the north and east, who, it was claimed, had signed it, hurriedly denied their involvement.[81] It was later revealed in *The Daily News* that the minorities' scheme was devised at the request of Manning and subsequently presented to the Secretary of State for the Colonies, Winston Churchill, on 31 August 1922. Manning proposed, with the connivance of the Minorities Conference, that membership should be composed of members from each community to serve in the Committee of the Legislative Council.[82] If this scheme were to be implemented in any future constitutional reform, the majority community, the Sinhalese, would become the sixth member of the family of minority groups in the island.

Ramanathan suffered a blow to his reputation and integrity. Even leading Tamil politicians wondered how he was able to commit such 'egregious blunders', given his standing as the patriarch of Ceylon Tamils. The most serious allegation levelled against him was that he had been guilty of using the signatures of other leading figures of community organisations. One such alleged signatory to the scheme, W. Duraiswamy, a member of the Jaffna Association, who protested to Ramanathan for wrongfully using his name, said:

> I had no hand whatsoever in the minorities Scheme. My telegram to Sir Ramanathan shows that I was opposed to the very essentials of the absurd scheme. If we have to hand the guidance of our political matters to the Minorities what is our political worth? I cannot understand how age and experience could have been guilty of such egregious blunders. I will never support any scheme of that kind that commits the Tamils to the backwaters of political uselessness. No sane Tamil unobsessed by personal magnificence could have been guilty of such a woeful exhibition of political absurdity.[83]

79 *Handbook*, p.447.
80 *Handbook*, p.445.
81 Vythilingam, *Ramanathan of Ceylon*, vol. 2, pp.594–595.
82 *Handbook*, p.439.
83 *Handbook*, p.439.

Criticising the Minorities' scheme, the Colombo Tamil Association said, 'The scheme formulated by the Minorities Conference . . . reduces the Tamils of the island to a position of political impotence. This Association expresses its unqualified disapproval of the scheme.'[84] The president of the Colombo Tamil Association, Dr E.V. Ratnam sent a cablegram to the Secretary of State for the Colonies alleging that his association had nothing to do with the scheme. 'The Colombo Tamil Association representing all Tamil sections, entirely disapprove of the scheme in the memorandum forwarded by minorities; be informed that the elected Council Members for Tamil Provinces have repudiated the Minorities' Memorandum.'[85] The Tamil elected member to the Legislative Council launched a scathing personal attack on Ramanathan calling him the 'nominated Knight' – which was intended both to insult and ridicule – and repudiated the claim that Ramanathan was entitled to represent the common views of the Tamils in the north and east. 'I say that the representation contained in the memorandum, which has been called the secret memorandum or memorial, does not represent the opinion of the Tamils. I do not deny for a moment that high position occupied, and rightly so occupied by the veteran Knight in our community. But it is one thing not to deny the high position, and another, to state that he represents all the people in the community. He did not represent the Tamil community for the reason that he was not elected by them.'[86]Another alleged signatory to the scheme, the Ceylon Muslim Association, in a letter to *The Ceylon Daily News* dated on 16 August 1922, disassociated themselves from the scheme, denying that they were involved in it in any way whatsoever.

The Congress was forced to take action to enlighten the Secretary of State and Colonies about the real force behind this scheme. In fact, it worried that this scheme could actually become a real threat to future constitutional reforms if the colonial officials at Whitehall believed that all the community groups, except the Sinhalese, wanted to maintain the communal representation in the LC. Its dispatch to Churchill on 20 September 1922 read as follows:

> Deep resentment was added to mistrust when through the enterprise of a newspaper – the Ceylon Daily News – this secret document saw, as stated above, the light of day and disclosed the fact that it had been prepared upon the advice of His Excellency the Governor. This disclosure has confirmed the popular suspicion that His Excellency's intention was not merely to thwart the aspirations of the large bulk of the people, but to make His Majesty's government renege upon the principle of representation which had been conceded, possibly against the Governor's wishes. His Excellency's advice to the authors of the Joint Memorandum cannot be regarded otherwise than as a hint, by whatever name the presentation might be called, that it was to be

84 *Handbook*, p.429.
85 *Handbook*, p.446p
86 Vythilingam, *Ramanathan of Ceylon*, vol. 2, 1977, pp.598–599.

> in substance and effect communal. In adopting this attitude the governor sought to arrest the growth of the sense of common citizenship and to give new life to the narrow communal spirit which was organized and fostered by the former system of racial representation in Council.[87]

Ramanathan and his co-writers were also criticised by another leading Tamil figure of the day, Mr Pasupathym, the representative of the Kurunegala Association. At a Congress meeting held on 20–21 April 1923 he said:

> A form of communalism, in any sphere, would benefit neither the granter nor the grantee, but would be a permanent source of friction and conflict. Communalism and national advancement were a contradiction in terms . . . *Communalism was the Spirit and the Handmaiden of that Doctrine of divide and rule.* It had become sanctified by the passage of time and was more powerful and destructive than the bomb or the bayonet. The amity of the races living in this island was a far greater treasure than the glimmering reforms that sought to erect communal camps. The ideas of race should be immolated at the altar of a motherland.[88]

Of course, criticism came from the Sinhalese as well. 'They (the Tamils) would soon realise', claimed H.J.C. Pereira, 'that the Salvation of Ceylon depended not on the growth of communalism or racialism but on the growth of the true national spirit'.[89] Thus, perhaps, one of the great political tragedies in the first half of the twentieth century was Ramanathan's shift from national to ethnic politics. According to Wilson, he became 'an indefatigable exponent of the rights of the Ceylon Tamils'.[90] In fact, as he was growing older, he became even narrower in his political outlook. His brother Arunachalam expressed his frustration to Ramanathan's son Vamadeva with the words, 'Your father is mad, stark mad.'[91] Ramanathan's biographer, M. Vythilingam, also reluctantly admitted that it was difficult to understand how he came to focus so exclusively on Tamil interests and only on one section of the Tamil population when, not long before, his political vision was grand and encompassing. 'It was a great paradox of Ramanathan's long and illustrious career, as it is the irony of all things human and mundane, that the most inveterate nationalist turned out to be the most hardened communalist; the most impassionate unionist was metamorphosed into the uncompromising separatist. Such alas, is the caprice of man's destiny.'[92]

Ramanathan's commitment to Tamil interests was unwavering. His closest associates became those who had devoted their political careers to Tamil interests

87 *Handbook*, p.439.
88 *Handbook*, p.513 (emphasis added).
89 *Handbook*, p.449.
90 Wilson, *Break-up of Sri Lanka*,1989, p.10.
91 Vythilingam, *The Life of Sir Ponnambalam Ramanathan*, vol. 1, 1971, p.536.
92 Vythilingam, *Ramanathan of Ceylon*. vol. 2, 1977, p.701.

only, for example, Sir Ambalavanar Kanagasabhai of the Ceylon Tamil Mahajana Sabhai and A. Sabapathy of the Jaffna Association.[93] Except for the brief period during the Sinhala–Muslim riots, his contribution to national politics, although extraordinary, was not as extensive as that of his brother, Arunachalam. Ramanathan's strong opposition to constitutional reforms and the campaign against territorial representation came to define his career.

Despite his national commitment in his early years, later he kept faith with the colonial administration so that 'the disproportionate advantage' enjoyed by the minority Tamil elite[94] could continue. In this endeavour, he became a follower of Manning. However, both Manning and Ramanathan's efforts failed. The Secretary of State for the Colonies appointed a commission, chaired by Donoughmore, to consider further reforms.

Naturally, Ramanathan took issue with the Donoughmore Commission and its commitment to territorial representation. He questioned why the Commissioners did not listen to the Ceylon Tamils and had failed to introduce balanced representation, which would maintain a proper balance between the Sinhalese and the Tamils. He argued that:

> There is also the well-known principle called the 'balance of power', which the Duke of Devonshire had in view when he considered the question of adequate representation needed for the majority and minority communities in order that one or two parties may not out vote the rest and dominate them.

But neither this expression nor the 'balance of power' can be applied to the Donoughmore Commissioners' scheme. For they have abolished communal representation, introduced territorial representation universally . . . There is nothing in this scheme to serve as a balance. On the contrary it has destroyed the final adjustment of political power conceived by Governor Manning, the Duke of Devonshire and the (British) Cabinet of 1923 and sanctioned by the King.[95]

Despite the strangeness of the minorities' scheme and the fact that reform along those lines would not, as the Commissioners pointed out, allow for a fully functional government, Ramanathan remained opposed to representative democracy in Ceylon since it would destroy any opportunity for Tamils to get elected to the Legislative Council on an equal footing with the Sinhalese. Such a system would sacrifice minorities on the altar of statistics without due consideration of the diverse nature of the island. He demanded to know what kind of offences minorities had committed to deserve such 'ill treatment, to be deprived of the work of winning the love and esteem of the people by an unceasing devotion to their welfare? These

93 de Silva, *A History of Sri Lanka*, 1981, p.393.

94 Wilson, *Break-up of Sri Lanka*, 1989, p.59.

95 Sir P. Ramanathan, *The Memorandum of Sir Ponnambalam Ramanathan on the Recommendations of the Donoughmore Commissioners by the Right Honourable the Secretary of State for the Colonies to Report upon the Reform of the Existing Constitution of the Government of Ceylon (1924–1930)*, London, 1930, p.11.

communities and their trusty leaders have always been helpful to the Government in its endeavour to administer the country soundly. It is wholly unjust to abolish their constituencies and enable indifferent men, versed in the art of currying favour to get themselves foisted into nominated seats'.[96]

Ramanathan was alive to the fact that if the territorial principle were introduced to the Legislative Council, it would make it extremely difficult for the elite groups of Ceylon Tamils to maintain numerical parity with the Sinhalese that they had enjoyed for over a century. In a memorandum sent to the Secretary of State for the Colonies on 18 July 1930, he urged the British administration to revert to communal representation:

> If, . . . these Unofficial Members had been elected by purely territorial constituencies, the Sinhalese community would almost certainly have been in a majority (disproportionate even to their numerical superiority in some respects) over all other sections of the Legislative Council including the Government. It would therefore appear to be clear that adherence, pure and simple, to the territorial basis of representation would be strongly opposed by all communities except the Sinhalese, and I am satisfied that the former are sincerely persuaded that their vital interests require a serious limitation of the territorial basis of representation.[97]

Ramanathan could not believe that, except for Sinhalese reformists, other minority groups would want any changes to the existing representation to the LC because the Manning Constitution was working smoothly and without a hitch 'and there was hardly any manner of disaffection [sic] anywhere'.[98] According to Ramanathan's biographer, Ramanthan believed that if the Donoughmore Commission's recommendations were to be implemented the minorities would run the risk of being submerged by the majority group. The government, without an adequate safeguard for minorities would, in his view, accelerate the process of 'total political extinction, a state of permanent national bondage and servitude'.[99] He strongly believed that a 'mathematical democracy', underpinned by territorial representation, would be the precursor to the total annihilation of the Tamil nation.

Ramanathan's submissions against territorial representation, as his biographer, notes were overly passionate. Most of his arguments sprang from the heart rather than from the head. He used the analogy of federal and international arrangements to argue his position:

96 Vythilingam, *Ramanathan of Ceylon 1977*, p.692.
97 Ramanathan, *The Memorandum of Sir Ponnambalam Ramanathan*, 1930, p.24.
98 Vythilingam, *Ramanathan of Ceylon*, vol. 2, 1977, p.686.
99 Vythilingam, *Ramanathan of Ceylon*, vol. 2, 1977, p.694.

> They say, let us not have communal representation at all; let territorial representation reign . . . Communal representation was, moreover, the system adopted by such great national and international organisations as the American Senate and the League of Nations wherein many peoples and many states were represented . . . Is this a faulty system? I do not think so, because the more powerful and more intelligent nations of the world have agreed to work together upon some righteous principle which admitted the rights of small communities as well as those of large communities. I do think that every minor community should be given a representation suitable to them in order that all the representatives may work together in a hearty way and arrive at conclusions that would ensure the safety of the whole community.

Ramanathan was deeply worried about the future of the Tamils as a nation if the Commissioners' recommendations were to be implemented. He remained committed to resistance by 'constitutional methods and by sound reasoning', since he was convinced that the Commissioners were 'implicating us in trouble without their knowledge'.[100]

Ramanathan, the 'paterfamilias' of secessionism

Ramanathan's biographer, Vythilingam, explained how Ramanathan came to entertain the notion that separateness was the only way to resolve the issue. 'It was at this dark hour of spiritual and moral travail, when all his passionate pleas for rudimentary justice and humanity had proved utterly unavailing, that the idea of a return to the pre-British order of things and the resuscitation of a separate Tamil State commended itself to him, as the only means of escape from what appeared to him to be an irretrievable disaster for the Tamils.' This is an extreme position to adopt and the first time any politician had suggested it in pre-independence Ceylonese politics. Secession was unthinkable among politicians. Indeed, the motto of patriots of both the Tamil and Sinhalese communities was, up to now, to serve the country in which you prosper: *ubi bene ibi patria.*

Ramanathan's partition theory was modelled on that of Ireland and he wondered why the Donoughmore Commissioners had not studied Ireland, which was next door to them? 'If they could confer separate states, one for the southerners and the other for the northerners, why were they reluctant to create a separate Tamil State comprising the north and east? Why did the (Donoughmore) Commissioners not think of that?' Why did they not? 'What is their excuse?' He also wondered why the British government did not follow the constitutional device implemented in British Canada. If the British government could agree separate governments, one for the French-speaking people and the other for the

100 Vythilingam, *Ramanathan of Ceylon*, vol. 2, 1977, pp.697–698.

English-speaking people in recognition of their racial, ethnic and linguistic differences, why could it not allow a separate government for the Tamils?[101]

Ramanathan's views were not popular and were publically criticised by both the Sinhalese constitutionalists of the Congress and by liberal Tamils as well. M.E.R. Tambimuttu, a member of the Legislative Council for the Eastern Province, in *The Ceylon Daily News* of 23 August 1922 said: 'So Sir P. Ramanathan cannot be said to represent the Tamils. Therefore, I fail to see how these minorities could boast that the Tamils are in agreement with them . . . that the Tamils and the Sinhalese should stand together in order to face the crisis that is looming ahead of us.'[102] Clearly, in his old age, Ramanathan had become irrelevant or had lost his preeminent position as both a national and Tamil leader. Evaluating the political career of Sir Ponnambalam Ramanathan, one Tamil scholar, S. Navasivayam, wrote:

> As has happened to so many before him, in his last years he was considered by the younger public men as a reactionary. Nurtured as he was in the political attitudes of the nineteenth century, he was not affected by the constitutional and economic developments of the latter day, and viewed changes like adult suffrage, and state ownership with deep suspicion. However, his contribution to the country's political advancement was great, and though he did not live to see the new Dominion of Ceylon, he contributed largely towards its making.[103]

When Ramanathan died, the great dynasty of Ponnambalam-Coomaraswamy in Ceylon politics ended and it is no exaggeration to say that from 1860 to 1930 it had dominated Ceylonese politics. The contribution to cultural, religious and national issues left its mark on the political map of the island forever. It was an unfortunate situation that they – Sir Ponnambalam Arunachalam and Sir Ponnambalam Ramanathan – found themselves in. National politics and freedom from colonial rule was so close to them as was the interests of their own community. However, it seemed impossible to secure the one without destroying the other, and both brothers opted to defend the interests of their own community.

Hindsight has not made it easier to evaluate the brothers' political legacy. Both brothers fearlessly stood up to British authority often alone and without support, and in the national interests. They were also right in recognising that representative democracy without built-in safeguards would make it impossible for minorities, including the Tamils to live and work in an independent Ceylon. They might have been prescient in imagining that the Tamils, who had ever lived as if they were a majority too, who were administered separately under different colonial regimes before the British brought the country under one central administration and who

101 Vythilingam, *Ramanathan of Ceylon*, vol. 2, 1977, pp.700–701.
102 *Handbook*, pp.443–444.
103 Navasivayam, *The Legislatures of Ceylon*, 1950, p.28.

were well represented as a community in British Ceylon, would now settle for minority status. The internal divisions in Tamil society, the privileged position of the upper class in national politics and the view of themselves as a separate community were going to present insurmountable problems. Yet, it is also true that charismatic leaders shape the political thinking of a people. There is no evidence that ordinary Tamils viewed the Singhalese as a real threat. The threat facing the Tamils, according to the brothers, was holding on to an equitable share of the political leadership, which, under the British, the Tamils had become used to enjoying.

7 Tamil 'communalism' rises with G.G. Ponnambalam as its impresario

Young blood against the old guard

The arrival of the Donoughmore Commission presented enormous difficulties for the traditional leadership of the Ceylon Tamil elite. There were on the horizon young hawks sharpening their beaks and keen to make an impression on the political scene. Any weakness in the traditional leadership would be exploited. But it was not easy given the prestige of the Ponnambalam-Coomaraswamy family in the country for over three-quarters of a century. Ramanathan himself had dominated Tamil politics for nearly half a century when he died in 1930, a remarkable feat no other Sri Lankan politician had ever achieved. It was no easy task for any potential leader from a non-Ponnambalam-Coomaraswamy clan to launch a successful fight for the leadership, given the fact that there were still politically experienced members of the second generation of the family on the scene. The Tamils could not so soon forget the indefatigable service rendered to them by Ramanathan in particular.[1]

After Arunachalam's failure to win the concession for an especially reserved seat for the Colombo Tamils in the Western Province, his brother, Ramanathan's prestige increased. Many in the Ceylon Tamil community admired Ramanathan's qualities; in particular, his remarkable foresight in forming a 'correct' opinion about the treacherous leadership of Congress. Therefore, it was only after the death of the Ponnambalam brothers the possibility for a new kind of leadership opened up.

The emergence of new forces, that is, the Jaffna Youth Congress and the appearance of a young man just fresh from Cambridge was to change the direction of Tamil politics radically. G.G. Ponnambalam came to dominate Tamil politics for the next two decades until S.J.V. Chelvanayakam successfully challenged him in the 1950s in favour of a more strident political approach.

1 He was renowned for his generosity in fighting for the cause of the Tamils and Education in general. The establishment of two Hindu schools in the Jaffna Peninsula, one for girls and the other or boys, is still remembered with gratitude by the ordinary people. In recognition of his service to education in general, one of the resident halls of the first university of Sri Lanka, the University of Ceylon, Peradeniya, was named after Sir Ponnambalam Ramanathan.

Immediately after his arrival home following study abroad, Ponnambalam sensed the change in the political wind which seemed to have caught the Ceylon Tamil political elite by surprise. For a while, he struggled to decide how and with which political group he should align himself. There were three obvious ways for him to enter the political scene. First, there were radical youth movements in both Colombo and in the Jaffna Peninsula. Such radicalism was not favoured by the young Ponnambalam who never appreciated lawlessness in politics. The second choice was perhaps joining the still 'quite dignified and respectable' elite political organisation that was Congress, which, since the departure of Arunachalam had become monopolised mainly by the low-country Sinhalese elite. There is, however, no evidence to suggest that Ponnambalam had ever seriously considered entering this charmed circle of cosmopolitan gentlemen. Finally, there were the traditional Ceylon Tamil parties, that is, the Jaffna Association and the Ceylon Tamil Mahajana Sabhai. But they were, by the time of Ponnambalam's arrival, not only moribund and weak but also in total disarray.

Surprisingly, Ponnambalam decided to begin his political apprenticeship in a party dominated by the low-country Sinhalese elite. He joined other rising men such as S.W.R.D. Bandaranaike, Francis de Zoysa and S.W. Disanaike. Bandaranaike and Ponnambalam had already met during their university days in Britain – the former at Oxford and the latter at Cambridge. Both were equally ambitious, politically. Thus, Ponnambalam's decision to join the Progressive Nationalist Party in which Bandaranaike was a leading player seemed logical. The new party proved to be a disappointment because it failed to challenge the hegemony of Congress or other Tamil parties. Most politicians were happy where they were. Even Bandaranaike and Ponnambalam did not sever their links with traditional political organisations. Ponnambalam himself kept a foot in both the Jaffna Association and the Ceylon Tamil Mahajana Sabhai. Both men had served in the Congress in the 1930s under the leadership of E.W. Perera's All-Ceylon Liberal League. Ponnambalam distinguished himself as a leading liberal, with broad national views but he was not afraid to articulate the particular interests of the Tamils as well.

When the Liberal League was established by ex-Congressmen as a political party to provide a common platform for the both Sinhalese and Tamil professionals to initiate new policies in the economic and social fields, liberalism, already a political force in Britain, was on the wane. The newly formed Labour Party successfully replaced the Liberal Party in British politics in the late 1920s. Liberals had not fared well in Ceylon. Liberalism could not take root in a country under imperial rule. The majority of the members of the Liberal League in Ceylon came from Congress and were mostly professionals. They were a colourful array of individuals with contrasting views. For example, there was Dr S.A. Wickramasinghe, who later formed the Ceylon Communist Party, and C.W.W. Cannangara, who was more of a pragmatist on social and political issues.

The Liberal League very soon proved to be a disappointment. There were no organisational structures or proper disciplinary machine to keep the members in its fold. In short, the Liberal League was weak and lackadaisical. This was a pity because the organisation could have been a counterweight to the ethnically based politics that came to divide the country. But the leading liberal's laissez-faire attitudes were not congruent with the majority of the population whether Tamils or Sinhalese.[2] Ironically, it was the ethnic interests of these liberals that surfaced as the main issue that divided Ponnambalam from his Sinhalese counterparts.

Ponnambalam was, by all accounts, a liberal in his politics but he was also loyal to his community. It is not surprising therefore, that his departure from the Liberal League was on account of his desire to take up the role in Tamil politics vacated by the Ponnamblam brothers. His insistence on a 'weighting' for the Ceylon Tamils in the reformed Legislative Council did not go down well with his 'learned friends' among the Sinhalese elite. Early in the 1930s he made a decisive break and located himself squarely in Tamil politics. This move allowed him to rise to political prominence within the Tamil community, which he dominated between the years 1934 to 1956, becoming identified with the Tamil cause in Ceylonese politics until he was replaced by his deputy, S.J.V. Chelvanayakam.

G.G. Ponnambalam forced to wait in the wings

In the aftermath of the Donoughmore Constitution, the Jaffna and Colombo Tamils were confused and divided. Most were resentful at having thrown away their opportunity by boycotting the elections to the State Council set up in terms of the Donoghmore Commission. They came to see this as a self-inflicted defeat. There was no Jaffna Tamil presence in the State Council apart from the little known Ananthan, the representative of the Mannar-Mullaitivu constituency who had beaten Ponnambalam in that election. Ponnambalam suffered the most, not because he had anything to do with the boycott, but because the election in the Mannar-Mullaitivu constituency was very closely fought. His defeat at the hand of a little known, humble Tamil politician in the Peninsula, S. Ananthan, dealt his leadership ambitions a severe blow from which he took a while to recover. However, a few years in the political wilderness did not do any lasting damage to his political career as the post-1931 years proved. But he had to wait.

A. Mahadeva, the son of Arunachalam, was still a towering figure among his contemporaries even though he had never been able to command the respect and allegiance of the Tamils as his father and uncle had commanded in previous decades. Mahadeva was, unfortunately, neither a shrewd politician nor a brilliant orator like Ponnamblam. While the former was principally resident in Colombo and struggled to converse in vernacular Tamil, the latter was conversant in Tamil and had close connections with the Jaffna Peninsula. Before he went off to Cambridge Ponnambalam had been educated in Jaffna and had retained many friends who could be useful in future elections. Still there were barriers

2 de Silva, *A History of Sri Lanka*, 1981, pp.426–427.

to overcome. In comparison with Mahadeva, he was a relative newcomer to Sri Lankan politics and regarded by the first generation of the Jaffna Association and the Ceylon Tamil Mahaja Sabhai as politically green. Furthermore, to the Tamils in both the Jaffna Peninsula and Colombo, the Ponnambalam brothers, Arunachalam and Ramanathan, were princes of the Tamil people and even though G.G. Ponnambalam shared the same name as the Ponnambalam brothers and Mahadeva, he was not a lineal descendant of the Ponnambalam-Coomaraswamy family. His rise to political prominence was due to his mastery of oratory both in English and Tamil, his education and his reputation as a brilliant lawyer.

Ponnambalam realised that liberal ideas did not have much currency in the Peninsula. In the undeclared battle between himself and Mahadeva for leadership of the Tamils, he needed a powerful platform and a credible cause to build up his political credentials to convince the uncommitted, the doubters and the fence sitters. He also realised that he needed to take up the cudgels on behalf of the Tamils since the stated purpose of the Jaffna Youth Congress was to *swaraj*. After Ramanathan's death, the next leader to be acceptable to both moderate and more radical Tamils was W. Duraiswamy, a leading figure in the Jaffna Association. He had managed to retain his popularity with the youth who remembered that he had given unstinting support to the Jaffna Youth Congress in the boycott of the elections held in accordance with the Donoughmore Constitution. The old guard of the conservative Tamil elite had lost their grip on ordinary people in the face of competition from the more vigorous and politically active Tamil youth and intelligentsia. After the debacle of the boycott the Jaffna Youth Congress also suffered a loss of credibility even among its own supporters. This created an ideal opportunity for a new man to lead the Tamils in the era of post-Donoughmore politics. But to be that man, Ponnambalam first had to win a seat in the State Council.

Ponnambalam takes up the Tamil cause

From 1921 onwards politics in the Jaffna Peninsula bifurcated into streams that both drew their inspiration from neighbouring India. Tamil politicians never shied away from expressing their gratitude to India even within the State Council (until 1924, the Legislative Council) as well, 'for the spiritual gifts and privileges which she gave us'.[3] One strand was the separatist aspirations of Ali Jinnah's Muslim League, and later other separatist Muslim organisations that were also sources of inspiration for the Tamil elite. Jinnah's demand for partition and a separate state for the Muslim community within a federation was an attractive proposition and it was adopted by the Ceylon Tamil groups from around the 1920s. The second generation of the Ceylon Tamil elite were enamored of his policies. The famous cry of a small caucus of Cambridge educated students (all of them in their 30s even

3 R. Sri Pathmanathan statement to State Council, cited in Russell, *Communal Politics*, 1982, p.149.

though they were called students) that the Muslim regions of India 'should have a separate Federation[4] of their own' and their defiant call that 'there can be no peace and tranquility in the land if we, the Muslims, are duped into a Hindu-dominated Federation where we cannot be the masters of our own destiny and captains of our own souls'[5] was the message that reverberated through the Jaffna Peninsula in the post-Donoughmore years.

Ponnambalam and his contemporaries were no doubt greatly affected by developments both within Congress and outside it. The local newspapers of the Peninsula were full of admiration for the Muslim agitators, especially Jinnah, who became somewhat of a cult figure in Jaffna politics. Whenever the Jaffna politicians failed to outmanoeuvre the Sinhalese they were often compared to Jinnah rather than with Gandhi or Nehru. Indeed apart from the Jaffna Youth Congress, Gandhi and Nehru never became political role models for the second generation of the Tamil elite.

Ponnambalam, who was unhappy with the boycotters for spoiling his chances of being elected to the Council, began his political campaign for the State Council immediately after the elections. His courage against the boycotters in the 1931 election actually won him many admirers because the majority of Tamils, including the Tamil media, had come to see that the boycott had effectively prevented representation of the Jaffna Tamils in the State Council. Ponnambalam thus, quite unexpectedly, became the hero and was commended in many of the local papers for his remarkable foresight. The consensus now was that the governor should hold elections for the four seats that had remained vacant on account of the boycott, as soon as possible. It was Ponnambalam who led this call.

The first State Council was a significant victory for the Sinhalese. There were 38 Sinhalese members (low-country Sinhalese 28 and Kandyans (up-country Sinhalese) 10). There were only four Tamils elected of whom only three were Ceylon Tamils and the other an Indian Tamil.[6] Out of seven executive councils,[7]

4 This name was given by a small group of students who studied in Cambridge in the 1930s. In a pamphlet published in 1933 the new Muslim State was to be named 'Pakistan' (the land of the pure). 'Pak' stands for 'pure'. Every letter in 'Pakistan' gives geographical identity of this new nation. Thus, P for Punjab, A for Afghanistan, K for Kashmir, S for Sind, Tan for the last part of Baluchistan. See A. Read and D. Fisher, *The Proudest Day, India's Long Road to Independence*, Pimlico: London,1998, p.234.

5 Read and Fisher, *The Proudest Day*, 1998, p.234.

6 See Jeffries, *Ceylon, The Path to Independence*, 1962, p.68. The total representation was as follows: Sinhalese 38 (both low country and Kandyans), Ceylon Tamils three, Indian Tamil two, European two, Moors one. In addition, the governor nominated two burghers, one Malay and one Indian merchant and four Europeans.

7 These were home affairs (police, prisons, excise), agriculture (agriculture, Crown lands, irrigation, food control), local administration (local authorities, motor transport, mines, mineralogy, fisheries), health (medical and sanitary services), education (control of primary and secondary education), communication and works (public works, railways, electrical undertakings, civil aviation, ports, postal and telegraph services). Although ministers' power was similar to that of a minister of cabinet, the body they formed was called a 'board'.

five Sinhalese members[8] were elected, four as ministers. Peri Sundaram, an Indian Tamil, and H.M. Macan-Marker, a Moor, were elected to the other two ministerial posts. In the eyes of the Ceylon Tamils, their worst fears had materialised. For the first time in pre-independence Sri Lanka, there was a Sinhalese-dominated State Council and no strong Jaffna Tamil presence. The boycott had cost the Jaffna Tamils four seats, all of which remained vacant until 1934.

Ponnambalam realised that if this situation were not rectified soon the position of the Ceylon Tamils would be considerably weakened. The four elected Tamils were not considered sufficient in number to be able to represent the viewpoints of the Ceylon Tamils. The two Indian members were not 'one of them' and could not act as representatives because they were descendants of low castes and tribal groups. Of the other two, the fact that one was from the Eastern Province and the other from the Western Province was sufficient reason for rejecting them as representatives of the Ceylon Tamils. They were outsiders and considered inferior to the more cosmopolitan Jaffna Tamil elite. Ponnambalam found many supporters among both the traditional and younger generation of Ceylon Tamils in his campaign to send Jaffna Tamil representatives to the State Council. A. Mahadeva, H.A.P. Sandrasegera, A. Kanagasabhi, J. Thiagarajah and others supported Ponnambalam's campaign. Their anti-boycott campaign of August 1932 was a success and in the following year, in January 1933, Ponnambalam was able to bring all the streams of Tamil politics under one umbrella except for the Youth Congress. The purpose of his campaign was to plead with the governor to hold elections for the vacant seats. More significantly, agitation within the State Council, for further constitutional reforms for the island caused grave concerns for the Tamils especially because the Sinhalese, notably D.B. Jayatilaka, the former Congressmen who now served in the State Council, were demanding more reforms.

Suddenly, in July 1932, the now famous 'Perera Resolutions' were presented by Perera, the rebel leader in the new Council, the leading figure of the Liberal League and an avowed opponent of the Board of Ministers. He quite unexpectedly seized the initiative to kick-start the next stage of political reform by presenting seven resolutions insisting on self-rule for the island. He argued, 'We have to fight . . . not with the carnal weapon, but with the sword of public opinion and constitutional agitation.'[9] D.B. Jayatilake, the Vice-Chairman, the leader of the House and the Minister of Home Affairs, and D.S. Senanayaka, the Minister of Agriculture, found themselves wrong-footed by the 'Perera Resolutions' and decided to set out their own demands in two memoranda. Thus, on 21 April 1933 and 28 July 1933 they demanded the abolition of the three officers of state, the reduction of the governor's powers, an increase in the power of the Council over financial matters, the abolition

8 They were, D.B. Jayatilaka, D.S. Senanayaka, T.B. Panabokke, C. Batuwantudawe, and C.W.W. Cannangara.

9 Hansard, 1932, vol. 1, pp.1625–1626, cited in Namasivayam, *The Legislatures of Ceylon*, 1951, pp.115–116.

of the executive council system, the introduction of a cabinet-style government and the reconstitution of the public service commission.[10]

The changes in the public service commission suggested by the Board of Ministers' memoranda gave serious concern to the Ceylon Tamils because employment in government service had become the bread and butter of the Jaffna Tamils especially after the Malays had placed restrictions on the employment opportunities in Malaysia hitherto open to Tamil professionals. It did not help matters that rumours about a secret pact between the governor and D.B. Jayatilaka and D.S. Senanayaka, about constitutional reforms, began in the Jaffna Peninsula ,[11] which worried the Tamils especially since they had no effective representation in the State Council to voice their concerns.

By October 1933, after the departure of Governor Sir Graeme Thomson (1931–33), there was a discernible change of attitude on the part of the Colonial Office at Whitehall, in respect of the by-elections to the four vacant seats in the Northern Province. Thomson was determined that the Jaffna Tamils should learn a lesson and had declined to make any overtures on their behalf. However, between 1931 and 1933, a huge effort was made by the Jaffna Tamils to convince the governor that they were 'reformed democrats'. The Colonial Office seemed satisfied that the Jaffna Tamils had proved their 'genuine desire' for representation, a condition that had been imposed on them after they had boycotted the previous election and before Whitehall would consider holding elections to those vacant seats.

With the new Governor Sir Edward Stubbs (1933–37) in place it was agreed by the Secretary of State for the Colonies that since the Ceylon Tamils were displaying a genuine desire to take part in the 'democratic process', elections to the State Council should be held immediately. Tamil politicians swung into action creating a political flurry in the Peninsula. Mahadeva took the initiative ahead of Ponnambalam to resuscitate the old All-Ceylon Tamil League, the leadership of which he had inherited from his antecedents, the Ponnambalam brothers. This was followed by the 'All-Ceylon Tamil Conference' convened by Mahadeva's Tamil League in November 1933, which was the first to devise strategies as to how to face the election and, more importantly, to confront Sinhalese domination in the State Council. The governor had demanded that there should be adequate representation entrenched in the Constitution to prevent minorities from being outnumbered by the majority Sinhalese. The demand for 'balanced representation' became the main issue for the Jaffna Tamil caucus. This was the brainchild of Ponnambalam even though he was forced to play second fiddle to Mahadeva since he had not yet been able to organise his own political party.[12]

10 See Namasivayam, *The Legislatures of Ceylon*, 1951, p.116, Jeffries, *Ceylon: The Path to Independence*, 1962, pp.69–70, de Silva, *A History of Sri Lanka*, 1981, p.432–433.

11 See Russell, *Communal Politics*, 1982, pp.59–60.

12 See Namasivayam, *The Legislatures of Ceylon*, 1951.

G.G. Ponnambalam vs Mahadeva

Ponnambalam entered the newly created State Council in 1934 as a representative of Point-Pedro in the Jaffna Peninsula. Two prominent members of the Arunachalam Ponnambalam dynasty, Mahadeva and Natesan, were also elected. Ponnambalam for the first time in his political career defeated a member of the Ponnambalam dynasty, Sri Pathmanathan. This was not only a significant turning point in Tamil politics but also the start of G.G. Ponnambalam's remarkable political career.

The gap between Mahadeva and Ponnambalam widened with the commencement of the election campaign of 1934. The former was a mature politician who believed that the best approach would be to build alliances between the Sinhalese and the Tamils for the betterment of both communities. In the three years between 1931 and 1934 he actively participated in promoting a national political agenda and kept in close contact with D.S Senanayaka, the leader of the House and the Vice-Chairman of the Board of Ministers, and D.B. Jayatilaka. It was Mahadeva who initiated the famous 'round-table conferences', the main objective of which was to bring the Tamils and Sinhalese under one umbrella organisation. He emphasised during his election campaign that constructive cooperation between the Sinhalese and Tamils was essential in the campaign for responsible government for the island. Ponnambalam, by way of contrast, campaigned on the platform that he would do whatever he could in the State Council to prevent any unjustifiable encroachment on the Tamils' rights by the Sinhalese. He also promised that he would make sure that the proper share in government services would be achieved for the Tamils.[13]

After entering the State Council, Ponnambalam gradually strengthened his position as the sole spokesman for the Ceylon Tamils by encouraging the impression that Mahadeva was a collaborator with the Sinhalese elite and not very interested in issues relevant to the Tamils. Some Jaffna local newspapers suggested that there was another personal reason for Ponnamblam's criticism of Mahadeva. In 1942 Mahadeva was appointed to the vacant post of Sir D. B. Jayatilake, Minister for the Home Office, with the majority vote of the Sinhalese members of the State Council. It was suggested that Ponnambalam had always aspired to high office in the administration. However, Ponnambalam was able to claim that only he could lead the Tamils into the next decade.

The second State Council (1936–39)[14] provided Ponnambalam's leadership campaign with a massive fillip. First, it was dominated by the Sinhalese, both the low country and Kandyan. The ratio was almost one Tamil to five Sinhalese.

13 Russell, *Communal Politics*, 1982, pp.74–76.

14 The elected members from each community were as follows: Sinhalese (low country) 31; Sinhalese (Kandyan) eight, Ceylon Tamils eight; Indian Tamils three (including a nominated member by the governor); Europeans five (including four Europeans nominated by the governor); Moors two (all were appointed by the governor); burgher one (nominated by the governor).

Second, the Singhalese held all the ministerial positions so the chairmen of the executive committees were all Sinhalese. None of the minorities was able to get elected even though in the first State Council (1931–36) two minority members did get elected. In the eyes of many political commentators the pan-Sinhalese Board of Ministries, excluding all minority candidates, was a constitutional blunder by the Sinhalese members.[15] The architects of the *coup d'état* were D.B. Jayatilaka and D.S. Senanayaka. The justification for a Sinhalese-only Board of Ministers was that they could, without the assistance of the Tamils, achieve 'responsible government'.[16] By this time the Sinhalese members of the Council felt that they were ready for self-rule. They had proved, having occupied various high posts in the colonial administration for the past decade or so, that they could govern without the help of the colonial administrators. But to achieve dominion status or independence for the island it was necessary for the Sinhalese and minority groups to work together.

The Board of Ministers in the first State Assembly (1931–36) had become aware that it was difficult to go forward in their campaign for greater constitutional reform because minority State Council members and three Ministers (one Indian Tamil, one Colombo Tamil and one Moor) were opposed to constitutional reforms that did not guarantee a weighted representation for minorities. This meant the kind of 'balanced representation' that had obtained since the time of Governor Manning. Yet the Board wanted to retain the Committee system under any future constitutional reforms. Both these demands were in conflict with the Sinhalese Ministers' constitutional reform plan.

The executive committee system, introduced under the Donoughmore Constitution was opposed by minorities when it was mooted. They argued that it would weaken the hands of the governor. Under the executive committee system, which was precursor to the cabinet system, ministers were given virtual power to run the island's affairs except for finance, defence, external affairs and legal matters. These areas fell under, respectively, the finance secretary, chief secretary and the legal secretary. These three officers together with the chairmen of the executive committees were entrusted with the administration of the island. Executive committee chairmen were elected by the ordinary members of the State Assembly.

G.G. Ponnambalam assumes the leadership role

The leadership baton of the Ceylon Tamils had passed to G.G. Ponnambalam, who is described by Wilson[17] as an orator without equal. He was ably supported by

15 Jeffries, *Ceylon, The Path to Independence*, 1962, p.76; see also Bailey, *Ceylon*, 1952, p.147. Namasivayam, *The Legislatures of Ceylon*, 1951, p.119.

16 Ceylon Sessional Paper XI of 1937, correspondence between the governor and the board of ministers, cited in Namasivayam, *The Legislatures of Ceylon*, 1951, p.119.

17 Wilson, *Break-up of Sri Lanka*, 1989, p.61.

a group of young professionals including the future leader, S.J.V. Chelvanayakam. Together they formed the All-Ceylon Tamil Congress (ACTC) in 1944 with Ponnamblam as its President. Very soon the ACTC began to dominate Tamil politics replacing the Ceylon Tamil Mahajana Sabhai and other smaller organisations, including the Jaffna Youth Congress. This new organisation seemed to have been established as a direct challenge to Sinhalese constitutionalists and to the Ceylon National Congress. Its main objective was to bring the Tamils living in Sri Lanka under its wing, a strategy different to that taken by the Jaffna Association and the Ceylon Tamil Mahajana Sabhai.

Ponnambalam's organisation represented exclusively Tamil interests. Unfortunately, some of its leadership were known for their reckless utterances. For example, in the aftermath of the Donoughmore Report, H.A.P. Sandrasegara was reported as saying 'I will make Jaffna an Ulster and I'll be its Lord Carson.'[18] When Ponnambalam and Sandarasagara campaigned on the lofty promise to resurrect 'the lost prestige' of the Tamils, it seems to have stuck a chord with Tamils who rushed eagerly to join the Tamil Congress.

With the formation of the ACTC, the animosity between the Sinhalese and the Tamil elites increased making it difficult to establish a united front with the Congress. Ponnamblam was more the spokesman for Tamil interests rather than its guiding light. He was never wholly committed to ethnically based politics for its own sake yet it was the road he chose to travel down.

All-Ceylon Tamil Congress (ACTC) rises to the occasion?

Ponnambalam resisted the efforts of the Sinhalese constitutionalist elite of the Congress to forge a new front with the Tamils.[19] The concept of a 'corporate unity in the minds of the Sinhalese is in the nature of a merger, an absorption of the minorities by the majority community. A just and more correct idea of a united Ceylon is that of a rich and gorgeous many-coloured mosaic, set and studded with the diversities of communal consciousness within a glorious one-minded solidarity'.[20]

Ponnambalam was opposed to further constitutional reforms on the grounds that such measures would weaken the position of Tamils in the State Council still further. In a strange way, they were now even opposed to the change in the executive committee system introduced by the Donoughmore Constitution.

18 *Ceylon Daily News*, 17 May 1931, cited in de Silva, *A History of Sri Lanka*, 1981, p.428.

19 Memorandum from the President of All-Ceylon Tamil Conference to the Secretary of State for the Colonies, 14 July 1937, CO, 54 Series, cited in Roberts, 'Problems of Collective Identity in a Multi-ethnic Society', in Roberts (ed.), *Collective Identities*, 1979, p.359.

20 Memorandum from the President, All-Ceylon Tamil Conference, to the Secretary of State for the Colonies, 14 July 1937, in CO 54, series, cited in Roberts, 'Problems of Collective Identity in a Multi-ethnic Society', in Roberts (ed.), *Collective Identities*, 1979, p.356.

The demand for further constitutional reforms, after the adoption of the Donoughmore Constitution, had come from E.W. Perera's Liberal League. He had insisted that the present constitution be replaced by 'orthodox constitutional machinery',[21] thus reducing the governor's reserve powers. Around 1934 the Board of Ministers also took the initiative to agitate for constitutional reforms but this initiative was opposed by the ACTC and other minorities in the State Council. This must have been a setback. It is likely that the Colonial Office was reluctant to interfere with a constitution which had taken three years to devise and which was in use for only three years. Also, the initiative would have had greater luck had there been a more diverse group agitating for it. The absence of minority support weakened the case for the ministers. Even a preparedness to consider changes to the system of executive committees by the Colonial office disappeared when the minorities claimed that their position, with respect to the dominant Sinhalese, would be imperilled should the executive committees be abolished.[22]

K.M. de Silva suggests that 'the minorities had by now the same strong faith in the Executive Committee system as a buttress of their inherently weak political position as they once had in communal (and weighted) representation, and were quite determined to resist any constitutional advance without a consolidation of such advantages as had accrued to them from the introduction of the Executive Committee system.'[23]

The ACTC received the support of several other minority groups and individuals. Of these, T.B. Jayah (leader of the Moors), K. Natesa Aiyer (Indian Tamil), C.G.C. Kerr, M.J. Cary, H.E. Newnham, J.W. Oldfield and C.J. Black (nominated European members to the State Council), especially the support given by the President of the European Association, Mr J. Morrison, ought to be mentioned. In addition, the British-owned *Times of Ceylon* and Tamil newspaper *Virakesari* were, from 1935 onwards, instrumental in building up the ACTC as a political force in pre-independence Ceylon politics.

Ponnambalam was able to forge a new alliance with the other minority groups including the burghers and Europeans against the Sinhalese-dominated political organisations.[24] Their attempts had some success. In 1935 the Ceylon Tamils came together with the Indian Tamils and the Moors, and presented a petition to the Secretary of State for the Colonies denouncing the new electoral system as being biased towards the Sinhalese.[25] The Moors, in particular, offered the greatest resistance to this built-in bias.

However, quite unexpectedly, divisions began to appear in the new alliance. Not all the Tamil politicians, especially some members of the State Council, were

21 de Silva, *History of Sri Lanka*, 1981, p.432.
22 de Silva, *History of Sri Lanka*, 1981, p.433
23 de Silva, *History of Sri Lanka*, 1981, p.433.
24 de Silva, *Managing Ethnic Tensions in Multi-ethnic Societies: Sri Lanka, 1880–1985*, University Press of America: Lanham, MD, 1986, cited in J.D. Rogers, 'Post Orientalism and the Interpretation of Pre-Modern and Modern Political Identities: The Case of Sri Lanka', *JAS*, 53(1), 1994, p.18.
25 Kearney, *Communalism and Language*, 1967, p.34.

in agreement with the ACTC's politics. For instance V. Nalliah (member for Jaffna, Northern Province), E.R. Thambimuttu (a leader of the Eastern Province), and Arunachalam Mahadeva, questioned the wisdom of the policies adopted by ACTC, which seemed detrimental to national unity. Ponnambalam's fifty-fifty campaign suffered a setback owing to these disagreements. This hampered his attempts to demonstrate to the British that the whole Tamil community was behind his organisation and united in opposition to the constitutional reforms of the Donoughmore Commission, which had been responsible for removing communal representation. ACTC also came under attack by the Jaffna Youth League, now a significantly weakened force. The demand for 'balanced representation' to the State Council was ridiculed as 'brand of communalism', which would harm any attempt to build a nation state. Mahadeva's acceptance of the portfolio of Minister of Home Affairs, in the Sinhalese-dominated Executive Committee was also a blow to Ponnamblam's 'uniting Tamil campaign'.

The 1947 general election showed that the 'betrayal of the Tamils' was never forgiven by the people of Jaffna. Mahadeva's famous statement that minority communities should 'join any endeavour with the Sinhalese to see the existing political bondage (colonialism) removed by joint action' did not go down well with the non-cooperative campaign of the ACTC. [26] Recognising that any demand for a fifty-fifty representation of the State Council would not materialise, Mahadeva asked his Tamil colleagues to abandon it even though he was a signatory to the 1937 *Minorities' Memorial*, the basic demand of which was to have equal representation with the Sinhalese. His famous remark, a fifty-fifty demand was 'dead as a dodo', upset Ponnambalam and his colleagues. Another dissenting Tamil politician, Tambimuttu, the representative of the Eastern Province, also questioned the necessity of engaging in communal politics to the detriment of national unity. He stressed that he was in the State Council to represent not only Tamils but other communities as well. He also pointed out that communal politics in favour of the Ceylon Tamils would not be tolerated by his constituency.

Clearly, there was a tension at the heart of Tamil political opinion. How to create an independent nation while at the same time ensuring that the interests of minorities are protected? That there was such a tension at all redounds to the credit of the leadership of the minorities who had already suffered a serious diminution of power under the new Constitution. However, this assessment is not shared by all. The nationalist stance adopted by Mahadeva, Nalliah and Tambimuttu has been branded, even by more recent Tamil scholars such as Wilson as the 'isolationist posture of middle-class Tamils' who displayed nothing more than prejudice and unfounded fear.[27]

26 Russell, *Communal Politics*, 1982, p.261.
27 Wilson, *Break-up of Sri Lanka*, 1988, p.65.

Bandaranaike's Sinhala Mahasabha

At the time that Ponnambalam's pro-Tamil stance was coming under attack from his own side, he unexpectedly found support from a leading Sinhalese politician. In 1937 S.W.R.D. Bandaranaike formed the *Sinhala Maha Sabha* to champion the cause of the Sinhalese Buddhists. This created a stir within liberal political circles. It was intended to be a continuation of the policies propagated by F.R. Senanayaka's *Mahajana Sabhas*, although this time with a more vigorous political agenda added to the religious and linguistic interests of Sinhalese Buddhists. With its formation and clear objectives, ethnicity became the cohering theme of the new organisation. Perhaps, the threat posed by the formidable Marxist organisation the *Lanka Sama Samaja Paksava* (LSSP), with its firebrand leaders Dr N.M. Perera and Philip Gunawardana, encouraged Bandaranaike to form an organisation to win back those who had flocked to the LSSP. The new Marxists had become a significant force among the labour movements in the island and Bandaranaike might have realised that they had alienated a significant section of Sri Lanka's voting population by their refusal to pander to a more parochial nationalism. The Sinhalese Buddhists' concerns were outside the LSSP's political agenda, which was to build an urban proletariat movement. The core of the Marxist leadership, like the Sinhalese constitutionalist leadership, was western-educated professionals, yet they used their social and professional status to take up the cause of the welfare of the 'common man' in the workplace. Nonetheless, they did not understand the quintessence of the day-to-day life of ordinary people, villagers and peasants. Most Sri Lankans, even during the great depression and war, were a cheerful lot with a happy-go-lucky attitude. A century ago, any idea of revolting against the Empire was abandoned after having felt its military might in the 1818 and 1848 great rebellions. Both ordinary Sinhalese and Tamils, unlike the urban labourers, showed no inclination to engage in a fight to the finish to win the kinds of concession new Marxists were demanding ever since they entered the political scene. Bandaranaike, by way of contrast, had never been a revolutionary and he never urged labourers and peasants to take to the street against His Majesty's Government. So quite naturally, there appeared a huge gap – a neglected sector of the population – which neither the new left nor the Congress leaders spotted. Also, with hindsight, it is now clear that it was difficult for Bandaranaike to stake a claim for the future leadership of the island without an organised and, to a certain extent, politicised mass behind him.

Bandaranaike came from 'a prominent aristocratic family' in the low country. His father was the Mahã Mudaliyãr, Sir Solomon Dias Bandaranaike, KCMG, the native chief and close collaborator of the colonial administration. His only son, S.W.R.D. Bandaranaike, had been groomed for a high post in Sri Lankan politics from his earliest years. Even with the right qualifications and credentials, Bandaranaike lacked the charisma with which D.B. Jayatilaka, D.S. Senanayaka and others of his contemporaries seemed to be blessed. This lack got in the way of his political ambitions. He became a Congressman, which provided the initial political credentials – a *sine qua non* in constitutionalist politics of the 1920s and 1930s. Then he was appointed joint Secretary of the Congress. He took part in many deputations to the governor and commissions (notably, the Donoughmore Commission), yet he was not able to win that prestigious title, President of the Ceylon National Congress. Maintaining one leg in Congress he tried other tactics. One such attempt was the formation of the Progressive Nationalist Party in the late 1920s. His attempt to woo all ethnic groups to his fold by advocating a federal structure for the island did not work. This was a pity since some sort of devolved power was probably the best solution to the problems that eventually developed on the island. Neither the Sinhalese nor the Tamils wanted a 'divided' country. Both sides believed that the other side was being difficult and that there could be a solution to the problem of the minorities within a unitary state. The tensions among the Tamils between nationalist and sectional sentiments prove this.

Had the Ceylon Tamils supported Bandaranaike's federal agenda, he could have made a play for the leadership. Instead, he had to watch less qualified and not so eminent people pass him by in the leadership race. After a long apprenticeship in Congress, and with his unassuming, charming and friendly manners with ordinary people, he might have understood more quickly than his contemporaries which way the wind was blowing. The birth of the *Sinhala Maha Sabha* was a natural move given the power politics of the day.[28] However, the *Sinhala Maha Sabha* never became a mainstream political party of the Sinhalese community. Congressmen D.B. Jayatilaka and D.S. Senanayaka – both of whom had never been advocates of Sinhalese interests alone – remained in charge. Even though they had virtually orchestrated a Sinhalese-dominated government, they saw themselves as representatives of the whole country, including minorities interests.

In a way, both Bandaranaike and G.G. Ponnambalam believed in parliamentary democracy. Both despised Marxism and showed no enthusiasm for labour movements or 'proletariat movements'. Both came from high-caste families and had reputations as great speakers. Both came to champion the causes of their own communities almost at the same time. Ponnambalam realised early in his political career that it was impossible for him to lead the Tamils if he did not identify with Tamil interests. Unfortunately, the parochial politics of the Jaffna Peninsula made it impossible for him to also become a national leader. Bandaranaike as well tried to adopt policies that would benefit all the communities but failing that he mobilised the Sinhalese Buddhists and came to identify with Sinhalese interests in a way that other leaders tried not to, even though, practically, their leadership depended on the Sinhalese majority as well. It was well known that Bandaranaike's activities within his new organisation were despised by Congressmen such as D.B. Jayatilaka, D.S. Senanayaka and even other rising stars such as J.R. Jayawardene. Bandaranaike was regarded as a liberal politician, yet this new organisation did

28 See J. Manor, *The Expedient Utopian: Bandaranaike and Ceylon*, Cambridge University Press: Cambridge, 1989.

concentrate on sectional interests and allowed Tamil politicians to point to 'Sinhalese communalism'.[29]

There are differences between Bandaranaike and Ponnambalam, the main one being that unlike Bandaranaike, Ponnambalam led the mainstream Tamil political party among the Ceylon Tamils that was exclusively centred on Tamil interests. Bandaranaike remained a member of the Congress.

Ponnambalam's reincarnation with the 'fifty-fifty' demand

Ponnambalam's political commitment to Tamil interests came under increasing criticism from some Tamil politicians. He was not, however, discouraged by this. He put forward his 'fifty-fifty demand' once again when the Governor Sir Andrew Caldicott (1937–44) began his inquiry into new constitutional reforms in accordance with the instructions given by the Secretary of State for the Colonies, W. Ormsby-Gore, in 1938. In order to protect minorities' interests, it was argued, there should be equal representation between the majority Sinhalese and minority groups. This mathematical solution had, however, been rejected by the Governor who had shown an interest in bringing speedy constitutional reforms to the country, thus guaranteeing greater political power to the native representatives of the State Council. Minorities' concerns, in his view, could be addressed by enhancing their representation not simply by adhering to any communally based mathematical formulae but by making changes to the boundaries of constituencies in which the minorities were concentrated. This, the Governor reasoned, would enable minorities to elect more members, but on a territorial basis. The Governor was a great believer in the political party system, which could not be developed without discarding communal elements from politics.

Ponnambalan's formulae for the election to the State Council could not simply be rejected as retrogressive and harmful to the developments of democratic institutions in the island since it highlighted for the Governor and Whitehall officials the fact that a new constitution could not be devised by neglecting minority interests in toto. New constitutional reforms could be introduced to advance the politics of the island to the next phase of democratic government, but only if they were supported by at least two major communities in the island. This allowed Ponnambalam and the leaders of other minority groups to foil attempts made between 1938 and 1940 by Mahadeva (Tamil State Council member) and his Sinhalese counterparts (in particular Sir D.B. Jayatilaka) in the State Council to forge a united front in the campaign for self-rule for the island. By 1944 constant attacks, in particular on Mahadeva, by his erstwhile Ceylon Tamil colleagues began to bear fruit. Succumbing to the pressure, Mahadeva, distanced himself from

29 See details, K.N.O. Dharmadasa, *Language, Religion and Ethnic Assertiveness: The Growth of Sinhalese Nationalism in Sri Lanka*, University of Michigan Press: Ann Arbor, 1992. See also M. Wickramasinghe, *Ethnic Politics in Colonial Sri Lanka 1927–1947*, Vikas: New Delhi, 1995.

Sinhalese members of the Board of Ministers. This change of mind by Mahadeva delayed the next phase of constitutional reforms and proved to be a barrier to a united campaign against British rule. The famous 'Draft of Ministers' (called the Draft Scheme of 1944) suffered a setback because of the insistence by Mahadeva that his dissention should be included in it. His dissension was recorded:

> The Hon. Mahadeva, Minister of Home Affairs, wishes it to be stated that he is not in agreement with the proposals regarding the question of representation and is of the opinion that the entirety of this question, which is a matter of considerable controversy, be settled by a Royal Commission. [30]

Mahadeva's attempt to work with the Sinhalese members of the State Council was seen as collaboration and was never forgiven by the Tamil leadership; neither were ordinary Tamils in the Jaffna Peninsula allowed to forget it. He was branded a traitor who had betrayed the cause of the Ceylon Tamils. Wilson concedes that the most treacherous act committed by Mahadeva was his decision to join the Board of Ministers after Sir D. B. Jayatilaka's resigned from the post of Minister of Home Affairs. The ACTC wanted to demonstrate to the British Ministers in London that there was no place for any Tamil in the executive committees (Board of Ministers) that operated under the Donoughmore constitutional reforms.[31]

The insistence of the ACTC, and other Tamil pressure groups, that any future constitutional reforms should entrench a clause guaranteeing equal representation between Tamils and the Sinhalese retarded the campaign of the Congress for self-rule for the island. Ponnambalam's politics were aimed at achieving an equal position for the Tamils *vis-à-vis* the Sinhalese but being a shrewd politician he did not want to be seen as a champion of exclusively ethnic interests, nor did he believe that such a position would win support among British officials in London. He presented his demands as an attempt at preserving the multicultural mosaic of the Ceylonese polity. Any constitutional changes, argued Ponnambalam, should be within a unitary framework in which both the Tamils and the Sinhalese should be placed on an equal footing. From his standpoint, it was suicidal for the Tamils to break away from the rest of the island by being confined to the barren lands of the north and east which were, during this time, underdeveloped and economically not viable. He knew very well that without the assistance of the Colombo based government it was impossible to run a separate administration in the Tamil-speaking area, let alone a separate state. Contrariwise, a separate Tamil state, in his view, would destroy the economic base of the Tamils living in the capital of the island. It should be noted that Ponnambalam, Chelvanayakam, Naganathan and many other members of the ACTC lived and earned their livelihoods in Colombo,

30 *Report of the Soulbury Commission: Constitutional Change in Ceylon*. Cmd. 6690 of 1945, Government Press: Colombo, 1946, p.121.

31 Wilson, *Break-up of Sri Lanka*, 1988, p.68.

and their connection with the Jaffna Peninsula was mainly political. It is therefore, not surprising that, as Michael Roberts has observed, the pluralist vision naturally attracted Ponnambalam.[32]

Ponnambalam wanted only limited constitutional reform with a balanced representation for both communities, the Sinhalese and the Tamils, with a governor presiding over the state mechanism with extensive executive powers.[33] More accurately, he saw the governor's role as similar to that of a cricketing umpire. With such a vision it was not surprising that the ACTC opposed the 'Ceylon Independence Bill' in the House of Representatives, arguing that it would not guarantee the rights of minority groups in the island.[34] Even Michael Roberts, a stern critic of the Sinhalese Buddhist ideology and the sympathetic to the separatist politics of the Tamils, had to admit that:

> Nor were the paths of those Sinhalese who supported appeasement made easier by strategies and tactics pursued by the Ceylon Tamil associations. For instance, in 1930–1931, at a time when the Congress leaders were disposed to permit concessions in the delimitation of territorial constituencies, the Ceylon Tamil leaders seem to have spurned co-operation. Again, from the mid-1930s, G.G. Ponnambalam's 'fifty-fifty' demand and his strategy of collaboration with the British created an unfavourable climate for accommodation.[35]

As leader of the ACTC, Ponnambalam, had actively sided with the colonial government by opposing every constitutional reform proposed by the Congress.[36] For this he and his advisers had been engaged in a robust campaign against any constitutional reform in which the dominance of the Sinhalese would be guaranteed.

Ponnambalam's 'fifty-fifty' demand as template for Governor Manning's balanced representation

With the appointment of the Soulbury Commission to examine constitutional reforms to the island, agitation along ethnic lines intensified. The ACTC wrote to the Soulbury Commission that '[T]he near approach of the complete transference of power and authority from *neutral British hands* to the people of this country is causing, in the minds of the Tamil people, in common with other minorities, much misgiving and fear'.[37]

32 M. Roberts, 'Ethnic Conflict in Sri Lanka and Sinhalese Perspectives: Barriers to Accommodation', *Modern Asian Studies*, 1978, p.359.
33 Wriggins, *Ceylon, Dilemmas of a New Nation*, 1960, p.84.
34 Bailey, *Ceylon*, 1952, p.153.
35 Roberts, 'Ethnic Conflict in Sri Lanka', 1978, p.375.
36 Roberts, 'Ethnic Conflict in Sri Lanka', 1978, p.360.
37 *Soulbury Report*, 1946, p.50 (emphasis added).

Governor Manning's 'balanced representation' became the mantra used by Ponnambalam, Chelvanayakam, Naganathan and others to justify the ACTC's demand for communal representation in the State Council. Its famous 'fifty-fifty' demand[38] presented to the Soulbury Commission involved 'fractional representation on a race basis'.[39] It proposed that the future State Council should have 100 elected members, half of whom would be elected from territorial constituencies, while 25 seats should be allocated to the Indian and Ceylon Tamils, and the remaining 25 to the other minority groups, that is, the burghers, the Moors and Europeans.[40] According to this proposal, any minority group could also contest the 50 seats allocated on a territorial basis while their own quotas remained intact. When this was opposed by the Sinhalese, the ACTC changed its fifty-fifty proposal to SC membership being divided equally among the Sinhalese and the rest of the minority groups. With this amended proposal of 'balanced representation' the ACTC tried to achieve two objectives: i) to secure a special status for the Tamil-speaking peoples in the island, ii) to reduce the influence of the majority community in the island. The leadership of the ACTC believed that the political power of the Sinhalese could be effectively curtailed by constitutional manoeuvring.[41] To his credit, Ponnamblam spent nine hours arguing his case, which Rajanayagam sums up as 'the Tamils fell under foreign rule as an independent kingdom; they became a privileged group under the British solely due to their own virtues of diligence and hard labour.[42] This position which is theirs by right must be kept up after independence.' His arguments did not go down well with the Commissioners. Rejecting this 'communal representation under another name',[43] the Soulbury Commission declared:[44]

> [I]t seems to us that under the 'fifty-fifty' scheme each General Election will inevitably produce a Legislature of the same complexion as its predecessor, and we cannot recommend a stereotype cast-iron division of the communities from which it would, in our judgement, be very difficult, if not impossible, ever to develop a normal Party system. But apart from a general consideration of this nature, we find it difficult to see how any stable Government could be formed or any head of a Government be able either to frame a policy or carry

38 *Soulbury Report*, 1946, p.68.

39 Governor Sir Andrew Caldecott's criticism, see *Soulbury Report*, 1946, p.20. The Governor, criticising this proposal, said that 'any concession to the principle of communalism would perpetuate sectionalism.' *Soulbury Report*, 1946, p.24.

40 *Soulbury Report*, 1946, prs.254–264, p.68. Bailey, *Ceylon*, 1952, p.149. See critical analysis, S.L. Gunasekara, *Tigers, Moderates and Pandora's Package*, Multi Packs (Ceylon) Ltd: Colombo, 1996, p.31.

41 Tremayne, *Sri Lanka: The Problem of the Tamils*, 1987, p.218.

42 Hellman-Rajanayagam, 'The Politics of the Tamil Past', in Spencer (ed.), *History and the Root of the Conflict*, 1990, p.115.

43 Wriggins, *Ceylon, Dilemmas of a New Nation*, 1960, p.91.

44 *Soulbury Report*, 1946, p.69.

> it out in a Legislature so constituted . . . We think that any attempt by artificial means to convert a majority into a minority is not only inequitable, but doomed to failure.[45]

The Commission could not see how the proposal would deliver effective government. This seems to be the basis for their rejection of the proposal. While Ponnambalam's idea may have had the virtue of curbing Sinhalese domination, it would also curb any possibility of effective policymaking.

Ponnambalam also proposed, inter alia, a 'balanced executive' in order to curb any future dominance of the Sinhalese in government affairs. He argued that 'a balanced Legislature with an Executive that leaves power in the hands of any one community would be a mere delusion and a snare.' Therefore, 'the Governor should choose the Council of Ministers in consultation with leaders of the various communities in the Legislature, but less than half the members of the Council of Ministers should be from any one community.'[46] If this proposal were to be implemented, argued Gunasekara, the Sinhalese would remain a perpetual minority in the island while representing more than two-thirds of the population.[47] For their part, the Sinhalese leaders rejected this proposal. Sir Ivor Jennings records:

> They were prepared for any compromise which gave the minorities adequate, or more than adequate, representation, provided that they were elected as representatives of the people and not as communal representatives.[48]

However, a very favourable representation of a 1:3 ratio was maintained for minorities under the Soulbury system. Out of 95 electoral seats, 37 were assigned to the minority communities. This electoral advantage or entrenched weighting in favour of minorities was secured by an especially designed delimitation of electorates securing the representation of minority communities without accepting communal representation.[49] Nonetheless, while under the new system the Tamils' representation reflected their proportion of the total population of the island, it was a significant weakening of their position in comparison with the Sinhalese. In fact, from 1833 to 1930, Tamils' representation in the LC far exceeded their ratio with regard to the whole population on the island. Navasivayam, a distinguished Tamil scholar observed:

> From the thirties of the last century to 1931, the minorities were very well represented in the Legislative Council; throughout the last century, indeed,

45 *Soulbury Report*,1946, p.70.
46 *Soulbury Report*, 1946, para. 258.
47 Gunasekera, *Tigers, Moderates and Pandora's Package*, 1996, p.31.
48 I. Jennings, *The Commonwealth in Asia*, Clarendon Press: Oxford, 1956, pp.75–76.
49 *Soulbury Report*, 1946, p.32.

> the native minorities had equal representation with the low country Sinhalese. The Ceylon Tamil representation was first equal to that of the low country Sinhalese and was subsequently in the proportion of 1:2; except for a short period during the operation of the 1920 Order in Council.[50]

The constant grumbling of the Tamil leaders about the dominance of the Sinhalese resulted in angry exchanges between the Sinhalese and Tamil members of the SC. The President of the Board of Ministers, D.S. Senanayake (a Sinhalese and a member of Congress) rebuked the Tamil members in the SC: 'Do you want to be governed from London or do you want, as Ceylonese, to help govern Ceylon',[51] he asked. Ministers in the SC firmly believed that eventually 'patriotism would transcend sectional difficulties.'[52] In a memorandum to the Colonial Office, a prominent leader of the CNC, George E. de. Silva, suggested that perhaps minorities might 'consider themselves as members of one Ceylonese nation owing allegiance to one common motherland'.[53] As Michael Roberts remarks, this theme was repeated over and over again to no avail.[54] Unfortunately, the dream did not materialise. Instead, from 1921 onward, every projected political reform became a contentious issue between the Tamils and the Sinhalese.[55]

Ponnambalam argues against 'legislative and administration discrimination'

Since the 1920s the leadership of the Ceylon Tamils had been considering a constitutional strategy that could be used to preserve the privileged position they had held so far in public life. Their most trenchant argument was the allegation of 'legislative and administrative discrimination' by the Sinhalese against the Tamils,[56] a strange notion in the politics of pre-independence Ceylon. The distribution of finances to the Tamil inhabited areas, it was alleged, was blocked by the Sinhalese members of the SC, an allegation that was later discovered to be unfounded by the Soulbury Commission. Another complaint was that the government, under the influence of the Sinhalese, was trying to promote cooperative movements throughout the island to the disadvantage of Tamil traders. These allegations were also rejected by the Soulbury Commission.[57] In fact, the Commission found after detailed investigation that, 'on the contrary, having

50 Namasivayam, *The Legislatures of Ceylon1928–1948*, 1951, p.59.
51 Ponnambalam, *Sri Lanka: The National Question*, 1983, p.65.
52 *Soulbury Report*, 1946, p.29.
53 Cited in M. Roberts (ed.), *Documents of the Ceylon National Congress 1929–1950*, vol. II, Colombo, 1977, p.962, Item 100.
54 Roberts, 'Problems of Collective Identity', in *Collective Identities*, 1979, p.344.
55 Mendis, *Ceylon Under the British*, 1944, pp.182–183; see, also, Kearney, *Communalism and Language*, 1967, p.29.
56 See Kearney, *Communalism and Language*, 1967, p.37. See, further, *Soulbury Report*, 1946, p.41.
57 *Soulbury Report*, 1946, p.43.

visited a number of these co-operative institutions, we are convinced that they are of great value, not only materially but educationally, to a large proportion of the poorer inhabitants of the island, Tamil as well as Sinhalese.'[58] The most serious allegation was that, in the service sector, Tamils were discriminated against and the Sinhalese favoured. However, although at no time since the first census were the Ceylon Tamils more than 10 to 13 per cent of the total population, the Tamils, mostly of the Jaffna Peninsula benefited most during the British colonial period.[59] They were well represented in the most sought after government services such as the Ceylon Civil Service and in such professions as medicine, engineering, accountancy, and law. For example, in 1921 there were 10,185 Tamils employed in 'public administration and the liberal arts'.[60] Pfaffenberger noted that 'at one time, for instance, it is said that every station agent on the Railway was a Jaffna Tamil.'[61]

According to the 1921 census, there were 861 barristers, advocates and proctors in the island, of whom 408 were Sinhalese (nearly 50 per cent) and 228 were Ceylon Tamils (28 per cent). The 1921 Census reported that 'the number of clerks supplied by Jaffna to the government services was out of all proportion to the size of population of the district.'[62] The representation of the Ceylon Tamils in the civil service and the Public Works Department exceeded their proportion in the total population as is shown in Tables 7.1 and 7.2.[63]

In the medical profession, the proportion of Tamils was extremely high. For example, in 1921, among physicians and other medical practitioners (not including native doctors) there were 281 Ceylon Tamils (44 per cent). By 1925 of provincial surgeons, and Grade I medical Officers, there were ten Ceylon Tamils to 21 Sinhalese. At Grade II level, there were 66 Sinhalese and 48 Ceylon Tamils. In

Table 7.1 Ceylon Civil Service, 1870–1946

Year	*Total*	*Sinhalese*	*Tamil*	*Burgher*
1870	81	7	not recorded	not recorded
1907	95	4	2	6
1925	135	17	8	14
1946	160	69	31	–

58 *Soulbury Report*, 1946, p.43.

59 S.J. Tambiah, 'Ethnic Representation in Ceylon's Higher Administration Services, 1870–1946', *UCR*, 12(13), 1955, p.127.

60 S. Arasarathnam, *The Historical Foundation of the Economy of the Tamils of North Sri Lanka*, Thantai Chelva Memorial Trust: Jaffna, 1982, p.40.

61 B. Pfaffenberger, 'The Political Construction of Defensive Nationalism: The 1968 Temple-Entry Crisis in Northern Sri Lanka', *JAS*, 49(1), 1990, p.84.

62 Census Ceylon, 1921, vol. 1, part II, p. 69.

63 Tambiah, 'Ethnic Representation', 1955, p.115.

Table 7.2 Ethnic representation in the Public Works Department, 1870–1946

Year	*Total*	*Sinhalese*	*Ceylon Tamil*	*Burgher*
1870	35	–	–	
1907	66	4 (district Eng)	2 (district Eng)	14
1925	73	6 (district Eng)	5 (district Eng)	13
1946	71	35 (Eng)	17 (Eng)	

the Home Office in 1935 there were 16 Europeans, 13 Sinhalese and 11 Tamils. This high rate of representation was also evident in the judiciary. Among the district court judges (DJ and ADJ) there were ten Ceylon Tamils to six Sinhalese and six burghers.[64]

As Tambiah demonstrated, these numbers clearly show that in the areas mentioned above, the Ceylon Tamils 'actually dominated' and 'their contributions were always in excess of their numbers in the total population.'[65] The Soulbury Commission, after investigating the complaints of the ACTC, reached a similar conclusion. It was held that, as late as 1938, the Ceylon Tamils occupied a disproportionate number of posts in the public services.[66] However, by the late 1930s the Sinhalese were making progress in medicine, law and the Civil Service due to the expansion of English education in the areas inhabited by them. For instance, in 1946 the Sinhalese secured 69 places in the Civil Service as against 31 by Ceylon Tamils. The Sinhalese were also able to increase slightly their representation in the Supreme Court. There were five Sinhalese and one Ceylon Tamil Supreme Court judges. If these data are analysed purely numerically, then there were more Sinhalese in these professions than Ceylon Tamils. But if these numbers are analysed proportionally it was the Ceylon Tamils who were greatly over-represented and were able to remain so for almost one and a half centuries. Analysing data from 1951, Wriggins says that 'a service-wide census taken in 1951 showed that out of a total of 123,194 reported as employed directly by the central government, those with Tamil backgrounds represented 21,768. Of the remaining 20,000 who had an exclusively English educational background, it would be plausible to assume that 10,000 were Sinhalese, 5,000 Burghers, and 5,000 Tamils. This would make a total of 27,000 Tamils out of total government strength of 123,000 or roughly 22 per cent.'[67]

If any significant advance was made by the Sinhalese, it was at the expense of the burghers, whose population and representation in the main professions

64 Tambiah, 'Ethnic Representation',1955, p.132.

65 Tambiah, 'Ethnic Representation', 1955, pp.129–130. See also H. Hannum (ed.), 'Sri Lanka', in *Documents on Autonomy and Minority Rights*, Martinus Nijhoff: Dordrecht/Boston/London, 1993, p.496.

66 *Soulbury Report*, p.49.

67 Department of Census and Statistics, Report of the Census of Government and Local Government Employees 1951, Colombo, cited in Wriggins, *Dilemmas of a New Nation*, 1960, p.235.

Table 7.3 Admission figures, 1981–1983

	S	T	O	S	T	O	S	T	O
Physics	63.5	31.8	4.7	61.1	33.5	5.5	73.4	23.1	3.6
Biology	72.5	24.3	3.2	71.7	26.1	2.2	70.3	23.1	3.6
Engineering	67.2	28.1	4.7	66.9	28.5	4.5	66.4	28.1	5.1
Medicine	72.7	23.1	4.3	72.4	25.3	2.3	72.8	22.1	5.1
Law	73.0	16.2	10.9	68.8	24.0	7.3	78.5	11.5	10.0

Source: Division of Planning and Research University Grant Commissions, 1983, cited in S.J. Thambiah, 'Ethnic representation in Ceylon's higher administration services, 1870–1946', 1955, p.154

decreased alarmingly. Yet the representation of the Ceylon Tamils remained virtually intact. Nonetheless, they feared that, in post-colonial independent Ceylon, their domination of the prestigious professions would not be maintained. (See Table 7.3.)[68] This was the strongest reason for their attempt to secure a balance of power in the public services as well as in the government.

Ponnamblam became a folk hero among the ordinary Tamils in Sri Lanka by the time the Soulbury Commission had left the island. His marathon nine-hour speech was heroic in the eyes of the ordinary Tamils in their campaign – this time not against British imperialism but against Sinhalese domination. His political achievement and his courtroom battles made him into a demi-god among the Tamil Hindu community. However by the time of the general election, held in accordance with the Soulbury Constitution, Ponnambalam had shifted his ground politically. His strong opposition to working with the Sinhalese-dominated government was beginning to mellow. He was by now not only a seasoned politician with 13 years' experience in the State Council, but also a mature politician ready to take on broader themes rather than represent Tamil interests only. However, his deputy, S.J.V. Chelvanayakam, watched his mellowing with utmost concern. G.G. Ponnambalam, KC, ironically, found that his destiny was to be determined by the 'hungry-looking'[69] Chelvanayakam, a King's Council as was Ponnambalam, rather than in a showdown with the majority ethic group.

The unhappy rounds of negotiations over constitutional reforms had increased tensions between the Sinhalese and Tamils. But this was not the only problem. Wilson's analysis of the political development during the years 1920 to 1947 noted that caste politics also played a not insignificant role in the collapse of unity between the elite groups of the Sinhala and Tamils. In the 1920s the entirety of the Ceylon

68 From the 1970s the Tamil leaders diverted their campaign alleging that the Tamil students were discriminated against in the university entry programme, an allegation that has no credibility, as will be shown later.

69 These were some of 'derogatory words' used by G.G. Ponnambalam in his election rallies against Chelvanayakam, his former deputy, in the 1952 general election. Chelvanayakam fought this election as a leader of the newly formed Federal Party against Ponnambalam's ACTC.

Tamil leadership was drawn from the highest *Vellala* caste equivalent to the *Goyigama* caste among the Sinhalese. Wilson claims that early in the 20th century, and again during 1930 to 1945, the Tamil elite suggested that the elites of the *Vellala* and *Goyigama* castes should form a united 'national front' against the politicians of inferior castes in the Sinhalese community such as members of the *Durave*, *Salagama* and *Karave* castes. According to Wilson (who belongs to the *Vellala* caste himself and is married to a daughter of the late Chelvanayakam), there was a meeting between these two groups in 1945 in Colombo to revive such a pact, but to no effect.[70] Leaders of the calibre of Marcus Fernando (*Karava*), Francis de Zoysa (*Salagama*), A.E. Goonesinghe (*Durava*), James Peiris (*Karava*) were already dominating Ceylon politics, and this could not now be broken by an alliance of the *Vellala* and the *Goyigama*. Moreover, a narrow political alliance between the two major castes of the island would have hampered any campaign for self-rule.

70 Wilson, *Break-up of Sri Lanka*, 1988, p. 60.

8 The passing of the baton

The rise of new leadership in the Jaffna Peninsula

National politics in the Jaffna Peninsula

The post-1925 years, in particular from 1926 to 1931, were remarkable for their impact on the island's political developments and their effects on traditional Ceylon Tamil politics. By this time both the Congress leadership and the traditional Tamil elite were coming under severe attack from Sinhalese and Tamil radical groups.

A.E. Goonesinha's (radical Congressman and leader of the Young Lanka League) vitriolic attack on the backwoodsmen of Congress for their conservative and imperialist attitudes was also a remarkable development in Sinhalese politics. The political atmosphere favoured radicals from both the Sinhalese and Tamils ethnic communities. Anti-British and anti-establishment slogans were frequently heard on the streets of both Jaffna and Colombo. While effigies of Congress leaders were ceremoniously burnt down by Goonesinha and his loyal followers in Colombo, in the town of Jaffna it was the effigies of British colonial officers instead and the Union Jack that were burned down by youngsters under the leadership of radical teachers and students.

Already by the late 1920s occasional rumblings were heard in the arid Jaffna Peninsula and even in the inner sanctum of the Colombo Tamil elite as to the next strategy to be adopted in their struggle. The need for new political strategies to face the threat of 'Sinhalese imperialism' was felt in many quarters since this posed a real threat to the position enjoyed by the elite Tamils, ever since the British conquered the island. The radical proposals presented by the Donoughmore Commission were a disaster for the Tamil elite of both the Jaffna Association and the Ceylon Tamil Mahajana Sabhai. As Judge C. Coomaraswamy had observed most *Vellalas* seemed unwilling to accept that the world was changing fast.[1] 'The political leadership of the Ceylon Tamils, the conservative section at least, was now left dumbfounded and in some confusion and dismay'[2] by the failure of the policies they had been pursuing. However, this could not be said of everyone in the Tamil elite and certainly not about G.G. Ponnambalam. A shrewd politician from the

1 *Hindu Organ*, 5 January 1934.
2 Russell, *Communal Politics*, 1982, p.18.

time of his entrance onto the political scene, he grasped the political opportunity offered by the fading star of the Ponnambalam-Coomaraswamy family.

His ascendancy to a leadership position had not been an easy task, since the political game has changed considerably. The question now was who could lead the Tamils in the next few decades not against British Imperialism – but against the threat from the south-west of the island – against Sinhalese dominance over the Tamils. While Ramanathan was leading a deputation to the Secretary of State for the Colonies against the Donoughmore Commission's recommendations, other leaders of the second generation of Tamil elite were meeting the Donoughmore Commissioners to represent the 'non-Ramanathan point of view'.[3] Of these, G.G. Ponnambalam was the most prominent.

Ponnambalam gains political ground but the Jaffna Youth Congress steals the political show

As the influence of Congress withered away, new radical movements emerged among the Jaffna Tamils. This young and radical youth movement comprising teachers and students began to cut the ground from under the traditional leadership of the Tamils. The 'monolithic dinosaurs' of Jaffna Tamil politics, that is, the Jaffna Association and the Ceylon Tamil Mahajana Sabhai, had, after the Donoughmore Commission, become unpopular with the masses in the Peninsula. The former was dominated by a small group of high-caste Jaffna Tamil *Vellalas*, some of whose members could not even speak the Tamil language. In the five years between 1926 to 1931, the traditional conservative leadership of the Ceylon Tamils lost their appeal among young Tamils, particularly the oppressed castes owing mainly to their parochial political outlook and social exclusivism. The ethnic focus of the old guard of the Tamil elite came under severe attack from the radicals especially the youth conference that had been sympathetically listened to by the Commission. Their focus was on national politics and constitutional reforms. From the point of view of Tamil politics, this was radical in that it broke ranks with the traditional concerns of the Tamils. Radicalism in Sri Lankan politics has meant different things at different times but it always implied a certain militancy.

Some of the leading lights[4] of this new organisation had cut their political teeth in early apprenticeship with the existing politics of the Jaffna Peninsula, but the rank and file had never had any political contact within the inner sanctum of the Jaffna elitists. It is noteworthy that the first President of the Youth Congress was the less well-known J.V. Chelliah, an outsider to the Tamil elite. He together with other members mentioned would never have been able to influence the existing political movements neither would they have ever been able to infiltrate the inner sanctum of the old guard, owing to their low social and caste status.

3 Russell, *Communal Politics*, 1982, p.18.

4 S.H. Perapanayagam, C. Balasingham, M.S. Balasingham, M.S. Balasunderam, P. Kandiah, T.N. Subbiah, J. Muttuswamy, T.C. Rajaratnam, M.S. Eliatamby and P. Nagalingam.

The Jaffna Youth Conference

The Jaffna Youth Conference tried to dictate the direction in which Tamil policies should go by ignoring sectional interests and advocating *swaraj*, the independence of the island, which had never been the political goal of anyone (except Arunachalam). The new leaders spoke with a new vocabulary that included 'boycotting' both elections and imported goods from the British Empire, and taking a stance against imperialism as the Indian National Congress had done. In fact, the Youth Congress became the centre of the attraction for the youngsters owing to its liberal and radical social and political outlook.

The Indian factor

The influence of the Indian National Congress was clearly evident in the formation of the Youth Congress and its political activities. In fact, between 1926 and 1931 some Conference meetings were addressed by prominent leaders of the Indian National Congress, including Kamaladevi Chattopadhya, Sarojini Naidhu, Nehru and Satyamurti.[5] It was recorded that one of the meetings that Nehru addressed was attended by over 10,000 people. If the Youth Congress were inspired by the ideology of any single Ceylon Tamil leader, it was certainly Ponnambalam Arunachalam. Most youths were exposed to the ideals of the Indian National struggle either when they were educated in Madras University or by following the activities of the Indian National leaders such as Gandhi and Nehru. Jane Russell describes the resolution adopted by the Youth Congress:

> A series of resolutions passed at its annual session in 1925 indicated the radical nature of its ideology: they called for the abolition of the dowry system; advocated open temple entry for the *harijans* and an end to disequalities based on caste; denounce a communal thinking and advocated full cooperation with the Sinhalese to bring about early self-government; advocated the adoption of national dress and the use of vernacular in place of English, and stressed the need for young men to involve themselves in social service.[6]

Coincidentally, when the Jaffna Youth Congress was beginning to raise its head in Peninsula politics, the whole of India was engulfed in protests and *hartal* against a Commission appointed by the Secretary of State for the Colonies to report on constitutional reforms for India. The Simon Commission began its two planned visits to India on 3 February 1928. But the commissioners soon realised how embarrassing it was to face angry protestors across all the main cities of India. Protests and *satyaghra* in Bombay, Maharashtra, Lucknow and Delhi, in

5 S. H. Perinpanayagam, *Handbook of the Jaffna Youth Congress*, 1939, cited in Russell, *Communal Politics*, 1982, p.27.

6 Russell, *Communal Politics*, 1982, p.26–27.

particular, should be mentioned here for their organisation and ferocity. There were well-organised protestors carrying black flags and banners inscribed 'SIMON GO HOME'. 'Nowhere could they escape the protestors – their train from Bombay to Poona was escorted by young Maharashtrians waving black flags at them from a lorry on the road, which ran alongside the track for most of the 70 miles between Poona and Lonavala. In Lucknow, the local Muslim League leader, Khaliquzzaman, conceived the brilliant notion of painting "GO BACK SIMON" on kites and balloons and flying them over the official reception organised by the taluqdars in the Kaiserbagh gardens.'[7] Violent clashes occurred between the police and protestors. Anarchy reigned during its stay in India. Protestors were hailed as national heroes by the leading Congressmen. The spiritual leader of the Indian nation, Gandhi, sent his 'congratulations to the organizers for the very great success they achieved'. He noted further, 'It did my soul good to see Liberals, Independents and Congressmen ranged together on the same platform.'[8] Gandhi and the anti-Simon Commission protestors made a deep impression on Jaffna Tamil youths. India is a close neighbour so political developments there did not go unnoticed and were monitored with keen interest by Tamil intelligentsia and the youths while the Sinhalese-dominated Congress appeared to take no interest in these developments whatsoever.

The uncompromising and revolutionary stance taken by the Indian National Congress in 1929 was admired by the Jaffna youth. The Indian National Congress's historical statement on the banks of the Ravi River on 31 December 1929 touched not only the hearts of the Indian independence movement but also the hearts of the Jaffna youths. Raising the tricolour flag of the Indian nation to the shout of *Inquilab zindabad* (long live the revolution!), Jawaharlal Nehru stated in particular that submission to 'a ruler that has caused fourfold disaster to our country' was a crime 'against man and God', finishing this famous 'Ravi River declaration' with the touching words, 'We believe, therefore, that India must sever the British connection and attain *purna swaraj* or complete independence.'[9]

Other forms of resistance against colonial rule in India were welcomed by the Jaffna Youth with enthusiasm. The 1930/31campaign against the Salt Tax, the 'most inhuman poll tax the ingenuity of man can devise',[10] and the boycott campaign against foreign clothes, British colleges, law courts, postal services and liquor shops had become a standard feature of the Indian political scene. During these years it was also a common occurrence that the Indian leadership of Nehru, Gandhi and Syed Mahmud were in and out of prison. In fact Motilal Nehru died while he was detained in prison with an estimated 60 to 90,000 fellow detainees.[11] No doubt the provocative speeches of the Indian National leaders reverberated in the hearts of young men, teachers and students of the Jaffna Youth Congress but

7 Read and Fisher, *The Proudest Day*, 1998, pp.211–225.
8 Cited in Read and Fisher, *The Proudest Day*, 1988, p.225.
9 Cited in Read and Fisher, *The Proudest Day*, 1988, p.225.
10 Read and Fisher, *The Proudest Day*, 1988, p.227.
11 Read and Fisher, *The Proudest Day*, 1988, pp.226–276.

the elderly Ceylon Tamil and Sinhalese elite who dominated Congress seemed impervious to these feelings.

The experience of the Donoughmore Commissioners visit to Sri Lanka from 13 November 1927 to 18 January 1928 was quite different to that of the Simon Commission. The Donoughmore Report mentioned with appreciation and with a 'lovely sense of gratitude' how wonderful their stay had been in Sri Lanka. They had heard about the traditions of Ceylonese hospitality yet they had never expected such a welcome by so many 'good people' and above all by members of the State Council. They recalled the 'universal desire of the people and the Council Members' to meet and discuss their grievances with the visiting commissioners. Above all, the Commissioners also especially mentioned that there were no difficulties placed in the way of the fulfilment of their task by the Ceylonese. Indeed it was the people's representatives who took pains to provide every comfort for the Commissioners. The Commissioners noted:

> Thus on arrival in Ceylon we found that the fullest arrangements had been planned for our convenience. Unasked, and under no obligation to do so, the Legislative Council had insisted that the best accommodation should be provided for us at public expense, that motor cars should be especially assigned to us for our sole use, and that all possible assistance should be given to us in the form of clerical staff, peons, messengers, and books and papers.[12]

The commissioners even mentioned the 'lovely entertainment' and the dinner with the Sri Lankan members of the State Council on the eve of their departure![13] These 'kindly people' were the political elite of the Sinhalese and Tamil *Vellalas.* Their approach was to plead and to hope for a sympathetic hearing from the visiting commissioners. There were neither protest marches nor any black flags waving in the capital or provinces of the island. Such actions would have gone against the grain of the cultured Sinhalese and the Tamil elite.

Youth Congress and its goal, swaraj

The main goal of the Youth Congress was to achieve *swaraj* status for Ceylon as well. Their struggles against British rule and its policies awakened the people who hitherto had been kept at arms' length from mainstream politics by the elderly gentlemen of the Ceylon Tamil elite. Many Tamil youths in the Jaffna Peninsula were ready to sacrifice themselves for the *swaraj* campaign and to follow boycotting campaigns against colonial rule. Their anti-British campaign commenced with the visiting Donoughmore Commission. Jane Russell points out that:

> Whilst the Tamil leaders in Colombo had been fighting the acceptance of the Donoughmore Constitution, and bickering amongst themselves about

12 *The Donoughmore Report*, 1932, pp.154–155.
13 *The Donoughmore Report*, 1932, pp.154–155.

> causeways, the young men of Jaffna had pre-empted the mass political basis in the peninsula. So when the conservative leaders finally came round to accepting universal franchise and territorial representation in 1930 and began to prepare to fight the elections in the northern constituencies, they found themselves at the mercy of the Jaffna Youth Congress for the votes of the villagers.[14]

However, the youth conference's only real, albeit dubious success, came with their success in forcing Tamil politicians to boycott the election to a newly established State Council that had been set up in accordance with the constitutional reforms introduced by the Donoughmore Commission. A week before the election was held the Youth Conference passed a resolution to boycott the election that was due to be held on 4 May 1931. The resolution was upheld at a specially convened meeting:

> This conference holds 'swaraj' to be the inalienable birth right of everyone and calls upon the youth of the land to consecrate their lives to the achievement of their country's freedom. Whereas the Donoughmore Commission militates itself against the attainment of 'swaraj', this conference further pledges itself to boycott the scheme.[15]

In this, they followed the example of the Indian National Congress's boycotting campaign.

After the resolution young men ran amok across the streets of Jaffna, tearing down Union flags and shouting slogans such as 'swaraj' and 'boycott'. They were able to force some 'confused' and bewildered leaders to withdraw from the election on the eve of it.[16] However, their attempts to persuade G.G. Ponnambalam's withdrawal from the election did not succeed. He refused to surrender to the boys on the street. Apart from the Mannar-Mullaitivu constituency, which was contested by G.G. Ponnambalam and Ananthan, the Youth Conference successfully stopped Tamil politicians in the Northern Province from taking part in the election on the grounds that the Donoughmore Commission's report did not guarantee *swaraj* status for the island.

Unfortunately, the boycotting campaign dealt a severe blow to the standing of established Tamil politicians. For a while there appeared to be a vacuum in the leadership of the Ceylon Tamils in the Peninsula. Some of the traditional political elite, for example Waitialingam Duraiswamy, appeared to make a comeback through the League, but others never regained their political footing.

The Youth Conference had its finest hours from 1927 to 1933. It successfully attacked the Donoughmore Commission's reports and was able to win over

14 Russell, *Communal Politics*, 1982, p.28.

15 Russell, *Communal Politics*, 1982, p.29.

16 Candidates who agreed to boycott the election were W. Duraiswamy, K. Balasingham, A. Mahadeva, S. Natesan, N. Selvadurai, Mudaliar Karalapillai, S. Rajaratnam, J. Tyagaraja and Dr I. Thambiah.

ordinary people to its ranks. 'The leaders who dressed in the *verti* and *banian*, talked freely with all, regardless of caste or social status, and were willing to enrol any person who wished to join.'[17] For the first time in Jaffna the rank and file of Tamils mobilized against British Imperialism. Also, for the first time in the twentieth century, the power base of the traditional political elite was broken. Jane Russell observed that 'As the Jaffna Youth Congress became more and more disillusioned with what they viewed as the opportunism extant in Ceylon politics, they leant increasingly towards the Indian movement, which they felt to be the fount of purity and idealism in politics . . . By adopting "Indian views" about politics, the Jaffna Youth Congress had necessarily abdicated any responsibility for the political future of the Jaffna peninsula and the Ceylon Tamils as a community.'[18]

The Tamil high caste did fight back but the Youth Congress held its ground in the interests of oppressed, low-caste Tamils. It was quite well known that it was Ramanathan's followers who initiated protests against equal rights for the low-caste Tamil students.

The Jaffna Youth Congress had also shown an interest in working with the Colombo based political reform organisations, in particular with E.W. Perera's All-Ceylon Liberal League, thus demonstrating its willingness to work with Sinhalese groups in the campaign for *swaraj*. It was less interested in the fate of the Tamils in a free and independent Ceylon than in freedom from imperial rule. In this respect, the younger Tamil leadership had a different agenda from that of the old guard.

The Youth Conference identified the struggle for nationalism as the more pressing issue. It believed that the interests of the ordinary people would be better served by enhancing 'political enlightenment' among the masses. The Tamil youths were invited to 'identify themselves with the independence movements in the island'.[19] Loyalty to the nation would defeat the need for concern about sectional interests.[20] The League's success as a political force was short-lived due to the absence of a charismatic leader who could take on the Sinhalese constitutionalists, and the lack of grassroots appeal because the ordinary people of the Peninsula were ultimately more concerned about their future in a Sinhalese-dominated country. The attempt to focus on the continuation of British imperialism that the Donoughmore Commission was not prepared to address did have temporary value in that it mobilised the Tamil masses, which was to have long-term consequences.

However, several things militated against any long-term success for the Youth Congress. The Tamils had perceived that their position was better under the former constitutional arrangement than what the Donoughmore Commission

17 Russell, *Communal Politics*, 1982, p.28.
18 Russell, *Communal Politics*, 1982, p.50.
19 *Morning Star*, 28 April 1933.
20 See *Communalism or Nationalism? A Reply to the Speech Delivered in the State Council on the Reforms Dispatched by G.G. Ponnambalam Esq*, Chunnakam: Thirumakal Press, 1939.

was proposing. They were going to suffer a radical loss of status with the new arrangements. Also, it later became obvious that the success of the boycott had left the Tamils without proper representation in national politics. It was a dreadful irony that the attempt to rise above ethnic interests for the national cause had actually placed the Tamils in a politically vulnerable position.

Fighting back

The old guard Tamil politicians were not so easily dislodged from their perch. It was by now clear that the Tamil political response to the elections had weakened their position. They were determined to regain the initiative from the Youth Conference. Organisations were set up to present the politicians as being more radical than the Youth Conference had ever been in its opposition to the Donoughmore Constitution. One such organisation was the All-Ceylon Tamil League. Another was the Tamil Conference. It was not surprising that it was the traditional leadership of Duraiswamy, Mahadeva and Natesan among others who came forward to lead the post-election boycott campaign. They sent a signed statement on 8 May 1931 to the Sinhalese elected members of the State Council, in particular to D.B. Jayatilaka, D.S. Senanayaka, S.W.R.D. Bandaranaike, Francis de Zoysa and E.W. Perrera, urging them to boycott the new State Council, which had been inaugurated on the previous day. Even though this was done at the request of the Jaffna Youth Congress the motives of these leaders were suspect because their withdrawal from the elections had been due to pressure from ordinary Tamils in the Peninsula and not because they were convinced that either the election was a bad idea or that the State Council should be made defunct. However, this was the time that the boycott campaigners were riding the crest of a wave of populist fame. Rather than distancing themselves from popular sentiment, the Tamil elite probably thought that it would be better to go with the 'lads'.

The boycott was a political disaster of the Ceylon Tamil elite. Only three Ceylon Tamils and two Indian Tamils, all of whom had refused to take part in the boycott, were elected. Thus there were Dr R. Saravanamuttu (Colombo North), M.M. Subramaniam (Trincomalee-Batticaloa), S.M. Ananthan (Mannar), Perry Sunderam (Hatton) and S.P Vytilingam (Talawakelle) in the first State Council, leaving Tamil representation very thin indeed. The Jaffna Tamil elite who had dominated the politics of the council for more than a century had been routed by its own hand. There was no representative from the Jaffna Peninsula. The nearest electoral seat to the Peninsula was Mannar but this seat was lost by G.G. Ponnambalam to Ananthan who was not a distinguished debater as was made clear in subsequent State Council debates. In fact, none of the Tamil representatives elected for the first State Council was equal in political skill or debate to the Sinhalese members. Often it was the Indian Tamil, Perry Sunderam, who rose on the floor to defend Ceylon Tamil interests. This was ironic since the Indian Tamils were despised by the Ceylon Tamils because they were considered 'coolies' – descendants from the lowest caste groups of south India. Those living in the Jaffna Peninsula would not have been allowed to enter the Hindu temples. This turn of events must no doubt have delivered a serious blow to *Vellalas* pride and social status.

Furthermore, the Tamil representatives of the State Council were not, as the governor admitted in his statement to the assembly, seasoned politicians who could defend Tamils' interests effectively. The governor, expressing his sympathy for the Tamils, said in the opening ceremony on 7 July 1931 that the whole debacle was due to 'hot-headed misrepresentations of the scope and spirit of the new constitution'. He could not understand why 'this very important section of the island should remain entirely without representation.'[21] He saw it as a loss to the Council and to the country.

Not long after the traditional leadership had had political power wrested from it than a chance came to reassert itself against the Youth Congress. In 1932 all those candidates who had boycotted the elections, except Duraiswamy and Balasingham, made a public statement condemning the boycott. In the following year, on 2 January 1933, they created a new organisation called the Tamil Conference to consolidate their position. There was another inducement for such urgent action to be taken – the governor's visit to Jaffna presented an opportunity for the Tamil elite to express its allegiance to the British Empire and colonial rule. They wanted to convey a clear message to the governor that they were now willing to return to democratic politics and to embrace the Donoughmore Constitution.

The feelings among many of the Tamil elite were that the new constitution, and in particular the committee system, should be given a fair trial. The meeting organised by the Tamil Conference was attended by the political luminaries of the day: G.G. Ponnambalam, A. Mahadeva, J. Tyagaraja, Sri Pathmanathan, H.A.P. Sandrasegara and N. Salvadurai. Almost all speakers in public admitted that they had made a mistake by not sending a strong group of Ceylon Tamil representatives to the State Council. Some tried to remind the audience that they were not engaged in any anti-British campaigners neither would they ever follow the path preached by the Indian National Congress. Tyagarajah was concerned that the 'Sinhalese brethren' may have misunderstood their actions. Finally, the Tamil conference issued a communiqué stating 'The earnest desire of the Tamil people to cooperate with the government in giving the Donoughmore Constitution a fair trial, notwithstanding the fact that Tamil representation has received a great setback under it.'[22]

Every effort was made by the Tamil elite to distance itself from the Youth Conference's political activities especially its anti-imperialist stance. Even those who had actually supported the boycott of the election to the State Assembly began to confess to the gathering that it was a serious mistake to take part in such a fruitless

21 Hansard, 7 July 1931, cited in Russell, *Communal Politics*, 1982, p.36.

22 *Morning Star*, 20 January 1933, cited in Russell, *Communal Politics*, 1982, p.60.

exercise. Youth Congress leaders were rebuked for their 'stupid' campaign. Those who supported the boycott A. Mahadeva, A. Kanagasabhai, Sir Pathmanathan and the non-boycotter, G.G. Ponnambalam, led the new organisation to secure a strong political footing for the future. Mocking the anti-British stance taken by the boycotters who had followed the example of the Indian National Congress, a leading Jaffna Tamil newspaper sarcastically recalled, 'Because the peacock danced, the Turkey cock tried too.'[23] The campaign to boycott western goods was also condemned. The new elite emerged victorious at the end of the conference heralding the end of the League's role. So the radicalism of the Jaffna Youth League never really recovered. The Youth Conference itself admitted that its boycotting campaign had been a 'blunder', because before taking such a drastic action: 'The country ought to have been more politically educated and organised on a large scale.'[24]

The clash between the traditional Tamil political class and the Youth Congress in political opposition often became violent. The tactics used to break the Youth Congress proved to be a turning point. Members of the youth movement were brutally attacked and their campaign centre burnt down. Their conferences and public meetings were broken up by especially deployed thugs. Jane Russell describes the pattern of this fighting:

> Throughout 1933, the peninsula was the scene of incidents of violence as boycotters and anti-boycotters clashed in demonstrations or at public meetings. Meetings were broken up by the opposing party. Fights and all kinds of thuggery broke out in these clashes. At the liberal league-Jaffna Youth Congress Conference in April, C. Balasingham's *pandal* was set on fire by anti-boycotters who tried to break up the meeting. The bitterness engendered in this year makes it a 'time of troubles' in Ceylon Tamil political history. In the process, the ideals and policies of the Jaffna Youth Congress were so discredited as to be finally extirpated from the mainstream of Ceylon Tamil politics. By mid-1934, the Youth Congress had ceased to command any influence.[25]

Thus the Tamil elite after a brief period of bewilderment and confusion, emerged victorious, once again defeating the radical and non-partisan national movement of the Youth Congress.

Youth Conference's failure

The Jaffna Youth Conference's failure to become a radical mass movement among Jaffna Tamils, and its inability forge a new alliance with radical and liberal Sinhalese organisations such as Goonesinha's Labour Party and E.W. Perera's Liberal League, dealt the final death blow to the forging of a national, anti-British

23 *Hindu Organ*, 10 March 1932, cited in Russell, *Communal Politics*, 1982, p.36.

24 Russell, *Communal Politics*, 1982, p.36.

25 Russell, *Communal Politics*, 1982, p.39.

movement in Ceylon, as events after the 1930s proved. Indeed, it was hoped by both the radical forces and the intelligentsia that an alliance with similar movements in the rest of the island, in particular with the Sinhalese, the Youth Congress would be able to forge a new radical front, comprising both the Tamils and Sinhalese, against the colonial administration in their campaign for *swaraj* for the island. Such a movement could have become a forum for ordinary Sinhalese and Tamils to learn their trade in politics and to challenge the domination of the Sinhalese constitutionalists in Congress and Tamil sectional politicians. Responsibility for the Jaffna Youth League's failure to become a formidable force among the Tamils in the Jaffna Peninsula is also the fault of radical and liberal Sinhalese organisations. The latter failed to make any meaningful effort to forge a joint front with the Jaffna Youth Conference, even though the conference had extended its hand to Sinhalese organisations. The Tamil Conference had to rise above its own interests to join with the Sinhalese but the Sinhalese majority did not need the Tamils to fight its own political battles. They could be anti-imperialist and sectionalist at once.

The Sinhalese liberal caucus distanced itself from the Youth Congress for several reasons. First, the Youth Congress had staked a claim for *purna swaraj*, which it could not realistically achieve, given its limited resources. Was theirs a case of imitating India without having fully appreciated the enormous responsibilities that accompany such actions? The Youth Congress did not have a long-term strategy to confront the colonial administration. For example, during the years 1926 to 1931 its final goal appeared to be to obtain *swaraj*. In the aftermath of the boycotting campaign, its ultimate political goal was to achieve *purna swaraj*. Yet it was not so sure how a complete severance from the British Empire could be achieved. For such bold action to succeed there should be a mass movement behind it. But neither the Moors nor the Sinhalese were prepared to support such a movement. Only the Tamil youth, teachers and students were ready to embark on this bold adventure.

Perhaps it was discouraging that even with the millions of followers behind the Indian National Congress, Nehru and Gandhi did not even manage to get internal self-government for India, even by as late as the 1930s but it is without doubt that mass political action against the British would not be contemplated by the Sinhalese.

Swaraj was itself a confused and nebulous concept. Was it to mean a total break from the British Empire and the British Commonwealth of Nations or was it instead a dominion status within a British Commonwealth of Nations that was being sought? Why then did the Youth Congress change its stance from *swaraj* to *purna swaraj*? *Purna* means 'complete' or 'total'. As stated in that famous Ravi River speech on 31 December 1929, Nehru interpreted *purna* as meaning 'complete independence'. Did this mean that the Indian National Congress wanted to sever every type of connection with the British Empire and the British Commonwealth of Nations? The speeches made by various leaders of Congress indicated that some wanted to retain membership of the British Commonwealth of Nations even after achieving *purna swaraj*. Indeed, that was the message given by Gandhi when he visited Britain to discuss the Indian situation with British parliamentarians in 1931.

He emphasised that what India wanted was equal status with other states in a commonwealth. This was reiterated in his address to the House of Commons when he said that he wanted to be a citizen of a Commonwealth of Nations.[26] Then *purna swaraj* did not mean a total break with the British Commonwealth of Nations. However, it did mean complete independence.

Second, the political influence of the Youth Congress was confined to a small area within the Jaffna Peninsula and its policies were very much peninsula-orientated ones. Third, its main inspiration was leading figures of the Indian National Congress, which no doubt alienated them from the majority community in the island. Contrary to what the Youth Congress thought about India, the Sinhalese viewed the Indian National Congress with suspicion. It should be remembered that when Sir Ponnambalam Arunachalam suggested in 1918 that Ceylon might consider federating with India and following the tactics adopted by the Indian National Congress he was subjected to a barrage of criticism for his 'unpatriotic' attitudes. Because of Arunachalam's reputation as an honourable statesman, he had been able to ride the storm with minimal damage. Such was the political temperament of Sri Lanka, that when the Youth Congress suggested, in the aftermath of the post-boycott phase, that Ceylon should be federated with India permanently, it was not surprising that even liberal Sinhalese politicians did not want to forge any alliance with the Youth Congress. The Youth Congress had given the impression that Sri Lanka was simply a part of India.

Third, their proposal that the Vanni be 'colonised' by the Ceylon Tamils did not go down well with the Sinhalese. The region of Vanni, a sparsely populated area south of the Jaffna Peninsula, was still considered by the Sinhalese politicians as part of the old kingdom of the Sinhalese, a part of *Raja Rata* (Kings' country) civilisation. All these policies and statements exposed weaknesses which were no doubt instrumental in alienating the other communities on the island.

Separatist elements within the Youth Congress

There were some separatist tendencies as well among certain of the leading figures associated with the Youth Congress, which had also, inculcated fear in the hearts of the Sinhalese elitists and liberal groups. Sandrasegara's famous statement that he would become Lord Carson and turn Jaffna into an Ulster did not bode well for any meaningful relationship with the Sinhalese. He even suggested that they not cooperate with the Sinhalese because 'the Tamils did not want to be submerged.' Furthermore, he warned the Sinhalese politicians that if they attempted to do so 'they would prefer to separate from the rest of the island.' He claimed that 'the Tamils as a race were different form the Sinhalese, and their habits and customs were entirely different.'[27] Sandrasegara was a loose cannon and his political colours anyone's guess but such talk gave offence to the Sinhalese even

26 D. Mercer (ed.), *Chronicle of the 20th Century*, Longman: London, 1988, p.407.

27 *Ceylon Daily News*, 24 March 1930, cited in Russell, *Communal Politics*, 1982, p.33.

though other leaders made overtures for a common struggle against the colonial administration.

Still, the liberal Sinhalese voices should have prevailed and the Sinhalese must also assume responsibility for not attempting a rapprochement with the Youth Congress. When Arunachalam, the Jaffna Association and the Ceylon Tamil Mahajana Sabhai left Congress in an acrimonious atmosphere, Congress leadership pursued the Jaffna Tamils for years, pleading with them to rejoin Congress. Deputation after deputation was sent to Jaffna to heal the rift between the 'warring parties' but to no avail. The Jaffna Tamil elite had already started an isolated path, distancing itself from mainstream politics. This was not the attitude of the Sinhalese to the Youth Congress. There is no evidence to suggest that Congress had ever tried to understand the Jaffna Youth Congress. There was not, on the part of the Sinhalese, any strong desire to work with the Youth Congress.

It was also unfortunate, from an ethnic harmony point of view, that some of the leading liberals of the Sinhalese camp rushed to condemn the election boycotting campaign of the Youth Congress, proclaiming it a total disaster and a futile exercise. A State Council member, S.W.R.D. Bandaranaike, said mockingly in a house debate that those 'self-sacrificing people' who ventured to boycott had ended up in a 'bleak desert'. Questioning the wisdom of resorting to such radical routes he asked how a small group of people could launch a boycott campaign in Ceylon when 'that enormously powerful body, the Indian National Congress' had failed in a similar campaign. He concluded, 'I venture to think that the boycott was not successful.'[28]

Another prominent Congressman and the new leader of the State Council, Sir D.B. Jayatilaka, could not understand why the Jaffna Tamils had ever resorted to such undemocratic, self-defeating and 'frivolous' actions.[29] The Youth Congress were also not spared by the Colombo based newspapers that vented their fury. According to the *Ceylon Daily News*, a boycott was a kind of 'virile politics' and those who 'exhilarated' in engaging in boycotting displayed only their foolish 'spirit'.[30] Jane Russell concluded that '[T]he "progressive" strand in the Tamil political woof was obfuscated by that of the "conservative" and the latter rapidly became the dominant force. The idea of Ceylonese or proto-Lankan nationalism was almost completely effaced by Tamil communalism within a few months, and the attempt to reform Hinduism in Ceylon and liberate the *harijans* became relegated to occasional platitudes uttered from election platforms.'[31] This assessment is only partly correct. The Jaffna Youth were genuinely concerned with the plight of the lower castes and their defeat impeded reform in this area. Also, they were more prepared that the older guard of Tamil politicians to forge alliances with Sinhalese groups of the same ilk. Russell's view is that the Tamils ought to have committed

28 Cited in Russell, *Communal Politics*, 1982, p.106.
29 Hansard, 1935, Col. 4283.
30 *Ceylon Daily News*, 5 May 1931.
31 Russell, *Communal Politics*, 1982, p.39.

themselves to the national cause of independence when such a cause had not really been embraced by the Sinhalese majority. Government under the Donoghmore Commission meant that power remained vested in the Sinhalese ethnic majority and there was no real urgency for change.

The Youth Congress made one final effort in 1931 to forge joint Sinhala–Tamil political organisation by seeking to replace the conservative Ceylon National Congress with the Northern Province National Association. This did not succeed either owing to a lack of support from the Sinhalese political organisations. Its last-ditch attempt to work in close cooperation with the Liberal League of E.W. Perera was also rebuffed. Thus, the only real attempt to forge a Sinhala–Tamil political party, after the departure of Sir Ponnambalam from Congress, disappeared into the sands of the Jaffna Peninsula. The parochial political outlook of the Sinhalese and conservative Ceylon Tamil elite were both at fault for failing to build a nationalist movement. Thus the traditional Ceylon Tamil elitists were replaced, not by the Jaffna Youth League, but by more sophisticated western-educated young blood of a second-generation Tamil elitists, but it took years for anyone to emerge as the obvious leader of the Ceylon Tamils.

The Jaffna Youth lost ground in the face of the ferocious protection of entrenched orthodoxy of *Vellalas* in the Jaffna Peninsula. Even though some hard-core activists were still around in the later years of the 1940s they were virtually 'finished' by the end of the third decade of the 20th century. It took another five decades for another youth movement to merge in the Jaffna Peninsula as a force to be reckoned with. Indeed, it became such a force that not only a small caucus of the *Vellala* elite, but also the whole socio-cultural-political configuration of the Tamils in the north-east, changed forever. The difference between the Jaffna Youth Conference in the 1930s and the current youth movements in the Peninsula was that the former was devoted to national, democratic politics, whereas the latter became a vigorous proponent of the Tamil cause and developed one of the most ruthless terrorist organisations in the world.

9 The winter of discontent in Tamil communalism

Congress's attempts at unity falls on deaf ears

In the late 1920s significant changes occurred among the constitutionalist reformists in Congress, most of whom were by now Sinhalese. With the departure of Sir Ponnambalam Arunachalam and a significant number of Jaffna Tamils, the Ceylon National Congress faced enormous challenges. Its unique position as a national organisation representing the natives had lost validity in the eyes of the colonial administration and other communities even though a significant section of the Colombo Tamils and Ceylon Moors still preferred to remain in its fold. Internal fighting between Ceylon Tamils and Sinhalese, and among the Sinhalese themselves, weakened Congress. Attempts to bring Arunachalam and the Jaffna Tamil leadership back to Congress by offering to support more members for the Northern and the Eastern Provinces did not materialise. The appointment of C.E. Corea (an outsider to the Colombo based Congress who had a good relationship with the Ceylon/Jaffna Tamils), as President of the Congress, to lure back the disenchanted Tamil elite also proved unsuccessful.

Sinhalese elites' opposition

There was a glimmer of hope in 1924, when Congress was able to reach an agreement with the leadership of the Ceylon Tamils over greater representation of the Tamils in the LC. It was agreed that future elections to the legislature should be based on a two-to-one representation, that is, for every two Sinhalese representatives there should be one Tamil.[1] Yet when it was debated in the Congress at its annual meeting in 1925, the newly elected President Francis de Zoysa (a leading Sinhalese) objected that a 'A unity brought about by pacts and agreements based on communal prejudices, communal distrust and communal selfishness is nothing but a pretence and a fraud . . . pacts between the two largest communities in the island guaranteeing to the other a certain proportion of the loaves and the fishes

1 *Donoughmore Committee Report*, CMND 4060, 1932 pp.92–93, *Soulbury Commission Report*, 1946, pp.66–67.

are extremely repugnant and deserve unqualified condemnation. The only real and lasting unity is a unity based on mutual trust, mutual good-will and recognition of the community of interest.'[2]

Nonetheless, there were significant developments. Giving evidence before the Donoughmore Commission in 1927, the leadership of Congress agreed that special representation could be permitted to continue if the Commission were satisfied that it was necessary, as a temporary measure, to redress genuine grievances of minority groups providing such measures would not be permitted to delay the establishment of self-government in the island.[3] These attempts did not materialise owing to the intransigence of both the men of Congress and the Ceylon Tamil leadership. It would appear that the leadership of the Tamils and Sinhalese was trapped in an unhelpful situation with any assertion of minority interests being seen as a lack of trust in the political leadership of the majority. Moreover, the Sinhalese were prepared to allow minority representation only as a temporary measure to address grievances. There does not appear to have been many in the leadership that gave serious thought to the sort of democracy that Sri Lanka needed.

As the years passed the authority of Congress dwindled. It also did not help that the rising star of the second generation of the Sinhalese leadership in the Congress, F.R. Senanayaka, died in December 1925. His untimely death affected not only his organisation, the Sinhala Mahãjana Sabhã, but Congress as well.

Sinhala Mahãjana Sabhã

Senanayaka's Mahãjana Sabhã was primarily a Sinhalese Buddhist organisation even though it remained a constituent part of Congress. In its formation and objectives it was an organisation committed to the interests of the Singhalese Buddhists and in this objective it was similar to the Jaffna Association. First, it emerged as a response to the Jaffna Association's 'communal' approach to national politics. Second, it gave Sinhalese Buddhists a national organisation through which to voice their concerns. The reluctance of the leadership of the Congress, most of whom were Christians and non-Buddhists, to propagate the rights and concerns of the Sinhalese Buddhists was instrumental in the formation of this new organisation. Since its inception in 1919 the Mahãjana Sabhã tried to reach out to the Sinhalese masses, but perhaps without a clear political objective. Branches of this new organisation appeared in most rural Sinhalese constituencies. It was an attempt at the politicisation of the masses but without any clear direction. Its limited political objective was compensated for by its commitment to the Sinhalese Buddhists' cause. The proceedings of the *sabhas* (branches) were conducted in Sinhala – they advocated Buddhist values very strongly and urged people to take a leading role in national life. Unlike the gatherings of Congress, the meetings held by the *sabhas*

2 Presidential address to the Congress, 18–19 December 1925, *Handbook*, p.686.

3 Evidence before the Commission at the Town Hall, Colombo, on 22 and 23 November 1927, *Handbook*, p.828.

were attended by hundreds of ordinary Sinhalese Buddhists, most of whom were rural peasants and the rising lower middle class.[4] Had Senanayaka survived longer the *sabhas* may well have become a political force in Sri Lanka. Senanayaka and the Mahãjana Sabhã were accused by the Jaffna Association and the Tamil Mahãjana Sabhã of promoting Sinhalese parochial interests.

With the death of F.R. Senanayaka, the traditional leadership of Congress lost ground. Most notably, Sir James Peiris's influence faded away alarmingly quickly. Although Sir Marcus Fernando was still able to be influential in the inner sanctum of the metropolitan circle he was never been able to establish himself as a figure of standing either within the Congressional circle or nationally. This cleared the way for a second generation of Sinhalese elite in Congress and in national politics. They were S.W.R.D. Bandaranaike, R.S.S. Gunawardana and J.R. Jayawardene; and among the Tamils, G.G. Ponnambalam.

S.W.R.D. Bandaranaike, a Sinhalese aristocrat and Oxford-educated scholar, became joint secretary of Congress in 1925. At the same time he formed various sub-organisations, consolidating his base for future leadership. Of these organisations, his short-lived Progressive Nationalist Party is worthy of mention because Bandaranaike used it as a vehicle for approaching the various community groups in the island. The main objective of this new organisation was to advocate federalism by recognising the racial and ethnic variety of the population of the island. He was unable to impress either the Sinhalese or Tamils with his approach.

With the governor on the top of the tree

Disunity between Congress and a section of the Ceylon Tamils had undoubtedly delayed constitutional reforms for the island;[5] the main reason being that the Ceylon Tamil leadership 'did not wish to exchange British domination for Sinhalese domination'.[6] They had always been self-consciously aware of their Jaffna Tamil identity and behaved as such.[7] Leaders of the Ceylon Tamils feared that, in an independent Ceylon, their position and prestige would be diminished in comparison to that of the Sinhalese.[8]

4 See, on the Mahãjana Sabhã, R.D. Gunawardena, *The Reform Movement and Political Organisations in Ceylon with Special Reference to the Temperance Movement and Regional Associations, 1900–1930*, unpublished PhD Thesis, University of Ceylon, Peradeniya, 1976, pp.74–156, cited in de Silva, *A History of Sri Lanka*, 1981, p.396.

5 Namasivayam, *The Legislatures of Ceylon*, 1950, 12, p.10; M. Roberts, 'Ethnic Conflict in Sri Lanka and Sinhalese Perspectives: Barriers to Accommodation', *MAS*, 12(3), 1978, p.355.

6 Jennings, 'Nationalism and Political Development in Ceylon. The Background of Self-Government', 1953, p.70.

7 Jennings, 'Nationalism and Political Development in Ceylon', 1953, p.68.

8 de Silva, *History of Sri Lanka*, 1981, p.78.

Separatist politics – the influence of the Muslim League

The politics of the Ceylon Tamils, after the first decades of the twentieth century, had a remarkable similarity to the Muslim League in India led by Mohamed Ali Jinnah. During the pre-independence period, Jinnah's advocated the partition of India so that Muslims would have their own state. Moreover, unlike the local Hindu Mahãsabhã in India, the Ceylon Tamils were not regionally interconnected with other movements. The Tamils' political approach was different to the kind of national politics advanced by the Indian Congress and other minority groups. The Jaffna Association and the later CTMS remained a provincial political organisation focusing only on securing electoral gains for Tamils. They should have attempted, in addition to advocating for the Tamil minority, a connection with the larger issues. Paradoxically, the nature of their politics meant that only the high-caste elitist group of the Jaffna Tamils and the Ceylon Tamils in Colombo benefitted and not members of the lesser castes. In fact, unlike non-Tamil regional organisations in the island, the Jaffna Association and the CTMS were not open to ordinary Tamils owing to entrenched caste divisions, and the Association was reluctant to accommodate other Tamils such as the Indian Tamils. Indian Tamils had also been marginalised by the traditional Tamil leadership for decades. The Ceylon Tamils had never, until recently, tried to entice other Tamil-speaking groups in the island to join them. Even the Moors had not been invited to join them on a wider platform in their campaign for minority rights. During the mid-nineteenth century the Ceylon Tamils had attempted to convince the colonial government that the Moors were originally Tamils who had converted to Islam, a claim rejected by the Moor community. Thus, the Jaffna Tamil elite enjoyed a monopoly of political activity while, at the same time, remaining detached from the bulk of the Tamil population in the island. The Tamils who lived in the Eastern Province only joined a nationwide movement in the late 1950s.

The egalitarian and non-sectarian ethos of early twentieth-century Sri Lankan politics gave way completely to sectional interests. From the Sinhalese point of view the Tamils appeared to be placing their own interests and the interests of their province above issues that affected the whole country. From the Tamil point of view the interests of the whole country simply translated into the interests of the Sinhalese majority.

The Donoughmore Commission and the end of communal representation

Until, perhaps, 1921, the year in which Ponnambalam Arunachalam left Congress, the Tamil leadership had proceeded on the basis that the Tamils and the Sinhalese were the *majorities* on the island,[9] with the Moors, burghers, and Europeans being

9 Rogers, 'Post Orientalism and the Interpretation of Pre-modern and Modern Political Identities', 1994, p.18.

lesser minorities ('three minorities').[10] The Jaffna Association's main purpose was to see that the Ceylon Tamils would be on an equal footing with the Sinhalese. In a memorandum to the Secretary of State for the Colonies on 2 January 1918, the Jaffna Association stated that, 'the Tamils of Ceylon have hitherto, in spite of their inferiority in numbers, maintained a position of equality with their Sinhalese brethren, whether in official or unofficial life.'[11] Governor Manning encouraged this perception, opening himself up to the charge that he was supporting emerging divisions between the Tamils and Sinhalese.[12] In fact, De Silva argues that the Jaffna Association and other Ceylon Tamil elite adopted this position as a political stratagem to agitate for a balanced representation between the Tamils and the Sinhalese in any future constitutional reforms. With the departure of Arunachalam from the Congress and the confrontational politics that ensued, the Ceylon Tamils accepted that they would have difficulty holding onto the political position they had hitherto enjoyed without significant opposition from the Sinhalese. From now on there would be two main categories of people in Sri Lankan polity, described by their numerical strengths as the majority Sinhalese and the minority Tamils, Moors, Malays and burghers.

The crisis in Tamil politics

Quite unexpectedly between 1924 and 1931, three separate events, occurring within a short space of each other produced a crisis for the Ceylon political elite. They were respectively, the deaths of the Ponnambalam brothers; the appointment of the Donoughmore Commission to report on further constitutional reforms for the island; and the emergence of a radical, nationalist orientated youth movement in the Jaffna Peninsula in the form of the Jaffna Youth Congress.

Ponnambalam Arunachalam died in 1924, a broken man, unable to achieve his ultimate political goal, which was to become the national leader of the country. Indeed, there was no one else, other than Arunachalam, to lead the country if the Sinhalese constitutionalist elite recognised the yeoman service rendered by him, when he put his distinguished career at the Ceylon Civil Service at risk. When the Sinhalese elite bent over backward to appease the colonial administration whenever the issue of constitutional reforms surfaced, it was Arunachalam – then serving as a registrar general – who led the agitation for self-rule. Before his death, he might have had sensed the difficulties that the Tamils would have had to confront as more constitutional reforms were being introduced. By then deep divisions had developed within the Tamil elites – mainly between the traditional elite group and the new generation of Tamil leaders whose political power bases were located elsewhere, far away from the seat of Tamil civilization, the Jaffna

10 P. Arunachalam's address to the Conference on Constitutional Reforms convened by the Ceylon Reform League and the Ceylon National Association on 2 April 1917, in *Handbook*, pp.86, 110.

11 de Silva, 'Formation and Character', 1967, p.90.

12 de Silva, 'Formation and Character',1967, p.100.

Peninsula. The Tamils, notably, of Colombo, Kandy and the Western and Eastern Provinces showed a greater willingness to work with the Sinhalese constitutional reformers in Congress. These regional divisions among the Jaffna Tamils and the Tamils in the rest of the island were played out publically during the 1920s and 1930s when the Colombo Tamils and the Jaffna Tamils hurled abuse at one another through the media. The Colombo Tamil, according to his northern cousins, 'is a man who (has) lost all pride of birth, pride of race, pride of history, and pride of his people's literature'.[13] These criticisms returned with remarks of similar harshness. The Jaffna Tamils were perceived by the Colombo Tamils as a 'Jingo(istic) Tamil whose only occupation is to glory in himself and especially his past. He, like the frog, knows only the wall he lives in . . . Burdened by the weight of his over-eating and over-storing in the capacious entrails, he sinks to the bottom of the stagnant well. The Jingo Tamil imagines that he became fat and rich in the world above because he fought his way there; "fight, fight, and you will get rich" he croaks.' The Jaffna Tamils' indiscreet loyalties to the colonial administration come under particular attack. From the standpoint of Colombo Tamils, the Jaffna Tamil 'is an Anglomaniac. The sign of a white epidermis inspires in the Jingo Tamils, the much preached of virtues of loyalty, servility and the like. He kow-tows before his lord and master, and renders him homage with his soul'.[14] Arunachalam's biographer noted with concern that:

> The members of the North chose to drive another wedge into the relationship of the Tamils by drawing a very subtle, insidious and far-fetched distinction between the Tamils of the north and the Tamils of Colombo who were none other than the Tamils of the north resident in Colombo for professional and commercial purposes. Instead of drawing them closer together and strengthening their ranks . . . the celebrity from the North was scattering them to the winds by drawing such mischievous and uncalled-for distinctions.[15]

The dichotomy that existed between the Jaffna and Colombo Tamils was a cause for concern for Arunachalam, which he knew militated against any united Tamil stance. However, Arunachalam was initially optimistic about the united future of the Tamil community. He believed that they 'will be saved by their sturdy common sense and marvelous industry, their innate disdain of comfort and Spartan simplicity, their love of knowledge and love of the mother-tongue'.[16]

Even before Arunachalam died the mantle of leadership fell to his brother, Ramanathan, who unashamedly took up the Tamil cause (as discussed in the previous chapter). However, during the last few years of Ramanathan's life, his authority was challenged by other less well-known Tamil leaders such as

13 *Hindu Organ*, cited in J. Russell, *Communal Politics*, 1982, p.79.

14 *Hindu Organ*, cited in Russell, *Communal Politics*, 1982, p.79.

15 Vythilingam, *Ramanathan of Ceylon*, vol. 11, 1977, p.596.

16 Cited in Russell, *Communal Politics*, 1982, p.8.

W. Duraiswamy of the Jaffna Association, E.R. Thambimuttu, from the Eastern Province and a representative to the Legislative Council, and some Colombo Tamils. Having criticised Ramanathan's role in the 'minorities' scheme', E. R. Thambimuttu even questioned his legitimacy to 'represent the opinion of the Tamils' from outside the Council since he was a nominated, not an elected, member. Ramanathan was frequently subjected to ridicule by people in his own community who referred to him gracelessly as the 'nominated Knight' and an old man 'obsessed by personal magnificence'. 'I do not deny for a moment', said Thambimuttu, 'the high position occupied, and rightly occupied by the veteran Knight in our community. But it is one thing not to deny the high position, and another, to state that he represents all the people in the community, for the reason that he was not elected by them.'[17] These 'corrupt' and 'selfish factions' of the north and the east, according to Vythilingam, exploited every opportunity to discredit and to oppose Ramanathan inside and outside the Council.[18] Vythilingam records in frustration the internal divisions among the Tamils:

> Attempts are being made to pin the blame for the complete collapse of Tamil fortunes on all and sundry, on the Britisher and on our Sinhalese Brethren. But when the tragic history of the Tamils comes to be written, as it must one day come, the world will know the truth, the stark and unflattering truth, that the Tamils were foiled not by enemies from without but rather by enemies from within, that they were their own undoing, that they have none else to blame but their own sweet selves.[19]

Even a local Tamil newspaper, *Morning Star*, noted that the Ceylon Tamil elite was not sure of their stance on socio-political issues since they wanted to be 'individualists in prosperity and communalists in adversity. Our people think very much in terms of individuals and families. We are communalists only when we stand to gain economically'.[20]

The Donoughmore Commission deals a blow to Tamil aspirations

When the Donoughmore Commission was appointed to look into constitutional reforms Ramanathan was approaching his final years. A leadership vacuum was created by the Ponnambalam brothers' deaths. Their decendants, A. Mahadeva (Arunachalam's son), R. Sri Pathmanathan (Arunachalam's son-in-law) and S. Natesan (Ramanathan's son-in-law) succeeded better than other Jaffna Tamil

17 Vythilingam, *Ramanathan of Ceylon*, vol. II, 1977, pp.598–599.
18 Vythilingam, *Ramanathan of Ceylon*, vol. II, 1977, p.595.
19 Vythilingam, *Ramanathan of Ceylon*, vol. II, 1977, p.592.
20 Cited in Russell, *Communal Politics*, 1982, p.24.

leaders to fill the gap but there seemed to be a general absence of direction and purpose. Sandarasegra, for example, an aspiring Tamil leader, was confused about the political direction the Tamil community should take. When among the Tamils in Jaffna, he proclaimed that, if necessary, the Tamil-speaking Northern Province should gain its independence by breaking away from the rest of the island, but when in Colombo, among the Sinhalese, he appeared ready to discard ethnic loyalties in the interests of the Ceylonese nation as a whole.

Thus by the time the Donoughmore Commission[21] came to review constitutional reforms for the island, the traditional Ceylon Tamil elite was in disarray. First, they lacked an imaginative and formidable leadership able to confront their political opponents – in this case, both the Commissioners and Congress. Second, there was no consensus among the Jaffna Association, the Ceylon Tamil Mahãjana Sabhã and the Tamils in the rest of the island as to how to deal with the possibility of Sinhalese hegemony. They were deeply divided in their approach to the constitutional reforms proposed by the Congress. It should be remembered that a significant section of the Ceylon Tamils, in particular, the Colombo Tamils and the Tamil elite in the eastern and the Kandyan districts, remained members of Congress even after the departure of Arunachalam from that body. Significantly, Arunachalam's son, A. Mahadeva, continued to work with the Sinhalese in the Congress becoming secretary in 1925. The leadership of the traditional Ceylon Tamil elite, as Jane Russell records, 'was characterized and debilitated by dissension, indecision and personal squabbles'.[22]

The Donoughmore Commission reforms

The Donoughmore Commission was appointed on 6 August 1927. The Commission, which was not a Royal but a special Commission, was appointed by the Secretary of State for the Colonies L.S. Amery. It was in Sri Lanka from 13 November 1927 to 18 January 1928. The President of the Commission was the Earl of Donoughmore. Other members were Sir Mathew Nathan, Sir Geofffrey Butler and Sir Drummond Shiels. The Commission's terms of reference were 'to visit Ceylon and report on the working of the existing Constitution and on any difficulties of administration which may have arisen in connection with it, to consider any proposals for the revision of the Constitution that may be put forward, and to report what, if any, amendments of the Order in Council now in force should be made'.[23] The deficiencies of the existing 'Manning Constitution'

21 See details, Namasivayam, *The Legislatures of Ceylon*, 1950, pp.24–25. See *The Report of the Special Commission on the Constitution*, London, 1928. See critical examination of the Donoughmore Constitution, I.D.S. Weerawardana, *Government and Politics in Ceylon 1931–1946*, Ceylon Economic Research Association: Colombo, 1951.

22 See, generally, Russell, *Communal Politics*, 1982, pp.79–80.

23 Donoughmore Report, 1932, p.3.

of 1924[24] was accepted by many – indeed by both the Tamils and the Sinhalese – except by Governor Sir Herbert Stanley (1927–1931), who felt that the Manning Constitution was 'a qualified success'. He believed that it should have been given a further trial. Nonetheless, he admitted that an 'intrinsically better and more liberal constitution' might be helpful in addressing certain issues in the island.[25]

With the arrival of the Donoughmore Commission, ethnic politics on the island gained a new lease of life with each group vying to make clear their respective community's views about representation to the Legislative Council.[26] It should be noted that most ordinary people of both Tamil and Sinhalese descent did not share the ethnically based political passions of their leadership.[27] It was evident that both the Sinhalese elite of Congress and the Ceylon Tamils were equally preparing the groundwork for the ensuing 'battle'. In fact, the Donoughmore Commission's report includes a mention of the fact that even before it had set foot in Sri Lanka, it had received 'some seventy memoranda from individuals and associations' each seeking to further its own cause.[28] A large number of these petitions came from those Tamil organizations opposing any significant changes to the existing constitution and, in particular, to the method of representation to the Legislative Council.

Both the Jaffna Association and the Ceylon Tamil Mahãjana Sabhã, the main Tamil political groupings were dissatisfied with any constitutional reforms that might weaken their position in the Legislative Council. They were determined to fight to protect what they considered their fair share in the Sri Lankan polity. The Manning Constitution of 1924, from their perspective, was operating perfectly well and should not be subject to wholesale change. With this Constitution their 'respectable' representation in the Legislative Council was guaranteed. The Manning Constitution had had the effect of reducing Sinhalese domination of the Council. With the proposed new changes, Tamil representation and influence

24 By the Order in Council of 1923 the Legislative Council was established. The Council was inaugurated in 1924. The constitution was popularly known as the Manning Constitution because most of the constitutional reforms were initiated by the Governor Manning.

25 Cited in Jeffries, *Ceylon: The Path to Independence*, 1962, pp.49–50.

26 Throughout the island various groups, many of which was previously unheard of, suddenly began to present themselves as representatives of a particular group/community that they represented. Of these, Negambo Baratha Association, Moors Political Association, Colombo Christian Chetties Association, Batticaloa North League, Batticaloa Peoples Association, Batticaloa Muslim Association, Kandyan National Assembly and Kandyan Union, Swajathi Abiwardhana Mahajana Sabha, Kandy Malay Club, Kandy Malay Association, Head Kanganies Association, Jaffna Association, Jaffna Rate Payers Association, Jaffna Catholic Diocesan Union, Jaffna Depressed Tamils Service League, Catholic Union of Ceylon, The Ceylon Tamil League, Swarajist Party, and branches of Sinhala Mahãjana Sabhã, should particularly be mentioned. See Donoughmore Report, 1932, pp.159–160.

27 It should be briefly remarked here until the later years of the 1950s ordinary Sinhalese and Tamils had not shown any interests in ethnically based politics neither were they convinced that it was worth engaging in.

28 Donoughmore Report, 1932, p.155.

would be severely reduced and the Sinhalese would enjoy hegemony through numerical superiority in perpetuity.

From the moment of the Donoughmore Commission's arrival, it was clear to the Ceylon Tamils that they were on a sticky wicket. Any credible defence for the retention of ethnically based representation would be a difficult task. The Manning Constitution's ethnically based representation was not a permanent solution since the leadership of Congress had cooperated with the Manning Constitution only when the governor promised its President, James Pieris and others that within a year a new commission would be established to introduce comprehensive reforms. According to the Donoughmore Commision, the Manning Constitution was no more than an interim arrangement in the political advancement of Sri Lanka:[29] 'Although communal representation was continued in the last revision of the constitution, a step in the right direction was taken by giving communities a territorial as well as a communal vote. This may have involved an apparent unfairness to the majority communities in that it gave a member of a minority community two and sometimes more votes.'[30]

If election to the Legislative Council were to be made on a territorial basis, then the Ceylon Tamils with just 11 per cent of the population could not defend any longer the position that they had held in the Council for over three-quarters of a century. When a new commission was appointed staffed with men of radical instincts, such as a Cambridge don and an MP, Sir Geoffrey Butler and Dr Drummond Shiels, a Labour MP with Fabian views,[31] the Ceylon Tamils elite knew that they were at the end of orthodox, elite politics. It was this fear that forced them to campaign, through various Tamil organisations, to preserve the status quo. When the Commissioner visited Colombo and Jaffna, there were myriad Tamil organisations petitioning him. Sir P. Ramanathan's newest organisation, the Ceylon Tamil League, the All-Ceylon Tamil Conference (which his nephew represented), the Jaffna Association, the Jaffna Rate Payers Association, the League of Christian Citizenship and the Jaffna Catholic Diocesan Union all expressed the same fears. The Tamil League was formed originally by Sir Ponnambalam Arunachalam, but when he died the Tamil League almost disappeared from the political scene. Ramanathan realised that this was the perfect opportunity to rescue it from its oblivion and to enhance the Tamil organisations. He did this on the eve of the arrival of the Donoughmore Commission. (It is noteworthy that, except for the Jaffna Depressed Tamil Service League and the North Ceylon Workers' Union, all these various Tamil organisations were represented by a small caucus of the Tamil *Vellala* elite. For example, Sir Ramanathan was a leading member of the Jaffna Association when he decided to resurrect his brother's organisation. It later emerged that one of its other leading members was Waitilingam Duraiswamy, a stalwart of the Jaffna Association. The previously unheard of All-Ceylon Tamil

29 Donoughmore Report, 1932, p.18.

30 Donoughmore Report, 1932, p.100.

31 Namasivayam, *The Legislatures of Ceylon*, 1950, p.24.

Conference was represented by Mr Sri Pathmanathan, a nephew of Ramanathan. Pathmanathan was a leading member of both the Jaffna Association and Ramanathan's Tamil League.) A group of Ceylon Moors also argued that without adequate safeguards for the minority communities in the island the existing constitution should not be changed. They urged the Commissioners to extend the communal representation based on ethnicity and religion to the Legislative Council.[32] A notable absentee from these discussions was the Jaffna Tamil Youth Congress, which campaigned against the visiting commissioners with the view to achieve *swaraj* for the whole island.

The Ceylon Tamil elite attempted to hold back any significant changes to the existing constitution. They had to convince the visiting Commissioners that it was necessary to retain communal representation in the Legislative Council as a counterpoise to future Sinhalese dominance. Any significant shift towards territorial representation, as they argued later, would be no more than a political windfall for the majority community, the Sinhalese. Unfortunately, their position was compromised by the fact that if they were successful, only the interests of a small caucus of the *Vellalas* would have been protected.

The members of the Commission were determined *ab initio* that the whole system should be underpinned by democratic institutions. In its view, the Manning Constitution did not have a 'complete and finished structure' to accommodate the Ceylonese who were politically ready for independence. 'Changes were needed', was the simple message of the Commissioners even before they set about their task. The existing political arrangement, namely, the Manning Constitution, was *a reductio ad absurdum*.[33]

Communal representation, 'one of the most difficult questions'

The perpetuation of communal representation in the State Council was 'one of the most difficult problems'.[34] Even though communal representation was introduced in many British colonies as a step towards the development of democratic institutions in the hope of eliminating clashes among the different 'racial' and communal groups, in the view of the Commissioners, the desired socio-political goal in Ceylon had not been achieved.[35] The Commissioners concluded that the former constitution was 'expected to provide, peacefully, an effective legislative assembly which would give a fair representation of the different elements in the population and would also tend to promote unity. Unfortunately, the experiment did not produce the desired results, but had had, if anything, the opposite effect.'[36]

32 Donoughmore Report, 1932, pp.94–95.

33 Donoughmore Report, 1932, p.19. See also Jeffries, *Ceylon – The Path to Independence*, 1962, p.50.

34 Donoughmore Report, 1932, p.90.

35 Donoughmore Report, 1932, p.90.

36 Donoughmore Report, 1932, pp.90–91.

The arguments of the representatives of the Congress, most notably of E.W. Perera, succeeded in swaying the Commissioners away from communal representation. According to Perera, racial representation was 'the barbaric survival of the original council of 1833 which gave unofficial recognition' to members on a racial basis. 'It was only a temporary measure to enable certain communities with historical traditions to have their voices heard in the Legislative Council'; the maintenance of communal representation against the wishes of the majority of the island, argued Perera, would be detrimental to national unity.[37] The Commissioners agreed with this view that the communal form of appointment to the Legislative Council was an 'evil' scheme[38] that should be eliminated from the future electoral process with a view to creating an environment wherein the different ethnic and community groups could work together irrespective of their differences. The Commission found that communal representation in Sri Lanka had no real antiquity to commend it, and its introduction into the constitution with the best of intentions had had unfortunate results in that it tended 'to keep communities apart and to send communal representatives to the Council with the idea of defending particular interests instead of giving their special contribution to the common weal'.[39] It concluded:

> We might have been encouraged to suggest the retention of some communal representation if there had been evidence of any diminution of the supposed necessity for it. We found however, that not only did those who already had communal seats desire that the number of these should be increased, but also that a number of other communities, religions, castes and special interests, not at present represented, came before us claiming that it was necessary for them to have seats in the Legislative Council and that they were as much entitled to this privilege as those who already possessed it. The result was that, so far from the demand being reduced, increased and new claims were put forward which would have made the number of communal seats more than 50, instead of the 10 already existing. Our investigations show that the desire for communal representation tends to grow rather than to die down, and, in these circumstances, it being in itself admittedly undesirable, it would seem well to abolish it altogether while the number of seats involved is comparatively small.[40]

Given the early careers of the Ponnambalam brothers this is a harsh assessment but the Commission was certainly correct that the form of representation meant that communities would be encouraged to expect their representatives to look after their own community's interests. More precisely, the Commissioners felt that 'the

37 Donoughmore Report, 1932, pp.90–91.
38 Donoughmore Report, 1932, p.99.
39 Donoghmore Report, 1932, p.99.
40 Donoughmore Report, 1932, pp.99–100.

very existence of communal representation' would obstruct any future co-habitation of the diverse communities in the island and prevent any formation of the democratic, political party system similar to that of Britain. The demands of both the Jaffna and Colombo Tamils for a special seat in Colombo, known as the Western Province Tamil seat, were also rejected by the Commissioners. The Tamil representatives argued that in the pre-1919 discussions between the Jaffna Association and the Sinhalese representatives of the Ceylon Reform League (E.J. Samarawickreme) and the Ceylon National Association (James Pieris), it was agreed by both parties for an especially reserved seat in the Western Province for the Colombo Tamils. But this agreement was rejected by the Commission. It noted that there were 'no good reasons for its continuance'. It was held that even though there might have obtained some understanding between the two major racial groups in the island such secret pacts 'cannot take precedence' over the interests of the Ceylon people as a whole.[41]

The Donoughmore Commission's 'utterly stupid' proposals

The radical reforms proposed by the Commissioners of universal adult suffrage and equality of opportunity were a bolt from the blue and dismayed the Tamil leadership. According to the Ceylon Tamil elite, universal adult suffrage and equality of opportunity were damaging proposals thrown at them by 'fumbling rulers' sent by Whitehall. The Commissioners were no more than 'misguided politicians who take pride in being the trustees of selfish suffragists who have been sent against the might of God'.[42] Vythilingam recorded the betrayed feelings of the Tamil elite who felt that the Commissioners were no more than a bunch of men from thousands of miles away, ignorant of local conditions, of the history, geography, and variety of races, religions, languages and traditions of the land, but 'presuming, after a hasty and superficial inquiry, to hammer out a constitution calculated to sustain the destinies of the heterogeneous elements comprising several millions of the country's population'. The report was simply a mass of 'impracticable, unrealistic, illusory ideological abstractions'.[43] The outraged feeling of a significant minority on the island boded ill for the proper working of the Constitution or the creation of feelings of amity between the different ethnic groups. The Commission had also neglected to address the matter of adequate safeguards for individual rights or for the rights of minorities.

When universal adult suffrage (voting rights for male above 21 and 30 years for the women) without qualifications such as literacy or property was pressed by the Donoughmore Commissioners so as to allow everyone to take part in the process

41 Donoughmore Report, 1932, p.93.

42 The Memorandum of Sir Ponnambalam Ramanathan on the Recommendations of the Donoughmore Commisioners appointed by the Right Honourable the Secretary of State for the Colonies to Report upon the Reform of the Existing Constitution of the Government of Ceylon, 1924–1930, London, p.20.

43 Vythilingam, *Ramanathan of Ceylon*, vol. II, 1977, p.679.

of electing their members to the Legislative,[44] Ramanathan led the protest arguing that this was a 'transfer of political power to a dangerous mob' and would destroy the fundamentals of the Jaffna Hindu Tamil society. Ramanathan passionately believed that the enfranchisement of the masses was a 'premature enthronement of the uneducated, unenlightened and indisciplined masses in the seat of power'.[45] This would, he argued, 'let loose dark and tyrannical forces and result in the helm of state being seized by ambitious and adventurous demagogues, power hungry mob-leaders and rabid, racialist party-bosses, men devoid of character or attainment'.[46] Ramanathan questioned the thinking behind this bold political move demanding to know whether there was 'anything sacrosanct about adult suffrage as a form of parliamentary representation?'. He declared that the 'leaders of the people did not ask for it nor could the commissioners feel in their heart of hearts that the country was ripe for it.' The fact was that 'illiteracy was rampant and political consciousness and experience confined to a very meagre section of the adult population.' In a memorandum to the governor, he stated his objections:

> What then would be the fate of the different races in Ceylon where only a very small percentage of the people have received elementary education, where the vast majority of the people have not learnt to manage their own affairs properly . . . ? Universal suffrage for a people who have not been given universal elementary education and sound training in business methods will assuredly lead to the filling of the legislature with speculators and schemers, skilled in robbing Peter to pay Paul.[47]

He expressed his extreme concern when he learnt that 'with one stroke of the pen' the Commissioners had 'recommended universal suffrage and the abolition of communal representation',[48] ignoring all the drawbacks that were brought to their attention by the leaders of the Tamil community.[49] He felt that the Commissioners' recommendations were acts of treachery, a gratuitous and wanton betrayal of the solemn trust the Tamil nation had reposed in the hands of the colonial government. When he found that his pleadings had fallen on deaf ears, he fulminated: 'Who are they, the Commissioners, to adjudicate upon what is good and what is bad for the country? What are their credentials for the very weighty and arduous task they had taken on themselves to perform? . . . Was it their motive to foist on the country a constitution that was beyond human ingenuity to work successfully and then

44 Donoughmore Report, 1932, p.97.

45 Vythilingam, *Ramanathan of Ceylon*, vol II, 1977, p.678.

46 Vythilingam, *Ramanathan of Ceylon*, vol.II, 1977, p.682.

47 Sir P. Ramanathan, The Memorandum of Sir Ponnambalam Ramanathan on the Recommendations of the Donoughmore Commisioners appointed by the Right Honourable the Secretary of State for the Colonies to Report upon the Reform of the Existing Constitution of the Government of Ceylon, 1924–1930, London, 1930 p.20.

48 Vythilingam, *Ramanathan of Ceylon*, vol. II, 1977, p.685.

49 Vythilingam, *Ramanathan of Ceylon*, vol. II, 1977, p.685.

proclaim to the wider world outside the inherent incapacity of subject peoples to rule themselves?'[50]

Ramanathan engaged in a futile visit to London to canvass against the Commission's Report, in particular its recommendation of the complete abolition of communal representation and the introduction of universal suffrage. His final public speech shortly before his death was about the Donoughmore Constitution and its negative bearing on traditional Hindu society. In the conference hall of 'Ramanathan College in Jaffna, he made his speech clad simply in a 'plain dhoti, a shirt and a shawl'. With no turban on his head, the little tuft of hair he had on his head all through his life, fitting for an orthodox Hindu, was visible. He looked melancholic and spoke in a voice charged with emotion. 'Gentlemen, dangerous times are ahead of us. The Donoughmore Commissioners have framed a constitution which will be the ruin of the country . . . The uninstructed masses will henceforth choose your rulers . . . I have before my eyes a surging mob . . . Beware; our future is in peril.'[51] Vythilingam, his biographer, says: 'His was a voice of a Cassandra prophesying doom, when he warned his countrymen against the wisdom of accepting a Constitution formulated by ignorant and self-opinionated foreigners whose sole motive was to create anarchy and chaos in a land where they were no longer welcome.'[52] The removal of the barriers with respect to voting rights was a 'kick in the teeth' for both the Tamil and Sinhalese elites. The latter had also expressed their own misgivings which were similar to Ramanathan's.[53]

Elite Tamil politics versus the depressed and low-caste groups

The Commissioners were also persuaded by the arguments presented by the 'depressed' Tamil groups in the Northern and the Eastern Provinces and in particular by the Young Lanka League of A.E. Gunasinghe for more rights for disadvantaged groups and equal opportunities for all, irrespective of wealth or prestige. Gunasinghe argued that if the existing franchise requirements were to remain in place in the aftermath of the Donoughmore Report at least 40,000 members of his labour union would be excluded from the political process in the foreseeable future. It was necessary, from the Commissioners' point of view, therefore to educate the ordinary people of the island about their rights, which were hitherto enjoyed only by elite males, irrespective of the vested interests of the oligarchic clans. For this, the Commissioner stressed that it was necessary to give ordinary people an opportunity to take part in public life, and most importantly they were persuaded of the need to eradicate communal representation.

50 Vythilingama, *Ramanathan of Ceylon*, vol. II, 1977, pp.683–684.
51 Vythilingam, *Ramanathan of Ceylon*, vol. II, 1977, p.732.
52 Vythilingam, *Ramanathan of Ceylon*, vol.II, 1977, pp.732–733.
53 Donoughmore Report, 1932, p.83.

The Commissioners found that of the island's population of over five million people – including 1,180,000 males and 975,000 females – only male citizens qualified to vote in elections in terms of Article XXVI of the *Order in Council* of 1923. Various criteria such as the literary test, age limit and property qualifications were barriers to low-income families, oppressed groups and low-caste people taking part in public life.[54] 'The present adult generations have', said the Commissioners, 'been denied education. Indeed it is only recently as a result of Government pressure, that a few of the present generation have been allowed to share the instruction of the more fortunate children, albeit under conditions which mark their inferior status.'[55] The Commissioners, in a sympathetic tone noted that they would be hesitant to recommend the imposition of any qualification that would have the effect of denying to these people the political status enjoyed by 'their more fortunate fellows and the opportunity of escaping from conditions some of which are incongruous in any country with established democratic institutions'.[56] As correctly observed by the Commissioners, it was only a small clique of the Sinhalese and Tamil elite who had benefited from close proximity to the colonial administration.

The predicament of the depressed and low-caste Tamils in the Northern and Eastern Provinces, as acknowledged by the Commissioners, 'has caused us some concern and anxiety'.[57] It was submitted on behalf of the low-caste and depressed Tamils in the Peninsula by the Jaffna Depressed Tamils Service League that they had been denied even their most fundamental rights by the high-caste Tamil *Vellalas*. Some castes such as *parayas*, for example, were not allowed to be seen in the daylight. Others were kept as slaves such as *koviyars* (domestic servants of the *Vellalas*), *chandars*, *pallas* (landless labourers), *vannars* (washermen), *ambattars* (barbers) and *nalavas* (toddy tappers).[58] Even though rãjakãriya (slavery) was abolished in the island in 1832 by the colonial government except for a small section of the *Karaiyar* (fishing caste) other low castes remained virtually enslaved even after a century of the promulgation of this law.[59] As a magistrate, C. Coomaraswamy, observed in a

54 According to Article XXVI (1) the following, among others, were disqualified: (b) a female; (c) is not the age of 21 years; (d) is unable to read and write English, Sinhalese, or Tamil; (h) does not have or hold one of the following qualifications, viz:- (i) the possession or enjoyment of a clear annual income of not less than Rs. 600 . . . (ii) the ownership of immovable property, either in his own right, or in right of his wife . . . situated within the electoral district . . . the value of which after allowing for any mortgage debts thereon is no less than Rs. 1,500.

55 Donoughmore Report, 1932, p.86.

56 Donoughmore Report, 1932, p.86.

57 Donoughmore Report, 1932, p.97.

58 See, on caste divisions on the Jaffna Peninsula, H.W. Tambiah, *Laws and Customs of the Tamils of Jaffna*, Times of Ceylon, Colombo, 1951; A. Wright (ed.), *Twentieth Century Impressions of Ceylon*, Lloyds Greater Britain Publishing Company: London, 1907.

59 It was reported in 1933 that several houses of *parayas* were burnt down when a *paraya* wore shoes in a church. See *Morning Star*, 26 May 1933. On another occasion it was reported, and even debated in the State Council, that two low-caste Tamil members of the village committee was not allowed to sit on the chairs in committee meetings. S.W.R.D. Bandaranaike, *Towards a New Era, Selected*

murder case in which a *Vellala* man was tried for murdering a *parayar* that the *Vellalas* were still unaware of the fact 'that the world is changing fast; that it is no longer possible for one class of people to dominate another, and that every individual, however humble, is entitled to the unrestricted exercise of his bare elementary rights.'[60]

The Commissioners found that there were between 70,000 to 80,000 persons of low-caste and depressed groups who were kept out of the socio-political life of the Jaffna Peninsula. To alleviate this social injustice it was necessary to introduce measures to enable them to 'gain a new status and self-respect as possessing one of the highest privileges of citizenship'.[61] The Commission's indictment was harsh. They noted the caste divisions among the Sinhalese as well but judged that the low castes among the Sinhalese were not subjected to the 'Peninsula treatment'. Attempts by the Ceylon Tamil elite to preserve the status quo in their representation in public life were also criticised: 'Tamils had obtained political influence somewhat disproportionate to their numerical strength.' This was, in the Commission's view, 'unfair to the majority community'.[62] The leadership of the Ceylon Tamil, quite literally, found themselves encircled on all sides, in a bleak winter from which there seemed to be no way out. With the implementation of a new constitution, it was clear that the Tamil elite faced two enemies – the Sinhalese elite and the depressed and low castes from within their own community.

The measures proposed by the Donoughmore Commissioners to take 'action to break down the social prejudices to emancipate the masses in the Northern Province',[63] also came under attack from Ramanathan who opposed such measures. He argued that the status quo was a kind of religious norm imposed on human beings by a supreme God. If such interventions took place in contravention of the island's social and religious norms, the 'Hindu way of life' would be in danger.[64]

The new measures empowered oppressed groups in the north and east to a degree that they had never previously experienced. Up until now, the representation to the Legislative Council from the Tamils seemed the natural birthright of the high-caste *Vellalas* of the Tamil elite both in the Jaffna Peninsula and Colombo. The Ponnambalam-Coomaraswamy clan (who came from the *Vellalas* of Manipay, considered the highest category among the *Vellalas* and close

Speeches in the Legislature of Ceylon, 1931–1959, Department of the Information of the Government of Ceylon: Colombo, 1961, p.68. All these cases are cited in Russell, pp.12–13.

60 In this case, a *Nalavas* was shot dead by a man who belonged to the *Vellala* caste, for trying to cremate a dead body of his own caste. See *Hindu Organ*, 5 January 1934, cited in Russell, *Communal Politics*, 1982, p.12.

61 Donoughmore Report, 1932, p.86.

62 Donoughmore Report, 1932, p.92.

63 Donoughmore Report, 1932, p.2.

64 P. Ramanathan, Memorandum on the Donoughmore Constitution, London, 1934, p.4, Russell, *Communal Politics*, 1982, p.16.

associates of the Tamil kings) had been able to hold to this position since the latter half of the nineteenth century until 1930. Any social and political reforms that might affect the socio-religious structure of traditional Hindu society would be a death blow to the pride and prestige of the Tamil elite. It was unthinkable even to suggest that a western educated, high-caste *Vellala* member should go to the doorsteps of 'abject and despised races begging their votes'? The effect of the Donoughmore Commission on the Tamil community was not forgotten by the Ceylon Tamils for years. The *Catholic Guardian*, a local newspaper in the Jaffna Peninsula, wrote about the Commissioners, alleging, that the reform 'suffers from having been framed by a man with socialistic views. Socialists are to a large extent idealists.'[65]

It is not difficult to understand, against this social background, that the campaign of the Ceylon Tamil elite would not have advanced all Tamils in the Jaffna Peninsula or the rest of the island. The Donoughmore Commision observed that the campaign was a 'noble' attempt to preserve the interests of the *Vellalas*.[66] The intervention by the Donoughmore Commissioners, at a time when the Ceylon Tamil elite enjoyed a unique social and professional status unchallenged by the oppressed low castes upset the whole social structure of the traditional Ceylon Tamil elite.

The Sinhalese and Tamils make common cause

The only course left to the Tamil leadership was to win the support of the Sinhalese representatives of the Legislative Council to defeat the Commission's Report. The principal argument presented by the Tamil members of the Legislative Council was free of communal interests and this point was emphasised during the debate on the Commission's report. They argued that the reforms did not go far enough in the campaign for self-rule for the island.[67] They also expressed their 'disgust' that the governor was still to retain an unacceptable level of executive power under the proposed constitutional reforms. The executive committee system and the adult suffrage were the other two proposals that were also severely criticised by the Tamil members of the Legislative Council. It should be mentioned that the Moor member of the Council, T.B. Jayah, agreed with these criticisms.

The Tamil members of the Legislative Council were well aware that the Sinhalese elite were also opposed to the introduction of universal suffrage for fear that their power base would also be eroded irreparably if ordinary people were given an opportunity to decide their representatives. These concerns were raised by a deputation of the Congress led by E.W. Perera (President), S.W.R.D. Bandaranaike and R.S.S. Gunawardana (joint secretaries), all of whom were

65 *Catholic Guardian*, 17 January 1936, cited in Russell, *Communal Politics*, 1982, p.83.
66 Donoughmore Report, 1932, pp.31–42.
67 *Ceylon Daily News*, 14 August 1929, cited in Russell, *Communal Politics*, 1982, p.20.

Sinhalese, to the Donoughmore Commission. Even though it was noted in their written documentation that they were not particularly concerned with the franchise, it was clear from their oral evidence that if the universal adult suffrage were conferred on ordinary men and women without strict qualifications, a class of person who did not have any qualities to uphold the high offices in the Legislative Council and whose vote could be 'bought' by interested parties, would be elected. It was further argued on the issue of the franchise for women that if they were to be enfranchised there should be in place 'rigid literacy or a property qualification'.[68] However, their opposition to universal, adult suffrage was not strenuously pursued. They were ultimately prepared to accept the reforms proposed by the Commissioners on a *quid pro quo* basis. They wanted their other, more important demand, that is, communal representation in preference to the territorial electoral principle, to be accepted.

If opposition to universal adult suffrage was continued by both the Sinhalese and the Tamil elite, it was conveyed through the governor by the Secretary of State for the Colonies, that the reforms proposed by the Donoughmore Commission report, would not be implemented. When some representatives of both Sinhalese and Tamils tried to vote for individual proposals, one at a time, during the debate of the Commissioners' Report at the Legislative Council they were told by the governor that the 'recommendations must be regarded as a whole'. It further transpired that the Secretary of State would not accept any proposals that 'would destroy the balance of the scheme'.[69] If the Sinhalese elite representatives succeeded in opposing the proposed reform because it would enable the ordinary people and low caste to take part in public life and in the elections to the Legislative Council, both the Tamil representatives and the Sinhalese would have achieved what each wanted.

Why did the Tamil members of the Legislative Council display such a radical outlook? Were they really dissatisfied with the fact that the governor would keep greater executive power in the aftermath of the reform? Were their protests based on the fact that the proposal would not accelerate the self-governing status for the island as some radical forces in the island complained?

If the Sinhalese Congressmen in the Legislative Council had risen to the patriotic arguments of the Tamil members it would have secured the latter's advantageous position in the Council but it would also have prolonged their leadership position in the Jaffna Peninsula. The Ceylon Tamils' opposition to the new Constitution was their fear that 'with the ratio vis-à-vis the Sinhalese being reduced from 2:1 to 5:1 under the Donoughmore Constitution, they would be unable to safeguard their position any more.'[70] If the Donoughmore Constitution was rejected by the Council members, the Manning Constitution of 1924 would remain – as warned by the Secretary of State for the Colonies.

68 de Silva, *A History of Sri Lanka*, 1981, pp.419–420.

69 Cmd. 3419, p.16, Correspondence regarding the Constitution of Ceylon, 1929.

70 Russell, *Communal Politics*, 1982, p.24.

However, the hopes of the Tamil representatives of the Legislative Council did not materialize. Only two Sinhalese, one of whom was E.W. Perera, a Congressman and former President of Congress, were opposed to the Commission Report agreeing with the Tamils that the reforms did not go far enough. A representative of the Moors, T.B. Jayah, also voted with Tamils because the Moors were put in a disadvantaged position by the proposed constitution.[71] One Tamil representative, E.R. Thambimuttu, voted with the Sinhalese representatives. The final vote was 19 to 17 when the draft proposal was put to the vote on 12 December 1929.[72] Even after this defeat, the Tamil members moved that the constitutional reform still be rejected since it was passed by only a single vote majority. By then, as Sir Charles Jefferies quite aptly observed, 'the die was cast.'[73]

At the end of the debate, there were winners and losers. The losers were the Ceylon Tamil elite who had enjoyed equal status at the State Council with the Sinhalese for most of the nineteenth century and the first two decades of the twentieth century. Nonetheless, some safeguards were entrenched in the constitution by requiring that the governor act as an umpire in cases where proposed legislation, in the opinion of the governor, might affect the rights of minority groups. In such instances, Royal Assent could be withheld by the governor. These are:

> Any Bill whereby persons of any particular community or religion are made liable to any disabilities or restrictions to which persons of other communities or religions are not also subjected or made liable, or are granted advantages not extended to persons of other communities or religions;
>
> Any Bill diminishing or prejudicing any of the rights or privileges to which, at the date of these Our Instructions, persons emigrating, or who have emigrated, to the island from India may be entitled by reason of such emigration;
>
> Any Bill the principle of which has evoked serious opposition by any racial, religious, or other minority and which in the opinion of the Governor is likely to involve oppression or unfairness to any such minority.

Communal representation, nearly a century later, in legal terms, disappeared. It was a happy day for the Sinhalese Congressmen in the Legislative Council since their most ardent wish – territorial representation to the Legislative Council – had become the cornerstone of the new Constitution. For the Tamils, their advantageous political position under the Manning Constitution disappeared. In its place was a few safeguards against encroachments on their rights by the electoral majority.

71 Jeffries, *Ceylon: The Path to Independence*, 1962, p.52.
72 See more details, Weerawardana, *Government and Politics*, 1951.
73 Jeffries, *Ceylon: The Path to Independence*, 1962, p.60.

10 Thamil Arasu and S.J.V Chelvanayakam

Emergence of federalism in Ceylon

According to the 1911 census, 14.8 per cent of Ceylon and Indian Tamils lived outside the north and east, in predominantly Sinhalese regions. By the time of the 1953 census this demographic had altered dramatically. Before the colonisation of the island, the Sinhalese and Tamils lived in different localities with implicitly demarcated boundaries. While the Ceylon Tamils inhabited the Jaffna Peninsula and surrounding regions, and some parts of the coastal areas of the east, the Sinhalese had settled in the south, west, east and the central-north. A few thousands of Sinhalese made their home in the Peninsula. The situation did not require any consociatonal structure to accommodate differences of race or ethnicity. The Tamils and Sinhalese lived largely in separate social spheres but interacted with each other in trade and in other commercial activities. This pattern changed dramatically with the conquest of the island, first by the Portuguese and then by the Dutch and finally with the arrival of the British in the first decade of the eighteenth century. Jaffna Tamils migrated in large numbers into areas previously inhabited mainly by the Sinhalese. This migration became significant from the middle of the nineteenth century. The Tamils went as traders and to take up positions in the colonial administration. Many Jaffna Tamils went south to practise in the medical, legal and engineering professions. The number of Tamils now living in Sinhalese-dominated areas had increased from 14.8 to 23.6 per cent. Migration of Sinhalese to predominantly Tamil- and Muslim-inhabited areas also gradually increased. There was only 1.8 per cent Sinhalese in the north and east in 1911 and by 1953 this increased to 6.6 per cent. Robert N. Kearney notes that the Tamils had become a significant section of the population in 12 of 15 administrative districts outside the Northern and Eastern Provinces.[1]

The determining factors behind these demographic shifts appeared to be professional and employment related as a result of the emergence of new trading and industrial possibilities. The increasingly southward movement of the Jaffna

1 E.B. Denham, *Ceylon at the Census of 1911 Government Printer: 1912; Census of Ceylon*, Department of Census and Statistics: Colombo, 1952 cited in Kearney, *Communalism and Language*, 1967, p.12.

Tamils to the Sinhalese-inhabited areas created an ethnically plural society of several languages and religions. In many places a transformation in the perception of group identity occurred. Gradually neighbours became competitors for limited resources and especially for government employment. This increased ethnic consciousness among competing community groups but not yet in a troublesome way. However, since the second decade of the twentieth century ethnicity had become enough of a problem for some to argue that only a federal system along the lines of communal and linguistic differences could solve the problem.

Federalism was not given any serious consideration at the beginning, however, since the 1940s the main objective of a new political movement led by S.J.V. Chelvanayakam was the equal rights of the Ceylon Tamils in a federal structure. The Tamils were initially unconvinced and remained sceptical of the suggestion that their future could only be secured in a semi-autonomous region of the island, but the political debate, involving community groups, academics and political parties in the island, has since been preoccupied with whether a unitary or federal model is better for Sri Lanka.

Sectional interests had gradually and decisively infiltrated national politics since the 1920s beginning with the reluctance of the Jaffna Tamils to accept constitutional reforms that did away with communal representation. Between 1920 and 1930 a virulent communal politics began to thrive among the Sinhalese as well. The aristocrats of the Kandyan Sinhalese insisted that they be regarded as a separate community different to that of the low-country Sinhalese, and their insistence on separateness hindered any attempt by Congress to bring all the communities under one umbrella organisation.

Kandyan aristocracy's campaign for a federal system of government

During the 1920s Congress faced a serious threat from the Kandyan Sinhalese aristocrats who in 1925, formed a separate organisation, rivalling Congress called the Kandyan National Assembly (KNA).[2] KNA was dominated by a number of people from the Kandyan aristocracy among whom were J.H. Meedeniya Adigar, P.B. Nugawela Dissawe, J.C. Ratwatte Dissawe, T.B. Panabokke, J.A. Halangoda, U.B. Dolapihille, P.B. Dolapihille, A.W. Mediwake, Dr T.B. Kobbekaduwa, W. Thalgodapitiya and W. Gopallawa. They argued for a federation of regions for the island along the lines of the US model. They were not willing to be governed by the low-country Sinhalese, neither did they want any Tamil involvement in their 'Kandyan Kingdom'. They claimed that low-country Sinhalese were a different ethnic group and different to that of the Kandyan Sinhalese. The Kandyan Sinhalese were the first to insist on separatism based on communal differences.

2 See Wickrameratne, 'Kandyans and Nationalism in Sri Lanka', 1975, p.59.

The KNA submitted its views in a memorandum entitled 'The Detailed Proposals for the Reform of the Constitution' to the Donoughmore Commission, in which it proposed that the island be divided into 'three parts' or three nationalities based on ethnically different regions, namely the Marttme province (where low-country Sinhalese lived), the Tamil province (which the Ceylon Tamils inhabited) and the Kandyan province (where the principal ethnic group were the up-country Kandyan Sinhalese). Each region, argued the KNA, should be composed of a legislative assembly with legislative and executive powers. There should be a central legislative council composed of the representatives of these three federal units to take decisions for the whole island in matters of national importance. KNA Wickremeratne described the federal structure proposed thus:

> [T]he Kandyan National Assembly declared that if the Low Country Sinhalese and the Tamils refused to join in the federal scheme, the Kandyans should notwithstanding be given local self-government with autonomy of the sort they would have had under a federal scheme. The Kandyans made it known that in such an eventuality they would also like to be represented in the central legislature on the same principles that would govern the representation of the other communities. Kandyan leaders however added that they did not think the Low Country Sinhalese would object to the federal scheme because some prominent countrymen – S.W.R.D. Bandaranaike for one – in their public pronouncements had themselves favoured the idea of a federal form of government for Sri Lanka.[3]

In its submissions to the Donoughmore Commission, KNA's representatives argued that they wanted to 'remain as Kandyans', as a separate nation otherwise '(T)hey would feel the loss.'[4] Any unitary system of government for the island based on territorial representation would' in their view, diminish the distinguished character of the Kandyan province and its people. They argued forcefully that theirs was:

> [N]ot a communal claim or a claim for the aggrandizement of a few: it is the claim of a nation to live its own life to realise its own destiny . . . We suggest the creation of a Federal system as in the United States of America . . . will enable the respective nationals of the State to prevent further inroads into their territories.[5]

As Wickremeratne states, the Kandyan aristocracy did not want to be governed by *outsiders*, that is, low-country Sinhalese or Tamils. They were afraid of being conquered in their 'own' country by the low-country Sinhalese and Tamils. A federal scheme along communal lines was rejected by the Donoughmore

3 Wickrameratne, 'Kandyans and Nationalism in Sri Lanka', 1975, p.62.
4 Wickrameratne, 'Kandyans and Nationalism in Sri Lanka', 1975, p.63.
5 Wickrameratne, 'Kandyans and Nationalism in Sri Lanka', 1975, p.63.

Commission owing to the objections of Congress. Neither did the Ceylon Tamils want to see their powers confined only to a small region of the north and east, most of which were sparsely populated, barren lands. The centre of politics and economic activities of the Ceylon Tamils always had been the capital of the island, Colombo. Tamils had, for a long time since the conquest of the island, been able to wield power in the civil and judicial administration. If they were to have only a small federal unit, most of which would be confined to the east and north regions of the island, they feared that they would lose their national standing and advantageous position they had enjoyed for nearly a century. The ideal solution, in their view, was to share the 'loaves and fishes of office' on an equal footing. The federal scheme of the KNA was given impetus by S.W.R.D Banadaranaike, a rising man in Congress and an aristocrat of an influential low-country family.

Bandaranaike enters the federal fray

Bandaranaike advocated federalism as a solution to potential communal strife on the island. In his view, while preserving their differences, communities on the island could work together without posing any threat to the unitary character of the island. In a series of articles that appeared in May and June of 1926 in the *Ceylon Morning Leader*, he argued that the best devise to achieve this was the introduction of a federal system for the whole island.[6] However, his proposal failed to muster support from either the Sinhalese or Ceylon Tamils. The leadership of Congress was, at the same time, trying hard to discourage any constitutional reforms that would divide the island because of communal or regional differences.

So while almost all the leaders of the Ceylon National Congress were promoting the idea of a 'one-nation' policy if any progression towards self-rule were going to be made, Bandaranaike was promoting communal politics among the Sinhalese, outside national politics. For instance, in April 1923, the then president of Congress reminded its members and the nation, 'Believe in one nation in Ceylon and that was the Ceylonese nation, the salvation of Ceylon is dependent not on the growth of communalism or racialism but on the growth of the true national spirit which the Congress . . . would always foster.'[7]

Bandaranaike faced criticism from both the Tamils and Sinhalese who branded his federal idea 'treacherous'. By then the 'sectional activities' of the Tamils and the Kandyan aristocracy had earned the pejorative epithet 'communalists' and were looked on with contempt by most Congressmen. As Michael Roberts writes, constitutionalist reformists who were trying to bring all the communities on the island to a common platform viewed 'communalism as a dirty word'.

6 Cited in Roberts, 'Ethnic Conflict in Sri Lanka', 1978, p.359. See also C. Vivekanathan, 'When Sinhalese Supported and Tamils Opposed Federalism', www.sundaytimes.lk/030119/column

7 *Handbook*, p.501.

Communalism was to be 'shunned, reviled and exorcised'; 'it does not square with liberal democratic nations.'[8]

When Bandaranaike formed the Sinhala Mahã Sabhã in 1935 (the Great Council of the Sinhalese) it was ridiculed as 'the local variant of brown Fascism',[9] 'a purveyor of romantic racialism' and 'another form of bourgeoisie reaction'. The communal politics of the Sinhala Mahã Sabhã were branded as a 'most rabid, most chauvinistic organization' the aim of which was to target the 'lowest and basest instincts' of the Sinhalese of both low-country and Kandyan origin. Angered by the communal politics of Bandaranaike, leading congressman, George E. de Silva commented that the Sinhala Mahã Sabhã was an 'invidious agency' and warned that those who preached communal sectionalism (including G.G. Ponnambalam) would never be considered 'true patriots or the true sons of our beloved Lanka'.[10] Indeed, there was an attempt between 1939 and 1942, by a few Congressmen such as J.R. Jayawardene, C.P.G. Abeywardena, A.W.H. Abeysundere, Stanley de Zoysa and the Corea brothers, to expel Bandaranaike from the Ceylon National Congress for his engagement in 'communal' politics. Bandaranaike defended his role in the Mahã Sabhã stoutly. In 1939 he wrote:

> We saw differences amongst our own people – caste distinctions, up-country and low-country distinctions, religious distinctions, and various other distinctions – and we therefore, felt that we should achieve unity, which is the goal of us all. Surely the best method is to start from the lower rung; firstly, unity among the Sinhalese, and secondly, whilst uniting the Sinhalese, to work for the higher unity, the unity of all communities . . . This is what the Sinhala Maha Sabha is trying to do. You will observe that the problem is twofold: a) to foster Sinhalese nationalism, b) to establish friendly relations with other communities.[11]

Bandranaike saw the communities as distinct. There is no feeling in his speech of 'one nation' and the argument itself is poor, unity is hardly achieved in this way and it is never initiated with one section of the community. What he really desired was Sinhalese nationalism. His notion of unity was formal – a harmony established

8 Roberts, 'Problems of Collective Identities', 1979, p.349.

9 Roberts (ed.), *Documents of the Ceylon National Congress*, 1977, pp.1294–95, Hansard, SC, July 1939, p.2294.

10 Roberts, 'Problems of Collective Identities', 1979.

11 The speech also contained the following sentiment: 'On the principle of first things first, Sinhalese must first try to unite the Sinhalese, remove from amongst themselves such meaningless differences as those of caste, and create the necessary enthusiasm and selflessness, by fostering a spirit of nationalism. Others should do likewise. While doing so, all must realise that there are common problems, arising out of residence in one country, that must be faced together, and strive to bring about mutual confidence and friendly co-operation, not by denying existing differences, but by admitting them and helping each other in the needs of each.' S.W.R.D. Bandaranaike, *Towards a New Era: Selected Speeches in the Legislature of Ceylon, 1931–1959*, Department of Broadcasting and Information: Colombo, 1961, pp.50–51.

among distinct and separate communities. Bandaranaike justified his federal system of government at the Executive Committee of the Congress, in the State Council, and at the Annual General Meeting of the Sinhala Mahã Sabhã when he tried to convince his followers that only their conception of nationalism would bring about 'true unity and progress in the country'.[12]

In the fine traditions of liberal democracy

During the heyday of Congress there was no violence between the Tamils and the Sinhalese. Their differences were aired within the liberal framework implicitly understood by both camps. The leaders of both communities came from the upper rungs of the society having an advantage over ordinary people through their English education. They were simply, as observed by the then Governor of the island, Sir Henry McCallum, 'a product of the European administration'.[13] Most of them appreciated the parliamentary traditions that operated in the Westminster parliament and themselves enjoyed the cut and thrust of debate in the State Council that their education had fitted them for. They engaged in debates in Council with admirable forensic skills.[14] Thus, their educational and aristocratic backgrounds shaped the conduct of their campaigns in accordance with the fine traditions of liberal democracy. Their approach to constitutional reform was in sharp contrast to that of their Indian counterparts in the Indian National Congress. Instead of non-cooperation with the colonial government and violence against its personnel, the leadership of the Tamils and Sinhalese adopted the approach of dispatches, memoranda and delegations to the Secretary of State for the Colonies and to the governor. Ordinary Sinhalese and Tamils coexisted in peaceful, mutual understanding. Governor Sir Andre Caldecott noted in 1938 that the civilian population in general seemed indifferent to communal politics:

> It is said on all sides that sectionalism has increased under the present Constitution, but my observation is that its increase is limited to the political field and has not extended to the everyday walks of life where there is a large measure of fellowship and understanding.[15]

Resurrection of federalism – Chelvanayakam's arrival

The non-confrontational style of engagement lasted a long while but the intensity of the debate changed when S.J.V. Chelvanayakam entered into the mainstream of Ceylon politics. Chelvanayakam was a Christian, Colombo Tamil, remarkably

12 S.W.R.D. Bandaranaike, *Speeches and Writings*, Department of Broadcasting and Information: Colombo, 1963, p.87.

13 See Dispatches from Sir Henry McCallum to the Earl of Crew, in *Handbook*, p.48.

14 Jennings, 'Nationalism and Political development in Ceylon', 1953, pp.81–82.

15 Great Britain, Colonial Office, Correspondence Relating to the Constitution of Ceylon, Cmd. 5910, 1938, HMSO: London, p.8.

slight and fragile in appearance, yet he headed an increasingly intense campaign matching the intensity of Sinhalese nationalism that was not satisfied with anything less than a Sinhalese Buddhist State. The politics of post-1950s Sri Lanka is mainly the history of how these two sides reacted to and responded to each other's demands.

The 1947 general election was an early indication of what was to come in post-independence Ceylon. Parliamentary elections in the north and east were fought and won by those Tamil candidates who were most convincing in their partisan message. The leadership for these 'tribal' politics was unpredictably provided by ACTC 'whipping up racial feeling' among Tamil voters.[16] The fear of the 'Sinhalese domination and the alleged demise of Tamil rights and Tamil culture'[17] was the core premise on which the ACTC fought its election campaign. The Tamil electorate was reminded that it was time that they should 'walk the land with their heads erect.'[18] None of the Tamil candidates attempted a broader, national appeal. Kearney commented, 'This election served as an early indication of the Tamil voters' preference for exclusively Tamil parties.'[19]

In fact, none of the candidates who fought the election on a non-communal platform succeeded in winning Tamil-dominated constituencies. For example, the son of Sir Ponnambalam Arunachalam, Arunachalam Mahadeva, was defeated by a fiercely fought election in Jaffna by G.G. Ponnambalam who, according to Wilson, defeated the former for his alleged betrayal of the Tamil cause. In fact, Ponnambalam left his safe electorate, Point-Pedro, and selected the Jaffna parliamentary seat to, it seems, 'exact revenge' for Mahadeva's betrayal. The latter fought the election as a UNP candidate emphasising the need for cooperation among ethnic groups. This was the common pattern of the 1947 elections across the Tamil-speaking areas of the north and east but it was not allowed to flare up into 'communalist' confrontations by either the Sinhalese or Tamils. With respect to this, S. Arasaratnam, a leading Tamil historian, made the following observation:

> After independence a conscious effort was made to lay finer foundations for nationhood. Political power was distributed among all communities to an extent that gave them all a sense of participation in the building of nation. National issues were placed in the forefront of political activity. Sectionalism and separatism preached by some groups in all communities were unpopular and did not gain widespread adherence. Admittedly communal issues flared up occasionally, such as over the disenfranchisement of Indian Tamils of the plantations. But protest over such questions was muted and it was generally recognised that direct appeals to communal loyalties should, as far as possible,

16 Kearney, *Communalism and Language*, 1967, p.66.
17 Wriggins, *Ceylon: Dilemma of a New Nation*, p.146.
18 Wilson, *Break-up of Sri Lanka*, 1989, p.75.
19 Kearney, *Communalism and Language*, 1967, p.45.

> be avoided. Communalism was held to be dirty politics and it was felt that it should not blemish the efforts, consciously made, to promote Ceylonese nationalism.[20]

In the immediate aftermath of the 1947 general election, D.S. Senanayake attempted to form a national government by offering cabinet portfolios to Muslim and Tamil MPs. In fact, a new political party, the United National Party (UNP) was launched to signal that the new political organisation was inclusive of all the people of the island. D.S. Senanayake, the former leader of the Board of Ministers which had operated under the Donoughmore Constitution, formed this new political party comprising all community groups.[21] In 1940 he had resigned from the Ceylon National Congress to demonstrate his commitment to a unified nation. It was his desire to inflict a deathblow to communalists, in particular against S.W.R.D. Bandaranaike and G.G. Ponnambalam. Even when he was leader of the Board of Ministers, he took every opportunity to assure all communities in the island that he would not lead or support any communal politics or organisations of which the main objective was to propagate a kind of politics detrimental to national unity.[22] It was a widely held view that Bandaranaike's communal organisation, the Sinhala Mahã Sabhã, was never appreciated by D.S. Senanayake who never encouraged anyone to indulge in partisan politics which would do irreparable damage to the building of a multicultural and multi-ethnic polity.

In the first government formed under the Soulbury Constitution with D.S. Senanayake as Prime Minister, two Tamil MPs, C. Sittamparam (MP for Mannar) and C. Suntheralingam (MP for Vavuniya), were offered cabinet portfolios, respectively Posts and Telecommunications, and Trade and Commerce, which they accepted. Ponnambalam's deputy Chelvanayakam was also offered a cabinet post, but he refused. Wilson claims that Senanayake sent one of his trusted deputies, Edwin Aloysius Perera, to meet Chelvanayakam *in pectro* informing him of the offer of a cabinet portfolio.[23] When Chelvanayakam rejected it, he was offered a seat on the Supreme Court Bench. He refused to accept any of these high offices since it would compromise his Tamil-only policy. G.G. Ponnambalam was not able to join the first cabinet of the Senanyake government due to enormous pressure being placed on him by a group in the ACTC of which S.J.V. Chelvanayakam played the role of 'the guardian of the communalist wing of the Tamil Congress'.[24]

Ponnambalam never quite shared the views of his deputy, Chelvanayakam. He expressed his willingness, during the 1947 election, to engage in 'responsive cooperation' with a future Sinhalese-dominated government providing it would

20 Arasaratnam, 'Nationalism, Communalism and National Unity in Ceylon', in P. Mason (ed.), '*India and Ceylon: Unity and Diversity*',1967, p.262.

21 Bailey, *Ceylon*, 1952, p.149.

22 See de. Silva, *A History of Sri Lanka*, 1981.

23 Wilson, *Break-up of Sri Lanka*, 1989, p.74.

24 Russell, *Communal Politics*, 1982, p.386.

address Tamil concerns.[25] Having realised that it was futile to be in the opposition forever he wanted to join the Senanyake government as a partner, because, under the prevailing Soulbury Constitution, it was impossible for a government to be formed by a Tamil-dominated party. However, a small caucus led by Chelvanayakam had decided on a stubborn non-cooperation stance. Cooperation could only be possible with the Sinhalese-dominated government if their demand for a Tamil state within a federal union was met. It was later revealed that Chelvanayakam and his supporters had sent a telegram after the 1947 election to the British government in London stressing that the Tamil people in the north and the east had rejected the Soulbury Constitution and that this was the platform on which members of the ACTC were elected to the parliament. The crux of their argument was that since they have not accepted the constitutional reforms proposed by the Soulbury Commission they were not bound to accept its legitimacy. It was also argued that the Tamil people were entitled to 'revert to their status before the advent of the Westerners in 1505 . . . by virtue of the right to self-determination'.[26]

On 26 November 1947, moving an amendment to the Crown speech in parliament, he asked, 'If Ceylon is fighting to secede [sic] from the British Empire why should not the Tamil people if they feel like it, secede from the rest of the Country?'[27] Two years later, on 15 February 1949[28] at a political rally in his constituency, Kankesanturai, he stressed that the 'Tamil must govern itself' and argued further that there was 'the elementary right of small nations to have self-determination'.[29] During the 1940s the concept of self-determination was not very clear even among international jurists and statesmen,[30] but Chelvanayakam was using the idea as a basis for securing the minority rights of the Tamils. In fact, by the 1950s self-determination was only just emerging as a nebulous concept in political science.[31]

The leader of the ACTC, Ponnambalam, did eventually accept a cabinet post in August 1948 believing that it was imperative for both communities to work together in post-independence Ceylon. He had never been an admirer of federalism since it would exclude the Tamils from the benefit of commercial and economic activities, which were all centred in the Sinhalese regions. Yet Chelvanayakam and

25 Wilson, *Politics in Sri Lanka*, 1974, p.163.

26 Wilson, *Break-up of Sri Lanka*, 1989, p.73.

27 Hansard, 26 November 1947, colmn. 232, cited in S.L. Gunasekera, *Tigers Moderates and Pandora's Package*, 1996, p.35.

28 The Tamil Federal Party was officially established on 18 December 1949.

29 A.J. Wilson, *S.J.V. Chelvanayakam and the Crisis of Sri Lankan Tamil Nationalism 1947–1977*, C. Hurst & Co.: London, 1994, p.29. See also Helmann-Rajanayagam, 'The Politics of the Tamil Past', in Spencer (ed.), *Sri Lanka: History and the Roots of Conflict*, 1990, p.116.

30 Cassese, *Self-determination of Peoples*, 1995; A. Rigo-Sureda, *The Evolution of the Right to Self-determination*, New York: TY Crowell, 1969.

31 R. Higgins, *The Development of International Law through the Political Organs of the United Nations*, Oxford University Press: London, 1963; D. Ronen, *The Quest for Self-Determination*, 1974.

his supporters were adamantly clinging to the notion that Tamils would be better off with a degree of autonomy.

For Chelvanayakam, the issues of state-aided colonisation, the national flag and the Indian Tamils had to be addressed and a permanent solution to Tamils' problems found. The most stringent demand of Chelvanayakam's group was that the provinces of East and North, which are more than one-third of the island's land, should be recognised by the government as traditional Tamil homelands. The notion of a homeland is the beginning of the alignment of territory with community. The land was never designated Tamil only and the constitution did not allow for discrete, demarcated areas for each community but the fact that Sinhalese peasantry was being encouraged to settle there gave the impression the Tamils were being colonised. It is also true that one of the ways of assimilating a minority people is to 'colonise' areas where they have traditionally lived ensuring that their numbers are diluted.

Clevanayakam laid down the condition that it should only be the Tamil-speaking people who should be allocated lands in any future irrigation or development project in these two provinces. If the government were to accede to this request, the landless peasants in the over-populated areas in the south and west would be permanently excluded from development programmes of the north and east. Chelvanayakam seems to have departed from Ponnambalam's policy of 'responsive cooperation'. Neither did his followers seem committed to a unitary state.[32] It was now Ponnambalam who was branded a traitor who had betrayed the Tamil nation for his personal benefit.[33]

Independence was granted to Ceylon on 4 February 1948 by the *Ceylon Independence Act* of 1947. A year later, the *Eelam struggle* was unofficially declared by a faction of the ACTC led by S.J.V. Chelvanayakam who established a new political party entitled *Ilankai Thamil Arasu Kadchi* (the Federal Freedom Party of the Tamil-speaking People of Ceylon – later known as the Federal Party) on 18 December 1949.

Ilankai Thamil Arasu Kadchi

Chelvanayakam had taken up the plight of the Indian Tamils for citizenship so when the government passed three acts dealing with this matter his partisan[34] approach sharpened and his campaign for a separate federal region emerged as a serious political movement and a threat to the territorial integrity of the island. The relevant pieces of legislation were:

1 the *Ceylon Citizenship Act* (no. J8 of 1949)
2 the *Indian and Pakistani Residence (Citizenship) Act*, no. 3 of 1949
3 the *Ceylon (Parliamentary Elections) Amendment Act*, no. 48 of 1949.

32 Kearney, *Communalism and Language*, 1967, p.46.
33 See Wilson, *Break-up of Sri Lanka*, 1989, pp.74–76.
34 Russell, *Communal Politics*, 1982, pp.321–322.

The objectives of the first two Acts were to regulate Ceylonese citizenship by curbing illegal immigration from South India to limit the influence exercised by the Indian labourers (nearly one million) who had not adopted Ceylonese citizenship when they rejected the opportunity offered by the *Indian and Pakistani Resident Act*. In particular, with the support of the majority of MPs in the ACTC, new laws were introduced regarding eligibility for the register of electors. S. 4 (1) of the *Ceylon Parliamentary Elections Act* postulated that 'no person shall be qualified to have his name enacted or retained in any register of electors in any year if such person – a) is not a citizen of Ceylon, or if he is by virtue of his own act, under any acknowledgement of allegiance, obedience or adherence to any foreign Power or State which is not a member of the Commonwealth.' Within the Indian and Pakistani Residence (Citizenship) Act, there were provisions that offered citizenship to the above individuals on proof of i) ten years' continued residence in Ceylon prior to 1946 without a break of more than 12 months in respect of unmarried persons, or ii) seven years' continued residence for married persons. Two years (the deadline being 5 August 1951) were given to those who wanted to apply for citizenship by registration. This was rejected at the insistence of the Indian Ceylon Tamil Congress (ICTC). which argued that the citizenship law violated s.29 (2) (b) and (c) of the *Ceylon (Constitution) Order in Council, 1946* of the Ceylon Constitution. s.29 (2) (b) states that parliament does not have power to make persons of any community or religion liable to disabilities or restrictions to which persons of other communities or religions are not made liable or (c) confer on persons of any community or religion any privilege or advantage that is not conferred on persons of other communities or religions.

The Indian Tamils challenged the validity of these provisions in *Kodokan Pillai v Mudanayake*,[35] alleging that the intension of the legislature was to prevent Indians acquiring Ceylonese citizenship. When the Attorney-General pointed out that the above citizenship Acts provided an opportunity for Indians to acquire citizenship the appellant surprisingly argued that the Indian and Pakistani Resident Act 'might be *ultra vires* as conferring a privilege upon Indian Tamil within s.29 (2) (c) of the Constitution Order-in-Council'.[36] Refusing the appeal the Privy Council held that 'It is a perfectly natural and legitimate function of the legislation of a country to determine the composition of its nationals . . . The migratory habits of the Indian Tamils are facts which, in the Lordships' opinion, are directly relevant to the question of their suitability of citizens of Ceylon and have nothing to do with them as a community.'[37] Their Lordships concluded that 'the Ceylon legislature did not intend to prevent Indian Tamils from attaining citizenship provided that they were sufficiently connected with the Island.'[38]

35 (1953) 2 WLR 1142, PC.
36 (1953) 2 WLR 1142, PC p.1148.
37 (1953) 2 WLR 1142, PC p.1149.
38 (1953) 2 WLR 1142, PC p.1143.

There is no doubt these three Acts affected a large number of Indian Tamils and Pakistanis who wanted to remain Indians or Pakistanis and have the right to live in Ceylon.[39] These Acts in no way affected the Ceylon Tamils who, like the Sinhalese, acquired their citizenship through birth by the operation of *jus soli.* However, Chelvanayakam took up the cudgels on behalf of the Indian Tamils declaring, 'Today it is the Indian Tamils. Tomorrow, it will be the Sri Lankan Tamils who will be axed.'[40] Not surprisingly, on 10 December 1948, he registered his strong opposition to the Citizenship Act: 'The only communities which are large enough like the Tamils, the Indian and the Muslims cause fear. It is such bodies that the Honourable Prime Minister wants to hit. He is not hitting us now directly. But when the language question comes up, which will be the next one to follow in this series of legislations; we will know where we stand.'[41]

In December 1949 Chelvanayakam, C. Vanniasingham and E.M.V. Naganathan (all of whom were MPs in the first post-independence parliament) with their followers formed the *Ilankai Thamil Arasu Kadchi* (or Federal Party, FP) breaking away from the ACTC. The term *Thamil Arasu* attracted controversy because of the ambiguity of its meaning. It has been pointed out by some that Thamil Arasu means 'Tamil sovereign independent state'. In other words, the principal aim of this political party was to establish a separate Tamil nation state carved out of Ceylon. However, this was disputed by the leadership of the Thamil Arasu, contending that the true meaning was *Tamil Federal State*, which was only one federal unit of Ceylon. A.J. Wilson, a Tamil scholar and son-in-law of Chelvanayakam, writes:[42]

> The English designation is not an exact transalation of the Tamil one. *Ilankai Thamil Arasu Kadchi* means 'the Ceylon Tamil State Party'. The word 'Arasu' could mean 'kingdom', 'government', 'administration', or 'state'. The Tamil opponents of the party have always accused the Federalists of trying to deceive the Tamil people by the use of the word 'Arasu' which they allege has connotations of a separate Tamil state or Kingdom. The federalist leaders, however, have made it very clear in all their pronouncements that what they mean by *'Thamil Arasu'* is an autonomous Tamil state within the framework of a federal state.[43]

However, Wilson points out that Chelvanayakam used 'Thamil Arasu Kadchi' 'to appeal to the nationalism of the Tamil people harking back to the days before the advent of the Portuguese, when there was a separate Tamil Kingdom in the north of Ceylon'. Indeed, the connotations associated with the Thamil Arasu, that is,

39 Wilson, *S.J.V. Chelvanayakam*, 1997, pp.30–31.

40 See Ponnambalam, *Sri Lanka: The National Question*, 1983, p.78.

41 Parliamentary Debates, 10 December 1948.

42 A.J. Wilson, 'The Tamil Federal Party in Ceylon Politics', *Journal of Commonwealth Political Studies*, iv(2), 1966, p.135.

43 Wilson, 'The Tamil Federal Party', 1966, p.118.

'sovereign independent Tamil state' cannot easily be erased in the light of the politics adopted by Chelvanayakam even before the island was granted independence.

In fact, the main goal of the FP was to create *two states* federated along Swiss lines, one for the Sinhalese and the other for the Tamil-speaking people in the north and east.[44] However, as Wilson concedes, the agenda behind the FP was to partition the island on linguistic and ethnic lines as envisaged by Ponnambalam Ramanathan during the 1920s and 1930s. The FP considered the pros and cons of an idea of a federation of the Tamil-speaking areas in the north and east with a future Dravidian sovereign state of Madras, now known as Tamil Nadu.[45] This would have been considered a brazen *irredentist* attempt by a political party in Ceylonese politics. It is noteworthy that in 1945 the Prime Minister of India, Jawaharlal Nehru, demanded that Ceylon should be a part of the Indian federation, 'since she was culturally, racially and linguistically as much a part of India as any province of India'.[46] Encouraged by such political statements coming from a person who was, by then, the Prime Minister of India, Chelvanayakam and some of his closest allies toyed with the idea of a federation with Greater India. However, when Nehru later abandoned this idea due to its impracticability and the political implications for the whole South Asian region, they began to consider the possibility that the future of the Ceylon Tamils lay in a separate Tamil state. In its first pamphlet, FP's future objective was declared as, 'the attainment of freedom for the Tamil-speaking people of Ceylon by the establishment of an autonomous Tamil State on a linguistic basis within the framework of a federal union of Ceylon'.[47]

Chelvanayakam had also invited other minority groups, notably the Muslims (also called Moors), to follow him. Addressing the Young Men's Muslim Association at Fort, Colombo, in 1945, he said: 'It is better to have our own territory, our own culture and self-respect than be a minority in the island living on the good fortune of the majority community.'[48]

FP's strategy

The FP had from its inception followed a totally different strategy to that of the policies adopted by, first the Jaffna Association, and then the Tamil Mahãjana Sabhã, which were dominated by the Tamil elites of the Jaffna Tamils during 1920–1930, and by the ACTC from 1930–1948. The traditional leadership of these groups often thought, as pointed out by Wilson, in terms of a partnership with their Sinhalese counterparts.[49] Their aims, as publicly stated, were to agitate for the

44 Tremayne, 'Sri Lanka: The Problem of the Tamils', in *Defense Yearbook*, 1987, p.219.

45 A.J. Wilson, *Politics in Sri Lanka 1947–1973* Macmillan:, London, 1974, p.165.

46 Bailey, *Ceylon*, 1952, p.158.

47 See *The Case for a Federal Constitution for Ceylon: Resolutions Passed at the First National Convention of the Ilankai Thamil Arasu Kadchi*, Ilankai Thamil Arasu Kadchi: Colombo, 1951 p.19.

48 Wilson, *S.J.V. Chelvanayakam*, 1997, pp.30–31, 50.

49 A.J. Wilson, 'Race, Religion, Language and Caste', in M. Roberts (ed.), *Collective Identities*, 1981, p.467.

political interests of the Ceylon Tamils. The next generation of the leadership of the Ceylon Tamils represented by the ACTC had followed this policy more aggressively and vigorously without posing any threat to the unitary character of the island, neither did it cause any serious damage to national harmony. Its sole aim seemed to be to compete with the Sinhalese on an equal footing, in particular in the areas of education, employment and trade and industry. Its primary objective was how it could preserve and protect the achievements of the Ceylon Tamils that they had gained during the past century or so through constitutional measures that ensured their protection in case a future Sinhalese-dominated government threatened to eliminate it.[50] The advantages achieved by the Ceylon Tamils they genuinely believed would be eroded once political power was transferred to the Sinhalese. This is why, argued Wilson, the ACTC tried to secure a 'balanced representation' in the legislative council.[51]

G.G. Ponnambalam's 'communal' ideas vs Chelvanayakam's separatist policies

The strategy adopted by the ACTC operated within clearly demarcated parameters of liberal democracy.[52] This was not surprising considering the educational and professional background of its leader, G.G. Ponnambalam. He was an eminent constitutional lawyer and regarded as one of the best jurists in Sri Lankan legal history. He used his skills in oratory to confront his opponents in both the courthouse and parliament. Apparently he enjoyed it and revelled in the discomfiture of his rivals. He had never been a strong supporter of civil disobedience neither did he resort to confrontational politics against the Sinhalese in his campaign for equal rights for the Tamil-speaking people. In fact, G.G. Ponnambalam was of the opinion, even in the 1960s that it was impracticable and unwise to engage in separatist politics since such policies might cause irreparable damage to national unity.[53] The reasonable demands of the Tamils, in his view, could be achieved only by working in close cooperation with the Sinhalese leaders. As already mentioned, at about the time that *Kandyan National Assembly* and Bandaranaike's Sinhala Mahã Sabhã were advocating federalism, the ACTC had not shown any interest in it at all. Even though ethnically based politics had always raised the tempo between the two major community groups, neither group had turned to violence; neither did they prefer non-constitutional measures to win the rights of their respective constituencies. Rivalries between Tamils and Sinhalese were demonstrated only

50 C.R. de Silva, 'Sinhalese-Tamil Ethnic Rivalry: The Background', in R.B. Goldman and A.J. Wilson (eds.), *From Independence to Statehood: Managing Ethnic Conflict in Five African and Asian States*, Frances Printer: London, 1984, p.116.

51 Wilson, 'The Tamil Federal Party in Ceylon Politics', 1966, pp.117–137.

52 Wilson, 'The Tamil Federal Party in Ceylon Politics', 1996, p.117.

53 See *Ceylon Daily News*, 30 May 1962, *Ceylon Daily News*, 16 June 1965, *Ceylon Observer*, 16 May 1965, cited in Kearney, *Communalism and Language*, 1967, p.96. See, further, Namasivayam, *The Legislatures of Ceylon*, 1951; Weerawardana, *Government and Politics in Ceylon*, 1951.

through constant constitutional wrangling resulting in major reforms in 1920, 1924, 1931 and 1946.[54] The ACTC never advocated regional devolution or federation but the foundation of the ACTC was loyalty to the Tamils. It was a 'communal' political party of the Jaffna Tamil elite.

Obviously there was not one view only on how to tackle the problem of the minority status and loss of prestige of the Tamils. The Tamil leadership at this time represented a range of opinion on the tactics necessary to secure their future prospects. Therefore, the emergence of the FP was not simply a natural development of the political aspirations of the JA, the CTMJ, and the ACTC even though the ACTC was as 'frankly communal' as the FP.[55] The FP in order to raise support needed a few 'burning' issues on which the Thamil Arasu campaign could be launched and to justify their breakaway from the ACTC. They managed to rally support around the issue of the national flag, the question of the undecided future of the Indian Tamils and the alleged state-aided colonisation by the Sinhalese of the traditional Tamil homelands.[56] The FP did not seem to want to address issues as they arise, but chose instead a confrontational strategy in the belief that issues might arise in the future that would weaken the position of the Tamil-speaking people, particularly in the north and west. Many of their demands were based on the potential threat from the Sinhalese to their culture, language, religions, and above all to their existence as a distinct nation.

The FP was not a party interested in making a contribution to the development of national politics in post-independence Ceylon, neither did it want to take part in national politics in conformity with the rules shaped by parliamentary principles. From the very beginning they believed that a strict parliamentary strategy would not be sufficient to win their legitimate demand, that is, Thamil Arasu Kadchi, a Tamil independent State. From 1956 the FP followed a path that made violence unavoidable. Wilson noted that '[T]he Party has employed two techniques to press home its demands. It has threatened and launched campaigns of non-co-operation and civil disobedience to embarrass the Government.'[57] This was unusual. Political parties usually use the parliament process, but Chelvanayakam was resorting to extra parliamentary 'pressure tactics' to force political change. European, Sinhalese and Tamil scholars agree that the tactics of the FP was a significant departure from the way politics, by all political factions, had been hitherto conducted on the island. Robert N. Kearney noted that 'Single-minded preoccupation with communal questions has caused the Federal party to ignore almost totally all other questions. A Federalist MP once explained that the party's members took little part in debates except on communal and language questions.'[58] Thus, the FP provided an organisation for more aggressive and uncompromising Tamils some with 'clearly

54 See Kearney, *Communalism and Language*, 1967, p.29.

55 Kearney, *Communalism and Language*, 1967, p.29.

56 Wilson, 'Tamil Federal Party in Ceylon Politics', 1966, p.118.

57 Wilson, 'The Tamil Federal Party in Ceylon Politics', 1966, p.119.

58 Kearney, *Communalism and Language*, 1967, p.95.

enunciated separatist objectives'.[59] As C.R. de Silva observed, when ethnic tensions were seriously exacerbated it was the FP around which even ordinary Tamils tend to rally.[60] According to Wilson it represented a 'different strand of communal politics' since its formation as a political party.[61]

Special mandate to speak for Tamil-speaking people?

At a time when the other mainstream political parties felt that it was uncivilized even to think in terms of ethnic politics, the FP unashamedly stated time and time again that its sole political goal was to work for the interests of the Tamil-speaking people, and 'of a Tamil homeland'.[62] It repeatedly stressed that it was the only true and genuine spokesman of the Tamil-speaking people, that is, Ceylon Tamils, Indian Tamils and the Moors. In fact, the FP stated in parliament, that it had 'a special mission, a special mandate to speak on behalf of the Tamil-speaking people and to give a certain message to this House and to the country'.[63] It never even tried to pretend that it was interested in debating questions of common interest for the island or its people. Only issues of linguistic and other rights of Tamil-speaking people engaged the interest of the FP. In brief, the preservation for Tamils of a separate existence as a distinct nation has been the mantra of the FP its whole political life. Without autonomy to Tamil-speaking areas, argued Chelvanayakam, 'the Tamil peoples' chances of continuing to exist as a different unit possessed of their cultures, habits, customs, religions and language will be lost.'[64] This threat of extinction was repeatedly stressed by Chelvanayakam whenever an opportunity arose. For example, in 1956 when the notorious *Official Language Act* was passed by parliament making Sinhalese the only official language he said, 'it is our bounden duty to continue the struggle for the preservation of our language rights lest we disintegrate and lose our national identity.'[65] The leadership of the FP repeatedly stressed, in and out of parliament, the distinctiveness of the Tamil nation and that it is different to the Sinhalese. At the first national convention of the FP it was pointed out that:

> The Tamil speaking people in Ceylon constitute a nation distinct from that of the Sinhalese by every fundamental test of nationhood, firstly that of a separate historical past in this island at least as an ancient and as glorious as that of the

59 Wilson, 'Race, Religion, Language and Caste', in Roberts (ed.), *Collective Identities*, 1979, p.468. See also Wilson, 'The Tamil Federal Party in Ceylon Politics', 1966, pp.117–137.

60 de Silva, 'Sinhala Tamil Ethnic Rivalry: The Background', in Goldman and Wilson, *From Independence to Statehood*, 1984, p.118.

61 Wilson, 'Race Religion Language and Caste', in Roberts (ed.), *Collective Identities*, 1981, p.468.

62 Wilson, 'The Tamil Federal Party in Ceylon Politics', 1966, p.118.

63 House Debates, vol. 38, col. 777.

64 Kearney, *Communalism and Language*, 1967, p.96; R.C. Oberst, 'Federalism and Ethnic Conflict in Sri Lanka', *Publius*, 18, 1988, p.183.

65 House Debates, vol. 39, col. 409.

> Sinhalese, secondly, by the fact of their being a linguistic entity entirely different from that of the Sinhalese . . . and finally by reason of their territorial habitation of definite areas which constitute over one-third of this island.[66]

The FP created the general impression that given the differences between the two nations, the Tamils and the Sinhalese, it was inconceivable even to think about working together within a unitary framework for the island.[67] In 1961 the President of the FP, S.M. Rasamanickam in his presidential address stated:

> We are a nation by all standards. We inhabit a geographically compact and well-defined territory; we speak a common language; we are proud inheritors of a common heritage and culture as ancient as man himself; and above all, we are bound together by that feeling of oneness which is a necessary ingredient for nationhood, that consciousness which you and I and all of us share whatever the part of the country we may live.[68]

Any idea of working together with another political party, dominated by Sinhalese was, in the view of the FP, detrimental to the future prospects of the Tamil-speaking peoples of the island.

Thus, not surprisingly, the membership of the FP was exclusively for Tamil-speaking peoples, and the highest level of leadership was occupied by the Jaffna Tamils. At its first business meeting held on 18 December 1949, explaining the aims and objectives of the FP, Chelvanayakam stressed, 'We have met together with the common aim of creating an organisation to work for the attainment of freedom for the Tamil speaking people of Ceylon.'[69] Justifying the communal character of the FP he said that 'as long as there are activities directed against communities and as long as those communities are minority communities, they must, for their self-protection bind themselves in a communal way.'[70] The speech is remarkable for its clear way in which it signalled a clear shift away from minority rights that would secure participation in national life to minority rights for a separate group. Also, from a political point of view Chelvanayakam was seeking to rally the Tamils, who were a disparate group politically, around a single clearly articulated idea. With the firm adherence to policies shaped by communal

66 The Case for a Federal Constitution for Ceylon: Resolutions Passed at the First National Convention of the Ilankai Thamil Arasu Kadchi, Ilankai Thamil Arasu Kadchi: Colombo, 1951, p.1

67 See also N. Thiruchelvam, 'The Politics of Decentralisaiton and Devolution: Competing Conceptions of District Developmental Councils in Sri Lanka', in Goldman and Wilson, *From Independence to Statehood,* 1984, p.199.

68 S.M. Rasamanickam, Presidential Address, Illankai Thamil Arasu Kadchi Annual Convention, Illankai Thamil Arasu Kadchi: Jaffna, 1961, p. 2

69 See S.J.V. Chelvanayakam, Presidential Address Delivered at the Inaugural and First Meeting of the Illankai Thamil Arasu Kadchi, Illankai Thamil Arasu Kadchi: Colombo, p.1.

70 House Debates, vol. 5, col. 491.

exclusivity and separatism, the concerns of previous generations of moderate Tamils for a bill of rights with constitutional safeguards for minorities, an independent judiciary, adequate representation in the legislature and in education and employment quickly disappeared.[71] Every step, every strategy and policy adopted by the FP aimed to strengthen its political power so that it could take defensive action against the threat posed by the Sinhalese majority.

'Our lands, our religions, our culture and our heritages'

The 1956 general election manifesto of the FP stated that their sole objective was to 'preserve our language, our lands, our religions, our cultures and our heritages. The one and only way . . . is to regain for us the right to be the ruler of ourselves in our own home.'[72] Even though Chelvanayakam was a devoted Anglican Christian, he was prepared to protect and preserve the 'Hindu religion' and 'Hindu culture' from 'Sinhalese linguistic and nationalistic imperialism'. His credibility on these issues was challenged again and again by Ponnambalam and others in every election fought since 1952.

Two states along Swiss lines

It was stated time and again in public by the FP that their aim was to work for the creation of two states, federated along Swiss lines (that is, separated along linguistic lines) with a separate legislature, within a framework of a federal union of Ceylon.[73] These two provincial legislatures should be 'entrusted with the administration of certain internal affairs relating to education, health agriculture, industries, law and order and similar subjects'.[74] Otherwise, argued leading figures in the parliamentary group of the FP, it was impossible to guarantee 'the Tamil peoples' chance of continuing to exist as a different unit possessed of their cultures, habits, customs, religions and language'.[75] Issues that were of national significance were simply not addressed.

The FP warmed to the theme of federation and 'began to think in terms of an economic future for the Ceylon Tamils . . . in the preservation and development in isolation of a Tamil homeland'.[76] In 1951 at the annual convention of the FP at Trincomalee, the leadership' emphasising that as a separate nation they had an

71 Wilson, 'Race, Religion, Language and Caste', in Roberts (ed.), *Collective Identities*, 1981, p.468.

72 *Ceylon Daily News*, Parliament of Ceylon 1970, Colombo, p.193, cited in Wilson, *Break-up of Sri Lanka*, 1988, p.83.

73 See *The Case for a Federal constitution for Ceylon: Resolutions Passed at the First National Convention of the Illankai Thamil Arasu Kadchi, 1951*, Illankai Thamil Arasu Kadchi: Colombo, p.9. See details, Kearney, *Communalism and Language*, 1967.

74 *Case for a Federal Constitution for Ceylon*, 1951, p.9.

75 House Debates, vol. 24, col. II.

76 Wilson, 'The Tamil Federal Party in Ceylon Politics', 1966, p.118.

'inalienable right to political autonomy', called for a plebiscite to determine 'the boundaries of linguistic states in consonance with the fundamental and inalienable principle of self-determination'.[77]

In its 1956 election manifesto, the FP spelt out the implications of its federalist agenda: wherever people of Tamil origin happen to live they should come under Tamil federal unit. It wanted 'Tamil pockets in Sinhalese areas like Puttalam, Wellawatta (urban cities in the Western Province), Nawalapitiya and Hatton' (up country) and the Tamil-speaking areas inhabited by the Moors in the Eastern Province to become cantons or half-cantons of the Tamil state.[78]

When the Official Language Act was passed in 1956, the FP adopted a resolution spelling out their demands. The following set of demands was presented as its immediate non-negotiable goals:

1 creation of one or more linguistic state or states . . . enjoying the widest autonomous and residuary powers consistent with the unity and external security of Ceylon;
2 bestowal on the Tamil language of absolute parity of status with Sinhalese as an official language;
3 fighting for the restoration of citizenship for the Indian Tamils on the basis of residence in the island;
4 ensuring the immediate cession of the colonisation of traditional Tamil speaking regions with Sinhalese.[79]

The Official Language Act of 1956 seemed to justify the FP's fears of the potential threat to their interests from the Sinhalese majority. The leadership of the FP realised that the language issue would rally all Tamil-speaking people to its banner in its struggle for a separate Thamil Arasu.

Chelvanayakam faced difficulties in convincing the Tamil electorate of the wisdom of adopting a federal model for the island. Ordinary Tamils as well as some Tamil politicians were puzzled by his insistence on ethnically based politics, which led one of the Tamil MPs, Ramalinkam, in 1951, to brand Chelvanayakam a 'fanatic' in a conversation with his future son-in-law, Wilson.[80] Chelvanayakam's arch-rival in the 1952 general election, Mr Natesan, ridiculed the 'separatist politics' of the FP because of its detrimental effect on the lives of Tamil entrepreneurs. 'Because the Tamil people are now under a unitary government', argued Mr Natesan, 'they are entitled to share all the amenities provided by a welfare state drawing most of its revenue from other than Tamil-speaking areas.' If the Tamils tried to confine themselves only to those barren lands of the north and east, he wondered, how an economic foundation would be built for the incipient Tamil

77 Gunasekara, *Tigers, Moderates and Pandora's Package*, 1996, pp.33–34.
78 Wilson, 'The Tamil Federal Party in Ceylon Politics', 1966, pp.123–124.
79 Wilson, 'The Tamil Federal Party in Ceylon Politics', 1966, pp.117–137.
80 Wilson, *Break-up of Sri Lanka*, 1988, p.102.

society.[81] The fiercest critic of the federalists' politics, Ponnambalam, also raised the economic argument contending that the federalists' policies would bring only disaster for ordinary Tamils in the north and east. He contended that: '[F]ederalism would confine Tamil employment to the two (Tamil) provinces to the exclusion of the vast-wealth-producing areas occupied by the Sinhalese and which now helped the economy of the Tamils.'[82]

Others were concerned about the possible consequences of a separate state governed by elite high-caste Tamils. The low-caste Tamils were worried about a situation where they would be ruled by the high-caste *Vellala* Tamils. Some prominent politicians of the Moor community in the Eastern Province were not convinced about how the federalists would achieve a federal state since there was no clear geographical demarcation between provinces or between the 'cantons', which are scattered in various provinces. One prominent independent candidate for Batticaloa (an electoral constituency in the Eastern Province), Mr Kadramer, questioned how a Tamil state could be created out of the east and north since there was no geographical contiguity between these areas:

> The Swiss ideal of federation provides no judicial safeguards to the minorities because the Supreme Court has no power to declare laws unconstitutional. The Swiss methods of initiative and referendum, i.e. majority rule, are the very things which the Federalists oppose in a unitary constitution. Let the Federalist produce a map of Switzerland. Does it make as ridiculous a map as the one of Ceylon produced by them? Does not even common sense suggest to them that there should be geographical contiguity among the cantons of the various states?[83]

These arguments meant that the FP was in a difficult position. There was little unanimity among Tamils that federalism was the solution and Chevanayakam was facing defeat at the hands of ordinary Tamils in the 1952 general election. In the years leading up to 1956, Chelvanayakam considered seriously how the island could be partitioned[84] without causing too many problems for the Tamils living in the Sinhalese-dominated regions. According to Wilson, Chelvanayakam started studying federal forms of government in particular reading reading with care K.C. Wheare's *opus magnum* on federalism entitled 'Federal government' (1951 edn.).

Wilson agreed that 'while the Federal Party insisted on a federal constitution, the voters were not clear in their minds as to what was meant by this newly introduced concept in their political vocabulary.'[85] The initial reaction from

81 Weerawardana, *Ceylon General Election*, 1956, p.201.
82 Weerawardana, *Ceylon General Election*, 1956, p.204.
83 Weerawardana, *Ceylon General Election*, 1956, 1960, p.200.
84 Wilson, *Break-up of Sri Lanka*, 1988, p.101.
85 Wilson, *Break-up of Sri Lanka*, 1988, p.84.

ordinary Tamils to the federal idea was a disaster for Chelvanayakam's campaign even though he had dreamt about 'reaping the harvest'[86] of his policies during the 1952 general election. Ironically, he reaped only 'the bitter harvest'. He lost in the 1952 general election to another distinguished Tamil politician, S. Natesan, who contested the seat as a candidate of the UNP, a national party.

Only two members of Chevanayaksm's party secured victory while another five members lost to the ACTC. However, Chelvanayakam did not take the defeat lying down. He submitted an election petition challenging the election of Natesan but not only did he lose his case, he was also asked to pay Natesan's legal costs, which was at the time an excessive amount. He also lost the election petition lodged against Ponnambalam, the leader of the ACTC. This, if Wilson's accounts of the events are accurate, shook his belief in an independent judiciary.

The election defeat and the ordinary peoples' reluctance to trust Chelvanayakam and his allies would have discouraged men with less courage. But Chelvanayakam was able to find other avenues and strategies to convince the Tamil electorates that the only alternative for the Tamils lay in the hands of the FP. He was driven by the stubborn belief that the Sinhalese would give in to Tamils demands for a separate Tamil state after realising that it was better to live without Tamils.[87] When a journalist in the *Guardian* (London) questioned Chelvanayakam about how he would win a separate Thamil Arasu in the aftermath of the Vaddukodai Convention he was quoted as saying that he and his followers would become a nuisance to ensure that the Sinhalese would ultimately give up hope of living together with the Tamils. His closes allies swallowed his prophecies *ad unem emnes*.

Chelvanayakam worked tirelessly, even though for most of his adult life he suffered from Parkinson's disease. He began to talk about 'the glorious' history of the Ceylon Tamils and their ancient culture which, in his view, was *nulli secundus*. Any scheme that did not further his political goals was rejected without consideration. Tamil politics, for the first time in the twentieth century, went to the 'grassroots', with new cadres from both the low and high castes being recruited. According to Wilson, between 1950 and 1956, 16 constituencies in the Northern and Eastern Provinces were targeted. Many of these were surprisingly located in the east, away from their power base, the Jaffna Peninsula. Various campaigns were launched to win the Tamil-speaking peoples in the Eastern Province. Friendly overtures were also made to Indian Tamil labourers who were identified as Hill Country Tamils, belonging to the lowest tribes of the Malabar and Koramandal coasts in India, and who until 1950, were excluded by the first generation of elite Tamil politi-cians. Chelvanayakam, however, realised that without 'great numbers' behind his party, it was futile to attempt to steer a mass movement against the government in his campaign for Thamil Arasu. It was *numbers* that were important in his political game. One of the strategies Chelvanayakam used was to encourage

86 This very word, according to Wilson, was used by Chelvanayakam just before the election took place in a conversation with one of his colleagues. See Wilson, *Break-up of Sri Lanka*, 1988, p.101.

87 Wilson, *Break-up of Sri Lanka*, 1988, pp.105–106.

Indian Tamil labourers to migrate to the dry zone, Vatmi, the north-central areas and to the Eastern Province to enhance the population size of the Tamils. He hoped that such a migration would help the Tamils defend themselves against any future attempt at domination of the area by the 'Sinhalese colonists'. He opposed any development scheme involving irrigation projects in the east and the north. Tamil engineers and labourers were asked not to participate or help in any development projects of ruined irrigation systems because he believed that ultimately it was the Sinhalese who would benefit from such endeavours.[88]

Grassroots politics

There was a precedent for Chelvanaykam's grassroots campaign. They were aware that the cadres to the Marxist political party, the LSSP, which had dominated the labour movements during the years 1930 to 1953, were recruited in secret. Mass agitation and demonstrations against the government and employers were frequent during those years.[89] Destruction of public property, hurling stones at police officers and employers, long and protracted strikes were tactics frequently deployed by the trade unions to weaken the state machinery. The second government of post-war independence Ceylon led by Dudley Senanayake was almost defeated by a massive *hartal* led by a Trotskyist LSSP in 1953. It was reported that cabinet ministers sought refuge from the protesters in a ship in Colombo harbour to save their lives. This led to the resignation of the prime minister in October 1953.[90] However, these extra-constitutional agitations were despised by every non-Marxist political party. Most importantly, G.G. Ponnambalam's ACTC condemned in the strongest terms the use of extra-parliamentary, violent activities to win demands. This was one of the reasons suggested for why Ponnambalam had joined the D.S. Senanayake government in 1949. He was keen to prevent the LSSP and the Communist Party gaining power. No one expected that a man of the calibre of Chelvanayakam, a QC and high-caste Jaffna Tamil, educated at the University of Cambridge would resort to such 'direct actions' that were supposed to be the *modus operandi* of the working class.

The theme of the discussions in the recruitment centres was to explain the 'dangers of responsive cooperation' with the Sinhalese and the nefarious effect on the Tamils of the colonisation scheme of the traditional Tamil homelands. The daily circulation of the Tamil newspaper entitled *Suthanthiran* (freedom) was instrumental in the federalist campaign in spreading the message. Most of the lessons and discussions in the recruitment camps and Tamil-speaking areas were, as admitted by Chelvanayakam to Wilson, no more than the 'indoctrination' of ordinary Tamils. There was a gigantic figure in this campaign in the form of

88 Wilson, *Break-up of Sri Lanka*, 1988, p.103.

89 See V.K. Jayawardene, *The Rise of the Labour Movement in Ceylon*, Duke University Press: Durham, NC, 1972.

90 See details, de Silva, *History of Sri Lanka*, 1981, p.449.

C. Vanniasingham, Chelvanayakam's deputy leader who, before his premature death at 49 due to high blood pressure, had single-handedly masterminded this 'indoctrination process'. Wilson records the following conversation:

> On the premature death and unexpected death of C. Vanniasingham, the deputy leader of the Party, in 1959, I asked Chelvanayakam, who was in poor health at the time, which of his lieutenants would help him to win again in the Eastern province. His answer was that Vanniasingham, the other members of his party and he himself has successfully 'indoctrinated' the Eastern province Tamils on the dangers of Sinhalese domination. Thus there was no compelling need to drive home the message again. Election results after 1956 showed that this was a correct assessment.[91]

In fact, both Wilson and Chelvanayakam are correct insofar as the indoctrination of ordinary Tamils is concerned. Not only the 1956 general election, but also in subsequent elections of March 1960, July 1960, 1965, 1970 and 1977 the FP had been able to 'reap the harvest' of their vision since it was the main political party behind which the Tamil electorates flocked in part to counter the Sinhalese threat. Chelvanayakam tackled the apathy of the Tamils with respect to the threat from the majority through several strategies. He argued that the future of the Thamil Arasu had to be the combined provinces of the north and east. He knew that without a combined north-east, he could not convince the Tamil electorate that it was worth fighting for a separate Tamil state. He realised that he had to weaken the Sinhalese electorate to achieve his goal. So he tried to win over the largest minority group (one million) who lived among the Sinhalese in the Hill Country, the Indian Tamils, to his side.

His strategy, as far as the Indian Tamils were concerned, did not work as he would have liked. First, he tried to coax the leadership of the Indian Tamils. The leader of the Ceylon Worker Congress, Thondaman,[92] who was a kind of *publilius yrus*[93] among the Indian Tamils, and another leader who represented a large chunk of the Indian labourers, Mr Abdul Aziz, were approached to join the FP, but to no effect. Then the FP decided to approach the labourers directly by forming trade unions in the tea states in direct challenge to Thondaman and Aziz.

The battle to win the Moors in the eastern region also did not succeed; this is discussed at length in the next chapter. Even though the FP did occasionally manage to recruit a few Muslim MPs, it was not a successful drive. To Chelvanayakam's frustration, Moor MPs who were elected from the FP joined the Sinhalese-led government as soon as they were elected to parliament. Therefore, finding and

91 Wilson, *Break-up of Sri Lanka*, 1988, p.104.

92 S. Thondaman, *Tea and Politics, My Life and Times, An Autobiography*, Navarang: New Delhi, 1994.

93 He lived in the first century BC. He came to Rome as a slave and subsequently became a prominent figure as a writer. Thondaman came to Sri Lanka as a labourer, subsequently became the undisputed leader of the Indian state Tamils and one of the most powerful politicians in the years from 1970 to 1999.

keeping Moor MPs loyal to the cause of the FP became a wasteful exercise. By the same token, the Moors were reluctant to place their trust in the FP for fear that they might become a minority in a Tamil state established in the north and east. They had also had some bitter conflicts with the Tamils since the middle of the nineteenth century.

The FP and secession

The leadership of the FP did sometimes entertain the idea of secession. For instance, in 1962, some members of the working committee, which was described by Wilson as the 'nerve centre of the FP' openly flirted with the idea that the party should move away from federalism to secession. According to Wilson, this was not adopted by the majority.[94] Thus, with the formation of the FP, ethnic politics intensified with the Tamil parties vying 'to assert adversarial courage toward the Sinhalese'.[95] However, it was the FP which emerged as the dominant force committed to winning autonomy for the Tamils.

In 1972 Chelvanayakam changed his strategy once again. He had managed to unite more or less all the Tamil political parties into a new party, the Tamil *United Front* (TUF) to achieve Thamil Arasu. In 1976 the TUF was changed to accommodate a new militancy that was manifesting among the younger generation of Tamils. So the Tamil United Liberation Front (TULF) came into existence. After winning his seat in the 1976 by-election he stated:

> Throughout the ages the Sinhalese and Tamils in the country lived as distinct sovereign people [sic] till they were brought under foreign domination . . . We have for the last twenty five years made every effort to secure our political rights on the basis of equality with the Sinhalese in a united Ceylon. It is a regrettable fact that successive Sinhalese governments have used the power that flows from independence to deny us our fundamental rights and reduce us to the position of a subject people . . . I wish to announce to my people and to the country that I consider the verdict at this election a mandate that the Tamil Eelam nation should exercise the sovereignty already vested in the Tamil people and become free. On behalf of the Tamil United Liberation Front, I give you my solemn assurance that we will carry out this mandate.[96]

There is in this quote a hint of the possibility of secession. This is not the first occasion in which the legitimacy of a united Sri Lanka (in 1972 Ceylon became Sri Lanka) was challenged by the Tamil-dominated parties in the north and east. However, this time around its significance was enormous given the fact that since the early 1970s, perhaps for the first time in the political history of the FP, its

94 Wilson, *Break-up of Sri Lanka*, 1988, p.122.
95 Sabaratnam, 'The Boundaries of the State', 1987, p.307.
96 Cited in Ponnambalam, 'Sri Lanka: The National Question', 1983, p.184.

authority as the sole Tamil political party was being subjected to a serious challenge by less privileged and low-caste Tamil youths. Perhaps the leadership of the FP realised that unless they take defensive action and accommodate the new voices the FPs elite groups would face the danger of elimination.

Chelvanayakam died in 1977 without realising his dream of Thamil Arasu, and perhaps never having to face the direction his party eventually took. A few years later his chosen successor, a hard-line young leader, Allapillai Amirthalingam, MP, was brutally murdered by a new generation of Tamil militants. The FP was proscribed by militant separatists calling themselves, the LTTE, and most of the parliamentarians of the FP were assassinated. However, it is said that he died not a disappointed man, but as a prophet who saw what was to befall the Tamils *ex ante* at the hands of 'Sinhalese linguistic and nationalist imperialism'.

11 Awakening the political consciousness of the Tamils

The Federal Party's modus operandi

Chelvanayakam[1] launched his *Thamil Arasu* campaign more vigorously during the years 1956 to 1961. There was wave after wave of *satyagraha* and civil obedience movements organised by him to force the government to yield to Tamil demands. Chelvanayakam argued that it was necessary to resort to extra-constitutional agitations because since the days of the Donoughmore Constitution there had been constant attacks on the Tamils and their civilisation. S*atyagraha* was the strategy used to awaken the political consciousness of ordinary Tamils who were lukewarm towards the whole business of federalism. Most Tamils were not convinced about the necessity for a federal state system on a small island nor were they convinced that that the Singhalese constituted a major 'threat'.

Chelvanayakam's entrance into politics

Opposition to separatist politics came from Tamil politicians themselves. G.G. Ponnambalam, a charismatic figure and leader of the Ceylon Tamils until the 1956 general election, was furious about the way in which 'this lean and hungry looking' Chelvanayakam[2] had tried to divide the nation along communal lines by resorting to language that could have far-reaching consequences for ethnic harmony on the island. Mahadeva and Natesan, other distinguished Tamil politicians of the day, publicly questioned the wisdom of the separatist politics advocated by Chelvanayakam. The aggressive stance adopted by the FP was not enough to bring the Tamil population into Chelvanayakam's fold, since they could not remember any serious conflict between themselves and the Sinhalese during the previous five centuries. Ordinary people of both communities had lived in harmony during or under foreign occupation without violence or even confrontational politics.

1 See A.M Rajendram, *S.J.V. Chelvanayakam: A Tribute*, Colombo, 1978; A.J. Wilson, *S.J.V. Chelvanayakam*, 1994.

2 These were the famous words used by Ponnambalam during the 1952 general election to ridicule Chelvanayakam, which to a great extent worked against the latter and his new political party, the FP.

However, matters became fraught when the newly formed *Mahajana Eksath Peramuna,* (MEP) the Peoples' United Front, a coalition of various Sinhalese factions including Sinhala nationalist groups and the SLFP, introduced, on 5 June 1956, a bill to make Sinhalese the sole official language, with a clause containing provisions for the reasonable use of Tamil.[3] This was a very unfortunate move, which gave Tamils a reason to believe that their progress in a unitary state was dangerously imperiled. This move gave Chelvanayakam and the FP the opportunity to win Tamil voters to their cause. On the same day that the bill was introduced into parliament, the FP staged a Gandhi-style *satyagraha* in Galle Face Green, challenging the legitimacy of the new laws as 'Sinhalese linguistic imperialism', which was ranged against the Tamils' wider interests. Large numbers of Tamils came to the rally travelling from the north and east. Violence followed in mixed Sinhalese and Tamil conurbations. It is estimated that at least 150 people from both communities were killed. Undeterred by these incidents a long march was undertaken from the north to the main city of the east, Trincomalee, in July and August 1956. The main purpose of this 'pilgrimage', according to Wilson was 'to alert the Tamil-speaking people to the dangers confronting them, making them aware that they belonged to a separate nation'.[4] The pilgrimage culminated in a mass rally where a strong warning was issued that if, within a year, the Sinhalese government failed to yield to their demands, the FP would resort to direct action.

The language issue in the Privy Council

Section 29 of the Constitution of Ceylon (the Soulbury Constitution) was debated in both the Privy Council and the Supreme Court of Sri Lanka. s.29 (1) provides that 'Subject to the provision of this Order Parliament shall have power to make laws for the peace, order and good government of the island.' s.29 (4) provides that 'In the exercise of these powers under this section, Parliament may amend or repeal any of the provisions of this Order, or of any other Order of Her Majesty in Council in its application to the island.'[5] However, these powers, as upheld in a Privy Council decision in *Liyanage et al v Regina* [1966] 2 WLR p.682, must be exercised in accordance with the terms of the Constitution from which they ultimately derive. Parliament could not amend or abolish existing provisions, nor could it introduce new laws or regulations in contravention of s.29 (2) (b) (c) and (d).[6] These provisions

3 This Act passed into law as the Official Language Act no. 33 of 1956.

4 Wilson, *Break-up of Sri Lanka*, 1988, p.109.

5 A similar provision was included in s.2 of the Ceylon Independence Act 1947.

6 Article 29 (1) provides, 'Subject to the provisions of the Order, Parliament shall have power to make laws for the peace, order and good government of the island.' Article 29 (2) provides, 'No such law shall - (a) prohibit or restrict the free exercise of any religion; or (b) make persons of any community or religion liable to disabilities or restrictions to which persons of other communities or religions are not made liable; or (c) confer on persons of any community or religion any privilege or advantage which is not conferred on persons of other communities or religions; or (d) alter the constitution of any religious body except with the consent of the governing authority of that body: provided that,

were incorporated so as to guarantee the rights of religious and racial minority groups in the island, and were 'cast-iron guarantees given to the minorities'.[7] s.29 (3) stipulates that any law made in contravention of subsection 2 of this section is *null* and *void* and has no legal effect.[8] Lord Pearce, interpreting this section, held in *Bribery Commissioner v Pedrick Ranasinghe* [1964] 2 *WLR* 1305, PC, that racial and religious matters coming under it 'shall not be the subject of legislation. It represents the solemn balance of rights between the citizens of Ceylon, in the fundamental conditions of which, *inter se*, they accepted the Constitution; and these are therefore unalterable under the Constitution'.

Thus, it is apparent that the *Official Language Act*, 1956 (Act no. 33) was in contravention of art. 29 (2) (b) and (c) of the Constitution of Ceylon. Not only did it impose certain conditions upon a section of the nation but its implications for minority groups, in general, were disastrous. The absence of entrenched protections for minority rights in the Sri Lankan constitution, which was in any case a new concept, had left the minorities at the mercy of policies that favoured the majority.

Indefatigable Chelliah Kodeeswaran

The legality of the regulations introduced by the *Official Language Act* was challenged not by the FP but by a humble government clerk of Tamil origin, a Mr Chelliah Kodeeswaran.[9] He refused to take the Sinhalese proficiency examination required by the Treasury Circular, no. 560 of 4 December 1961, which was issued in order to implement the Official Language Act. Kodeeswaran was, therefore, denied a salary increment on 1 April 1962. By challenging this unjustifiable requirement in the District Court, his counsel argued that the regulations in question were in violation of art. 29 (2) (b) and (c). His complaint was subsequently upheld by the District Court. The Attorney-General appealed to the Supreme Court arguing that the Crown could not be sued by its employees. In the Privy Council,[10] it was held that according to Roman-Dutch law employees could sue their employers. Other constitutional issues were, therefore, not considered and the case was remitted to the Supreme Court to hear the constitutional issues raised by the appellant. The government, realising it had made a serious error, repealed the regulations in question. Kodeeswaran was promoted.[11] However, the validity of the Language Act was never seriously challenged by Tamil political parties in the courts, *coram judice*. The FP, with brilliant QCs at its disposal, many of whom were experts in

in any case where a religious body is incorporated by law, no such alteration shall be made except at the request of the governing authority of that body.' Article 29 (3) stipulates that 'Any law made in contravention of subsection(2) of this section shall to the extent of such contravention, be void.'

7 M.L. Marasinghe, 'Ethnic Politics and Constitutional Reforms: The Indo-Sri Lanka Accord', *ICLQ*, 37, 1988, p.557.See also R. Edirisinha and N. Selvakumaran, 'Constitutional Changes since Independence', *Sri Lanka Journal of Social Sciences*, 1(2), pp.79–103.

8 Marasinghe, 'Ethnic Politics and Constitutional Reforms', 1988, p.556.

9 *Kodeeswaran v AG of Ceylon* [1970] AC 1111, PC.

10 *Kodeeswaran v AG of Ceylon* [1970] AC 1111, PC.

11 Marasinghe, 'Ethnic Politics and Constitutional Reforms', 1988, p.561.

constitutional and civil law,[12] sought redress through extra-judicial means. They did not see the matter as strictly a legal issue. It was a question of majority domination and an attack on Tamils. Moreover, a minority would view such a policy as an attempt at assimilation. No doubt the issue could have been fought and won legally but the policy itself had a deleterious effect on the perceptions of minority Tamils signalling to them that the majority is a threat, which increased their feeling of vulnerability.

The *Kodeeswaran* case eventually had a revolutionary effect on language policy in the island which had hitherto favoured only the Sinhalese. In 1966 the right to use the Tamil language in the north and east of the island was regulated in terms of the *Tamil Language (Special Provisions) Act* 1958. The Tamil language was recognised by the 1972 Constitution as a national language as well. In 1988, by the 13th amendment to the Constitution of the Democratic Socialist Republic of Sri Lanka, 1978,[13] it was upgraded to the status of 'an official language'. The demands for regional government along federalist lines were also by 1978 constitutionally recognised, thereby establishing provincial government in accordance with the Indo-Sri Lanka agreement.[14] The 13th amendment resolved most of the pressing problems facing the Tamils as far as minority rights were concerned. Ironically, the 13th amendment was nobody's child except India's although its father Rãjiv Gãndhi was killed by the LTTE for introducing it.[15]

Sinhalese frustration in the run up to the 1958 ethnic violence

The political landscape gradually changed within a few years of S.W.R.D. Bandaranaike's premiership due to his maladroit handling of almost every issue he laid his hands on. Inter-rivalries between government ministers spread with some resorting to 'dirty tricks' to undermine one another's credibility. The Prime Minister himself did not escape these attacks. The divisions between the right and left within the same government surpassed issues of national import. Phillip Gunawardene's people friendly policies were attacked by right wing ministers of the Bandaranaike government. Senior ministers such as C.P. de Silva, Wijayananda Dahanayake and Wimala Wijayawardene spearheaded the attack against left wing ministers. There were also rumours about the boycotting of cabinet meetings by some senior cabinet ministers.

12 Chelvanayakam was himself a QC. Most of the senior members of his party were eminent civil and constitutional lawyers in the island.

13 See art. 18 (2). Article 19 reads that 'the national languages of Sri Lanka shall be Sinhala and Tamil.'

14 See Chapter XVII A, *The Constitution of the Democratic Socialist Republic of Sri Lanka*, 1978, amended by the 13th amendment.

15 See, on this, R. Gonsalkorale 'Changes to the 13th Amendment', *Asian Tribune*, 10 June 2013. See also L. Fernando 'Provincial Councils in Sri Lanka from a Political Economy Perspective', *Asian Tribune*, 15 April 2011.

The new government thus faced major difficulties. First, the conservative faction were united in their opposition against any progressive actions launched by their left leaning colleagues. In particular, the laws introduced by Phillip Gunawardane regulating paddy fields hit the rural aristocrats hard. Those who had supported Banaranaike during the 1956 general election campaign came to realise that their demands were not being met owing to the lukewarm attitudes of senior ministers. The demands made by the Sinhalese, for the implementation of the Official Language Act without delay, did not materialise. The implementation of the Language Act was to be delayed for another five years. The *lingua franca* among the elites was English. The bureaucracy inherited from the colonial administration remained intact in the eyes of ordinary people. This frustrated the hopes of those who had sought a quick solution by supporting Bandaranaike and displacing the United National Party (UNP). Contrariwise, the due place of Buddhism, promised by the Bandaranaike coalition before the 1956 election, was not fulfilled even after two full years of government. Buddhist monks and other Sinhalese Buddhist organisations expected that the new government would follow in the ancient traditions of the Sinhalese kings to once again create a Sinhala Buddhist country. Those who opposed western culture and the pre-eminence of the English-educated elitist groups soon realised that the new government was not very different to its predecessor, the UNP, which from 1947 to 1956 was led first by D.S. Senanayake and after his death by his son, Dudley Senanayake. The influence of the Catholic and Anglican churches was still palpable.

The government in disarray – Chelvanakam takes his chance

Chelvanayakam observed this situation with interest. He realised that the government was in strife, unable to focus on issues of national significance. It was clear that they had lost control. Industrial strikes led by the Marxist political parties, in particular the Lanka Sama Samaja Party (LSSP), were regular occurrences putting the whole economy at grave risk. Chelvanayakam seized the opportunity presented by a haphazard government.

By now Tamils were willing to support action taken by the FP. Chevanayakam's policy, as recorded by his son-in-law, Wilson, namely 'the indoctrination of the Tamil masses' had begun to bear fruit by the late 1950s. By 1958 those who took part in training sessions, and others who supported the federalists' cause, showed a willingness to confront 'Sinhalese linguistic and nationalist imperialism'. Those who took part in recruitment drives became an army of foot soldiers more than willing to give up everything for the federalist cause.[16]

Confrontational tactics were seen by the FP as the most desirable route to achieve a *federal*-style government – the Thamil Arasu – from an unwilling government of

16 See S.K. Hennayaka, 'Interactive Ethno-nationalism, An Alternative Explanation of Minority Ethno–nationalism', *Political Geography*, II(6), 1992, pp.526–549.

'Sinhalese chauvinists'. Thus, it was not surprising that the FP abandoned its *satyagraha* campaign by 1958 in preference to *direct actions*. By 1958 the scene was set for a new kind of politics in which the main weapon would be extra-constitutional methods, *hartal*. Although this was in effect civil disobedience/direct action, Chelvanayakam's *hartal* became violent, sometimes involving attacks against government property.

The communal violence of 1958 which engulfed the north, east, west and other conurbations of Tamil settlements in the upper reaches of the Hill Country[17] was the result of direct action and involved Tamils and Sinhalese extremists. The FP made several demands including a resolution to the language issue, the alleged colonisation of traditional Tamils' homeland by Sinhalese peasants, the Indian citizenship issue and the demand for regional assemblies in the north and east. The confrontation between Chelvanayakam and Premier Bandaranaike intensified when the latter unilaterally abrogated the agreement he had entered into with Chelvanayakam.

In April 1961 violence again spread among the Sinhalese and the Tamils owing to the FP's *hartal* and its attempt to setup a symbolic Tamil government by establishing a 'Thamil Arasu Postal Service'.[18] Sinhalese communalists reacted to this. This was, as stated by the FP, a stark reminder to the government that any action that might put the Tamils in a disadvantaged position would not be tolerated.

Intensification of Direct Action and the threat to territorial integrity and the sovereignty of the island

The 1961 civil disobedience campaign was launched as a direct challenge to the sovereignty and the territorial integrity of the island owing to the failure of the ruling Sri Lanka Freedom Party (SLFP) to implement the *pactum* entered into between Chelvanayakam and the leaders of the SLFP, C.P. de Silva, Felix R. Dias Bandaranayake and A. Jayasuriya. However, Mrs Sirimao R. Dias Bandaranaike, the newly elected Prime Minister, was reluctant to implement this, saying that she knew nothing about such an agreement between her political party, SLFP and the FP. Let down and betrayed by the new government, Chelvanayakam declared in April 1961 that the edict of the Sinhalese government would not be obeyed by Tamil-speaking people in the north and east. A long-awaited declaration of the formation of Thamil Arasu was declared. Its principal public service, the Thamil Arasu Postal Service, was established with new stamps bearing the faces of famous Tamil heroes. Measures were quickly taken to distribute crown lands among landless Tamil peasants. Chelvanayakam gave orders to establish a Tamil police force. Many of his supporters questioned the wisdom of these hasty measures and the confrontational policy which they did not feel they could win.

17 See, on this, T. Vittachi, *Emergency '58: The Story of Ceylon Race Riots*, Andre Deutsch: London, 1958.
18 Ponnambalam, *Sri Lanka: The National Question*, 1983, p.122.

'The third tactic', little now and later more

Chelvanayakam tried to use his personal and political contacts with the Sinhalese to win back the lost sovereignty of the Tamils. To this end he continually sought what became known as 'interim adjustments' with successive governments. On some occasions such 'adjustments' led to agreements and understanding between Chelvanayakam and the leaders of the main political parties in the island, the SLFP and the UNP. One such famous agreement was when the Bandaranaike government agreed to introduce devolution of powers to the Tamil-speaking areas of the north and east in 1957. The second agreement was reached between the Dudley Senanayake government and the FP in 1965 in which it they agreed to introduce a power sharing scheme at district level, although this agreement was not as extensive as the agreement of 1957. Neither of these agreements was acted on because of extreme opposition from the Sinhalese Buddhists.

The Bandaranaike–Chelvanayakam Pact 1957

The first historic step to find a solution to the reasonable demands of the Tamils was taken in 1957 by the government led by S.W.R.D. Bandaranaike. Many people close to Bandaranaike agreed that a solution had to be attempted. Of these, Wilmot Perera (a prominent Sinhalese parliamentarian), Sir Edward Jayatilake (the former retired Chief Justice), P. Navarathna Raja, QC, and the influential Catholic priest, Dr Stanislaus Xavier Thaninayagam should be mentioned. According to the personal accounts of Wilson, they played a major role in softening Bandaranaike's opposition to federalists' demands. When Thaninayagam met with the Premier to discuss the seriousness of communal tensions in the Tamil-dominated areas Bandaranaike was quoted as saying, 'Father, I would rather have this issue decided by the sword.'[19]

Bandaranaike was bewildered and infuriated by the tactics employed by the FP to achieve its ends even though he himself was once a prominent federalist especially in the 1920s and again in the 1940s. It was in disbelief that he watched the way Chelvanayakam resorted to *satyagraha*, which sometimes ended violently, on the eve of the passage of the Official Language Act, in June 1956. He was a believer in Westminster-style liberal democracy; the tradition in which the elite groups engaged in national politics. It remained, until Chelvanayakam resorted to *direct action*, a game played out between gentlemen. They frequently settled their differences at social gatherings of the high society of Colombo, the epicentre of elite politics in post-independence Ceylon.

Bandaranaike ultimately succumbed to friendly pressures applied by 'gentlemen of the elite groups' from both the Tamil and Sinhalese sides. The FP, meanwhile, issued an ultimatum to the government, threatening that it would launch a massive campaign of civil disobedience unless its demands were met within a reasonable

19 Wilson, *Break-up of Sri Lanka*, 1988, p.110.

length of time. The result was an agreement entered into between Prime Minister Bandaranaike and the leader of the FP, S.J.V. Chelvanayakam, concerning the demands of the Tamils on 26 July 1957 (popularly known as the B-C Pact). The language issue, the state-aided settlement of the Tamil regions, and the devolution of power to the north and east were the main focus of this *pactum*. It was agreed that the Tamil language should be the language of administration of the north and the east. According to the provision of the B-C Pact, regional assemblies would be established both in the north and the east, of which the Northern Province was to form one regional council while the Eastern Province was to be divided into two or more regional councils, taking into consideration ethnic diversities within the province – this Chelvanayakam resented. Significantly, provisions were also made in the bill to enable two or more regional councils to amalgamate even beyond provincial limits, thus giving the impression that in the future, it would be possible for both the north and east to merge as one territorial unit. The B-C Pact also enabled a single regional council to divide itself into sub-units, subject to proper ratification by parliament. The regional councils would have powers over agriculture, cooperatives, lands and land development, colonisation, education, health, industries and fisheries, housing and social services, electricity, water schemes and roads. It was also envisaged that further provisions would be made in the bill for two or more regions to collaborate on matters of common interest.

It also envisaged that further details about the scope of the devolution of powers to the regional councils would be made in due course. In respect of the allocation of state lands located in the north and the east, the B-C Pact virtually made provisions to grant full powers to the regional councils 'to select allottees to whom lands within their area of authority shall be alienated and also to select those personnel to be employed for work on such schemes'. Taxation and borrowing also came under the remit of regional councils.

Explaining the main issues contained in the B-C Pact, Bandaranaike assured the Sinhalese Buddhists that there was nothing to fear, because the necessary constitutional measures would be entrenched in any constitutional reform so as to preserve and 'safeguard the position of the Sinhalese while, at the same time, reasonably meeting the fears of the Tamils'.[20] The B-C Pact was hailed, even by a staunch separatist such as Tambiah as 'far-seeing' constitutional reform,[21] which, if implemented, would enable the Tamils to reconstruct their national and linguistic identity within a federal structure. In fact, the scope of the B-C Pact was so extensive that Tambiah says it could have settled the problems of the Tamils forever.[22] Many others agreed. The Committee for Rational Development (in Sri Lanka),

20 S.W.R.D. Bandaranaike, 'Message by the Prime Minister', in the Sri Lanka Freedom Party Annual Conference, SLFP: Colombo, 1958, p.15.

21 S.J. Tambiah, *Sri Lanka: Ethnic Fratricide*, University of Chicago Press: Chicago, 1986, p.30. See also S.J. Tambiah *Buddhism Betrayed – Religion, Politics and Violence in Sri Lanka*, University of Chicago Press: Chicago, 1992.

22 Tambiah, *Ethnic Fratricide*, 1986, p.71.

the organisation comprising Tamil, Sinhalese, Moor and burgher intelligentsia, called it 'the most comprehensive federal model' ever attempted in the years 1957 to 1987.

However, widespread protest against the implementation of the B-C Pact was abundant. It was unthinkable for many Sinhala Buddhists to countenance the possibility of a division of the island along linguistic lines. In their view, this was no more than acquiescence to the federalists' territorial claim for the north and east, which is one-third of the land of the whole island and more than half of the territorial waters. The plan was opposed by most of the prominent organisations of the day; Eksath Bhikku Peramuna (United Front of Buddhist Monks), Jathika Vimukthi Peramuna (the National Liberation Front led by K.M.P. Rajarathne), Tri Simhala Peramuna (the organisation comprising Sinhalese living in the three provinces, namely, Ruhuna, Maya, Pihiti, which cover the whole island) and the UNP. If the B-C Pact were implemented, it was claimed, the Sinhalese, Moors and burghers would themselves become minorities in these two provinces – the worst scenario would be the mass expulsion of Sinhalese peasants settled in the state-aided irrigation schemes from the 1930s.

Eventually the B-C pact was not implemented because of strong opposition from both the Buddhist clergy and Sinhalese 'communalist' groups, including some sections of the UNP led by Dudley Senanayake and his deputy, J.R. Jayawardene (JR). Any solution involving federalism would be seen as Bandaranaike's 'abject surrender' to the extremist demands of the FP.[23] JR led a long, high-profile march opposing the B-C Pact and this created fear among the Sinhalese Buddhists. His extra-parliamentary actions were approved of by the acting leader of the UNP, Dudley Senanayake, who became Premier in 1965. Opposing the B-C Pact, Mr Senanayake said 'I am prepared to sacrifice my life to prevent the implementation of the B-C Pact, which is a racial division of Ceylon under the guise of a Regional Council system. It is an act of treachery on the part of the Prime Minister Bandaranaike.'[24] The FP's claim, especially, for one-third of the island on a communal basis was seen by Dudley Senanayake as an unjustifiable demand. Criticising the territorial claims of the FP, Senanayake said, 'It is anti-national to take up the attitude that any area of Ceylon is to be specifically reserved for any particular community or that any particular community should be excluded from any part of Ceylon.' 'It is the Federal Party that is taking a communal stand', said Senanayake.[25]

The B-C Pact was eventually abandoned[26] and Bandaranaike was later assassinated by a Buddhist monk, the Rev. Somarama, in 1959.

23 Tambiah, *Ethnic Fratricide*, 1986, p.73.

24 See Senanayake's comment in parliament, House Debates, vol. 38, col. 884.

25 *UNP Journal*, 28 April 1961, cited in Kearney, *Communalism and Language*, 1967, p.119.

26 See Kearney, *Communalism and Language*, 1967, pp.85–87. See also Wriggins, *Ceylon*, 1967, pp.266–267.

Bandaranaike's failure in the communalist adventure

It was not surprising that the B-C Pact collapsed. The way in which the process was conducted between Bandaranaike and Chelvanayakam must take at least some of the blame. The former was a scholar of Christ Church, Oxford and chose politics as his profession after returning to Ceylon in the 1920s. After completing his apprenticeship with Congress for a few years he proved to be opportunistic in his political decisions to the surprise of many national leaders. First, he presented federalism to the whole nation as the only way forward for a pluralist country such as Ceylon. Few showed any interest in this solution. Having failed to win over supporters from the main communities to his federalist ideas he then committed himself to the policies adopted by Congress. He became Secretary of Congress in the late 1920s. Suddenly, in the mid-1930s, he began to espouse narrow, ethnically based sentiments.

In the first cabinet of D.S. Senanayake's government, Bandaranaike was given an important portfolio and was appointed to be leader of the House, but as soon as it became apparent that his chances of succeeding D.S. Senanayake as prime minister were minimal, he crossed over to the opposition side. He later formed a political party with other members of the UNP who had crossed over with him. Sinhalese sectional interests became an important policy of this newly formed political party. Within a few years of its formation, Bandaranaike's political party, the Sri Lanka Freedom Party (SLFP), won the support of most Sinhalese Buddhist leaders. These developments served to demarcate and widen the divide between the Sinhalese and Tamils and increased tensions between the groups.

Bandaranaike predictably fought the 1956 general election on a communal platform, making a number of promises to Sinhalese Buddhists thus alienating the Tamils further. Immediately after his election victory, he set about fulfilling his electoral promises. He made the Sinhalese language the official language of Ceylon but retained some statutory provisions for the reasonable use of the Tamil language. This created problems for both communities. The FP's threat of civil unrest unsettled Bandaranaike, returning him to his federalist ideas as a solution. The acknowledgement of the FP's territorial claims to the north and east enraged the Sinhalese and for the first time in post-independent Ceylon, the Tamil claim to the north and east was given legitimacy.

S.W.R.D. Bandaranaike: political and personal paradoxes

Bandaranaike was indeed a paradox in this critical phase of Ceylon politics. The contradictory approaches he adopted demonstrated that he had never, during his whole career, been able to stick to a coherent policy. In hindsight, it might appear that he was a political opportunist. His embrace of communal politics in the 1930s and later in the 1950s was a mere stepping stone to power. He was a shrewd political operator who could sense the mood of the country and he used his political instincts to become prime minister – unfortunately, his personal ambition took precedence over his political convictions. He made changes on the personal level as well that appear calculated to impress Sinhalese voters – he changed from Catholicism to Buddhism, rejecting his western attire for the *jathika anduma* (the traditional clothes of the Sinhalese), worn by ordinary Sinhalese people.

These personal modifications were mirrored on the political level when he showed himself unable to stay with parties and policies for more than a few years. He also unsuccessfully tried to appease the both the Sinhalese and Tamils, which created further divisions between these two communities. This was vividly demonstrated by his behaviour during and after the communal violence of 1956 and 1958. He travelled the country during 1957, promoting the B-C Pact and federalism. When violent protests started in the Jaffna Peninsula against the use of *sri*, a Sinhala letter that the government had insisted be painted on the buses belonging to the Ceylon Transport Service, he failed to take timely steps to contain it. He also failed to establish direct communication between Chelvanayakam and himself. When the Sinhalese in the south and west began to respond to Tamil protests in the north and east and painted over Tamil signs on streets and on Tamil-owned businesses, Bandaranaike was not able to contain them either. As opposition to the B-C Pact spread among the Sinhalese, he unilaterally abrogated the Pact without even informing Chelvanayakam. Thus, the federal solution, which Bandaranaike championed as a solution to communal harmony on the island, appeared and disappeared within the space of a few months. The consequences of this aborted pact have reverberated in the politics of the island ever since.

Identity, history and political narrative

The claim that there was a Tamil kingdom[27] covering the north and the east was very important to the consolidation of Tamil identity. To some scholars, it is an 'exaggerated historical claim', to others it is grounded in fact.[28] It is not the purpose of this book to adjudicate or settle this matter. What is important is the significance of history to stake a territorial claim so that the argument for autonomy can be strengthened. Chelvanayakam needed all the tools at his disposal to woo the Tamil-speaking people in both these provinces and to strengthen the power base of the Tamils. For this, he needed a territory on which his future Thamil Arasu was to be established.

He warned his followers that 'like the Irish nationalists they must remain dedicated and avoid compromise or the lure of office until their goal was won.'[29]

27 It was a senior lecturer in history at the University of Ceylon (Peradeniya campus) who, for the first time, presented as a theory that there was a kingdom in the Jaffna Peninsula. See Pathmanathan, *The Kingdom of Jaffna*, Colombo, 1978. See also Indrapala, 'Dravidian Settlements in Ceylon and the Beginning of the History of Jaffna', 1965.

28 Helmann-Rajanayagam, 'The Politics of the Tamil Past', in J. Spencer (ed.), *History and the Roots of the Conflict*, 1990, p.116.

29 Chelvanayakam, Presidential Address, 1949, cited in Kearney, *Communalism and Language*, 1967, p.108.

This uncompromising stance was shaped and conditioned by other socio-religious factors as well. Professor Tambia's analysis is that social upbringing, experience of social dominance; Hinduism and caste supremacy made the Jaffna Tamil feel superior to that of the Sinhalese. The Tamils, 'whose experience of social dominance in their own region and whose sense of greater "orthodoxy" and "orthopraxy" in matters of castes and religious observances made it impossible for them to accept a position of subordination in a polity composed of a Sinhalese majority, who by their standards were inferior in their purity of customs, inferior in talent, and had no historical claim to rule or encompass them.'[30]

Some Tamil historians', notably Dr K. Indrapala and S. Pathmanathan's, research on the Tamil settlements on the Jaffna Peninsula shows,[31] that there was a Tamil kingdom during the thirteenth–fifteenth centuries around the Jaffna Peninsula even though the chronological order of the kingdom could not be established.[32] The limits of the territory, however, were never extended beyond the isthmus of the Elephant Pass to the south. The Eastern Province had never been a constituent part of this short-lived Tamil kingdom as acknowledged by many Tamil scholars.[33] Even a staunch federalist, severe critic of the Sinhalese Buddhists and a distinguished Tamil anthropologist at the University of Harvard, Professor Tambiah, refuted the accuracy of the concept of the 'traditional Tamil homeland', which was alleged to have been located in the north and east. He writes:[34]

> The political and social heart of the Sri Lankan Tamils has been and continues to be the Jaffna peninsula, because there alone a Tamil polity was established: the kingdom of Jaffna, which thrived in the centuries before the arrival of the Portuguese; its history is more accurately known from the third quarter of the fifteenth century until the time of its Portuguese subjugation in the 1620s. It is doubtful whether the Tamils of the Eastern Province were subjects of this kingdom: traditionally, that region lay at the outer perimeter of the Kandyan kingdom, enjoying much autonomy as did many of the Vanniyars from the centers of political influence like Kandy and Jaffna. Thus traditionally, and especially after the kingdom of Jaffna was overtaken by the Portuguese and thereafter by the Dutch, the Tamils of the north and east had neither strong social interconnections nor acted as political collectivities – though no doubt

30 Tambiah, *Sri Lanka, Ethnic Fracricide*, 1986, p.106.

31 Indrapala, 'Dravidian Settlements in Ceylon and the Beginning of the History of Jaffna', 1965. Pathmanathan's methodology of research to assert that there was a well-established Tamil kingdom is severely criticised by some historians. See P.A.T. Gunasinghe, 'Review Article of S. Pathmanathan's Kingdom of Jaffna', 1978, pp.99–112. See Pathmanathan's answer to Gunasinghe's criticism, 'The Kingdom of Jaffna – Propaganda or History?', *Sri Lanka Journal of the Humanities*, 5, 1979, pp.101–125.

32 See de Silva, *History of Sri Lanka*, 1988.

33 See Indrapala, and Helmann-Rajanayagam, 'The Politics of the Tamil Past', 1990, p.117.

34 Tambiah, *Sri Lanka: Ethnic Fratricide*, 1986, pp.102–103.

their speaking a common language, worship of the same or similar 'Hindu' deities, and practice of similar cults and customs gave them a recognizable affinity.

The kingdom of Jaffna Peninsula disappeared with the Portuguese conquest of the Peninsula. The whole idea behind this concept was to create a historical foundation for the FP's argument for autonomy for the Tamil region.

Tamil Eelam

The conception of a traditional *Tamil homeland* is now referred to as *Tamil Eelam* by both terrorist secessionist group and moderate Tamils. Rajanayagam states that Tamil Eelam was the ancient name used by the Tamils for Sri Lanka and it was interchangeably used with *Illankai* in the old Tamil literature.[35] This much abused word was resurrected by Ponnambalam Arunachalam in the 1920s in his political speech and memoranda. By the 1930s it was widely used, in particular, by Tamil historians who began to engage in the construction of Tamil identity in direct response to Sinhala Buddhist revivalism. It formed the political and historical base on which the demands of the Jaffna Tamils for equal share of the political power in the colony was justified.

In its contemporary sense Tamil Eelam was revitalised by the former Professor of mathematics and a parliamentarian, C. Suntharalingam, between 1955 and 1964 in a series of articles and letters. As Rajanayagam describes he, initially, used '*Eylom* to identify the Tamil kingdom'.[36] The present political connotation, however, was given by Chelvanayakam in the 1970s. He used *Eelam Tamil kingdom* and *Tamil Eelam* interchangeably. After this Eelam became a standard term for the independent sovereign Tamil state. To awaken Tamil consciousness, as Rajanayagam, points out 'mythical and mystical qualities' were deliberately added to Eelam.[37]

Chelvanayakam's Failure to Unite the Tamils

The link between territory and the language was important to make a credible claim for separation. Why did Chelvanayakam emphasise linguistic traits instead of ethnic differences? Was it a mistake or masterly strategy? If Chelvanayakam genuinely wanted to liberate only Tamil-speaking people of Dravidian stock then his movement would not take off as he wanted. By the same token, Ceylon Tamil alone could not launch any strong and meaningful attack on the Sinhalese-dominated government given the fact that they never represented more than

35 Helmann-Rajanayagam, 'The Politics of the Tamil Past', 1990, p.117.
36 Helmann-Rajanayagam, 'The Politics of the Tamil Past', 1990, p.114.
37 Helmann-Rajanayagam, 'The Politics of the Tamil Past', 1990, p.117.

11 per cent of the population of the island. In the Eastern Province, their representation was not strong in comparison with the combined Sinhalese and Moor populations. If the Moors were to be excluded from any future Dravidian state in the east then the FP would face an insurmountable barrier in relation to land because large areas of the east was inhabited by both the Sinhalese and the Moors.

The identity of the Moors as a separate nation had been frequently questioned by the Jaffna Tamil elite politicians. In the 1880s when the British governor tried to nominate a Moor to represent the Moor community in the legislative assembly in an unofficial capacity, the Ceylon Tamil elite group objected arguing that the Moors were in fact Tamils who had migrated from south India and later converted to Islam. This assertion had been made by Sir Ponnnambalam Ramanathan.[38] The Moors rejected this pointing out that their ancestors came from the Arabic countries and they were a different racial and ethnic group.[39] However, this view was again questioned by the Jaffna Hindus who pointed out the similarities between the Tamils and the Moors.[40] Even today Tamil politicians and some Tamil scholars challenge the Moors' claim and this is the reason why the FP continually referred to the Moors as the Tamil-speaking people.

Opposition from the lower castes: edging toward secession. From Thamil Arasu to Tamil Eelam (final)

Since the late 1970s militant secessionist movements among Tamil youths began to surface on the political scene of the Jaffna Peninsula, first, as pressure groups against the elite Jaffna Tamil politicians and, later, developing into a secessionist armed struggle against the Sri Lankan government. The oppressive caste system prevalent on the Peninsula was a significant factor in these developments.

There had been for centuries a deep division between high caste *Vellalas* and low caste Tamils, mainly *Pallavar*, *Nalavar* and *Karaiyar*. These last castes were considered 'non-Tamils or aboriginal people of a despicably low status'.[41] They were socially excluded by the *Vellalas* in almost every aspect of day-to-day life. Holmes describes the condition of the low-caste Tamils thus:[42]

> In Jaffna in the 1940s and 1950s, for instance, minority [sic] Tamils were forbidden to enter or live near temples; to draw water from the wells of

38 P. Ramanathan, 'Ethnology of the Moors in Ceylon', *Journal of the Royal Asiatic Society* (Ceylon Branch), X(36), 1888, pp.234–62. See, also, V. Samaraweera, 'The Muslim Revivalist Movement, 1880–1915', in Roberts (ed.), *Collective Identities*, 1979, pp.261–263.

39 Rogers, 'Historical Images in the British Period', in Spencer (ed.), *Sri Lanka, History and the Roots of Conflict*, 1990, p.98.

40 *Hindu Organ*, Jaffna, 13/vi/1900, cited in Rogers, 'Historical Images in the British Period', in Spencer (ed.), *Sri Lanka, History and the Roots of Conflict*, 1990, p.106.

41 Pfaffenberger, 'The Political Construction of Defensive Nationalism', 1990, p.82.

42 W.R. Holmes, *Jaffna (Sri Lanka)*, St Joseph's Press: Jaffna, 1980; Pfaffenberger, 'The Political Construction of Defensive Nationalism', 1990, p.82.

high-caste families; to enter laundries, barbershops, cafes, or taxis, to keep women in seclusion and protect them by enacting domestic rituals; to wear shoes; to sit on bus seats; to register their names properly so that social benefits could be obtained; to attend school; to cover the upper part of the body; to wear gold earrings; if male, to cut their hair; to use umbrellas; to own bicycles or cars; to cremate the dead; or to convert to Christianity or Buddhism.

This practice of caste exclusion gave rise to violent incidents in the 1960s and 1970s directed against high-caste Jaffna Tamils. Trade and industry and jobs in government service remained the monopoly of the upper-caste groups and attempts by the *Pallars* and *Nalavars* to improve their position resulted in violence, long drawn-out *hartal*, and in extreme cases, killings by both high- and low-caste Tamils. Any sign of upward mobility by untouchable groups was quickly suppressed and repressive social customs were enforced through intimidation and violence.[43] *Vellalas* often fielded thugs to punish attempts by *Pallars* or *Nalawars* to improve themselves, forcing them to conform to the social stratification. According to Pfaffenberger: 'Minority Tamils who attempted to raise their position would find their communities victimised by Vellalar-organised gangs of thugs, who burnt down properties and poisoned wells.'[44]

Gradually, in the 1960s, oppressed Tamils began to voice their anger against these discriminatory practices. They organised under the umbrella group 'All-Ceylon Minority Tamils' United Front'. One of the protest campaigns organised by minority Tamils with the help of Shanmuganathan, a Tamil politician, and his Communist Party was 'the Maviddapuram Temple-entry movements' which shook the fabric of the Jaffna Tamil society. Low-caste Tamil campaigners tried to enter the Maviddapuram Hindu Temple hitherto reserved for the worship of high-caste Tamils only, by force. This campaign resulted in a drawn-out and violent struggle between high- and low-caste Tamils attracting wide publicity in the Colombo-based newspapers.

In response, high-caste Tamils of the Jaffna Peninsula organised against low-caste Tamils by setting up a new organisation in 1968, the 'All-Ceylon Saiva Practices and Observances Protection Society'. Chelvanayakam's Federal Party failed to provide any leadership or viable solution to this crisis. In fact, in 1968, Chelvanayakam was confronted by low-caste Tamils challenging him to stand down from his parliamentary seat and contest it again. Other Federalist leaders, S. Nadaraja and A. Amirthalingam (who succeeded Chelvanayakam as leader of the FP, and later the Tamil United Liberation Front (TULF)) also failed to respond to the frustrated youth faction of the low-caste Tamils. By 1968 low-caste Tamils lost almost all faith in the FP to move in a new direction.[45]

43 17 Feb. 1968, *Times of Ceylon*, cited in Pfaffenberger, 'The Political Construction of Defensive Nationalism', 1990, p.82.

44 Pfaffenberger, 'The Political Construction of Defensive Nationalism,' 1990, p.80.

45 *Times of Ceylon*, 9 Aug. 1968, cited in Pfaffenberger, 'The Political Construction of Defensive Nationalism', 1990, p.92.

Colombo based political parties volunteered to support the All-Ceylon Minority Tamils' United Front. The SLFP, the main opposition party in parliament, introduced a parliamentary bill in 1968 urging the government to inquire into discriminatory practices perpetrated against low-caste Tamils. It wanted the *Prevention of Social Disabilities Act* of 1957 to be amended to include oppressive practices and discriminatory customs.[46] Unsurprisingly, low-caste Tamils were not in favour of devolution of power to the regions. They knew that power would be concentrated in the Jaffna high caste and that their position would become worse. Therefore, when the *District Development Council Bill*, which aimed to devolve power to the regions at district level, was wending its way through parliament, they demanded that the opposition parties oppose the bill. Low-caste Tamils argued that if political and administrative power devolved to the Jaffna Peninsula and to other Tamil conurbations in the coastal area in the north-east, this would operate to the detriment of the oppressed Tamil groups.

The *District Council Bill* also attracted widespread protests from the Sinhalese. They made the, by now standard, argument that the devolution of power to the north and east would result in the erosion of the sovereignty of the island. Large gatherings and marches were organised in Colombo by the Sinhalese to register their opposition to the bill, and in the resulting commotions a Buddhist monk died.[47] The concerted opposition of both Sinhalese-dominated political parties and oppressed Tamil groups in the Jaffna Peninsula resulted in the abandonment of the District Council Bill in 1968, an event regarded by both the elite of the Ceylon Tamils and its youth league as an act of betrayal by the Sinhalese.

Federalists' last ditch attempt

These crises culminated in the withdrawal of Chelvanayakam's FP from the coalition government in September 1968 saying that they needed time and space to focus on the unity of the Tamils. The federalist leadership made a concerted effort to recruit low-caste Tamils to its ranks and some did indeed join the FP. A few individuals were even selected to stand as FP's candidates in the parliamentary elections so the FP did succeed, at least temporarily, in uniting the various factions. The decline in government employment opportunities for Tamil youth and the discrimination against Tamils also helped coalesce the various groups. It had become too clear that only if Tamils of all political beliefs come under one wing would Sinhalese chauvinism be defeated and the way to do this was to build up a Tamil state (Thamil Arasu) in the north and east where the traditional Tamil homeland was believed to have been established. Many considered this to be a 'politics of defensive nationalism' and it was branded by some as 'a last ditch

46 Pfaffenberger, 'The Political Construction of Defensive Nationalism', 1990, p.90.

47 This tragic incident was immediately exploited by the main opposition parties (SLFP, CP and the LSSP) who set up a monument in memory of the monk on the place at which he was killed by a policeman.

attempt to unite a community that would otherwise fall to pieces'.[48] Nonetheless, the FP had to pay a price. It was forced to accommodate the disgruntled low caste while continuing to rely on the high-caste, landowning *Vellalas* who held high government positions.

In spite of the FP trying to create a broad base for Tamils of all castes, low-caste Tamils remained dissatisfied and became increasingly militant. Their opposition to both the traditional leadership of the FP and to non-Tamil nationals on the Peninsula was vividly demonstrated in the 1970 general election. The FP suffered the heaviest losses for the first time since the 1956 general election. Both the Chairman of the FP, S.M. Rasamanickam and his deputy leader, E.M.V. Naganathan, were defeated while the leader, Chelvanayakam, barely managed to avoid defeat.[49]

FP's six-point plan

In 1972 the coalition government led by the SLFP enacted a new constitution by which Ceylon became a republic, the Republic of Sri Lanka. During the deliberation on the constitutional reforms, the FP put forward a six-point plan that they hoped would be included in the proposed republican constitution. They were:

1. equal status for Tamil and Sinhala languages;
2. extension of citizenship for all Indian Tamils who had settled in Sri Lanka and who had been deprived of citizenship;
3. equality of religion;
4. fundamental rights and freedoms for every citizen group irrespective of ethnic and cultural differences;
5. abolition of caste and untouchability;
6. decentralisation of power to the regions on linguistic lines.

These demands, according to a leading Tamil theorist, Neelan Thiruchelvam, encompassed 'the lowest denominator of Tamil needs and aspirations'.[50] Did the FP leadership consider these to be the basic building blocks of a future Tamil state?[51] Neelan Thiruchelvam denied this stating that the FP wanted to 'work towards equality within a pluralistic society'.

The FP had also proposed that there should be five federal states in the new republic, one for the Tamils, one for the Moors and three for the Sinhalese. These demands were rejected by the Constitutional Assembly which had been convened

48 Pfaffenberger, 'The Political Construction of Defensive Nationalism', 1990, p.80.

49 Ponnambalam, 'The National Question', 1983, p.154.

50 N. Thiruchelvam, 'The Politics of Decentralisation and Devolution: Competing Conceptions of District Development Councils in Sri Lanka', in Goldman and Wilson (eds.), *From Independence to Statehood*, 1984, p.197.

51 In the 1970s the future Thamil Arasu was synonymously identified with Eelam Tamil nation state. From about 1980s the term used for a Tamil state is Tamil Eelam.

to draft the new constitution.[52] Article 2 of the new Constitution of 1972 proclaimed that 'the Republic of Sri Lanka is a unitary State' thus, much to the dismay of the federalists, proposals for the federal elements were rejected. In response to these developments, a new political movement, the 'Tamil United Front' (TUF) was hastily launched on 14 May 1972. It brought the FP, ACTC, Ceylon Workers Congress (CWC) and other smaller factions of the Tamil movement into one Tamil organisation to achieve Tamil Eelam. This new political party even allowed untouchable Indian Tamils (who lived in the Hill Country) to become members. In fact, the leader of the Indian Tamils, S. Thondaman, was elected as one of the leaders of the TUF. In 1975, in order to appease militant Tamil youths and other Eelamists, the TUF declared that its main goal would be to achieve an independent Tamil Eelam.[53]

Kankesanthurai gospel

The Kankesanthurai by-election proved to be one of the most significant turning points in the Tamil struggle in post-independence Sri Lanka. Chelvanayakam fought this election with Tamil self-determination as his main goal. After his victory he declared, 'I wish to announce to my people and the country that the Eelam Tamil Nation should exercise the sovereignty already vested in the Tamil people and become free.'

Neelan Thiruchelvam, one of the leading theorists of the TUF and its successor bodies until his death, did indeed interpret this statement as an assertion of the right of self-determination.[54] By 1977 the influence of the radical Tamil youth movements, many of whom were, by this time, actively engaged in secessionist activities, was evident within the TUF. To ensure that they kept faith with this increasingly dominant, unorthodox faction, within their ranks, the leadership of the TUF felt that they had to do something dramatic. The result was the historic Vadukoddai Resolution of 14 May 1976 where they resolved to work for the independence of the Tamil nation. Secession was officially adopted as the TUF's legitimate goal. The resolution stated:[55]

> The Tamils of Ceylon, by virtue of their great language, their religion, their separate culture and heritage, their history of independent existence as a separate state over a distinct territory for several centuries till they were conquered by the armed might of the European invaders and above all by

52 Thiruchelvam, 'The Politics of Decentralisation and Devolution' in Goldman and Wilson (eds.), *From Independence to Statehood*, 1984, p.162.

53 See Chelvanayakam's statement in Jan. 1975, cited in Ponnambalam, 'The National Question', 1983, pp.182–183.

54 Thiruchelvam, 'The Politics of Decentralisation and Devolution', in Goldman and Wilson (eds.), *From Independence to Statehood*, 1984, p.198.

55 Resolution Unanimously Adopted at the First National Convention of the Tamil United Liberation Front held at Vaddukoddai, Tamil United Liberation Front, Jaffna, 1976.

their will to exist as a separate entity ruling themselves in their own territory as a nation distinct and apart from the Sinhalese . . . (who) are using the power they have wrongly usurped to deprive the Tamil nation of its territory, language, citizenship, economic life, opportunities of employment and education thereby destroying all the attributes of nationhood of the Tamil people. This convention resolves that restoration and reconstruction of the Free, Sovereign, Secular State of Tamil Eelam.

The Vadukoddai Resolution was a turning point in the Tamil struggle and translated the 'vague and disconnected aspirations' of the Tamil-speaking people into a concrete political programme'.[56] TUF's name was changed to the Tamil United Liberation Front (TULF), adding a flavour of secessionism. The 1977 general election was fought by TULF on the platform of Tamil Eelam, comprising both the Northern and Eastern Provinces of the island.

The radical and subversive nature of the political slogans by the leadership of TULF during the general election of 1977 encouraged the creation of militant Tamil movements. Already an underground guerrilla movement was organising to force a separation from the Republic of Sri Lanka. According to Pfaffenberger, many Jaffna Tamil youths were convinced that the moderate and conservative policy of the Tamil elite was not working in achieving their rightful place in Sri Lankan polity. Some even criticised the old federalist leaders for their failure to achieve a Tamil State after four decades of 'futile politics'. The policies of the Tamil leadership in post-independence Ceylon were seen as timid, self-serving and neglectful of the interests of ordinary Tamils.[57]

In fact, most of the leaders of the newly emerged guerrilla groups were lower caste Tamil youths. The leader of what was to become the Liberation Tigers of Tamil Eelam (LTTE), V. Prabhakaran, was a *Karaiyar*. The new militant Tamil guerrilla groups turned violently against the traditional Tamil leadership of TULF first and to the shock of the Tamils, Thiagarajah, an MP, and Alfred Duraiyappah, the former mayor of Jaffna and a liberal Tamil politician were both assassinated in 1978. The reasons offered by the radicals for these murders were that the former had joined the UNP after deserting the TULF, while the latter had attempted to convince Tamil voters that for the betterment of both communities the Tamils should abandon isolationist and communal politics and join the 'mainstream of Ceylonese politics'.[58] The time for moderate cooperation was over.

The violent campaign for a Tamil homeland dates to the late 1970s when 13 Sinhalese soldiers were killed in Thinnevely on the Jaffna Peninsula.

56 Thiruchelvam, 'The Politics of Decentralisation and Devolution', in Goldman and Wilson (eds.), *From Independence to Statehood*, 1984, p.198.

57 A. Balasingham, *Liberation Tigers and Tamil Eelam Freedom Struggle*, Jaffna Liberation of Tigers of Tamil Eelam, Jaffna, 1984, p.25. Balasingham is the chief theoretician to V. Prabhakaran, the leader of the LTTE.

58 Kearney, *Communalism and Language*, 1967, p.29.

The July 1983 riots

On the night of 23 July 1983 there followed bloody violence against the Tamils by Sinhalese mobs instigated by a section of the government.[59] This appeared to be in retaliation to the killing of the soldiers. According to Wilson 'the violence of Sinhalese Buddhist nationalism took the Tamil militants by surprise.'[60] The effect of the riots was large-scale migration out of Sri Lanka and the recruitment of foot soldiers to the Eelamists. Thereafter a cycle of violence followed. Wilson records that a Jaffna army commander, in a letter to a friend, said that the LTTE who were actually guerrilla fighters were placed on a 'war footing'.

Separatism through violence

The strategy adopted to achieve a Tamil Eelam was twofold due to the total transformation of the political infrastructure in the Jaffna Peninsula. During the 1980s the power held by the traditional leadership of the high-caste *Vellalas* over Tamil constituencies changed dramatically. The traditional Tamil leadership of the Ceylon Tamil parties suddenly disappeared – some were killed and others forced to flee the region. Dr Neelan Thiruchelvam, Kumar Ponnambalam (the leader of the ACTC and the son of the late G.G. Ponnambalam), A. Amirthalingam (the former leader of the TULF), and many other distinguished Tamil parliamentarians were killed by the LTTE. In fact, the old Tamil political parties were banned and its leaders identified as traitors by the radical Tamil youth movements. Terrorism became the main strategy of the new Eelamist secessionist groups and was a strategy that was justified on the grounds of the right to self-determination.

Since the 1980s only armed secessionist groups[61] dominated the politics of the Jaffna Peninsula and other Tamil conurbations. From 1986 the LTTE began to consolidate its political position through the indiscriminate use of violence. All other Tamil political parties, including the TULF, were proscribed by the LTTE in the north and east. Tamil politicians, including a number of MPs were mercilessly assassinated. In 1986 Sabarathnam, and the entire leadership of the TELO (Tamil Ealem Liberation Organisation) another secessionist group, were wiped out. Seventy senior members of the EPRLF (a rival secessionist armed group) were also killed in the same year. The leader of the People's Liberation Organisation of Tamil Eelam (PLOTE), Uma Maheswaran, was killed while trying to hide in Colombo. Disobedience of LTTE's edicts inevitably resulted in death. Particular

59 E. Meyer, 'Seeking the Roots of the Tragedy', in Manor (ed.), *Sri Lanka in Change and Crisis*, 1984, p.139.

60 A.J. Wilson, *Sri Lanka Tamil Nationalism: Its Origins and Development in the Nineteenth and Twentieth Centuries*, Hurst & Co.: London, 2000, pp.125–127.

61 See details, O'Ballance, *Cyanide War: Tamil Insurrection in Sri Lanka*, 1989; A. Shastri, 'The Material Basis for Separatism: The Tamil Eelam Movement in Sri Lanka', *JAS*, 49(1), 1988, pp.56–77. A. Bandarage, *The Separatist Conflict in Sri Lanka*, Routledge: New York, 2009.

targets were government agents, headmasters, judges, and leading members of the citizens' committee and members of parliament.[62] Thus the modern era of political killing spread like a cancer engulfing every community on an island once described as a pearl in the Indian Ocean and its inhabitants as friendly, peace-loving and civilised people, having 'a highly productive and culturally rich civilisation'.[63]

62 See more details, Gunasekera, *Tigers, Moderates and Pandora's Package*, 1996, pp. 24–25.

63 Wriggins, *Ceylon, Dilemmas of a New Nation*, 1960, p.11.

12 The role of Sinhalese nationalism

The Tamils always saw themselves as a separate nation in the same way as the Sinhalese did. However, the emergence of the *Illankai Thamil Arasu Kadchi* (FP) was certainly a Tamil reaction to the attitude of the Sinhalese to Tamil aspirations. The formation of the TUF and later the TULF were responses to both a resurgent Sinhalese nationalism as much as a response to internal pressures within Tamil society in the Jaffna Peninsula.

'Sinhalese communalism'

Several eminent Tamil scholars as well as a few western political commentators prominent among whom are Tambiah, A. Jayaratnam Wilson, Dr Arasaratnam, Dr Sabaratnam, Dr Neelan Thiruchelvam, Michael Roberts and Robert R. Kearney claim that the emergence of a clear ethnic consciousness and the politics that gave expression to that development as a defensive stance by the Ceylon Tamils whose future as a distinct nation was in danger of extinction in the face of an aggressive Sinhalese nationalism.

Dr. Thiruchelvam argues that the FP had, until 1975, tried to secure the basic rights of the Tamil-speaking people on the island in conformity with pluralist, multi-ethnic polity. However, the discriminatory and repressive policies against the Tamils adopted by successive Sinhalese-dominated governments in post-independence Ceylon forced the leadership of the FP to adopt a separatist stance. These events 'had an important bearing on the emergence of a new Tamil awareness'. It forced 'a shift from the struggle for equality to an assertion of self-determination, from the acceptance of the pluralist experiment to the surfacing of a new corporate identity'.[1] A.J. Wilson agrees with the argument that Sinhalese Buddhist sub-nationalism ultimately gave rise to the separatist policies of the FP. Unlike Dr Thiruchelvam, Wilson does not try to hide the fact that from the very beginnings of the FP, the politics of self-determination was the central theme of the

1 Thiruchelvam, The Politics of Decentralisation and Devolution: Competing Conceptions of District Development Councils in Sri Lanka', in Goldman and Wilson, *From Independence to Statehood*, 1984, pp.198–199.

new party.[2] However, he justifies the separatist struggle of the FP as a reaction to a series of 'ethno-centric polices adopted by successive government in the post-independence Ceylon'. In addition, other factors such as the failure to honour agreements entered into between the leadership of the Tamils and the Sinhalese pushed the FP into favouring separatist politics. Another determining factor behind the emergence of the FP and its subsequent political manoeuvring was the fear of the Tamil-speaking people in the north and east that they would become a minority in their own traditional Tamil homeland because of resettlement policies of their lands by state-aided Sinhalese settlements.[3]

Tambiah, a proponent of the federal solution and a stern critic of the Sinhalese Buddhists, has been firm in his justification of the separatist polices of the FP. In his view, it was the Sinhalese Buddhists who were responsible for the path taken by the FP and subsequent Eelamist groups. He poses the question thus:

> The chief question I feel impelled to pose and answer . . . in terms of the motives and intentions of the actors and the logic of the situation in which they find themselves, is how it is that Sri Lankans – literally, genial, friendly folk – can have come to this sorry pass. Why, on the one side, should an elected majority government committed to liberal democracy have become in its own eyes so righteously authoritarian, an attitude directly or indirectly assented to by large numbers of the Sinhalese populace? And on the other side, why should the Tamil minority, who have by and large considered themselves rightful citizens of Ceylon, have bred terrorist groups, hell-bent on achieving an independent Tamil state, and whose aspirations increasing numbers of Tamil support? Why is it that the Sinhalese, the 'lion race', find themselves confronted, till death do them part, by the 'tigers'?[4]

Tambiah asserts that the proximate reason for the Federal Party's desire for separation was a 'persistent, unfair, and sporadically terrorizing campaign of discrimination' against the constitutional, democratic and lawful actions of Tamils by Sinhala Buddhist chauvinism.[5] In brief, the emergence of the FP and other militant Tamil organisations was mainly due to 'the post-independence boiling over of the pot of Sinhalese nationalism' against the Tamils.[6]

These theories for the formation and the rise of the FP as a militant organisation are supported by many western political commentators as well. Indeed, it is not difficult to prove that when a resurgent Sinhalese nationalism influenced public policy, such as the language issue, this had a direct effect on the fortunes of the Tamils, and produced extremism in the Tamil political class. However, it is too

2 See, for example, Wilson, 'The Tamil Federal Party in Ceylon Politics', 1966, pp.117–137.
3 See Wilson, 'Race, Religion, Language, Caste', 1979, p.464.
4 Tambiah, *Sri Lanka: Ethnic Fratricide*, 1986, p.3.
5 Tambiah, *Sri Lanka: Ethnic Fratricide*, 1986, p.17.
6 Tambiah, *Sri Lanka: Ethnic Fratricide*, 1986, p.71.

simplistic a conclusion given the history of events, to argue that Tamil 'communalism' was merely a reaction to Sinhalese chauvinism. To understand the events that brought the parties to this unfortunate pass it is necessary to examine the impact of Sinhalese nationalism on the Tamils and on the emergence of the FP and other separatist and secessionist Tamil groups and the self-understanding and social hierarchy of the Tamils themselves.

Sinhalese identity reconstructed?

The differences in approach taken by the elite clans of both the Sinhalese and the Ceylon Tamils, especially between 1920 and 1946, did not emerge suddenly. Viewed historically, it has to be acknowledged that these two communities lived in exclusivity until the arrival of the Europeans. Their respective existence as separate communities dates back centuries with each community developing a rich culture and heritage with a different ethos and values, independently of one another. This has influenced the way the elite groups of the Sinhalese and Tamils advanced the constitutional reforms and self-government for the island. Moreover, both the Sinhalese and the Tamils, as Sir Ivor Jennings noted, operated as two separate linguistic communities.[7] Thus, all the ingredients for ethnic tension existed even before the emergence of Congress. This was especially obvious in the 1930s, during the debates in the State Council, on the due status of the Sinhala and Tamil languages. The language issue gradually crept into the national political debate eventually becoming the main catalyst of ethnic conflict from the 1950s onward.[8]

The leadership of the Sinhalese in Congress campaigned to build up one nation, the Ceylonese nation. They were determined to have a unitary state with one government for the whole island based on elections that would take place in geographically defined constituencies. The approach of the Sinhalese elite in Congress was ostensibly nationalism, when it would be better described as an amalgamation of Sinhalese Buddhist culture and western liberalism. This, in effect, influenced the Sinhalese to accommodate different communities, provided the minority communities were prepared to respect majoritarian rule and the tradition of the island, as defined by the majority, which has existed for most of its history apart from the fifteenth to the sixteenth centuries.

Sinhalese identity is inextricably woven into a long history, rich culture and Buddhist religion. The Sinhalese understand their history and the history of the island as follows: Sri Lanka was identified as *Sihadeepa* (the island inhabited by the Sinhalese) and *Dhammadeepa* (island of Buddhism) in early monastic *chronicles*.[9] During this long history the island was one political entity governed by a king whose

7 See I. Jennings, *The Approach to Self-Government*, Cambridge University Press: Cambridge, 1956.

8 The major conflicts between the Sinhalese and the Tamils occured in 1958 in post-independence Ceylon. See Vittachi, *Emergency '58: The Story of the Ceylon Race Riots*, 1958.

9 *Mahavamsa* and *Chulawamsa* were the greatest chronicles in Ceylonese history. Both were recorded by the Buddhist monks.

uppermost responsibility was to protect Buddhism and Dhammadeepa. The island, as a single entity, is comparable to the post-Westphalian concept of a nation state. Ceylon was governed, before colonisation by the Europeans from the fifteenth century onwards, as one territorial unit (for some time there were three principalities in the island) with one supreme sovereign although there had been a Tamil principality since the thirteenth century in and around the Jaffna Peninsula and which in the fifteenth and sixteenth centuries functioned as a separate political entity. Sihadeepa was also a synonym for *Thri Sinhale,* three larger principalities, Ruhuna, Maya and Pihiti. Central to the idea of Sinhalese Buddhist identity is the notion of the island's historic role as a receptacle of Buddhism. Therefore, it must be maintained as a single unit.

Unlike the Tamils in the Jaffna Peninsula, the Sinhalese had been fighting ever since the island came under the threat of the Europeans, first, against the Portuguese, then the Dutch and later against British colonialism. Only in 1815 were the British able to defeat the Sinhalese kingdom. But Sinhalese determination was so strong that they launched rebellions against the colonial administrations one after another with serious rebellions occurring in 1818, 1820, 1823, 1824, 1834, 1848 and 1858. These were patriotic wars against western imperialism to liberate the island and its people. After 1858 there was no significant armed rebellion in the island. Changes to the traditional leadership and the spread of European education were instrumental in reconditioning the thinking of the locals towards colonialism.

Since the 1870s a renaissance in the religious and cultural spheres, in particular, in the coastal areas south of Colombo began to emerge. This was not a political movement but a reassertion of the value and significance of Buddhism. This resurgence was not uninfluenced by the fact that by the 1860s Sinhalese leadership had passed decisively from the highest caste of *Goyigama* up-country Sinhalese to low-country, low-caste English-educated, new elite groups who were principally from the *Karava, Durava* and *Salagama* castes. Commenting on the anti-imperialist and anti-western movements, de Silva writes that it was 'primarily religious in outlook and in content, a re-assertion of Buddhist values, a re-action against Christian missionary enterprise',[10] thereby challenging Christian proselytisation and its attendant ethos and values. Michael Roberts also noted that the revival of Sinhalese Buddhist movements was a backlash against Christian missionaries and western values that had begun to infiltrate the island since its defeat in 1815.[11] When Christian missionaries ridiculed and attacked Buddhism and Buddhist institutions, Buddhist monks felt that the island's historic role as a receptacle of Buddhism was threatened. Various movements sprang up to protect and nurture religion, artistic and cultural values and traditions in the face of the Christian adversary.

Sinhalese Buddhists also gained in confidence and found reasons to be proud of their history due to new archeological discoveries in the middle of the nineteenth

10 de Silva, 'The Formation and Character', vol. x, 1967, parts 1–2, p.70.
11 Roberts, 'Ethnic Conflict in Sri Lanka and Sinhalese Perspectives', 1978, p.365.

century. Most of these finds proved the accuracy of the great chronicles of the island, *Mahavamsa* and *Culavamsa*. It virtually proved that the Sinhala Buddhists' claim to a great civilisation and history was not exaggerated. New texts of Sri Lanka's history were written first by the Europeans followed by indigenous, western-educated scholars.[12] William Knighton's *History of Ceylon from the Earliest Period to the Present Time* (1845), James Tenant's *Ceylon* (1859), much later Arnold Wright's *Twentieth Century Impressions of Ceylon* (1907) are important works. Among the Sinhalese scholars (both Buddhist and Christian) are counted James D'Alwis (1823–78), C. M. Fernando, E.W. Perera and Sir D.B. Jayatilake. Alwis, who had challenged previously held views about the history of Sri Lanka by European writers, concluded that 'it is a remarkable fact that no country in the East possesses so correct a history of its own affairs and those of Asia generally, as Ceylon.'[13] It was further pointed out that the Sinhalese were from Indo-Aryan origin, aware of electricity and had maintained a well-defined polity with the rule of law and freedom of religion. He also claimed that the Sinhalese were of a different racial stock to the Tamils, and the latter was referred to as the rival group who invaded the island from time to time from their south Indian base and had been instrumental in the destruction of the *Raja Rata* Sinhala Buddhist civilisation.[14]

The resurgent Sinhalese Buddhist nationalism was led by Buddhist monks. Of them, Rev. Miggettuwatte Gunananda (1832–1890) and Rev. Battaramulle Subuthi (1845–1915) were both renowned as frontline leaders in the campaign against Christianity. Their anger and criticism were directed towards western imperialism, its values and their baneful impact on the Sinhalese Buddhists.[15] These movements spawned a new generation nationalist movement, the temperance movement between 1900 and 1916. The external appearance of the movement suggests that it was opposed to the excise policy of the colonial government, yet its propaganda was directed towards Christianity and colonialism. The temperance movement was a largely Buddhist-led mass, popular uprising against some policies of the colonial government predominantly in the Sinhalese Buddhist areas, both rural and metropolitan, although a few Ceylon Tamil leaders, among them A. Kanagasabai, Sandaresegara, Mrs Dr Ratnam, P. Ramanathan and S. Rajaratnam, addressed public gatherings in support of the movement.[16] Some speakers at these gatherings were reported as saying that the Ceylonese should

12 Of these pioneering scholars, James d'Alwis (1823–78), C.M. Fernando and later E.W. Perera should be especially mentioned.

13 J. d'Alwis, 'The Attanagalu-Vansa or the History of the Temple of Attanagalle', translation, Colombo, 1866, cited in Rogers, 'Historical Images in the British Period', in Spencer (ed.), *Sri Lanka, History and the Roots of Conflict*, 1990, p.94.

14 The greatest Sinhala civilisation took place in the dry zone of which the centre was Anuradhapura. Codrington, Paranavitane, Sinhalayo.

15 G. Obeysekere, 'Personal Identity and Cultural Crisis: The Case of Anagarika Dharmapala of Sri Lanka', in F. Reynolds and D. Capps (ed.), *The Biographical Process: Studies in the History and Psychology of Religion*, Mouton: Hungary, 1976, p.225.

16 Fernando, 'Arrack, Toddy and Ceylonese Nationalism: Some Observations on the Temperance Movement, 1912–1921', 1971, p.145.

govern Ceylon. Although the temperance movement never developed into a political organisation that agitated for self-government or constitutional reforms, it was able to rouse national consciousness.

Its character, functions and, above all, style of leadership provided a training ground for Sinhalese political activists who would later supply the future leadership of Congress. The temperance movements[17] against the toddy taverns introduced by the British appeared to be the only bridge between nationalist movements and the constitutionalist elite of the Sinhalese. It was, in fact, an ancillary movement of Buddhist revivalism that emerged during the middle of the nineteenth century. One of its most prominent leaders, Anagarike Dharmapala, urged the Sinhalese Buddhistst not to be frightened by the presence of Christian 'beef-eating' whites and his writings were laced with a vitriolic anti-imperialist tone:

> This ancient, historic, refined people, under the diabolism of vicious paganism, introduced by the British administrators are now declining and slowly dying away . . . the sweet gentle Aryan children of an ancient, historic race are sacrificed at the altar of the whisky drinking, beef-eating, belly-god of heathenism.[18]

Their campaigns were in essence against western imperialism, including a rejection of western religion and culture and they were supported by the rising middle-class elite.[19]

In the 1930s Walisingha Harrischandre and others such as John de Silva and Piyadasa Sirisena, writers of novels and drama, carried the Sinhala Buddhist revival campaigns further. Buddhist influence became a source of inspiration for several political movements agitating for the self-government of the island among which were the Young Lanka League, the Ceylon Reform Society, the Ceylon Reform League and the Ceylon National Association, Lanka Mahãjana Sabhã. These organisations emerged at the same time as the Sinhalese commemoration of the centenary of the Kandyan Convention when the Sinhalese kingdom was ceded to the British government.

The principal constitutionalist organisation, Congress, operated in parallel to the above nationalist organisations. However, in contrast to the nationalists, constitutionalists focused only on constitutional reforms and the limited issues

17 See on this R.D. Gunawardene, *The Reformist Movement and Political Organizations in Ceylon*, 1976, pp.14–73; P.V.J. Jayasekera, 'Social and Political Change in Ceylon, 1900–1919', unpublished PhD Thesis, University of London, 1969. Both these are mentioned in K.M. de Silva, *A History of Sri Lanka*, 1981, pp.374, and 376, respectively.

18 A. Guruge (ed.), *Return to Righteousness: A Collection of Speeches, Essays and Letters of Anagarika Dharmapala*, Colombo, 1965, p.484, cited in K.N.O. Dharmadasa, 'Nativistic Reaction to Colonialism: The Sinhala Buddhist Revival in Sri Lanka', *Asian Studies*, xiii(1), 1974, p.165, cited in G. Obeysekare 'Personal Identity and Cultural Crisis', in Reynolds and Capps (eds.), *The Biographical Process Studies*, Mouton: Paris, 1976, p.243.

19 Dharmadasa 'Nativistic Reaction to Colonialism', 1974, p.163.

associated with it. Although the Sinhalese Buddhist organisations' impact on Congress and its Sinhalese leadership was evident, this did not change the secular character of Congress neither did it stand in the way of the Sinhalese and Tamils working relationship in Congress. The influence of Sinhalese Buddhist ideology did not, contrary to the views of some Tamil scholars, notably, Sabaratnam, exacerbate ethnic differences.[20] The Sinhalese elite were representative of both Buddhists as well as Christians. Their allegiance to the traditions of Sinhalese Buddhism was not as entrenched as that of rural Sinhalese. In fact, Anagarika Dharmapala's public insults and his ridiculing of the Sinhalese for not following the traditional Sinhalese Buddhist way of life, was often directed against the cosmopolitan Sinhalese, bourgeois clique. Thus, between 1920 and 1946, Sinhalese Buddhist ideology did not dominate the constitutional strategies adopted by Sinhalese leaders in Congress.[21] However, its ultimate influence cannot be ignored.

Sinhalese Buddhist revivalism emerged as a political force much later in response to the notion that the UNP had betrayed the Sinhalese Buddhists. There was a deeply entrenched opinion among Buddhists that the non-Sinhalese Buddhists and Catholics had been favoured at the expense of the Sinhalese Buddhists. The separatist politics of the Ceylon Tamil political parties, and their close association with south Indian Dravidians frightened them. The campaign for Dravidastan (a separate Tamil state covering Madras, parts of both Andrapradesh and Kerala – Tamil-speaking areas of Malaya, and Ceylon) during the 1950s, stoked the fear that the Ceylon Tamils would ultimately capture the whole island unless Sinhalese Buddhists united. As Sabaratnam states, ethnic politics intensified each trying to dominate the other. 'Among the Tamil parties, there was a competition to assert adversarial courage toward the Sinhalese.'[22] The FP aggressively asserted that they would fight for the autonomy of the Tamil-speaking areas in a federal structure. Among the Sinhalese, a determined and united Buddhist movement, *Eksath Bikkhu Peramuna* (the United Front of Buddhist Monks) was organised, and they began to dictate terms to political parties dominated by the Sinhalese elite groups, mainly the SLFP and UNP.

Sinhalese Buddhist leaders and Buddhist monks claimed that it was their historical and religious responsibility to protect the Sihadeepa from foreign forces, impliedly, Catholicism and Christianity. Their anger came to be directed against the Ceylon Tamils later. Sinhalese Buddhists' fear was expressed by the chief Buddhist priest in the *Ramanya Nikaya* (one section of the Buddhist clergy) that, 'If the Tamils get hold of the country, the Sinhalese will have to jump into the sea. It is essential, therefore, to safeguard our country, the nation, and the religion and to work with that object in mind.'[23] Roberts argues that Sinhalese nationalism,

20 Sabaratnam, 'The Boundaries of the State', 1987, p.303.
21 Sabaratnam, 'The Boundaries of the State', p.307.
22 Sabaratnam, 'The Boundaries of the State', p.307.
23 Cited in S.U. Kodikara, 'Communalism and Political Modernization in Ceylon', *Modern Ceylon Studies*, 1, 1970, p.103.

particularly during the period 1919 to 1946 was influenced by the Gandhian idea of a one-nation policy.[24] But de Silva points out that the Sinhalese elite of Congress were not ardent admirers of Gandhi or the Indian Congress. In fact, the Gandhian strategy of *satyagraha* movements was criticised by many Congress leaders including James Pieris. It was Ceylonese history, culture, and religion that dominated the consciousness of the Sinhalese Buddhists but they did not influence the direction of Congress due to the broad, secular approach and liberal views of the leaders of Congress. Ceylon was always considered one territorial unit and one nation. Within this polity, the presence of other smaller communities were tolerated and accepted.

Tamil history and identity

The Ceylon Tamil constitutional reformists argued that constituencies should be based on communal differences to guarantee balanced representation between the majority and minority communities. They appeared to be insisting on political parity with the Sinhalese. Moreover, the Ceylon Tamils in Congress were Jaffna high-caste Tamils who were naturally reluctant to tolerate the domination of others. Their upbringing and thinking were molded within a Hindu religious and cultural ethos. Hinduism was deeply interconnected with caste. 'The Jaffna Tamil' is a status attached with honour and pride – connected with lands and social elevation. It is true that they absorbed elements of western civilization, such as western education and the English language before the Sinhalese did. Yet, a Jaffna Tamil is a Jaffna Tamil, even if he is in Cambridge or Oxford. When they retired from highly successful careers in the colonial government they retreated to their ancestral lands in the Jaffna Peninsula. Elite Jaffna Tamils always preferred the name 'Ceylon Tamils' rather than Ceylonese. Indian Tamils or low-caste Tamils living in the Jaffna Peninsula were excluded from their social and political milieux.[25] This heritage contributed to a certain stubbornness and unwillingness to compromise with the Sinhalese. Rajanayagam writes:

> Tamils were free to view and define their identity in quite different ways, without losing their identity as Tamils . . . Even more importantly for Tamil identity, history was not confined to the island of Sri Lanka, but could always be found in India in Tamil Nadu. One could perhaps even say that history held little importance for the Tamils because their identity did not depend on it exclusively. It still does not, but history's significance has without doubt increased since independence. This fact of having a choice of pasts also partly explains why the Christians were in the forefront not only of historical writing,

24 Roberts 'Ethnic Conflict in Sri Lanka'. Unfortunately, Robert's methodology in analysing Sinhalese nationalism suffered from his attempt to compare it with the African ideologies.

25 Sabaratnam, 'The Boundaries of the State', 1987, pp.291–316.

> but also of Tamil nationalism; they had a choice of pasts, too, and being Tamil, or even being Tamil nationalist, was not tied to being Saivite; other identifications existed.[26]

According to Rajanayagam, the Singhalese always feared that Tamils look more towards India and the Tamil mainland, Tamil Nadu than towards Sri Lanka and that they therefore, could not be trusted. How was it possible to be both a Sri Lankan nationalist and a Tamil nationalist at the same time?

Rajanayagam concludes that: 'By the late 1930s the scholarly "histories of Jaffna" intended for schools fizzled out: instead we see a spate of "Eelam" or great Tamils of Jaffna in general, and their achievements for the glory of its history, its culture, its ancient greatness, and most of all, its Tamilness.'[27]

Already, in the writings of Sir Ponnamblam Arunachalam's on the history of Sri Lanka, *Sketches of Ceylon History*,[28] and his article on 'Population' in *Twentieth Century Impressions*,[29] he, contrary to what James D'Alwis said, contended that the Sinhalese were a mixed race of Aryan, Dravidian, Veddha, Mongolian and Malay.[30] It was also argued that the glorious, ancient civilisation of the island was not solely the product of the Sinhalese. In his early writings as well as in speeches made in his later years, he emphasises Tamils' contribution to various aspects of social, economic and political life. These ideas have subsequently been embellished to augment the contribution of Tamils while belittling that of the Sinhalese. Rajanayagam states:

> The Tamil use of history to justify and defend their position shows decisive differences from that of the Sinhala. While the latter pursue an exclusive strategy, denying the standing of Tamils in the country *per se*, and labeling them alien and foreign intruders, the Tamils followed an inclusive strategy until the 1930s. They tried to prove that the Sinhala were in reality not Aryans, but Dravidians in disguise, and thus had nothing to be snooty about. This did not go down well with those Sinhala who prided themselves on their alleged 'Aryan' ancestry. But by the 1930s and 1940s, an argument had gained weight that it was immaterial whether the Sinhala were Dravidians or not – if they were, they were an inferior sort of Dravidian. The important claim was that the Tamils had been the first people in Sri Lanka, theirs was the highest culture and civilization from which others only copied, and everything great and good in both Sri Lankan and Sinhala culture was by definition originally Tamil. This related not only to language, literature, and architecture, but even to

26 Hellmann-Rajanayagam, 'The Politics of the Tamil Past', 1990, pp.113–114.

27 Hellmann-Rajanayagam, 'The Politics of the Tamil Past', 1990, pp.113–114.

28 See P. Arunachalam, *Sketches of Ceylon History*, Asian Educational Services: Colombo, 1906.

29 It was a collection of articles written by Europeans and elite Sinhala and Tamil scholars and professionals. See Wright (ed.), *Twentieth Century Impressions of Ceylon History*, 1906.

30 See Arunachalam, 'Population', in *Twentieth Century Impressions*, cited by Rogers, 'Historical Images in the British Period', in Spencer (ed.), *Sri Lanka, History and the Roots of Conflict*, 1990, p.97.

> religion: attempts were made to prove that the Sinhala, far from being Buddhists, were in reality Hindus, or that Buddhism was just an inferior kind of Hinduism. The Tamils had created progress and development in the country under the British, and the Sinhala therefore, if not acceding them the right to rule, would at least have to grant them equal political representation.[31]

Such uses and abuses of history are not uncommon when communities are locked in mutually exclusive nationalistic claims. Since the first decade of the twentieth century, the engagement of the Ceylon Tamils in national politics was on the basis of being an independent nation on the island, albeit small in number, but whose contribution matched that of the Sinhalese. Their engagement with Congress and their political organisations had a remarkable similarity with the pre-independence Muslim League in India, in particular, in the 1920s. The Jaffna Association had of its own volition remained a provincial political organisation representing mainly Jaffna Tamils. The paradox was that it was an exclusive body as well, representing in reality only the high-caste Tamils in the Jaffna Peninsula and Colombo. It was late in trying to encourage other Tamil-speaking people in the island, notably, the Moors to join them on a wider political platform.

Unlike other regional non-Tamil organisations in the island, the Jaffna Association was not open to a large number of ordinary Tamils owing to deeply inherent caste divisions in the Peninsula. They struggled to accommodate other Tamils in the Jaffna Peninsula itself and elsewhere on the island. The Tamils living in the Eastern Province were not made welcome until later parts of the 1950s. The Indian Tamils were intentionally marginalised and excluded from mainstream politics for decades, even after independence. They were not invited to join, or more correctly, their cooperation was never sought between 1900 to 1946. Unlike local Hindu *Mahã Sabhãs* in India in the 1920s, Ceylon Tamils did not have regionally interconnected popular political movements that would have strengthened and legitimised their claim to speak on behalf of the Ceylon Tamils. Yet, the Jaffna Association and later the Tamil *Mahãjana Sabhã*, subsequently All-Ceylon Tamil Congress, exploited prejudices associated with religion and race to the electoral advantages of the Ceylon Tamil elite. Thus in effect the Jaffna Tamil elite claimed to be speaking in the name of the Tamil community while remaining detached from the bulk of the Tamil population in the island.

Not surprisingly, deep knowledge and understanding of their (Sinhalese and Tamil) respective cultures, history, religions and centuries old civilisations made the two communities realise their differences which played a major role in separating them from one another.

31 Hellmann-Rajanayagam, 'The Politics of the Tamil Past', 1990, pp.114–115. Still, some Tamil politicians tried to convince, in particular, the western audience that it was Tamils who inhabited the island. Some of these Tamils later converted to Buddhism and adopted Pali as their *lingua franca*. Those great monuments of Sinhala civilisation, according to these writers, were the work of Tamils. See Ponnamabalam, *Sri Lanka, The National Question*, 1989, p.19.

Ceylonese nationalism?

Beginning in the nineteenth century and extending into the 1920s the campaign against the Catholics/Christianity by the Sinhalese Buddhists took on a new dimension. Sinhalese Buddhists influenced the political parties dominated by the Sinhalese to change their politics in terms of ethnicity, religion and language. At the beginning they proceeded by way of persuasion, public speeches, novels, short stories and dramas.

No inclusive Ceylonese identity developed naturally on the island. Any attempt at developing a national consciousness, such as developed in India through mass movements involving all communities and creeds against the British, was thrown off course even before independence (between 1919 and 1946) by the parochial interests of the Ceylon Tamils and intransigence of Sinhalese leaders in Congress to accommodate the Ceylon Tamils. The Ceylonese identity that eventually emerged was largely a Buddhist Sinhalese identity. Sinhalese preference for territorially based constituencies and Ceylon Tamils' preference for constituencies based on communal differences were the inevitable result of ethnic loyalties. The elite clan of the Ceylon Tamils, as Sir Ivor Jennings pointed out, from the very beginning cooperated with Congress while self-consciously preserving their Ceylon Tamil (Jaffna Tamil) identity. The Tamils did cooperate with the Congress, says Jennings, like the Scots' cooperation with the conservatives.[32]

Any closer cooperation among these majority national groups, as was proved by later events, was conducted while preserving their differences. With this background, both communities began to work within set agendas without compromising their positions. There were personal motivations too behind their campaign. The new Congress could be, or as Mendis[33] and de Silva[34] correctly explained, and was indeed, used by leaders of both communities as chariots for their own political ends.

There was, however, no violent politics during the heyday of Congress. Congress was dominated by upper- and middle-class western-educated professionals and gentlemen. Many were lawyers, doctors, businessmen and civil servants. The rivalry initially developed during the 1920s for greater political power among the leaders of both communities. However, the competition was conducted in a most civilised way. The leaders of both communities emerged from the upper rung of the society gaining ascendancy over ordinary people due to their English education and connection with the civil servants of the British Raj. The elite of the Tamils and the Sinhalese operated within the same social circle, played cricket together, and

32 Jennings, 'Nationalism and Political Development', 1953, p.68.

33 Mendis, *Ceylon Under the British*, 2nd rev. edn., 1948, pp.120–123. G.C. Mendis was an eminent historian in pre-independent Ceylon. He was a lecturer in history at University College, Colombo, when this article was written, and closely watched the growth of communal politics in the 1930s and 1940s.

34 de Silva, 'The Formation and Character', 1967, p.70.

practised their professions in a friendly way. (Ordinary peoples of both communities had, over the centuries, also developed a mutual understanding and tolerance in a spirit of 'live and let live' which helped maintain the peace in the island.) They were simply, as recorded by Governor Sir Henry McCallum, 'a product of the European administration'.[35] Most leaders of Congress were either Oxford or Cambridge educated and shared a deep admiration for some of the finest traditions of the Westminster parliamentary system, in particular for a single government for the whole country based on territorially elected membership to the House of Commons. This is why it was natural for the leadership of Congress to conduct their campaign for self-government in conformity with the traditions of liberal democracy which they had learned during their studies in Britain. Their approach to constitutional reforms was in sharp contrast to their Indian counterparts in the Indian National Congress. Instead of non-cooperation with the colonial government or mass protests, Congress leaders selected a path that involved sending dispatches and delegations to the Secretary of the Colonial Office and memoranda to the governor, engaging in skilful debates in the Legislative Council (most of these leaders were subsequently appointed KCs and honoured with knighthoods). In fact, as Sir Ivor Jennings[36] described:

> The fact is that the nationalists have never encouraged violence or even 'non-violence'. Their arguments have been, so to speak, academic and reserved mainly for the middle-class. No doubt religion has played a larger part; for Buddhism even more than Hinduism encourages passivity. Possibly, too, the westernization of the middle-class, which has proceeded much further than India, has been important . . . Even more importance would perhaps be attributed to the people involved. They were teachers, lawyers and landowners, men of a conservative trend of mind whose patriotism had made into politicians but who were generally happier in doing other things like writing about religion and the peoples of the island (Sir Ponnambalm Ramanathan), editing Sinhalese literature (Sir Baron Jayatilaka), or conducting agricultural experiments (Mr D.S. Senanayake).[37]

In fact, it was former high-flyer of the Ceylon Civil Service and a distinguished Tamil politician, Sir Ponnambalan Arunachalam, who became the first President of Congress. However, this friendly atmosphere changed dramatically after 1949 when the FP was formed by S.J.V. Chelvanayakam and a breakaway faction of the ACTC.

35 See 'Dispatches from Sir Henry McCallum to the Earl of Crew', in Bandaranaike, *Handbook of the Ceylon National Congress*, p.48.

36 Sir Ivor Jennings played a prominent role in the drafting of the Constitution of independent Ceylon and was the first Vice-Chancellor of the University of Ceylon, the highest seat of learning of Ceylon in the 1950s.

37 Jennings 'Nationalism and Political Development', vol. III, 1953–1954, pp.81–82.

Their foremost demand was for a federal union of Ceylon that guarantees virtual self-rule for the Tamil-speaking people in the north and east. However, to both communities federalism was at first a curious and nebulous concept. Also, they were not sure how a federal union of a state could be formed, as the FP's leaders were insisting, along linguistic and ethnic lines without endangering the territorial integrity of the island.

Opposed to the federalists was an emerging Sinhala Buddhist movement, which saw it as their historical and religious responsibility to protect the island from subversive forces. They opposed federalists' demands fearing that the Tamils would subsequently secede or join the south Indian Tamils with a view to creating a Tamil state that in the 1950s was called *Dravidastan* (a Tamil state covering Madras, parts of both Andrapradesh and Kerala, and the Tamil-speaking areas of Malaya, and Ceylon). In particular, the FP, and its close association with the south Indian Dravidian separatist movement frightened the Sinhalese Buddhists. The south Indian separatist political party *Dravida Munnetra Kalazagam* (DMK) set up branches in Ceylon in the 1960s.[38] Sinhalese Buddhists now feared that the Ceylon Tamils would ultimately capture the whole island unless the Sinhalese Buddhists united against separatist Tamil forces.

38 Ponnambalam, *Sri Lanka: The National Question*, 1983, p.142; Farmer, *Ceylon: A Divided Nation*, 1960, p.69.

13 The government considers devolution of power as a solution to the ethnic conflict in Sri Lanka

Accommodation through constitutional reforms

Since 1977 there has been a change of attitude on the part of successive governments towards the idea of the devolution of powers to the north-east regions of Sri Lanka. However, early experiments with devolution showed a half-heartedness on the part of the Sri Lankan government. In 1980 the UNP government led by J.R. Jayawardene enacted the *District Development Councils Act*, no. 36, guaranteeing limited delegated power to the north and east. However, in the view of some constitutional experts, the proposed councils had 'the same constitutional structure as the municipal councils and other local bodies'.[1] The Act did not alter the constitutional structure of the island in any way, since it could be amended or abrogated at any time following a normal procedure with a simple majority of parliament. Predictably, Tamil political parties did not show any interest since the 'devolution' appeared token and reluctant.

Indo-Sri Lanka Accord and its aftermath

In 1987 by the 13th amendment to the 1978 Constitution in pursuance of the *Indo-Sri Lanka Accord*, the Sri Lankan government introduced new provisions to accommodate Tamil demands for greater autonomy within a *quasi-federal* structure.[2] The proposed constitutional bill, which amended the constitution of Sri Lanka,[3]

1 Marasinghe, 'Ethnic Politics and Constitutional Reform', 1988, p.564.

2 See arts 154 A to 154 T of the Constitution of the Democratic Socialist Republic of Sri Lanka, 1977 as amended by 1987, published by parliamentary secretaries. See also map 2, *Provinces in Sri Lanka*.

3 The proposed constitutional reforms were contained in Chapter XVIIA containing arts 154A to 154T after art. 154 of the Constitution. Chapter XVIIA commences: 'The provisions of this Chapter shall be subject to Articles 1, 2, 3, 6, 7, 8, 9, 10, 11, 30 (2), 62 (2) and 83 and shall not affect or derogate from, or be read or construed as affecting or derogating from, any such Article, but, save as aforesaid, nothing contained in the Constitution or any other law in force on the date on which this Chapter comes into force shall be interpreted as derogating from the provisions of this Chapter. The provisions of such other law shall *mutatis mutandis*, apply.' See also Marasinghe, 'Ethnic Politics and Constitutional Reform', 1988, pp.551–587.

was referred to the Supreme Court to establish whether the bill had to be put to a referendum after it had won a two-thirds majority of parliament. The government was aware that given the opposition to any devolution of power, it would have been difficult to win any referendum. The judgment was a close call. The bench was divided 5:4. The minority opinion of the justices was that the devolution amounted to 'an erosion of the sovereignty of the people' and had 'to be passed by the two-thirds majority approved by the people at a referendum'.[4] However, the other five justices held that the provincial councils would only be granted delegated legislative powers similar to that of municipal councils, which would not affect the sovereignty of the country and, therefore, did not need to be approved by referendum of the people; a two-thirds majority of parliament would suffice.

The Indo-Lanka Accord accepted that the North and East Provinces would be Tamil *homelands*,[5] a scenario that scared both the Sinhalese and the Moors. In fact, the Jayawardene government wanted to grant much more powers to the Tamils in the north and east, but powers short of an independent, separate state. Jayawardena was said to have bitterly regretted his failure to do more to address the concerns of the Tamils during his tenure.[6] The Indo-Sri Lanka Accord went right to the heart of the problem by tackling two crucial issues:

1 the re-adjustment of the territory along ethnic and linguistic lines;
2 a solution to the language issue.

The language issue was addressed through the recognition of Tamil as an official language alongside Sinhala.[7] Both the Sinhala and Tamil languages of Sri Lanka shall be national languages (art. 19) and 'Sinhala and Tamil shall be the languages of administration throughout Sri Lanka' (rt. 22 (1).[8]

The more controversial provision was the introduction of the provincial councils. This was more in keeping with the B-C Pact of 1957 than any other constitutional arrangements envisaged by previous governments. The provinces of the north and east were to be merged to function as one territorial unit,[9] with the important proviso that one year after the merger a referendum for the Eastern Province be held[10] to determine whether to retain the north as one territorial unit. As provided

4 See parliamentary debates, Hansard, 10 November 1987, cited in Marasinghe, 'Ethnic Politics', 1988 p.578.

5 Art. 1.4 of the Indo-Sri Lanka Agreement states, 'Also recognizing that the Northern and the Eastern provinces have been areas of historical habitations of Sri Lankan Tamils speaking peoples, who have at all times hitherto lived together in this territory with other ethnic groups.'

6 Tambiah, 'Ethnic Fratricide', 1986, p. 30. See also Fred Parkinson, 'Ethnicity and Independent Statehood', in Jackson and James (eds.), *States in a Changing World*, 1995.

7 Art. 18 (1) provides, 'The Official Language of Sri Lanka shall be Sinhala.' Art. 18 (2) states, 'Tamil shall also be an official language.' See also art. 23 (1) (language of legislation), art. 24 (1) (language of the courts). The corresponding provision in the Indo-Sri Lanka Accord, art. 2 (18).

8 See corresponding provision in the Indo-Sri Lanka Accord, art. 2 (1) and 2 (2).

9 See corresponding provision in the Indo-Sri Lanka Accord, art. 2 (3A).

10 See corresponding provision in the Indo-Sri Lanka Accord, art. 2 (3A).

by art. 154 A (3),[11] a single territorial unit would be formed by merging both the north and the east.[12] A notable omission in the amended constitution was any reference to the 'Tamil homelands'. The demand for a homeland had been accepted in the Indo-Sri Lanka Accord by the Sri Lankan government amid strong protest from the Sinhalese Buddhists. The chief reason for leaving out any reference to a Tamil homeland was the Moors' insistence that the Eastern Province be their traditional homeland, which is now identified as *Nazaristan*. Even though the Accord ensured 'the unity, sovereignty, and territorial integrity of Sri Lanka',[13] the 'structure of the Accord shifted towards the Tamil demand for a greater autonomy within a federal structure'.[14]

The 13th amendment to the Constitution met many of the demands and addressed several of the grievances of the Tamil political parties although a majority of the Tamil secessionist movements rejected the amendment in its entirety. The provincial councils[15] were empowered to make laws 'applicable to the Provinces for which it is established', thus, every provincial council had a regional government with executive,[16] legislative and judicial powers.

For the first time in post-independence Sri Lanka, there was a genuine devolution of powers to the provinces of the north and east, creating a quasi-federal structure. It was greeted with strong protests despite the fact that the Jayawardene government excluded from the competence of the provincial councils[17] defence, national policy, foreign affairs, posts and telecommunications, broadcasting, television, aviation and airports, national transport, minerals and mines, immigration and immigration and citizenship, elections to parliament, provincial councils, local authorities and professional occupations and training. All these came under the sole authority of the central government. The central government even retained the power to make laws when they overlapped with the provincial council's powers in particular areas, after consultation with the provincial councils.[18] Also, the

11 It provides, 'Notwithstanding anything in the preceding provisions of the Article, Parliament my by, or under, any law provide for two or three adjoining Provinces to form one administrative unit with one elected Provincial Council, one Governor, one Chief Minister and one Board of Ministers and for the manner of determining whether such Provinces should continue to be administered as one administrative unit or whether each such Provinces should constitute a separate administrative unit with its own Provincial Council, and a separate Governor, Chief and Board of Ministers.'

12 See corresponding provision in the Indo-Sri Lanka Accord, art. 2 (2). See, further, Wilson, *Break-up of Sri Lanka*, 1988, where he stated that JR has confided him that he was confident that he was able to win the proposed referendum. And JR suggested that after partition, United Nations Peace Keeping Force should be brought into island.

13 See art. 1 (5) of the Accord.

14 Jackson and James (eds.), *States in a Changing World*, 1995.

15 They are elected legislative assemblies with the powers to enact statutes as provided by the Constitution. See art. 154A (1) and (2).

16 Executive powers of the provinces, according to art. 154C, were to be exercised by the governor appointed by the president ;either directly or through the Board of Ministers, or through officers subordinate to him, in accordance with Article 154F.

17 See art. 154G (7).

18 See art. 154G (5) (a).

national parliament retained the right to make laws in a wide range of areas directly affecting provincial affairs. The full legislative powers of the provincial councils were limited since the president could withhold his consent to any statutes passed by the provincial councils. He also retained power to 'give directions' to any provincial governor to exercise executive power if the 'security of Sri Lanka is threatened by war or external aggression or rebellion'.[19] Above all, the president had the power to dissolve any provincial council if 'a situation has arisen in which the administration of the Province cannot be carried out in accordance with the provisions of the Constitution'.[20]

Although this attempt at devolution suffered from a lack of clarity about the sharing of sovereignty between the centre and the provinces and was therefore, dismissed by many as similar to those operating in municipal councils,[21] this was the first occasion when political power at the provincial level was conferred on the areas inhabited by the Ceylon Tamils. The north and east were merged, on a temporary basis, into one territorial unit and an election was held for the merged North-east Province of the island. The provincial election was won by the EPRLF, a Tamil secessionist group. The combined province was governed by a Tamil chief minister with a cabinet-style government. The most powerful secessionist group, the LTTE, refused to take part in the provincial election neither would it allow the elected government to function, challenging it directly.

Inevitably, a power struggle ensued between the newly elected North-east Province government and the LTTE. The president, in the meanwhile, had managed to secure the removal of the Indian Peace Keeping Force who had provided protection to the chief minister. In order to avoid repeated allegations made by the LTTE that they had abandoned the Eelam struggle by participating in the election and accepting limited devolution, the chief minister, within a few months of the EPRLF's election, and shortly before leaving the country, made a unilateral declaration of independence. The chief minister, his cabinet and other supporters later fled to south India to escape the LTTE. They were killed while in hiding in Tamil Nadu by the LTTE with the suspected complicity of the Dravida Munnetra Kalazagam Party, DMK.[22] The government immediately dissolved the provincial government in 1990.

The Jayawardene government's provincial councils and especially the north-east merger, were rejected by almost all Sinhalese-dominated political parties and Sinhalese Buddhist activist groups. They claimed that the merged north-east might, in the course of time, become an ethnically defined sub-state barring other ethnic groups, notably the Sinhalese. According to Fred Parkinson: 'As things stand, it is to be feared that one day the Eastern province could be the scene of massive ethnic

19 See art. 154J (1). See also Chapter XVIII, Public Security.

20 See art. 154K and 154L.

21 Marasinghe, 'Ethnic Politics and Constitutional Reforms', 1988, p.568.

22 *Sri Lankan Monitor*, 1 September 1997, p.4.

resettlement, or, infinitely worse, massacres of Indo-Pakistani proportions of 1947, all in the name of the hallowed principle of ethnic homogeneity.'[23]

Tamil political parties, both moderate and Eelamist groups, were not satisfied with the limited powers granted, which they regarded as no more than the venerable district development scheme first suggested by the Senanayake government in 1966. The demands of all Tamil political parties since then have been based on greater autonomy within a confederation, that is, the division of sovereignty between the merged northeast and the central government.

From provincial councils to the Union of Regions, Chandrika's 'three Ds'

In 1985, claims D.L. Horowitz, the Sri Lankan government was forced to abandon its policy of seeking an agreement or a pact with the minority Tamils because of the fierce opposition of Sinhalese mass opinion led by politically active Buddhist monks; in this case 'the elite interests were overridden by mass concerns that ran counter to them.'[24]

This could not have been a more correct assessment on the repeated attempts by the Kumaratunga governments to solve the problem with constitutional amendments offering far-reaching devolved powers.

In 1995 the government presented to the country the 1995 *Devolution Proposals*. After this there were two more sets of proposals, the legal draft of 1996 and the proposals for constitutional reform of 1997 followed by the 2000 constitutional amendment bill.

President Chandrika Kumaratunga was sympathetic to the demands of the Tamils in the north and the east. She believed that it was her historic destiny to find a solution to the island's tribal conflicts and was all for 'devolving power to the Tamils'.[25] She was prepared to go beyond any previous governments' experiments with devolution of power. As her 1995 revised constitutional bill indicated she was prepared go beyond a federal structure to confer powers to the north and the east within a loose confederation.

Kumaratunga won the 1994 and 2000 presidential elections promising a peaceful solution through constitutional means. Addressing the General Assembly of the United Nations, she said, 'We have been traumatised by forces of terrorism and chauvinism. Nonetheless, my Government is resolved to fulfill its mandate by seeking, through political negotiations, solutions to our problems that would enable our people to live in peace, security and freedom.'[26] In 1996 she declared that her government would pursue peace for the island through 'three Ds' –

23 Parkinson, 'Ethnicity and Independent Statehood', in James and Jackson (eds.), *States in a Changing World Contemporary Analysis*, 1995, pp.336–340.

24 Horowitz, *Ethnic Groups in Conflict*, 1985.

25 P.K. Balachandran, 'Constitution: Chandrika Loses Faith in the UNP', in *The Hindustan Times* online, 30 July 2000.

26 A/50/PV.35, 22 October 1995, p.9.

devolution through dialogue, development in war-torn areas and devolution of power. Even though she considered the violent campaign of the LTTE and other armed groups as terrorism,[27] she was willing to talk and unwilling 'to settle this by war'.[28] However, her dilemma was how to devolve power within a loose confederation without compromising the sovereignty and territorial integrity of the island and with the blessings of both the LTTE and the Sinhalese hardliners. In a revealing statement made to the UN General Assembly, the Minister for Foreign Affairs, Laxman Kadiragamar, attempted to balance sovereignty with some form of self-determination and minority rights. 'Any fashionable theories about the need to limit national sovereignty' would be disastrous; however, the legitimate genuine 'grievances of the Tamils' could be addressed 'through democratic means'. He claimed that, 'We are working on a set of proposals introduced by my Government to address minority grievances, which includes far reaching constitutional changes.'[29] The government was willing to consider a constitutional solution to the problem of minority grievances.

The 1997 Constitution Amendment Bill

By the mid-nineties, the Kumaratunga government had introduced into the political language the concept of power sharing. The 1995 Constitution Amendment Bill (as revised in October 1997, popularly known as 'the constitutional package')[30] was presented as a solution to the ethnic conflict in the island. In her speech in February 1995, the President expressed her intention thus:

> One of the principal objectives of the proposals is the settlement of the ethnic crisis. However, there is a wider aim sought to be achieved. It is the empowerment of all Sri Lankans, wherever they live, to wield the authority to make decisions relating to their future. The ideal of democracy is better served, we feel, by *the sharing of power* with local representative units which will enable persons to determine their own destiny . . . The Government is resolved to secure a victory for democracy and peace.[31]

The 1965 District Council Bill aimed to delegate power to Tamils in the north and east at district level. The Jayawardene government's provincial councils took this a step further. The 1995 constitutional package moved away from the delegation

27 President Chandrika Bandaranaike's statement, A/50/PV.35, 22 Oct. 1995, p.9.

28 See her interview with the Indian journalist Ram, 'Constitution: Chandrika Loses Faith in the UNP', 2000, pp.2–6.

29 Statement made by the current Minister for Foreign Affairs, Laksman Kadiragamar (distinguished Tamil lawyer), during the GA debate. A/51/PV.II, 26 September 1996, p.3.

30 Select Committee's Report on Constitutional Reforms presented to parliament on 24 October 1997. See a critical examination of the package in Gunasekera, *Tigers, Moderates and Pandora's Package*, pp.116–221.

31 See http://members.tripoid.com/~sosl/devlou.html, 26 March 1999.

of powers contending that such limited powers would not suffice to meet the just and reasonable demands of the Tamils. It wanted to devolve power to the north and east (seven other provinces in the island were also involved) at the provincial level within a confederal structure. Each autonomous province will have its own governments with executive, legislative and administrative powers.[32]

The constitutional package signalled the government's determination to shift away from the unitary system to a confederal structure in which the Tamils in the north and east would share sovereignty with the central government. The chief architect of the 'package', Professor Peiris,[33] spoke in terms of current thinking on devolution and minority rights when he explained the need for devolution: It was necessary to 'bypass certain constitutional, legal and practical constraints' to achieve multi-ethnic polity in which the minority groups in the island would be able to find 'space' to develop their identity and nurture their culture and religions. The working assumption of the package was that a unitary model could no longer work in Sri Lanka, because such as model constrains the implementation of policies that affect different ethnic and linguistic groups.[34]

Peiris was no longer struggling with the dilemma of reconciling state sovereignty with the aspirations of minorities to determine their own future. The difficult question was to find an appropriate constitutional solution acceptable to all the parties.

While the Constitution still maintained that 'Sri Lanka is one, Sovereign and Independent Republic, being an *indissoluble Union of Regions*' (art. 1),[35] a regional council would have its own governor (art. 127 (1)),[36] an executive committee for each ministry,[37] regional attorney-general (art. 136) and the judiciary (art. 146). The regions were even granted power to borrow money from international and domestic institutions (art. 210). With the exception of defence, national security and foreign affairs, all other powers are vested with the regions.[38] One of the most important differences between the 1978 Constitutional Amendments and the 1995 one is that the devolved power to the regional councils could not be abrogated by the central government. The most controversial proposal was art. 144, which provided that state lands within the each province 'shall vest in the Region and shall be at the disposal of the Regional Council'. Thus, the constitutional package facilitated the merger of the north and east into one territorial unit/sub-state constituted along ethnic lines. This allowed the Tamils in the merged North-east

32 See Chapter XV, The Devolution of Power to Regions.

33 He drafted this constitutional bill together with late TULF member of parliament, Dr. Neelan Tiruchelvam, who was gunned down by the LTTE for his alleged 'collaboration' with the government.

34 See ACSLU, 'The Devolution Law of Sri Lanka: A Critique', 3 March 1999.

35 Emphasis added.

36 See art. 134 (1).

37 Art. 135 (1).

38 See critical analysis on this, Gunasekera, *Tigers, Moderates and Pandora's Package*, 1996, pp.115–234. See also Australian Centre for Sri Lankan Unity (ACSLU), 'A Critique', http://www. member. tripod. com /~ sosi/devolu.html.

Province to control virtually one-third of the land and slightly more than half of its territorial waters.

This package was a 'progressive attempt',[39] having gone further than anything attempted by the B-C Pact of July 1957,[40] the Dudley Senananayake-Chelvanayakam Pact of 1965[41] and the provincial councils of the Jayawardene government in 1987. Academics and civil rights activists also supported the 1995 constitutional package arguing that it provided the best constitutional mechanism to address the *just demands* of the Tamils in the north and the east.

Charles Abeysekara, President of the Movement for the Inter-Racial Justice and Equality (MIRJE) and the International Centre for Ethnic Studies, captured the radical change in thinking about ethnicity, minority rights and even the hegemony of ethnic majorities when he said: 'Majority decision cannot be used to deny rights to the minority. This is certainly what has been done in the past and continues to be done with regard to the rights of ethnic minorities in this country. Sinhalese' claims to decide the fundamental character of our polity – simply on the basis of their being a majority should be challenged. They define our polity as Sinhala Buddhists and require it's accepted by all other ethnic groups, who must live within its overarching ambit.'[42] In his view, the current system denied democracy to ethnic groups and was neither a civilised nor a democratic system.

This attitude is a major departure from former ideas of nationalism. In order to create a nation, it was necessary, in a unitary state, to insist that a nation subsume ethnic minority identities into the national character, which was often simply the culture of the majority that was identified with the state. Now, consistent with changes in the international political environment, where the concept of a nation had undergone a metamorphosis, Sri Lankans were willing to countenance changes to constitutional arrangements that would be better suited to a multi-ethnic society, but without sacrificing the idea of a single nation. The government appeared willing to sacrifice the unitary state for a lasting peace.

The 2000 Constitution Amendment Bill

The 2000 Constitution Amendment Bill planned to devolve even more powers to the regions so the government made a concerted effort to prevent the Bill from being blocked through a series of legal and constitutional manoeuvres, but in so doing fatally damaged the chances of the Bill being passed. The government first tried to circumvent the legal barriers entrenched in the 1978 Constitution by trying

39 See Ram, 'Constitution: Chandrika Loses Faith in the UNP', p.2. See also CFSP presidency statement, Brussels, 30 July 1996, Nr 9455/96 (Presse 224) CSFP: 66/96. It says that the European Union remains of the view that the Sri Lankan government's wide-ranging proposals for constitutional reforms could constitute a solid basis for a peaceful solution.

40 Wriggins, *Ceylon, Dilemmas of a New Nation*, 1960, pp.265–266; Ponnambalam, *Sri Lanka: The National Question*, 1983, pp.110–112.

41 Ponnambalam, *Sri Lanka: The National Question*, 1983, pp.135–136.

42 *Daily News*, 17 July 1996.

to block the involvement of the Supreme Court (SC) arguing that the SC had no jurisdiction over the Constitutional Bill. The Minister of Sports, S.B. Disanayake, even threatened that if the High Court judges were to block constitutional amendments the government might be forced to sack judges who did not toe the line.[43] Except for the President, Peiris and a few of their close allies, including a few Tamil political parties, others were kept in the dark about the process the government intended to follow.

The other option considered by the President and Peiris was to convert parliament into a Constitutional Assembly thereby allowing its members to agree a new constitution, bypassing the constraints of the current constitution. The government did make its intention clear in the run-up to the 2000 general election but it was still a gamble for it to insist that it had received a popular mandate[44] in the 2000 election to introduce a new constitution. Such a specific mandate was never sought by the President at any elections held during her tenure.

Did the government want a referendum if it was able to get a two-thirds majority of parliament, given the overwhelming opposition to it from the majority Sinhala Buddhist electorate? The evidence suggests that the leadership of the ruling party decided that a two-thirds majority of parliament would be enough to implement the Bill while the Bill was being drafted and even when it had been placed on the Order Book of parliament.

The dilemma of the *People's Alliance* (PA): devolution of power without altering state structure and alienating the sovereignty of parliament

The 1978 Constitution provides that: 'Parliament shall not abdicate or in any manner alienate its legislative power, and shall not set up any authority with any legislative power.' To get around this the government argued that the proposed amendments would delegate only limited legislative powers for institutions at regional level. If this is the case then, of course, the ruling party the Peoples' Alliance (PA) would have had no difficulty in passing the Bill without referendum. It was normal practice in Sri Lanka that the government would delegate some of its powers to the local level without having to share sovereignty between the centre and the regions.

However, such an argument would have been difficult to make given the significant alteration of the state structure by the proposed Constitution Bill. In summary, the powers conferred to the regional councils cannot be abrogated; parliament's power to make legislation in respect of the regional councils cannot

43 For this he was prosecuted for contempt of court and subsequently found guilty. He escaped a prison sentence after pleading that he did not mean what he uttered through his counsel, Fais Mustapha PC. However, he was severely reprimanded (by the Appeal Court) for his foolish utterance and warned not to resort to such action in future.

44 *The Lanka Academic*, 4 August 2000.

be exercised unless the regional assemblies agreed to such proposals and the President's power to dissolve the regional councils is confined to situations where the regional council does something drastic, like secede. The main difference between this constitution and any other is that the island ceases to be a unitary state after the Bill becomes law.

Manoeuvring in parliament: the president is trapped in the constitutional web woven by former President J.R. Jayawardene

However, as it turned out the government was unable to get over even the first hurdle when it failed to secure the two-thirds majority needed for the Bill to pass. On 4 August 2000 the Bill was 'temporarily' withdrawn from the Order Book of parliament.

When President Kumaratunga presented the Constitution Reform Bill to a specially convened session of parliament on 3 August she said that it was imperative to have a proper legal framework guaranteeing the basic rights of the Tamils to live as 'decent human beings'. The main purposes of the Draft Constitutional reforms, argued the President, were to guarantee an environment in which the Tamils' rights are secured through a legally binding document; to solve the ethnic problem by 'bringing an end to the present bloodshed for the sake of future generations' and to usher in lasting peace and economic prosperity.[45] Otherwise, it would be impossible either to secure the unitary character of the island or to protect and preserve the rightful place of Buddhism in the nation.[46] Most importantly, there is no 'way out', she argued, other than through the present proposals which avoids a division of the country and 'further strengthened the unitary character'.[47]

It is undeniable that the proposed Constitutional Bill 2000 went far beyond the 1995/1997 constitutional package. It aimed at a restructure of the territory of the island within a confederal structure along ethnic and linguistic lines, even though President Kumaratunga denied this in her address to parliament. If it were enacted the island would become a *confederation* of states, except in name. The most controversial provision of the Constitutional Bill was that the provinces of north and east would be merged forthwith. An interim government would be established with the representatives nominated by the President from among the representatives of Tamil political parties and other organisations that represent Tamils' interests, in addition to representatives from other ethnic groups in these two provinces thus conferring self-rule on the Tamils. Five years later an election will

45 See 'President Presents Historic Draft Constitution', in *Daily News*, 4 August 2000.

46 See 'Buddhism can't be preserved without protecting minority rights', http://in.news.yahoo.com/000804/20/3dvs.html, 4 August 2000.

47 See 'President Presents Historic Draft Constitution, 4 August 2000.

be held for the merged North-east Province. After a ten-year period a referendum will be held in the Eastern Province only to determine whether the people of that region would like to merge with Northern Province permanently. In fact, this latest constitutional draft offered extensive autonomous powers to the 3.3 million ethnic Tamil populations of the north and east covering virtually every aspect of legislative, executive and judicial powers, short of independence.

The press, particularly *The Hindustan*, reported that 'the devolution proposals will turn the country into a de facto federal state. It was also widely rumoured that the constitutional bill will be used as a basis of peace negotiations with the LTTE.'[48] Although the Bill was drafted after reaching an agreement with the United National Party (UNP), the UNP suddenly developed cold feet and refused to support it. However, the President of the Tamil United Front (TUF) claimed that 'the President is quite determined to dispose of this very early and she is confident that she can get the support she needs.'[49]

Rejection of confederalism

The amendment changed the words 'indissoluble Union of Regions' to 'Sri Lanka is one, free sovereign and independent state consisting of the Centre and of the Regions which shall exercise power as laid down in the constitution.'

Predictably, the Constitutional Bill has attracted more criticism than any other previous constitution amendment bills had done. It was opposed by most of the Sinhalese Buddhists and even by some impartial observers. It suffered, according to journalist Kishali Pinto Jayawardene, from 'constitutional fraud' because of the way it was presented to parliament and the way the public was kept in the dark.[50] The country's highest court, the Supreme Court, was given only 24 hours to determine the constitutionality of the Bill, and on the following day, 3 August 2000 the bill was presented to parliament by the President herself in a hurriedly summoned special session of parliament on an emergency basis, stressing that it was urgent and in the national interest.

The influential Buddhist clergyman, the Ven. Madihe Pannaseeha Mahanayaka Thero, the Chief Prelate of the Amarapura Nikaya, branded the attempt of President Kumaratunga as the betrayal of the country and of the Sinhala Buddhists:

> We are against the war. At present we are living without much racial disharmony. But with the new Constitution there will be a big problem. The North will be taken over by the Tamils, the East will be taken over by the

48 C. Jayasinghe, 'Chandrika Confident of Getting Peace Plan through Parliament', http://www.asianage.com/asianage/30072000/detsou03.htm, 29 July 2000.

49 Jayasinghe, 'Chandrika Confident of Getting Peace Plan through Parliament', in http://www.asianagenews.com/asianage/30072000/detsou03.htm, 30 July 2000.

50 Kishali Pinto Jayawardene, 'No Greater Crime than this Occurs', in *The Sunday Times*, 6 August 2000.

> Muslims and the hill country will also be taken over by the Tamils. What is left for the Sinhalese majority of 74 percent in a Buddhist country?[51]

Buddhist monks opposed any devolution to the north and east arguing that it would erode the island's sovereignty. They claimed that 'the enactment of this constitution will finally result in Sri Lanka getting divided and dilute the ancient civilization and heritage of the Sinhala people.'[52] The government was warned that the proposed constitutional changes could only be implemented over the dead bodies of the *mahasangha* (Buddhist clergy). At a demonstration held at Colombo, one of the leading Buddhist monks said 'we will not allow anyone to split this country.' The proposed reform allows too many concessions to Tamil terrorists.[53] The Ven. Hendigalle Wimalasara Thero, a member of the National Council of Sangha (Buddhist monks) threatened to kill himself saying that 'I would sacrifice myself to save the unitary character of Sri Lanka.'[54] More significantly, for the first time in the post-colonial era, the chief heads of four influential Buddhist sects issued 'a religious decree' against President Chandrika Kumaratunga ordering her 'to roll back the bill'.[55] Such a decree was the equivalent of a kind of *fatwa*.

There were trenchant constitutional criticisms as well. S.L. Gunasekara, a lawyer, President of Sinhalese Heritage and a campaigner for the rights of Sinhalese Buddhists and against the division of the country along ethnic lines, claimed that the central government's powers had been severely reduced since there was an absence of any constitutional corrective measures to avoid a repeat of Vartharaja Perumal's unilateral declaration of independence in 1990. He insisted that 'the Government is setting in motion a process which would be irreversible, regardless of the consequences . . . It is said that more power to the North and East is only a stepping stone to a separate State.'[56] The majority view of the Sinhalese is that 'this country does not want a division of Sri Lanka whether by force or legislative process.'[57]

Many Sinhalese-dominated political parties were unwilling to support the 'constitutional package' owing to a perennial fear that once the Tamils are granted political power at provincial level within a loose federation they will secede from Sri Lanka. Also, the way in which the ruling PA tried to secure the two-thirds majority in parliament, disillusioned many people. It was widely rumoured that MPs who crossed over to the ruling party from the opposition parties were offered

51 Shelani de Silva's interview with Ven. Madihe Pannaseeha Mahanayake Thera, reported in *The Sunday Times*, 6 August 2000.

52 Christine Jayasinghe, 'Lanka Monks call for Protest Meeting', in http://news.indiaabroad.com/2000/07/31/31coloíbo.html

53 'Buddhist Monks Protest New Constitution', *The Lanka Academic*, 1(115), 2000.

54 Sri Lanka Academic Net, 8 August 2000.

55 *The Hindu*, 8 August 2000.

56 *The Sri Lankan Monitor*, no. 97, Feb.1996, published by British Refugee Council: London, p.1.

57 P. Gunawardhana, 'Chandrika Has Mismanaged N-E Crisis', *The Island*, 30 April 1995.

money.[58] 'It was politics at its worst with the government leaving no stone unturned as they fixed their sights on unprincipled opposition members who could be persuaded to vote for the constitution with the right offer.'[59] In spite of the ruling party, PA, securing the defection of seven MPs from the main opposition party, the UNP, resistance to the bill was strong.

The Bill failed to find a broad consensus of communal organisations and political parties.[60] Opposition to the Constitution Amendment Bill also came from the Moors who represent around 7 per cent of the population of the island. The majority of Moors in the eastern region, in particular in Trincomalee, Amparai and Batticaloa districts, were opposed to the proposed constitutional reform arguing that permanent merger of the east with the north will reduce them to a minority within the new predominantly Tamil administration. It is expected that 70 per cent of the representation to the interim north-east would be of Tamils, even though in the eastern region both the Sinhalese and Moors represent 56.42 per cent of the total population (respectively 30 and 26.42 per cent).

In the end, the deep divisions within the ruling PA were the main reason for the withdrawal of the Constitutional Bill. It was widely reported that a powerful and popular Minister, Mahinda Rajapakse, sided with the Buddhist monks threatening that, together with at least another seven MPs of the PA, he would vote against the Amendment Bill. Two MPs had already resigned from the ruling party.

Tamil political parties rejected the Bill because it did not go far enough. The Secretary-General of the TULF, Mr Sambandan, MP, said, 'It is generally watered down and we cannot go before the Tamil people with this package. We cannot accept this.'[61] The LTTE rejected the Bill since it fell short of full independence for the Tamil regions. In an interview with the Tamil *Guardian International*, the LTTE's theoretician, Dr. Anton Balasingham, said: 'The PA government and the UNP in an attempt to reach a consensus engaged in deliberations for the last several months diluting further the constitutional reform proposals of 1997. Having sucked the blood and flesh out of the original package, a skeleton now remains as the final draft.'[62]

The LTTE did not accept this package because 'it did nothing substantial to provide a foundation for a permanent solution to the Tamil national question.'[63] It failed to address the key demands articulated in the Thimpu declarations. The

58 'Lankan MPs for Sale', *Times of India*, 8 August 2000. See also Sri Lanka Academic Net, 15 August 2000.

59 *Sunday Leader*, 6 August 2000.

60 *The Hindu*, 7 August 2000.

61 R. Denish, 'Tamil Parties Say Reforms a Farce', *Sunday Leader*, 16 July 2000.

62 A. Balasingham, 'The Tamil People Will Determine Their Own Destiny', http://www.eelam.com/interviews/asb_tag_010700.html, 18 August 2000.

63 Namini Wijedasa, 'Sri Lankan Government Draft Constitution', http://dailynews.yahoo.com/h/ap/2000=803/wl/sri_lanka_civil_war_3.html

most controversial issue was state structure. Even though the Bill did not use the term unitary, in their view, the state structure remains unitary.

The main supporters of the Constitutional Bill were most left-leaning Sinhalese academics and Tamil academics. At a rally organised by pro-Constitutional Bill supporters, the professor of political science of the University of Peradeniya argued that all rational thinking people should hail this as a sincere effort to address a national disaster.[64] He asked, 'there are over 3,000 races in the world speaking different languages. Can each race claim a separate State?' Professor S.T. Hettige of the University of Colombo also believed that a new constitution was necessary to solve ethnic conflict on the island.[65]

The Tamils also contributed to the failure to find a solution

First, the FP and later other Eelamist and secessionist Tamil parities contributed to the lack of progress in devolving political powers to the north and east. Even though Ceylon Tamils in both these regions are no more than 11 per cent of the total population of the island their claim to one-third of the island and more than half of territorial waters has been unacceptable to moderate Sinhalese political parties and other Sinhalese Buddhist organisations. The FP presented to successive governments their territorial claims to the north and east on the basis that these two regions are traditional Tamil homelands. Since the late 1970s demands for a federal solution turned to secession. Any other solution after that was resisted.

The 1995/2000 constitutional reforms, according to several impartial observers, not only created a *de facto* federal state but it gave greater political autonomy to the Tamil-speaking people in the north and east. The merged North-east Province enjoyed a fair degree of self-government but was not independent. The new Constitution went beyond even the Indian federal model. However, moderate Tamil political parties' were not happy with the constitutional reform. It was only a starting point to negotiate the shape of a future Tamil Eelam[66] which raised the question as to the future envisaged by the Tamils.

The terrorist tactics of the LTTE did not inspire confidence in devolving greater autonomy to the north and east. The LTTE had rejected successive governments' constitutional reforms criticising them for not granting full independence to the Tamil-speaking regions.

64 L. Yodasinghe and J.S. Nissanka, 'Thousands Picket for New Constitution', in *News Lanka*, 3 August 2000.

65 S.T. Hettige, 'Understanding the Current Socio-Political Crisis in Sri Lanka', *The Island*, 19 August 2000.

66 *The Hindu*, 7 August 2000.

Conclusion

After Chief Minister Wardaraja Perumal's brief reign over the Northern Province, a democratically elected provincial council was not favoured by the Sinhalese government for over a decade. The provincial council had been dissolved following the unilateral declaration of independence by the Chief Minister. The pro-provincial lobby was unable to criticise the Rajapakse government for neglecting to restore the cprovincial Council since such democratic measures were vehemently opposed by the LTTE. In fact, no dialogue was allowed in the Northern Province about a constitutional mechanism to devolve power since it would frustrate the Tamil peoples' desire for an independent Tamil Ealam.

However, during the war with the LTTE, the Rajapakse government set up a committee comprising 'all party representatives' to find a political solution to the 'ethnic issue'. The committee, popularly known as APRC and headed by the leader of the Lanka Sama Samaja Party (LSSP), Professor Thissa Vitharana, submitted its report in 2009. President Mahinda Rajapakse has not shown any interest in implementing the APRC's proposals.[67]

After Nandikadal

The leader of the LTTE, Prabhakaran, was killed at a place hitherto unheard of – Nandikadal lagoon perhaps on the evening of 18 May 2009. His body was unceremoniously cremated and violence disappeared from the island after almost four decades. Prabhakaran's death changed the political landscape of the island giving an opportunity for the moderate Tamil leaders of the Northern region to re-evaluate the pros and contras of a provincial council government for the region. Having realised that there would be no armed struggle by Tamil youth in the foreseeable future, they are, quite justifiably, demanding the implementation of the provincial council in accordance with the 13th amendment to the Constitution. Encouraged by the military victory over the LTTE, the Rajapakse government has shown no interest in holding an election in the Northern Province with full powers accorded by the 13th amendment.

However, pressured by India, USA and the European Union, the Rajapakse government has appointed a commission of inquiry entitled, 'Lessons Learnt and Reconciliation Commission' to investigate the circumstances that led to the failure of the ceasefire agreement of February 2002; the lessons that should have been learned from those events; the institutional, administrative and legislative measures that need to be taken in order to prevent any recurrence of violence in the future and to promote further national unity and reconciliation among all communities. This Commission submitted its report to the President in November 2011 but its recommendations have to date not been implemented either.

67 *The Sunday Leader*, 'APRC Proposal was Completely Forgotten by the Rajapakse Government'. *The Sunday Leader*, 1 June 2013, 'Rajapaksa Government Playing Pandu with 13th amendment'.

Instead, the government is preparing to alter the 13th amendment to curtail powers accorded to the Province, especially land and police powers as well as the right to merge with any other province on the island. In what is perceived to be a shrewd move to silence his critics, the President appointed a parliamentary select committee to address issues arising out of the 13th amendment. Opposition to the full implementation of the 13th amendment has come from various political parties[68] in the south in this seemingly unending 'ethnic drama' of the island. The full implementation of the provincial council in the Northern Province, in their view, would pose a threat to national security and the sovereignty of the country.[69] It is evident that some senior ministers of the coalition government have been urging the President to either annul the 13th amendment or else severely restrict its powers. The objections seem to be that powers over police and allocation of lands in the Northern Province would strengthen separatist movements similar to the LTTE. In accordance with these views, the President told cabinet in June that any failure to address the irregularities contain in the 13th amendment, in particular, police powers to the Northern Province, would enable the Northern Province to operate as a rival power base thus posing a threat to sovereignty of the island.

Meanwhile, the JHU (a coalition partner) has already submitted a constitutional amendment to parliament to annul the 13th amendment. Nonetheless, there is considerable opposition to tampering with the 13th amendment from within the senior ranks of the Rajapakse government. Even some of its constituent parties,[70] have stressed their opposition to any proposed change arguing that such an undemocratic measure would undermine the legitimate interests of the minorities in the Northern and the Eastern Provinces of the republic. The National Languages and Social Integration Minister Vasudeva Nanayakkara threatened to leave the government if the PC system is abolished.[71]

Both the Tamil and Muslim political parties in the north and east have opposed any restrictions to the powers accorded by the 13th amendment. Any such undemocratic move will be opposed with the support of ministers of left wing political parties in the coalition government. Rauff Hakeem, leader the Sri Lanka Muslim Congress (SLMC) and the Justice Minister of the present government has confirmed recently that his party would defeat any undemocratic and anti-minority measures taken by the coalition government to curtail powers vested with the provincial council.[72]

68 Among these, Wimal Weerawansa's National Front, Jathika Hela Urumaya, Minister Dinesh Gunawardene's Mahajana Eksah Peramuna.

69 See *Sunday Leader*, leader article, 'Rajapakse Government Playing Pandu with 13th amendment', 1 July 2013.

70 The Democratic Left led by Vasudeva Nanayakkara, Professor Thissa Vitharana's Lanka Sama Samaja Party, the Communist Party of Sri Lanka led by Minister D.E.W. Gunasekera, and the Muslim Congress leader Rauf Hakeem.

71 *Ada Derana*, 1 June 2013.

72 See D.B.S. Jeyaraj, 'Muslim Congress Parliamentary Group Unanimously Resolve to Oppose Government Move', 11 June 2013.

There is also a great deal of support for the full implementation of the 13th amendment. Dr Dayan Jayatilleke, a former diplomat and well-known political scientist, argued in his recent publication that in future a northern provincial council government run by moderate Tamil political party such as the Tamil National Alliance (TNA) will have an opportunity to operate as a counterbalance to any authoritarian regime in the south. In an article published in a leading newspaper, *Colombo Telegraph*, he pointed out that 'a TNA led by a Sampanthan run Provincial Council will be good for democracy and therefore, for all the people of the island. The Northern Provincial Council will be an opposition led Council and will provide a much needed counterweight in a situation in which the traditional checks and balances including the separation of powers are being eroded and fundamentally questioned.'[73]

It would appear from the aforementioned discussion that there is no imminent solution to the ethnic question in Sri Lanka. The current government seems to have found a temporary solution through military victory but defeating the LTTE does not address the ethnic problem. Sri Lanka is a stubbornly multi-ethnic society. The willingness of the government to repeatedly give in to Buddhist nationalism seemed to have turned the clock back from the 1995 attempts at a solution.

In hindsight, and with the benefit of international human rights norms, secessionist wars and perennial problems with minority groups, it is still difficult to see what political options the Tamils or the Sinhalese should have exercised. One option for the Tamil leadership was to accept that majority rule would mean the domination of the Sinhalese in perpetuity and an attempt should have been made to try to ensure a more equitable national language policy, better protection for human rights and regional powers. But the Tamils as a minority behaved in exactly the same way as minorities elsewhere in the world and refused to be subsumed by another national group. Horowitz has observed that 'again and again in divided societies, there is a tendency to conflate inclusion in the government with inclusion in the community and exclusion from government with exclusion from the community.'[74] It could be argued that the loss of political representation diminished the influence of Tamils in government but did not necessarily exclude them from the 'community'.

Whenever separatism raises its head the question has to be posed about whether the 'only right a minority seems to want is the right to become a majority' by 'changing the political context',[75] or whether the majority Sinhalese refused to recognise the legitimacy of the Tamil point of view and accommodate moderate Tamil aspirations. Indeed, policies such as language policies and educational opportunities weighted in favour of the Sinhalese majority did exclude the Tamils from the community as well.

73 D. Jayatilleke, *Long War, Cold Peace : Conflict and Crisis in Sri Lanka*, Vijitha Yapa Publication: Colombo, 2013.

74 Horowitz, 'The Challenge of Ethnic Conflict Democracy in Divided Societies', 1993, p.18.

75 O'Brien, 'What Rights Should Minorities Have?', in Whitaker (ed.), Minorities: a Question of Human Rights, 1984, p.11.

Partition or assimilation is not the only options left to states and ethnic minorities. Assimilation denies that the other cultures are worth preserving and partition refuses to recognise the problems that are bound to attend small and non-viable political entities. Moreover, it is impossible, in principle, to create a world of ethnically homogenous states.

Forced assimilation has been abandoned as a good idea and international politics has accepted that minority groups endure and are making serious attempts to accommodate the aspirations of the minority within democratic systems, either through the protection of minority rights or through a devolved constitutional settlement. The 2009 war which eliminated the armed Tamil opposition has not resolved the problems of the Tamil minority nor addressed the issues facing a fatally divided society. Arguably, the manner of the victory may have destroyed a political resolution in the short term.

Bibliography

T.B.H. Abeysinghe (1966) *Portuguese Rule in Ceylon 1594–1612*, Lakehouse Investments: Colombo

Linda Martin Alcoff and Eduardo Mendieta (eds.) (2003) *Identities: Race, Class Gender and Nationality*, Blackwell Publishers: Oxford

S.M. Ali (1993) *The Fearful State: Power, People and Internal Wars in South Asia*, Zed Books, London

B. Anderson (1991) *Imagined Communities: Reflections on the Origin and Spread of Nationalism*, Verso Books: London

S. Arasatatnam (1964) *Ceylon*, Englewood Cliffs, NJ: Prentice Hall

S. Arasaratnam (1982) *The Historical Foundation of the Economy of the Tamils of North Sri Lanka*, Thantai Chelva Memorial Trust: Jaffna.

R.A. Ariyaratne (1973) 'Communal Conflict in Ceylon and the Advance Towards Self-government 1907–32', unpublished PhD thesis: Cambridge

P. Arunachalam (1906) *Sketches of Ceylon History*, Asian Educational Services: Colombo

E. Aspinall and E. Berger (2001) 'The Breakup of Indonesia Nationalism after Decolonization and the Limits of the Nation State in Post-Cold War South East Asia', *Third World Quarterly*, 22(6), 1003–1024

Ronald Axtmann (2004) 'The State of the State: The Model of the Modern State and its Contemporary Transformation', *International Political Science Review*, 25(3), 259–279

S.D. Bailey (1952) *Ceylon*, Hutchison University Library: London

A. Balasingham (1984) *Liberation Tigers and Tamil Eelam Freedom Struggle*, Jaffna Liberation of Tigers of Tamil Eelam: Jaffna

A. Bandarage (2009) *The Separatist Conflict in Sri Lanka*, Routledge, Contemporary South Asia Series: New York

S.W.R.D. Bandaranaike (1928) *The Handbook of the Ceylon National Congress, 1919–1928*, H.W. Cave & Co.: Colombo

S.W.R.D. Bandaranaike (1961) *Towards a New Era: Selected Speeches in the Legislature of Ceylon 1931-–1959*, Department of Broadcasting and Information: Colombo

S.W.R.D. Bandaranaike (1963) *Speeches and Writings*, Department of Broadcasting and Information: Colombo

A.L. Basham (1952) 'Prince Vijaya and the Aryanisation of Ceylon', *Ceylon Historical Journal*, 1(3), 172–191

S.M. Birgeson (2002) *After the Breakup of a Multi-Ethnic Empire. Russia, Successor States, and Eurasian Security*, Praeger Publishers: Westport, CT

C.T. Blackton (1979) 'The Empire at Bay: British Attitudes and the Growth of Nationalism in the Early Twentieth Century', in M. Roberts (ed.) *Collective Identities, Nationalisms and Protest in Sri Lanka*, Marga Institute: Colombo

Y.Z. Blum (1992) 'UN Membership of the New Yugoslavia: Continuity or Break?', *AJIL*, 86(4), 830–833.

L. Bremmer and A. Bailes (1988) 'Sub-Regionalism in the Newly Independent States', *International Affairs*, 74(1), 131–147

L. Brilmayer (1991) 'Secession and Self-Determination: A Territorial Interpretation', *YJIL*, 16, 177–201.

C. Brölmann, R. Lefeber and M. Zieck (eds.) (1993) *Peoples and Minorities in International Law*, Martinus Nijhoff: Dordrecht

A.E. Buchanan (1991) *Secession: The Morality of Political Divorce: From Fort Sumter to Lithuania and Quebec*, Westview Press, Boulder, CO

L.C. Buchheit (1978) *Secession: The Legitimacy of Self-Determination*, Yale University Press, New Haven, NJ, and London

C. Chapman and K. Ramsay (2011) 'Two Campaigns to Strengthen United Nations Mechanisms on Minority Rights', *International Journal on Minority and Group Rights*, 18, 185–199

A. Cassese (1995) *Self-Determination of Peoples*, Cambridge University Press: Cambridge

Naomi Chazan (ed.) (1991) *Irredentism and International Politics*, Lynne Rienner: Boulder, CO

S. Choudhry (2009) 'Managing Linguistic Nationalism through Constitutional Design: Lessons from South Asia', *International Journal of Constitutional Law*, 7(4), 577

K.P. Clements (ed.) (1993) *Peace and Security in the Asia-Pacific Region: Post-Cold War Problems and Prospects*, United Nations University Press and Dummove Press: Tokyo

A. Cobban (1994) *National Self-Determination*, Oxford University Press, London

D. Demissie (1997) 'Self-Determination Including Secession vs The Territorial Integrity of Nation-States: A Prima Facie Case for Secession', *Suffolk Transnational Law Rev*, 20, 165

B. Denitch (1994) *Ethnic Nationalism: The Tragic Death of Yugoslavia*, University of Minnesota Press: Minneapolis and London

K.M. de Silva (1967) 'The Formation and Character of the Ceylon National Congress 1917–1919', *CJHSS*, 10, 70–101

K.M. de Silva (1972) 'The Ceylon National Congress in Disarray, 1920–1921: Sir Ponnambalam Arunchalam Leaves the Congress', *CJHSS*, 2(2), 97–117.

K.M. de Silva (1981) *A History of Sri Lanka*, C. Hurst & Co.: London

K.N.O. Dharmadasa (1974) 'Nativistic Reaction to Colonialism: The Sinhala Buddhist Revival in Sri Lanka', *Asian Studies*, xiii(1)

K.N.O. Dharmadasa (1992) *Language, Religion and Ethnic Assertiveness: The Growth of Sinhalese Nationalism in Sri Lanka*, University of Michigan Press: Ann Arbor

Christa Diewiks, Lars-Erik Ciderman and Kristian Skrede Gleditsch (2012) 'Inequality and Conflict in Federations', *Journal of Peace Research*, 49(2), 289–304

B.H. Farmer (1963) *Ceylon: A Divided Nation*, Institute of Race Relations: London

P.T.M. Fernando (1970) The Post-Riots Campaign for Justice, *JAS*, xxix(2). 255–266.

T. Fernando (1971) 'Arrack, Toddy and Ceylonese Nationalism: Some Observations on the Temperance Movement, 1912–1921', *Modern Ceylon Studies*, 2(2)

T.M. Franck (1993) 'Postmodern Tribalism and the Right to Secession', in C. Brölmann, R. Lefeber and M. Zieck (eds.) *People and Minorities in International Law*, Martinus Nijhoff: Dordrecht, pp. 3–28

P. Gilbert (1994) *Terrorism, Security and Nationality: An Introductory Study in Applied Political Philosophy*, Routledge: London and New York

N. Glazer and D.P. Moyniham (eds.) (1976) *Ethnicity, Theory and Experience*, Harvard University Press: Cambridge, MA

R.B. Goldman and A.J. Wilson (eds.) (1984) *From Independence to Statehood: Managing Ethnic Conflict in Five African and Asian States*, Frances Printer: London

S.L. Gunasekara (1996), *Tigers, Moderates and Pandora's Package*, Multi Packs (Ceylon) Ltd: Colombo

P.A.T. Gunasinghe (1978) 'Review Article of S. Pathmanathan's Kingdom of Jaffna', *Sri Lanka Journal of the Humanities*, 4, 99–112

R.D. Gunawardene (1976) 'The Reformist Movement and Political Organizations in Ceylon with Special Reference to the Temperance Movement and Regional Associations, 1900–1930', unpublished PhD thesis: University of Sri Lanka, Peradeniya

Raymond L. Hall (ed.) (1979) *Ethnic Autonomy – Comparative Dynamics. The Americas, Europe and the Developing World*, Pergamon Press: Oxford

M.H. Halperin, D.J. Scheffer with P.L. Small (1992), *Self-Determination in the New World Order*, Carnegie Endowment for International Peace: Washington

D.C.H. Hannum (ed.) (1993) 'Sri Lanka', in *Documents on Autonomy and Minority Rights*, Martinus Nijhoff: Dordrecht/Boston/London, p. 496

S.K. Hennayaka (1992) 'Interactive Ethno-nationalism, An Alternative Explanation of Minority Ethno-nationalism', *Political Geography*, II(6), 526–549

A. Heraclides (1991) *The Self-Determination of Minorities in International Politics*, Franc Class and Co. Ltd: London

R. Higgins (1963) *The Development of International Law through the Political Organs of the United Nations*, Oxford University Press: London

W.R. Holmes (1980) *Jaffna (Sri Lanka)*, St. Joseph's Press: Jaffna

H. Hongju Koh and R.C. Slye (eds.) (1999) *Deliberative Democracy and Human Rights*, Yale University Press: New Haven, NJ

D.L. Horowitz (1985) *Ethnic Groups in Conflict*, University of California Press: Bekerley

D.L. Horowitz (1993) 'The Challenge of Ethnic Societies: Democracy in Divided Societies', *Journal of Democracy*, 4(4), October

K. Indrapala (1965) 'Dravidian Settlements in Ceylon and the Beginnings of the History of Jaffna', unpublished PhD thesis: University of London

R.A. Jackson and A. James (eds.) (1993) *States in a Changing World: A Contemporary Analysis*, Clarendon Press: Oxford

J. Jackson Preece (2005) *Minority Rights*, Polity Press: Cambridge

J. Jackson Preece (1998) *National Minorities and the European Nation State System*, Clarendon Press: Oxford

V.K. Jayawardene (1972) *The Rise of the Labour Movement in Ceylon*, Duke University Press: Durham, NC

C. Jeffries (1962) *Ceylon: The Path to Independence*, Pall Mall Press: London

I. Jennings (1953) 'Nationalism and Political Development in Ceylon. The Background of Self-Government', *CHJ*, 3, 70

I. Jennings (1956) *The Commonwealth in Asia*, Clarendon Press: Oxford

I. Jennings, (1956) *The Approach to Self-Government*, Cambridge University Press: Cambridge

S.J. Kaufman (2001) *Modern Hatreds: The Symbolic Power of Ethnic War*, Cornell University Press: Ithaca, NY

R.N. Kearney (1967) *Communalism and Language in the Politics of Ceylon*, Duke University Press: Durham, NC

R.N. Kearney (ed.) (1973) *Political Mobilization in South Asia*, Syracuse University Press: Syracuse, NY

E. Kedourie (1960) *Nationalism*, Hutchison: London

S.U. Kodikara (1970) 'Communalism and Political Modernization in Ceylon', *Modern Ceylon Studies*, 1(1–2), 94–114

A. Kohli (1997) 'Can Democracies Accommodate Ethnic Nationalism? Rise and Decline of Self-Determination Movements in India', *JAS*, 56(2), 326

H. Kohn (1965) *Nationalism, Its Meaning and History*, Van Nostrand Rand, Princeton, NJ

P.G. Kreyenbroek and S. Sperl (eds.) (1992) *The Kurds, A Contemporary Overview*, Routledge: London and New York

W. Kymlicka (ed.) (1989) *The Rights of Minority Cultures*, Oxford University Press: Oxford

W. Kymlicka (2008) 'The Internationalisation of Minority Rights', *International Journal of Constitutional Law*, 6(1)

S. Lawson (1993) 'Ethno-Nationalist Dimensions of Internal Conflict: The Case of Bougainville Secessionism', in K.P. Clements (ed.) *Peace and Security in the Asia-Pacific Region: Post-Cold War Problems and Prospects*, United Nations University Press and Dummove Press: Tokyo

S. Lawson (1996) 'Self-determination as Ethnocracy: Perspectives from the South Pacific', in M. Sellers (ed.) *The New World Order, Sovereignty, Human Rights and the Self-Determination of Peoples*, Berg: Oxford and Washington, DC, pp. 153–175

C.F. Leff (1999) 'Democratization and Disintegration in Multinational States: The Breakup of the Communist Federation', *World Politics*, 51(2), 79–92

I.M. Lewis (ed.) (1983) *Nationalism and Self-Determination in the Horn of Africa*, Ithaca Press: London

G. Lyons and J. Mayall (eds.) (2003) *International Human Rights in the 21st Century: Protecting the Rights of Groups*, Rowman & Littlefield: Oxford

J. Manor (ed.) (1984) *Sri Lanka in Change and Crisis*, Croom Helm: London and Sydney

J. Manor (1989) *The Expedient Utopian: Bandaranaike and Ceylon*, Cambridge University Press: Cambridge

M.L. Marasinghe (1988) 'Ethnic Politics and Constitutional Reforms: The Indo-Sri Lanka Accord', *ICLQ*, 37, 551–587

P. Mason (ed.) (1967) *India and Ceylon: Unity in Diversity, A Symposium*, Oxford University Press: London and New York and Bombay

S. May (2001) *Language and Minority Rights: Ethnicity Nationalism and the Politics of Language*, Longman: Harlow

J. Mayall (1990) *Nationalism and International Society*, Cambridge University Press: Cambridge

G.C. Mendis (1952) *Ceylon Under the British*, 2nd rev. edn., Apothecaries Co. Ltd: Colombo

D. Mercer (ed.) (1988) *Chronicle of the 20th Century*, Longman: London

D.E.M. Mihas (1997) 'Romania Between Balkan Nationalism and Democratic Transition', *Politics*, 17(3), 175–181

D.P. Moyniham (1994), *Pandemonium: Ethnicity in International Politics*, Oxford University Press: Oxford

R. Müllerson (1994) *International Law: Rights and Politics: Developments in Eastern Europe and the CIS*, LSC and Routledge: London

R. Müllerson (1993) 'Minorities in Eastern Europe and the Former USSR: Problems, Tendencies and Protection', *MLR*, 56, 799

S. Namasivayam (1951) *The Legislature of Ceylon*, Faber & Faber Ltd: London

E. Nissan and R.L. Stirrat (1990) 'The Generation of Communal Identities', in J. Spencer (ed.) *Sri Lanka: History and the Roots of Conflict*, Routledge: London, pp. 19–44

G. Obeysekere (1976) 'Personal Identity and Cultural Crisis: The Case of Anagarika Dharmapala of Sri Lanka', in F. Reynolds and D. Capps (eds.) *The Biographical Process Studies in the History and Psychology of Religion*, Mouton: Hungary, pp. 221–252

E. O'Ballance (1989) *Cyanide War: Tamil Insurrection in Sri Lanka*, RUSI and Brassey's Defence Publishers: London

R.C. Oberst (1988) 'Federalism and Ethnic Conflict in Sri Lanka', *Publius*, 18, 183

G. Ostby (2008) 'Polarisation , Horizontal Inequalities and Violent Civil Conflict', *Journal of Peace Research*, 45(2), 143–162

B. Pfaffenberger (1990) 'The Political Construction of Defensive Nationalism: The 1968 Temple-Entry Crisis in Northern Sri Lanka', *JAS*, 49(1)

C. Palley (1978) *Constitutional Law and Minorities, Report no. 36*, Minority Rights Group: London

S. Ponnambalam (1983*) Sri Lanka: The National Question and the Tamil Liberation Struggle*, Tamil Information Centre with Zed Books: London

P. Radan (2002) *The Breakup of Yugoslavia and International Law*, Routledge: London

P. Ramanathan (1888) 'Ethnology of the Moors of Ceylon', *Journal of the Royal Asiatic Society* (Ceylon Branch), 10(36), 234–262

P. Ramanathan (1915) *Riots and Martial Law in Ceylon*, St Martin's Press: London

P. Ramanathan (1930) 'The Memorandum of Sir Ponnamablam Ramanathan on the Recommendations of the Donoughmore Commissioners appointed by the Right Honourable the Secretary of State for the Colonies to Report upon the Reform of the Existing Constitution of the Government of Ceylon 1924–1930', London

A. Read and D. Fisher (1998) *The Proudest Day, India's Long Road to Independence*, Pimlico: London

Report of the Soulbury Commission (1946) *Constitutional Change in Ceylon*. Cmd. 6690 of 1945, Government Press: Colombo

A. Rigo-Sureda (1969) *The Evolution of the Right to Self-determination*, TY Crowell: New York

M. Roberts (ed.) (1977) *Documents of the Ceylon National Congress and Nationalist Politics in Ceylon: 1929-1950*, vol. II, Department of National Archives: Colombo

M. Roberts (1978) 'Ethnic Conflict in Sri Lanka and Sinhalese Perspectives: Barriers to Accommodation', *Modern Asian Studies*, 12(3), 353–375

M. Roberts (ed.) (1979) *Collective Identities, Nationalism and Protests in Sri Lanka*, Marga Institute: Colombo.

M. Roberts (1979) 'Problems of Collective Identity in a Multi-ethnic Society: Sectional Nationalism vs Ceylonese Nationalism 1900–1940', in M. Roberts (ed.) *Collective Identities, Nationalism and Protests in Sri Lanka*, Marga Institute: Colombo, pp. 337–360

P.G. Roeder (2007) *Where Nation-States Come From: Institutional Change in the Age of Nationalism*, Princeton University Press: Princeton, NJ

J.D. Rogers (1990) 'Historical Images in the British Period', in J. Spencer (ed.) *Sri Lanka, History and the Roots of Conflict*, Routledge: London, pp. 87–106

J.D. Rogers (1994) 'Post Orientalism and the Interpretation of Pre modern and Modern Political Identities: The Case of Sri Lanka', *JAS*, 53(1), 10–23

D. Ronen (1974) *The Quest for Self-Determination*, Yale University Press: New Haven, NJ, and London

J. Russell (1982) *Communal Politics under the Donoughmore Constitution 1931–1947*, Thisara Prakasakayo: Colombo

L. Sabaratnam (1987) 'The Boundaries of the State and the State of Ethnic Boundaries: Sinhala-Tamil Relations in Sri Lankan History', *Ethnic and Racial Studies*, 10, 291–315

V. Samaraweera (1979) 'The Muslim Revivalist Movement', 1880–1915' in M. Roberts (ed.) *Collective Identities, Nationalism and Protests in Sri Lanka*, Marga Institute: Colombo, pp. 261–263

V. Samaraweera (1981) 'Land, Labour, Capital and Sectional Interests in the National Politics of Sri Lanka', *MAS*, 15(1), 127–162

M. Saul (2011) 'The Normative Status of Self-Determination in International Law: A Formula for Uncertainty in the Scope and Content of the Right?', *Human Right Law Review*, 11(4), 609–644

C. Schreuer (1993) 'The Waning of the Sovereign State: Towards a new Paradigm for International Law', *EJIL*, 4(4), 447–471

M. Sellers (ed.) (1996) *The New World Order, Sovereignty, Human Rights and the Self-Determination of Peoples*, Berg: Oxford and Washington, DC

M. Shahabuddin (2012) 'Ethnicity in the International Law of Minority Protection: The Post-Cold War Context in Perspective', *Leiden Journal of International Law*, 25, 885–907

A. Shastri (1988) 'The Material Basis for Separatism: The Tamil Eelam Movement in Sri Lanka', *JAS*, 49(1), 56–77

K.S. Shehadi (1993) *Ethnic Self-Determination and the Break-up of States*, Adelphi Papers 283, Brassey's: London

F.L. Shiels (ed.) (1984) *Ethnic Separatism and World Politics*, University Press of America: Lanham, MD, New York and London

P. Sieghart (1984) *Sri Lanka, A Mounting Tragedy of Errors*, Report of a Mission to Sri Lanka in January 1984 on behalf of the International Commission of Jurists and its British Section, Justice, Dorchester

J.A. Sigler (1983) *Minority Rights: A Contemporary Analysis*, Greenwood Press: London

W. Soyinka (1996) *The Open Sore of a Continent*, Oxford University Press: Oxford

J. Spencer (ed.) *History and the Root of the Conflict*, Routledge: London

H. Spruyt (2002) 'The Origins, Development and Possible Decline of the Modern State', *Annual Review of Political Science*, 5, 127–149

E. Stein (1994) 'International Law in Internal Law: Towards Internationalization of Central-Eastern European Constitutions', *AJIL*, 88, 427–450

R. Sterling (1979) 'Ethnic Separatism in the International System', in R.L. Hall (ed.) *Ethnic Autonomy – Comparative Dynamics. The Americas, Europe and the Developing World*, Pergamon Press: Oxford

M. Suksi (ed.) (1998) *Autonomy: Applications and Implications*, Kluwer Law International: The Hague

J.L. Talmon (1967) *Romanticism and Revolt: Europe 1815–1848*, Harold Brace and World: New York

H.W. Tambiah (1951) *Laws and Customs of the Tamils of Jaffna*, Times of Ceylon: Colombo

S.J. Tambiah (1955) 'Ethnic Representation in Ceylon's Higher Administration Services, 1870–1946', *UCR*, 12(13), 113–134

S.J. Tambiah (1986) *Sri Lanka: Ethnic Fratricide and the Dismantling of Democracy*, University of Chicago Press: Chicago and London

S.J. Tambiah (1992) *Buddhism Betrayed – Religion, Politics and Violence in Sri Lanka*, University of Chicago Press: Chicago

Sor-Hoon Tan (ed.) (2005) *Challenging Citizenship, Group Membership and Cultural Identity in a Global Age*, Ashgate: Farnham

C. Taylor (1992) *Sources of the Self: the Making of Modern Identity*, Cambridge University Press: Cambridge

S. Thondaman (1994) *Tea and Politics, My Life and Times, An Autobiography*, Navarang: New Delhi

M.D. Toft (2012) 'Self Determination, Secession and Civil War', *Terrorism and Political Violence*, 24(4), 581–600

C. Tomuschat (ed.) (1993) *Modern Law of Self-Determination*, Martinus Nijhoff: Dordrecht

P. Tremayne (1987) 'Sri Lanka: The Problem of the Tamils', in *Rusi and Brassey's Defence Yearbook*, Royal United Services Institute for Defence Studies: London, pp. 217–237

D.S. Treisman (1997) 'Russia's Ethnic Revival, The Separatist Activism of Regional Leaders in a Post Communist Order', *World Politics*, 49(2)

K.C. Vadlamannathi (2011) 'Why Indian Men Rebel? Explaining Armed Rebellion in the North Eastern States of India,1970–2007', *Journal of Peace Research*, 48(5)

A. Varshney (2001) 'Ethnic Conflict and Civil Society: India and Beyond', *World Politics*, 53(3)

T. Vittachi (1958) *Emergency '58: The Story of Ceylon Race Riots*, Andre Deutsch: London

E. Vulliamy (1998) 'Bosnia: The Crime of Appeasement', *International* Affairs, 74(1)

M. Vythilingam (1971) *The Life of Sir Ponnambalam Ramanathan*, Ramanathan Commemoration Society: Colombo

M. Vythilingam (1977) *Ramanathan of Ceylon: The Life of Sir Ponnambalam Ramanathan*, vol. II, Chunnakam: Colombo

I.D.S. Weerawardana (1956) *Ceylon General Election*, Gunesena: Colombo

I.D.S. Weerawardana (1951) *Government and Politics in Ceylon: 1931–1946*, Ceylon Economic Research Association: Colombo

G. Welhengama (2000), *Minorities' Claims: From Autonomy to Secession, International Law and State Practice*, Ashgate: Aldershot

B. Whitaker (ed.) (1972) *The Fourth World: Victims of Group Oppression*, Sidgwick & Jackson: London

B. Whitaker (ed.) (1984) *Minorities: a Question of Human Rights*, Pergamon Press: Oxford

L.A. Wickramaratne (1975) 'Kandyan and Nationalism in Sri Lanka: Some Reflections', *CJHSS*, 5, 49–67

M. Wickramasinghe (1995) *Ethnic Politics in Colonial Sri Lanka 1927–1947*, Vikas: New Delhi

A.J. Wilson (1974) *Politics in Sri Lanka, 1947–1979*, Macmillan: London

A. J. Wilson (1979) 'Race, Religion, Language and Caste in the Sub-nationalisms of Sri Lanka', in M. Roberts (eds.) *Collective Identities, Nationalism and Protests in Sri Lanka*, Marga Institute: Colombo

A.J. Wilson (1988) *The Break-up of Sri Lanka: The Sinhalese Tamil Conflict*, C. Hurst & Co.: London

A.J. Wilson (1996) 'The Tamil Federal Party in Ceylon Politics', *Journal of Commonwealth Political Studies*, 4(2), 117–137

A.J. Wilson (1994) *S.J.V. Chelvanayakam and the Crisis of Sri Lankan Nationalism 1947–1977*, London: C. Hurst & Co.

A.J. Wilson (2000) *Sri Lanka Tamil Nationalism Its Origins and Development in the Nineteenth and Twentieth Centuries*, Hurst and Co.: London

W.H. Wriggins (1960) *Ceylon: Dilemmas of a New Nation*, Princeton University Press: Princeton, NJ

A. Wright (ed.) (1907) *Twentieth Century Impressions of Ceylon*, Lloyds Greater Britain Publishing Company: London

Index

For Product Safety Concerns and Information please contact our EU
representative GPSR@taylorandfrancis.com
Taylor & Francis Verlag GmbH, Kaufingerstraße 24, 80331 München, Germany

www.ingramcontent.com/pod-product-compliance
Ingram Content Group UK Ltd.
Pitfield, Milton Keynes, MK11 3LW, UK
UKHW022223190926
475702UK00003B/483

* 9 7 8 0 4 1 5 8 5 4 8 6 3 *